D0386434

PROLOGUE: The Great Hall of Justice

DEEP in the sprawling Washington complex that is home to the Department of Justice is the cavernous room called the Great Hall of Justice. Its neoclassical architecture, marble floors, columns, high coffered ceiling, and huge seal of the Republic tend to inspire a sense of awe no matter what one's politics or degree of patriotism. The room is dominated by two large statues. One is a bare-breasted woman standing on clouds from which Moses' tablets protrude. The other is a man wearing a loincloth, holding aloft a cluster of oak branches and arrows. The woman is called "the spirit of justice"; the man, "the majesty of law." While the precise symbolism escapes many observers, the sculptor's intent is clear: The figures personify a justice that is magisterial, serene, nonpolitical.

In October 1982, nearly two years into the Reagan presidency, the United States Attorneys gathered here for the first of the administration's meetings with the nation's top federal prosecutors, usually held once a year. There are ninety-four U.S. Attorneys, one for each of the federal judicial districts in the country. By virtue of geography and population, U.S. Attorneys for some of the districts command more power and prestige than others.

The U.S. Attorney for the Southern District of New York, based in Manhattan, for example, has long been considered the premiere prosecutor after the top Justice Department officials themselves. U.S.

Attorneys located in key cities such as Boston, Miami, Chicago, Los Angeles, and San Francisco typically wield enormous power. The U.S. Attorney for the District of Columbia is unusual in that he presides over a force of what are essentially local prosecutors, since all criminal law in the District is federal.

The U.S. Attorneys are, first and foremost, prosecutors. In other words, they are lawyers who represent the United States in criminal proceedings against those accused of crime. Like other lawyers, they gather evidence, study judicial opinions and statutes, examine witnesses, and file appeals. Their "clients" are government officials—the Attorney General and the President—and, by extension, the people of America.

For that reason, it is the President who appoints the U.S. Attorneys and is ultimately responsible for their behavior. But partly for administrative reasons, partly because of custom, and partly because U.S. Attorneys serve the judicial districts located within the fifty states and the District of Columbia, the prerogative of selecting them has largely shifted to the senators from the same political party as the President.

In practice, the degree of senatorial control over their appointment has varied widely, depending on the interest of particular senators, on their political power, prestige, and seniority, and on the degree to which the President and his top aides want to exercise control over the appointment process.

The prosecutors who gathered for their first Reagan administration annual meeting included a few holdovers from previous administrations, a few of whom had become near-legends. H. M. Ray, a U.S. Attorney from Mississippi, had held his office for twenty years. Sidney Lezak, from Oregon, had been attending these meetings for over eighteen. Their careers dated to the early sixties, and no subsequent President had dared replace them.

But to a greater degree than in nearly any other administration, the group gathering for the first Reagan administration meeting consisted of new faces in Washington. In the case of the Reagan administration, the President and his aides took an unusually keen interest in these appointments. Edwin Meese, counselor to the President and one of his top advisers, was himself a former prosecutor who considered criminal prosecution one of the nation's top priorities. The result had been the wholesale replacement of most U.S. Attorneys who had served in the Carter administration—even some Republican holdovers from earlier administrations.

That President Reagan and Meese took such an interest in the U.S. Attorneys was fully consistent with the President's politics and priorities. On the surface, the function of the federal prosecutors is straightforward: they decide who should be charged and with what federal crime. In practice, their work is complex and their influence far-reaching. Simply launching a federal investigation can have major, even dire, consequences for their targets. In deciding what crimes to prosecute—and what crimes to ignore—they make vitally important decisions about the fundamental values that will be reflected in administration policy.

And yet their function has been deemed essentially nonpolitical. This theory posits that it is Congress that defines what is a crime. Prosecutors simply prosecute them—all crimes, whatever the prosecutors' own feelings about the wisdom of Congress's criminal statutes. It is a theory that has been embraced publicly by Republicans and Democrats alike when it has been expedient to do so.

For many of the new federal prosecutors, the gathering was their first opportunity to meet in person the men who headed the hierarchy of criminal prosecution in the country and were their current bosses.

The U.S. Attorneys were greeted by the Attorney General himself, William French Smith, by virtue of his office the nation's top prosecutor. He was ultimately responsible for all their activities, answerable directly to the President. The remarks by the silver-haired former partner in Gibson, Dunn & Crutcher, a large and prestigious Los Angeles law firm, were fittingly brief. Although Smith had an unusually close relationship with the President and had been his personal lawyer for years, he had virtually no experience in law enforcement or criminal law and made no secret of the fact that he planned to delegate responsibility for those areas to his top aides.

Next came speeches from the two men most directly involved with the U.S. Attorneys: D. Lowell Jensen, the Assistant Attorney General in charge of the Criminal Division, and Rudolph ("Rudi") Giuliani, the Associate Attorney General, the third-ranking official in the Justice Department. It hadn't taken long for the U.S. Attorneys with even one ear to the ground to realize that Jensen and Giuliani were locked in some kind of power struggle within the still-new administration.

The two men seemed opposites, in both appearance and temperament. Jensen is tall, clean-cut, square-jawed, quiet and thoughtful. A native of Utah who spent most of his life in California, he had an instinctive affinity for the Reagans. Nonetheless, he is at least nominally a member of the Democratic Party. He was already a popular figure with the U.S. Attorneys who knew him. He was an experienced state prosecutor in one of the busiest criminal districts in the country—Alameda County, California, which includes both Oakland and Berkeley. He had been a prosecutor during the turbulent late sixties, and worked closely at the time with Meese, who was an Assistant District Attorney in the office. Since then Jensen had become known as a strictly professional prosecutor, one who let few, if any, political ideologies interfere with a zealous determination to convict criminals. He was the administration's symbol of a bipartisan commitment to fight all kinds of crime.

Giuliani, by way of contrast, is stocky and dark-haired, a flamboyant, aggressive, voluble New Yorker. His words pour forth in a torrent. He seemed at first glance out of place in the Reagan administration. He was largely an outsider, once a protégé of Harold Tyler, Deputy Attorney General in the Ford administration. He had worked in the Justice Department then and had been an Assistant U.S. Attorney in the Southern District of New York.

In those positions he had developed a reputation for hard work, political savvy—and an enormous ego. Those who knew Giuliani doubted that he would settle for any role out of the limelight, even if it meant stepping over a few of his colleagues in the administration.

Indeed, Giuliani had already scored what many deemed a political coup by being named Associate Attorney General, a position that ranked above Jensen. Moreover, as the highest-ranking Justice Department official with experience in criminal law, Giuliani had been given greater responsibility than had previous Associate Attorneys General in the criminal arena. Although Jensen had direct responsibility for criminal cases, Giuliani had seized responsibility for overseeing the appointment of the U.S. Attorneys. As a result, it was Giuliani rather than Jensen to whom the prosecutors owed their jobs.

The gathering of U.S. Attorneys should have been a triumphal appearance for Giuliani. But the case being most avidly discussed among the prosecutors as they convened in Washington had cast a shadow on his career. Already, the opinion of many of the U.S. Attorneys at the meeting was that Giuliani had blundered.

The case was *United States* v. *McDonnell Douglas Corporation*, the result of an enormous investigation begun during the Carter administration; it involved foreign payments, bribes, and fraud, and was aimed at one of the country's largest and most visible corporations. It was a case that had the potential to be a significant, even decisive, battle in the struggle for power within the Reagan Justice Department. And it was a case that might decide early on the role of politics in this administration's prosecutions.

BRIBERY AT
McDONNELL DOUGLAS

THOUGH darkness had descended, traffic still choked the narrow, dusty streets of Rawalpindi, close to the capital city of Islamabad, in northern Pakistan. Charles M. Forsyth, vice president for marketing of Douglas Aircraft Company, the commercial aircraft manufacturing division of St. Louis–headquartered McDonnell Douglas Corporation, wondered anxiously if his contacts were going to deliver on their promise: an audience with a high-ranking member of the government of Ali Bhutto, the president of Pakistan.

Forsyth's mission was an unusually important one. Pakistan International Airlines was on the verge of making a substantial order for wide-body jets, and the McDonnell Douglas DC-10 aircraft was a contender—in large part because the company had waged an aggressive, persistent campaign to win the order, carried out with the exactitude of a military mission. More than the sale of a few aircraft was involved. McDonnell Douglas had never before succeeded in cracking the rapidly growing, lucrative Middle Eastern market dominated by archrival Boeing Company. If successful, McDonnell Douglas's Pakistani campaign could usher in a new era for the DC-10 and McDonnell Douglas.

Leslie Sequeira reassured Forsyth. Sequeira, operating through his company, Sequeira Brothers, was McDonnell Douglas's agent in Pakistan. Nearly all foreign sales of aircraft are made through agents whose functions vary depending on the country. In most cases, one of their principal functions is to provide access to the decision makers involved in the purchase of so substantial an asset as a wide-bodied jet aircraft; in countries like Pakistan, with state-owned airlines, those decision makers are invariably high-ranking members of the government, in some cases the president, prime minister, or dictator.

Sequeira had been promised $100,000 in U.S. dollars for every aircraft McDonnell Douglas sold. But that money alone, it seemed, wasn't going to buy the kind of access McDonnell Douglas wanted and needed to defeat Boeing. Sequeira, Forsyth had concluded, simply didn't have enough clout.

If all went well tonight, Forsyth thought, that problem would be solved. Sequeira had managed to schedule a meeting with Ashiq Ali Bhutto, the president's cousin. And Bhutto had promised to bring an even more important contact: Rafi Raza, President Bhutto's chief of staff.

Forsyth had already reviewed the top-secret memo prepared by the McDonnell Douglas sales staff in anticipation of this meeting. Dated December 9, 1972, the memo made clear that Bhutto and Raza had the clout Forsyth wanted—and maybe the inclination to help as well, as long as their price was met.

With respect to Bhutto, the memo read:

> This man controls family lands in province of Siad [Sind] on behalf of entire family, including the President; he has immediate access to all current high government officials because of his family position; land-holding system here has not progressed much beyond Feudal system, and thus his position in the family cannot be underestimated, as he controls the family wealth.

The memo then took a significant turn:

> However [underlined], family wealth includes current political assets, plus much land and considerable local cash BUT no convertible [underlined] currency; as a locally wealthy landowner he and other family members cannot travel abroad, and his primary motivation now is to receive some external cash or negotiable assets.
>
> He is not comfortable in his present commercial posture, but the situation has progressed far beyond his capacity to change it; while his contacts are impeccable, and his associates highly placed, his resolve

might weaken in this regard, except for his personal family obligations: his wife is quite obviously a strong-willed girl, and her brother ASIF MAHMOUD is a partner in this venture.

The memo's thrust was obvious. Although it didn't say it directly, it was clear that Bhutto, though reluctant, could be bribed. So too might Raza.

Probably the most highly placed government official we can contact [the memo had explained]. His U.S. equivalent has to be Kissinger, as he has the complete confidence of the President in all affairs of State, mainly in foreign negotiations such as People's Republic of China, India and the U.N. He is married to an English girl, and apparently has a young family . . . His object is unknown, but his foreign marriage may clue this.

And the groundwork for the clandestine meeting had been laid for Forsyth.

Meeting in Rawalpindi will have to be rather late at night, and should involve only four persons (possibly five); principals have agreed to a frank [underlined] discussion [underlined] of mutual interests.

Despite the traffic, Forsyth arrived at the appointed time and place. As instructed, he had his driver turn off the headlights as they approached. Bhutto arrived soon after, accompanied, as he had promised, by Raza. Forsyth was struck by the urbanity of the young men. Both were handsome, though Bhutto was dark and Raza so pale he could easily have passed for European. Both had been educated in the U.S.; Raza in particular spoke impeccable, unaccented English. Forsyth's mission was to bring them into the McDonnell Douglas fold.

There seemed to be a rapport among the men. Forsyth is an impressive man himself—a former air force officer with combat experience who was as comfortable with heads of state as with other airline executives. Their discussion was, indeed, frank. When it was over, Forsyth agreed to pay an additional $500,000 per airplane purchased by the Pakistani airline, to be funneled to Mahmoud and Bhutto through Sequeira. It isn't known what, if anything, Raza received.

The effort paid off for McDonnell Douglas and their Pakistani allies. Less than two years later, Pakistan International Airlines bought four DC-10 aircraft at a cost of over $80 million. President Bhutto was overthrown in a coup in 1977 and was executed in 1979; his cousin, Mahmoud, and Raza fled the country, presumably relying on the contents of their Swiss bank accounts.

The agreement with Forsyth was to remain top secret. It was never put in writing. The $500,000 was simply tacked onto the sale price of each aircraft, and was never allocated as a commission expense. After the aircraft were sold and the payments made, Forsyth ordered one of his assistants to take documents related to the Pakistan transactions and hide them under his bed.

Years later, when Forsyth's secret meeting became the focus of the government's first major criminal prosecution for illegal foreign payments, Forsyth would claim he was merely doing business in the time-honored way for that part of the world. To Justice Department prosecutors, however, Forsyth's actions smacked of a different kind of time-honored conduct: crime. Specifically, fraud.

FIVE years after Forsyth's clandestine meeting in Rawalpindi, Michael Lubin sat at his desk in the Department of Justice building in Washington, shaking his head over the stacks of files. Lubin, then twenty-eight years old, is still boyishly handsome, and exudes energy and enthusiasm. But he wondered if this assignment was going to be too much even for him. A prosecutor in the criminal fraud section of the department, he had joined forces with five other prosecutors to form a task force. Their mission: to find and prosecute any violations of criminal law that may have occurred in conjunction with the payment of foreign bribes, then one of the hottest topics in Washington.

His problem wasn't a lack of leads. On the contrary, approximately one hundred American corporations, nearly all in the *Fortune* 500, had already admitted paying foreign bribes in submissions to the Securities and Exchange Commission. Some of them had been paying bribes in as many as twenty-five or thirty countries, and each instance could form the basis for a separate investigation by Lubin and his colleagues. If that wasn't daunting enough, Lubin wasn't even sure what, if any, criminal laws had been violated. The lawyers were embarking on investigations where they weren't even sure what to look for.

Lubin's predicament had its roots, as did so many legal and political currents of the late seventies, in the Watergate crisis. A Senate investigation by the so-called Church Committee into secret corporate payments to the Nixon campaign fund uncovered what one commentator called a "sickening trail" of covert payments by American corporations to foreign agents and government officials.

While not directly related to Watergate, the foreign payments fell well within the sense of public outrage that has since come to be known as post-Watergate morality. Congress reacted by passing the Foreign Corrupt Practices Act in 1977, making such payments not only unlawful, but criminal. The Church Committee also passed its findings on to the Securities and Exchange Commission, where the enforcement director, Stanley Sporkin, picked up the crusade and made foreign payments a top priority of the commission under President Jimmy Carter. The commission's attack wasn't on the payments per se—there wasn't any law expressly forbidding them when they were made—but on the companies' failures to disclose the payments to investors and the public. Hundreds of investigations were launched and scores of companies amended their SEC disclosure forms to acknowledge the payments, amid much public hand wringing and promises of reform.

Attorney General Benjamin Civiletti, who was named to the top post at the Justice Department after Griffin Bell resigned in 1979, decided that the resources of the Justice Department too should be brought to bear on the problem, and urged the Assistant Attorney General for the Criminal Division, Philip Heymann, to investigate possible prosecutions. A genial, low-key intellectual, Heymann had been a professor of criminal law at Harvard, and colleagues say one of his strengths as a prosecutor was his ability to recognize creative applications of existing statutes. Many of his colleagues in Washington referred to him as "the professor." Heymann recognized that the department might not be able to rely on the relatively new Foreign Corrupt Practices Act, which clearly didn't apply to bribes that occurred long before the statute was passed. Rather, he thought the department could go a step further than the SEC had—the concealment of the foreign payments from stockholders, regulatory agencies, and foreign governments might be treated simply as criminal fraud, a crime that could be prosecuted under laws in existence at the time most of the payments had occurred.

Lubin was brought into the department's effort at an early stage. He'd reached the Justice Department through something of a side door. After graduating in 1974 from the University of Miami Law School, where he concentrated on the unusual combination of criminal and international law, Lubin had landed a job with the U.S. Customs Service. There he'd worked on international currency transactions, which frequently involved criminal aspects, and he became the service's liaison to the Justice Department. That led to the prosecutor's job at Justice. Lubin also had an esoteric area of expertise because of his work on a case involving the currency reporting statute (then a sleepy backwater of law enforcement; it's since been revived by recent massive violations by major banks, such as the Bank of Boston). Currency reporting violations tended to be investigated by customs agents rather than by agents of the Federal Bureau of Investigation. One of the major problems faced by the fraud unit in pursuing foreign bribes was a lack of investigators—the FBI didn't have the manpower for such a massive undertaking—so the department had decided to enlist the help of customs agents. Lubin, therefore, was a natural for the assignment, even though he'd never handled a grand jury investigation.

As he sifted through the files, Lubin tried to focus on a target, or at least a group of targets. He began by looking at the amount of the foreign payments involved, which led him to companies like McDermott, the Louisiana oil services concern; Sea-Land, then a unit of R. J. Reynolds, Inc.; Westinghouse; and Raytheon. It also brought him with increasing frequency to one industry group: aircraft. No doubt about it, it was an industry that had come to depend on such payments to an extraordinary degree. The biggest offender seemed to be Boeing Company, followed closely by Lockheed and McDonnell Douglas.

Some investigations that looked promising were farmed out to various U.S. Attorneys, but Lubin and his colleagues detected a distinct lack of enthusiasm for foreign payments cases in their regional offices. Not surprisingly, U.S. Attorneys were concerned about the budgetary impact of wide-ranging investigations that often had to be conducted overseas. And Lubin thought that, generally speaking, the U.S. Attorneys resisted what he calls the "big paper" cases. "They were afraid of these cases," he says. "Paper fraud just wasn't a priority for them. So the big national cases all stayed with us."

Those included the aircraft cases, and Lubin began concentrating on Boeing and McDonnell Douglas. Lockheed went to other prosecutors in the office. As a group, the prosecutors decided to convene a grand jury to investigate the whole area of foreign payments; the aircraft manufacturers would be part, though not all, of the inquiry.

Grand juries serve many functions in the modern criminal justice system, but essentially their function is a simple one: to listen to evidence in order to determine if criminal charges should be brought. They do not determine guilt or innocence. (Trial juries, which do make that determination and are far more familiar to most Americans, are often called petit juries, to distinguish them from their preindictment counterpart.)

Grand juries are, as a result, a crucial interface between government authority and the private citizen, and provide a recognition that even the bringing of criminal charges is a momentous step that can have dire consequences for the accused. Despite this overriding function as a bulwark against government's overreaching, grand juries are often, and increasingly, used by prosecutors as a means of conducting investigations, because grand juries have the subpoena power—the power to compel testimony. Grand juries do not themselves investigate, but subpoenas are issued in their name, thus providing a powerful tool for investigators.

When the foreign payments grand jury first convened, it had neither a specific target for indictment nor specific charges under consideration. The facts that would emerge before the jury would be used by the prosecutors to determine who, if anyone, should be indicted and what they should be charged with.

It was an unusually active grand jury session. Most grand juries sit one or maybe two days a week. The foreign payments grand jury met three and four days a week as a parade of witnesses from a wide range of companies began to appear.

As for McDonnell Douglas, Lubin began at an obvious place for anyone looking into the matter of foreign bribes: the McDonnell Douglas salesmen in the various countries where, because of the SEC investigation, the company had already admitted making payments. Lubin subpoenaed witnesses from Mexico, Venezuela, Zaire, Congo, South Korea, the Philippines, and Pakistan.

Although they spent most of their time outside the U.S., most of the company's salesmen were available to testify. A federal grand jury has the power to serve potential witnesses with subpoenas only within the United States or its territories and protectorates within the jurisdiction of the U.S. courts. A major problem in prosecuting international crime is that potential witnesses who reside abroad can't be compelled to testify unless they travel into the jurisdiction of the U.S. courts. Fortunately for Lubin, McDonnell Douglas salesmen were required to make regular visits to company headquarters in St. Louis. He also assuaged their concerns by giving the salesmen letters of immunity, assuring them that they wouldn't be prosecuted themselves for any testimony they gave before the grand jury. Appearing was therefore an opportunity for any salesman who feared that his behavior might be deemed criminal, since he could insulate himself from prosecution by cooperating.

Lubin didn't worry much that he was protecting people who would later appear to be guilty of crimes. He handed out such immunity with little hesitation, although he did provide the FBI with a list of names of those he wanted to immunize, to make sure they weren't already under investigation for some other alleged crime. "At this level it didn't bother me at all," Lubin says. "It wasn't the decision of any salesman to make foreign payments of this magnitude." Lubin wanted to use the resources of the Justice Department only to land those he considered most culpable—the corporations themselves and their top officers. And, as a practical matter, his investigation would go nowhere unless he secured the cooperation of the salesmen. Even then, he couldn't be sure he would get true cooperation. He knew from experience that loyalty to a corporation can be deeply ingrained, and that corporate executives have been known to choose perjury over what they deem to be betrayal, even when they have been immunized and risk a perjury trial. (Letters of immunity for testimony generally do not protect witnesses from prosecution for perjury or obstruction of justice.) Lubin specifically warned his witnesses that despite their letters they could be prosecuted if they lied in their testimony.

The salesmen didn't make easy witnesses. "They were very impressive people," Lubin recalls. "We're not talking Fuller Brush salesmen. These people were tough, polished witnesses, accustomed to dealing with top executives in countries all over the world. Many had distinguished records in the U.S. military. In fact, after I'd met a wide range of top executives in these companies, I thought some of these salesmen were the most impressive, competent people in the organization."

One of the most impressive was Lubin's third witness before the grand jury, a McDonnell Douglas salesman named Sherman Pruitt. Pruitt had volunteered for combat duty during World War II even before the U.S. officially entered the war. He was decorated for heroism after flying scores of combat missions over Germany and other parts of Europe during the battle for Britain. Later, he had been a test pilot, flying daring missions in California. Now he was a salesman for McDonnell Douglas, with sole responsibility for sales in Pakistan.

Pruitt was consequently a key witness with respect to sales of the DC-10 to Pakistan International Airlines, and Lubin had granted Pruitt the standard letter of immunity in return for his testimony. Lubin knew already, based on the files from the SEC, that McDonnell Douglas had paid more than the $100,000-per-plane commission to its agent, Sequeira, disclosed in the airplane sales documents. He knew too that substantial, unreported payments had gone to Bhutto and Mahmoud. He also had a document turned over by McDonnell Douglas which was a memo from Pruitt indicating that others in addition to Bhutto and Mahmoud had received payments, and Lubin was anxious to learn the scope of the payments in Pakistan.

"Who else did Sequeira pay out money to?" Lubin asked Pruitt on the witness stand.

"I don't know . . . I don't have any knowledge of who his payees were other than Asif Mahmoud and Ashik [sic] Bhutto," Pruitt answered.

With the document in mind, Lubin asked, "Do you have any knowledge that he paid money to people other than Asif Mahmoud or Ashik Bhutto?"

"No, I do not," Pruitt replied.

Lubin was very skeptical of the testimony. It wasn't just that he had a document indicating that Pruitt did know more, or at least at one time knew more. It was Pruitt's demeanor—something that Lubin, as an experienced prosecutor, knew was as important as what Pruitt said. As the questioning had moved closer to the actual details of the payments, Pruitt's confidence had seemed to erode slightly. And during those last two questions, he had seemed nervous. He started tapping his fingers rapidly. He was perspiring. His answers were slower in coming. Then Lubin confronted Pruitt with the document, and Pruitt asked to confer with his lawyer, then asked to go to the bathroom. Lubin felt he was on to something.

When Pruitt returned to the stand, Lubin began again. "So you were aware of Sequeira paying out money to people . . . ?"

"That's what I've reported," Pruitt acknowledged. "But I don't know the amounts or to whom . . . I don't know whom he paid or how much."

Lubin was disappointed in the answer; he also remained skeptical. Who might Pruitt be trying to protect? Himself? Lubin took another stab, asking Pruitt if he himself had any foreign bank accounts. Pruitt said no. Lubin wondered about that too. As he brought his questioning of Pruitt to an end, he felt sure he would be talking to the salesman again.

Lubin's activities before the grand jury, however, were not the focus of attention of the Justice Department and the fraud section of the Criminal Division at that moment, for another investigation—Lockheed—had taken precedence.

The Lockheed investigation—arising from a scandal involving the Dutch royal family that had erupted in 1976—had now rocked the Japanese government of Kakuei Tanaka. Lubin could feel a chill toward foreign bribery cases begin to emanate from the State Department, which was horrified at the prospect of one U.S. ally after another falling victim to Justice Department probes. In fact, in another case Lubin and his colleagues had already developed enough evidence to implicate the elected head of one of the U.S.'s major allies. In the wake of Lockheed, some pleas were arranged and the rest of the case was quietly dropped. The identity of that official has never been disclosed, and prosecutors say they are bound by the laws of grand jury secrecy from disclosing his identity. These details are known: the official was an elected president, he is no longer in office, and the bribe was paid before he became president.

Despite State Department concerns, the parade of witnesses continued before the grand jury. Increasingly, Lubin's attention returned to McDonnell Douglas and its dealings in Pakistan. Pakistan, Lubin thought, offered a unique prosecutorial opportunity, especially in light of concerns arising from the fate of the Tanaka government. In Pakistan, President Bhutto had been swept out of office and power had been seized by General Muhammad Zia. Zia was in no way threatened by an investigation of events that occurred during the regime of his predecessor—indeed, Lubin hoped he might persuade the present Pakistani government that it was in its own interest to investigate and publicize corruption in the previous regime.

Lubin began by calling the Pakistani embassy in Washington. He wasn't terribly optimistic—he'd tried calling embassies of other countries implicated in bribery schemes and had gotten nowhere. But in this case, he was put in contact with a Pakistani diplomat named Zafar Hilaly, who was at least willing to listen to Lubin.

The two began a series of meetings which gradually turned into a friendship. Hilaly's father was a former Pakistani ambassador to the U.S.; Hilaly spoke impeccable English and was familiar with the ways of both the current and former Pakistan regimes. He listened sympathetically, Lubin thought, as the prosecutor explained his investigation and emphasized how scandal in the Bhutto regime could redound to the benefit of Zia. He emphasized, too, his sense that it was Pakistan itself that was the victim of the fraud—the state-owned airline had paid $500,000 more per plane than necessary.

After a number of conversations with officials in Islamabad, Hilaly informed Lubin that the Zia government was prepared to cooperate. Hilaly thought that a number of relevant documents could be produced from government files, and that witnesses might be made available if Lubin wished to travel to Pakistan. Lubin was excited by the prospect—he hadn't yet managed to interview one of McDonnell Douglas's foreign agents. And he was elated that his campaign to win over Hilaly and the Zia government seemed to be working.

Lubin asked for and received government approval for the trip to Pakistan. On Thanksgiving eve 1978 he arrived in Karachi, where he discovered that Hilaly had already intervened on his behalf. As he stepped onto the tarmac of the airport he was greeted by a chauffeur who took him immediately through customs and to a waiting car. Lubin, who thought of himself as a comparatively low-ranking prosecutor, felt he was being treated like a visiting head of state.

It also made him a bit leery. "I was mindful of the fact that I was a representative of the United States, and I was dealing with a repressive dictatorship. I didn't want to be set up," he says. He assumed his chauffeur was an internal security agent, reporting on his every move. His telephone, Lubin says, was tapped.

By comparison to the effusive greeting he received from his Pakistani hosts, the reaction at the U.S. embassy was cool. Lubin made a courtesy call to the U.S. ambassador, who, it turned out, had been in the U.S. embassy in Japan when the Lockheed scandal broke there. "I know why you're here," he told Lubin. "But I don't want to know what you're doing. It was a mess in Japan."

One of Lubin's first interviews was with the finance minister at the time of the McDonnell Douglas transactions, Mubashir Hassan. He was a potential witness who had to be handled carefully, because he had survived the Bhutto purge and was still finance minister under Zia. He was a former member of the board of governors of the World Bank, and a financier-statesman with world stature. Any criticism of his role, or suggestion that he was responsible for the scandal, could obviously backfire.

Lubin's evidence, however, suggested that Hassan was not responsible for what had happened. On the contrary, one of the most important documents Lubin had obtained was an internal McDonnell Douglas memo summarizing a meeting with the finance minister held near the outset of the company's campaign to sell DC-10s to Pakistan International Airlines. The document indicated that the finance minister had expressly forbidden precisely the kind of under-the-table payments that had later occurred. In a letter written after the meeting with the minister, Pruitt, the McDonnell Douglas salesman, said that "the M of F laid down the law to all of us to the effect that everything was going to be aboveboard, honor bright, and Eagle Scout with no deals, no kickbacks, no commissions, payoffs, etc. That this was the new law of the land."

Lubin had questioned Pruitt about the letter, and the salesman insisted that while the minister had made such remarks, they weren't meant to be taken seriously. Indeed, Lubin had obtained a copy of another letter from Pruitt that closely followed the previous one. In it, Pruitt described a meeting he had had with Rafique Saigol, the managing director of the airline, who told Pruitt not to take the minister's remarks at face value. "While at his home, [Saigol] opened up on the deal to me and admitted that it was a wholly staged operation for appearances to make sure that they, the airline and the government, present a clean image."

Lubin was eager to know how the finance minister would react to these missives. When he told him about Pruitt's conclusion that the remarks were merely window dressing, Hassan seemed genuinely indignant, insisting that a consistent theme during his tenure as finance minister had been to bring Pakistani business practices into line with the highest international standards. Of course, under the circumstances, it would have been foolish for the minister to admit that his remarks weren't meant seriously, but Lubin was convinced by Hassan's demeanor. Nor was there any plausible motive for him to have made such a statement at the time. In his remarks to the McDonnell Douglas representatives, he could simply have ignored the subject of payoffs.

Lubin was pleased by the interview, and thought it added a significant dimension to the potential case against McDonnell Douglas. It and other companies had repeatedly insisted that they had simply followed accepted business practices in the countries where they did business; that bribes were not only essential but were encouraged by some foreign governments. In Pakistan, however, Lubin was convinced that the contrary was true. It appeared to him that the company had defied an order from the highest financial authority in the country. It added what he believed could be an important moral aspect to the company's behavior, one that might have a significant impact on a jury's deliberations.

Lubin had taken care before leaving Washington to make sure that McDonnell Douglas knew nothing about his trip to Pakistan, for fear that the company and its agents would get to witnesses there before he had a chance to interview them. He'd instructed his secretary to tell no one about his whereabouts—not even to say that he was out of the country. But when he returned to his hotel after the interview with the foreign minister and placed a call to his office, he learned that his secretary had already been deluged with calls from lawyers representing McDonnell Douglas, demanding to know what he was doing in Pakistan and whom he was planning to see. The news was upsetting for Lubin. McDonnell Douglas had hired some top defense counsel, but he was amazed at their ability to gather such intelligence. And he hadn't yet interviewed Leslie Sequeira, McDonnell Douglas's agent in Pakistan and one of Lubin's most crucial potential witnesses.

Sequeira's interview was scheduled for the next day at the elaborate former presidential palace in Karachi, now used to house visiting foreign dignitaries. When Lubin arrived for the interview, his fears were confirmed: Sequeira didn't show up. Lubin assumed he'd been tipped off by McDonnell Douglas operatives. The Pakistani investigators assigned to the matter seemed acutely embarrassed, almost as though the national honor depended on their being able to produce Sequeira. They told Lubin they'd find Sequeira. Given their grim determination, Lubin thought they probably would.

A day went by; Lubin was reassured that Sequeira would be produced. The next day he was. Much to the embarrassment of the Sequeira family, their house had been ringed twenty-four hours a day by Pakistani security agents, and the minute Sequeira reappeared, he was nabbed. It turned out that he hadn't been contacted by McDonnell Douglas. He was simply on a hunting expedition in a remote area of Pakistan, and hadn't even gotten word that he was expected for an interview. He was profusely apologetic toward Lubin.

With the not-so-subtle encouragement of the Zia government, Sequeira proved to be a cooperative witness, confirming much of what Lubin had learned about the secret payments and adding valuable details about how the payments had been made and who inside McDonnell Douglas had been responsible for approving them. It was becoming obvious that responsibility for the payments went far beyond Pruitt.

One key witness, however, eluded Lubin during his trip to Pakistan: Rafique Saigol, the airline's managing director who, according to Pruitt, had made light of the foreign minister's remarks urging an aboveboard, Eagle Scout transaction. Saigol always seemed to stay one step ahead of Lubin, usually by being far away from Pakistan. (The Zia government, however, finally persuaded Saigol to fly to Washington to meet with Lubin. "Mr. Lubin I presume," Saigol said with a twinkle in his eye when the two finally met. Lubin found him charming, and he proved to be a valuable witness before the grand jury, contradicting Pruitt's account and confirming the finance minister's remarks and sincerity.)

By the time Lubin returned from Pakistan in late 1978, he had a pretty good idea about what had happened in the transaction with Pakistan International Airlines and who at McDonnell Douglas were involved.

Following Forsyth's visit to Rawalpindi, Lubin had learned that McDonnell Douglas formally modified its contract with Sequeira, adding to the $100,000-per-plane commission it was already going to pay an additional payment of $500,000 per plane. The $500,000 was to be divided between Ashiq Ali Bhutto, the president's cousin, and Asif Mahmoud, Bhutto's brother-in-law. According to Sequeira, the $100,000 commission was a "visible" arrangement, to be disclosed publicly if required. But the other commissions were to be "invisible," and no agreement with Bhutto and Mahmoud was put in writing. (It was amply documented, however, by scores of memos written by Pruitt and other employees.) The $500,000 was simply tacked onto the price of each plane. All this had transpired in late 1972 and early 1973.

Then, in May 1973, the finance minister had held his meeting with Pruitt and other McDonnell Douglas representatives, asking specifically for the names of the company's sales agents and the amounts of the proposed commissions. Similar requests had been made of Boeing, and it was clear that the government was factoring in the expense of sales commissions in deciding which plane to purchase.

Pruitt had communicated this information to his superiors inside the company, specifically, Forsyth and John Brizendine, the president of Douglas Aircraft Company. The executives decided not to disclose the arrangements with Bhutto and Mahmoud to the Pakistan government, instead reporting only the $100,000 payment agreement with Sequeira. In response, the Pakistan government asked McDonnell Douglas to reduce the price of each plane by $100,000—it didn't intend to pay the company's commissions—and McDonnell Douglas agreed to do so.

The company's effort to win the sales, however, hadn't stopped with the payments to Bhutto and Mahmoud. Another major effort had been mounted to secure the cooperation of Afsar Hussain, the airline's director of planning.

Hussain had not, at the outset, seemed a promising target. A McDonnell Douglas memo described him as a

long-time airline employee who graduated to present position, probably on merit; educational background unknown; he is only Bengali [underlined] in the airline management, and his position may be tenuous; he will (apparently) write the airline in-house aircraft selection recommendation, drawing on the evaluations of his own Department, plus inputs from Operations and Engineering, but there seems little doubt that he is not [underlined] friendly to Douglas; this report will go to Saigol very soon (if not already submitted); he appears to favor B-747 . . . It is probably correct to assume that he is personally committed to one or both of our competitors, but we have made no direct or indirect response to this possibility.

Pruitt and Forsyth soon remedied the failure to make a response. They secretly offered to pay Hussain as a McDonnell Douglas "consultant," and later the company paid more than $100,000 into Hussain's Swiss bank account. Hussain not only switched abruptly from opponent to ally in promoting the DC-10—he handed over the confidential sales proposals of McDonnell Douglas's competitors.

The evidence also implicated McDonnell Douglas executives higher than Forsyth and Pruitt. After the company had won the competition, Brizendine had signed the purchase agreement, a document that continued the deception. The commission arrangement persisted through additional sales of aircraft, and was explicitly approved by Robert C. Little, a corporate vice president. It was also approved by James S. McDonnell III—the son of the company's founder and chairman, and the most sensitive name to have emerged in the investigation.

The size of the secret payments caused them to be questioned by McDonnell Douglas's auditors; nonetheless, Brizendine and Forsyth decided to continue them so as not to jeopardize any sales. McDonnell Douglas executives also participated actively in plans to make the payoffs. At times, in fact, the McDonnell Douglas officials seemed like little more than couriers for their foreign agents. In one instance, Pruitt hand-carried a cashier's check for $395,500 from Long Beach, California, to Sequeira in Karachi, then took the check from Karachi to Geneva where he negotiated it at Sequeira's bank. He returned to Pakistan carrying Bhutto's and Mahmoud's share of the commission payment.

Just why Pruitt was so cooperative had also become apparent, and it added another potential crime to any indictment: perjury. Before embarking on his trip to Pakistan, Lubin had made requests for documents related to the case in various countries, one of which was Switzerland. Working closely with another lawyer in the Justice Department who specialized in foreign discovery requests, Lubin carefully drafted the request so as to characterize the suspected activity as a violation of Swiss law. Under an existing treaty with the U.S., the Swiss would cooperate with requests for evidence if the U.S. charges were also a violation of Swiss law. Foreign bribery isn't a crime in Switzerland, so the prosecutors characterized the offense as fraud. Lubin also worried that he was being forced to disclose to the Swiss authorities some confidential information from the grand jury testimony, but decided he had little choice but to comply with their requests.

His careful planning eventually paid off. On the way back from Karachi, he had a stopover in Rome, where he picked up the Swiss documents from the Swiss consulate there. Among those documents were the bank records of Sequeira and Mahmoud.

Lubin was also carrying documents back from Pakistan, which he'd obtained in much the same way. Pakistan, however, hadn't had a treaty with the U.S. governing the exchange of documents needed in judicial proceedings, so Lubin drew one up. "It had lots of ribbons and seals—it was suitable for framing," Lubin recalls proudly. In another example of the importance of Pakistani cooperation, the government readily approved the agreement and granted Lubin's requests while he was in the country.

A close examination of the bank records when Lubin got home showed that whenever a McDonnell Douglas check was deposited by Sequeira, another check was paid out. What made Lubin suspicious was that the amount of the payment was always the same percentage of the McDonnell Douglas deposit, suggesting that Sequeira was making a kickback to an as-yet-unnamed accomplice in the scheme. Lubin suspected Pruitt.

Sure enough, when Lubin made another document request to the Swiss, a bank account belonging to Pruitt showed up at the same bank as Sequeira's, with deposits in the amounts indicated on Sequeira's statements. It was now obvious to Lubin that Pruitt had lied in his grand jury testimony at exactly those points where his demeanor had suggested the possibility.

Lubin was growing increasingly confident that he could make out a criminal case against McDonnell Douglas, and some of its officers too. In order to pick up the pace of the investigation and speed the progress of the grand jury, Lubin enlisted the assistance of another prosecutor in the fraud unit, George Mendelson. Mendelson had been a prosecutor in New Jersey, and had come to the Justice Department to prosecute offshore banking cases. With the rise to prominence of the foreign payments cases, however, he was diverted to assist Lubin.

Both found the McDonnell Douglas case to be the most challenging they had worked on. "You really want this kind of case in the sunset of your career," Lubin says. "You need to apply every skill developed over a lifetime of practice. It's not really for the sunrise of your career—I mean, we'll probably never have another case like this in our lives. I was drinking this in. I was living with new revelations every day. It was intoxicating."

As intensely as Lubin and Mendelson were pursuing the case, however, events in the Lockheed investigation moved ahead of them. Prosecutors in that case were ready to obtain indictments of individual officers, arguing that the evidence was sufficient to establish individual, as opposed to corporate, culpability. But Lockheed subsequently agreed to plead guilty and pay $647,000 in fines and penalties.

The effect on the Lockheed prosecutors and their colleagues in the fraud section was demoralizing. The fine Lockheed paid seemed like a slap on the wrist—an insignificant amount given that the company's illegal behavior had resulted in $430 million in sales of Lockheed aircraft. They didn't see how the result would deter any other companies from engaging in bribes.

Nor did Lockheed provide much of a precedent for other prosecutions. Although the company pleaded guilty to fraud charges, based on the same theory that Lubin and Mendelson were developing in McDonnell Douglas, there had been no court ruling validating the theory.

Most of all, Lubin and Mendelson were disappointed at the decision not to seek individual indictments for corporate officers. They saw such charges as the key to deterrence, and it was a major focus of their own investigation. "We could have gotten a corporate plea like Lockheed's out of McDonnell Douglas a year earlier," Lubin says. "What the hell were we working so hard for if that's all we'd end up with?"

Indeed, Lubin had first discussed the possibility of a plea bargain with McDonnell Douglas officials in January 1979, shortly after he returned from Pakistan. Veryl Riddle, general outside counsel to McDonnell Douglas and a partner in Bryan, Cave, McPheeters & McRoberts, St. Louis's most prominent law firm, told Lubin bluntly that the company wanted to "shut down" the investigation and was willing to consider guilty pleas to various statutes.

During the same month, Lubin met with lawyers for Brizendine and Pruitt, also to talk about pleas. They were less amenable—their lawyers found it difficult to accept the fact that the government would seriously consider charging individuals in the case, when it had never done so before. Lubin warned them, however, that their clients could very well end up as defendants if the case reached the indictment stage.

The case against Pruitt, in particular, had been strengthened by the information Lubin had gathered in Pakistan and from other witnesses. He had become convinced that Pruitt lied in his testimony before the grand jury, at precisely those points where Lubin had noticed a pattern of nervousness and tension. Not only did Lubin believe that Pruitt knew more recipients of payments than just Bhutto and Mahmoud, but Pruitt himself was one of the recipients. Pruitt's share went into his own secret Swiss bank account. Even though Pruitt had been granted immunity for his testimony, Lubin warned Pruitt's lawyer that it was likely Pruitt would be indicted for perjury.

Those discussions went nowhere, but talks resumed in mid-February with the lawyers for the corporation. At the February series of meetings, the lawyers for McDonnell Douglas asked specifically for a "Westinghouse" plea, named after a case in which Westinghouse Electric Corporation agreed to plead guilty to felony charges and pay a fine, and in return the government agreed not to prosecute individuals involved in the crime. Lubin and Mendelson, however, balked at the prospect of a Westinghouse plea—it was precisely what they didn't want. Heymann had made clear that the government, as a general policy, shouldn't allow corporations to "buy off" the criminal liability of their officers and employees with corporate pleas and fines, for obvious reasons: the department didn't want to have what seemed a double standard for employees of corporations wealthy enough to engage in such tactics, which had happened all too often in the past. Lubin and Mendelson insisted that any plea reached with McDonnell Douglas would have no bearing on the individuals being investigated, and they refused to discuss those individual cases with the lawyers representing the corporation.

In late February, the corporation tried another approach: it offered to enter into plea negotiations with respect to its submissions to the U.S. Export-Import Bank, which had financed the sale of the planes to Pakistan International Airlines. (The company's submissions had been false, since they concealed the secret commission payments.)

Lubin and Mendelson rejected this too, saying that pleas to Eximbank violations certainly wouldn't be enough to dispose of the case. But they promised to make recommendations with respect to proposed pleas and submit the whole question to an indictment review committee within the Justice Department. Such committees are formed from time to time to provide prosecutors involved in the day-to-day investigation of a case with an objective appraisal of the merits of pursuing an indictment. They are frequently used in cases such as McDonnell Douglas, where the charges are unusual or unprecedented, or likely to generate political controversy.

Lubin prepared a thick, top-secret review memorandum that summarized all the evidence that had so far been presented to the grand jury. The memo was circulated to seven other prosecutors in the department, including Heymann and JoAnn Harris, the head of the fraud section. When the review committee convened in late February,

Lubin and Mendelson made oral presentations in favor of seeking indictments, and then were grilled extensively by the members of the review committee.

Harris, in particular, asked probing questions. She had come to the Justice Department in 1979, the first woman to head a section in the department's history. A native of Macomb, Illinois, who had already had a successful publishing career before entering New York University Law School at age thirty-six, Harris had graduated near the top of her class and had compiled an impressive record as one of the first women prosecutors in the Southern District of New York U.S. Attorney's office.

Harris says she was therefore shocked when she reported for her first day of work in Washington and was told that "the entire section was in open revolt over my appointment." The entire section at the time consisted of sixty-seven lawyers, 85 percent of them male, who had apparently concluded that Harris had been hired only to carry out affirmative action policies of the Carter administration.

Lubin and Mendelson hardly knew Harris, but they had heard those reports. Her performance in the review committee, however, started to lay those concerns to rest. Harris's demeanor is impressive—she's tall, and has a strong, resonant voice. Her questioning also revealed a well thought out sense of the appropriate role of prosecution.

In my view, [prosecution] was where the power to do justice rested, not with the defense bar . . . [she has written]. It really didn't occur to me until much later, when I was exercising this power, that in addition to all of this, responsible prosecutors have a far simpler ethical road to travel. My client has always [underlined] been served when I do the right thing even if it means dismissing or losing a case. Indeed, one of the major satisfactions of the various roles I have played in the Department of Justice has come from the responsibility to use this power in the public up to its very limits, and no [underlined] further [underlined]; to exercise it in decisions not to prosecute as firmly as in decisions to indict. It is easy to get up and go to work every day to a job that not only permits that sort of righteousness, but demands it.

Several factors emphasized by Lubin and Mendelson during their presentation and the questioning finally convinced Harris and the other committee members that indictments of both McDonnell Douglas and some of the individual officers would not constitute overreaching. First, there was the opposition of the Pakistan government to bribes, a policy that had been clearly stated to Pruitt and passed on to other officers. McDonnell Douglas couldn't persuasively argue that it was simply following the customs of the countries in which it did business.

Secondly, there was the secrecy with which the company and officers wrapped the payments and tried to conceal them—even to the point where Pruitt had lied to the grand jury.

Especially in cases where the criminal charges are novel, such evidence that the defendant thinks what he did was wrong can be crucial. One of the most publicly misunderstood aspects of the criminal law is the perception that one must know a criminal law is being violated in order to be guilty of the crime. That isn't usually the case: one must simply act with what is known as "mens rea"—a guilty mind. Many criminals would never have been convicted if they hadn't tried to hide their misconduct, thereby undercutting their subsequent claims that they didn't know they were doing anything wrong.

Despite these factors, McDonnell Douglas was not an easy case for the committee to resolve. Lubin and Mendelson strongly took the position that both corporate and individual indictments should be recommended, but others weren't as certain.

As Harris recalls, "Everyone really agonized over this. It was a really close call. This wasn't, after all, a murder case. The question wasn't simply, 'Is the evidence sufficient?' Even if you have the evidence, there's still the question of whether this is a crime. Should you stretch the mail fraud statute? Is criminal prosecution the appropriate thing to do? These factors are often present when considering white-collar crime—they certainly were in this case."

After several long discussions, however, a consensus emerged: indictments against both the corporation and individuals should be pursued. At the same time, the investigation should continue to seek more and stronger evidence for a case that would undoubtedly be fought with all the resources that one of the country's largest corporations could muster. For that reason, it was only prudent to at least consider the possibility of a plea bargain. These recommendations were sent on to Assistant Attorney General Heymann, who approved them.

Lubin and Mendelson were pleased by the review committee's decision, even though they felt they could have obtained indictments from the grand jury immediately based on the evidence that had already been submitted. Given the outcome of the Lockheed case, they were relieved that their prosecution was still on track and that they had the backing of the administration. But the committee's decision to keep investigating the case did pose one practical problem: the term of the grand jury, which lasts six months, was about to expire. The prosecutors had no choice but to empanel a successor grand jury to continue hearing testimony.

They did so in April, knowing that they would almost certainly be challenged later by McDonnell Douglas if indictments resulted. The problem is that members of the second grand jury could have the testimony of earlier witnesses read to them, but they couldn't observe their demeanor and reach conclusions about their credibility. Defense lawyers could be expected to claim that the second grand jury couldn't perform its function of independently weighing the evidence. But this was a risk the prosecutors had to take.

The results of the review committee's deliberations also had the effect of stepping up the pressure on McDonnell Douglas and the potential individual defendants. In March, formal letters were sent to Pruitt, Forsyth, and Brizendine, notifying them that they had become targets of the grand jury's investigation.

At the same time, Lubin and Mendelson indicated to the McDonnell Douglas lawyers that they were interested in resuming plea negotiations. As an inducement, they said that they would be willing, for the first time, to discuss some kind of a Westinghouse plea in which the corporation would be allowed to plead guilty and no individual indictments would be sought. The prosecutors made clear that they personally remained opposed to any Westinghouse plea, but that they would negotiate and pass the results on to their superiors in the department, who, they indicated, might find it acceptable.

In fact, Lubin and Mendelson had initially been adamantly opposed to any talk of a Westinghouse plea; they thought the matter had been laid to rest in the earlier, abortive plea discussions. But their views had been softened somewhat by introducing a new aspect to the discussions: the prospect that McDonnell Douglas could be induced to plead guilty to criminal violations of the Racketeer Influenced and Corrupt Organizations Act, popularly known as RICO. Not only might McDonnell Douglas be publicly branded a racketeer for its conduct, but the statute also provides for triple monetary damages, giving it a far more potent deterrent effect.

The RICO statute is part of the Organized Crime Control Act, and grew out of congressional hearings in the late sixties into the inadequacy of federal laws intended to curb unlawful activities of the Mafia. Despite the act's name, the final legislation wasn't limited to Mafia activities, but was designed to reach all types of sophisticated criminal behavior, particularly fraud. As one commentator noted, "Victims of crime rightly care little that their life savings are stolen by mobsters wearing black shirts and white ties or by accountants while dressed in Brooks Brothers suits."

Lubin and Mendelson thought that if McDonnell Douglas could be persuaded to plead to a RICO charge with substantial money damages, the hundreds of other potential foreign payments cases might produce similar results, which would vastly enrich the U.S. Treasury and at the same time create a real deterrent to future violations.

Plea discussions between the prosecutors and counsel for both McDonnell Douglas and possible individual defendants resumed in late April, and initially made little progress. At the same time, the prosecutors called some of the company's key executives before the grand jury. In early May, two of the chairman's sons, John and James III, the latter known as "Jimmy," came to Washington and testified before the grand jury. Though they were represented by counsel, neither was given any immunity in return for his testimony. Both were assured that at that time they weren't targets of the investigation.

John McDonnell, the eldest son and a corporate vice president, testified first, on May 1 and 2. Lubin thought he was a strong witness. Bright, confident, and apparently a natural leader, he seemed his father's obvious heir apparent. He wasn't directly involved in the incidents in Pakistan, and contributed little to the case. Nor did he say anything that made Lubin suspect he was dissembling or evading questions.

Jimmy McDonnell was scheduled to testify on Tuesday, May 15. The evening before, Lubin was still at the office when his pregnant wife called, asking to be taken to the hospital. The next day, their first child was born, and Lubin was at the hospital. "It killed me to miss Jimmy's first day of testimony," he says. But Mendelson handled the questioning, and Lubin was back at work the following day. The grand jurors gave him a card congratulating him on the birth of his daughter, signed by each of them. "By then, we'd spent so much time together that we were like a family," Lubin says.

JIMMY McDonnell's testimony was a sharp contrast to that of his brother. Though he bore his father's name, Jimmy displayed little of his father's drive. He seemed ill at ease and restless, frequently pausing, and indicating many lapses of memory on crucial events. McDonnell also indicated that he had direct personal involvement.

"On the basis of what I know today," he testified, "we did at that time have a sales agent in Pakistan. I believe his name was Sequeira Brothers and we had agreed to pay him a certain amount of commission . . . The airline had also been told that . . . our only agreement with Sequeira was for $100,000 commission payment, which they . . . said they would deduct from their price from the airplane, whereas at one time we had an agreement up to $500,000 per airplane with Sequeira . . . Some letters to the airline had been signed stating that, as I say, our only agreement with Sequeira was for $100,000 . . . In fact payment was made to Sequeira for the full amount. I was told or acquired the knowledge that Sequeira said he had so-called commitments with, I believe, it was the nephew of the president of the country at that time," he testified with a halting cadence.

In other words, McDonnell's testimony indicated he personally knew of the payments, knew they were misrepresented to be $100,000 when they were actually $500,000, and knew that Sequeira had "commitments," i.e., bribes, with the "nephew" of the president.

Nonetheless, it was what McDonnell didn't say as much as what he did say that caused the prosecutors to focus new suspicion on him. On key points, for example, he couldn't recall what had happened, even though documents indicated he had been personally involved. Altogether, he said more than 250 times in the course of his testimony that he couldn't remember. Alleged failures of memory alone have formed the basis for prosecutions for perjury and obstruction of justice.

Lubin and Mendelson carefully reviewed McDonnell's testimony, and eight days later, his lawyers were notified that McDonnell's status in the case had changed: henceforth, the chairman's son was also a target of the grand jury's investigation. Jimmy's lawyers were furious. Jimmy's testimony was supposed to resume at the end of the month but was canceled. His lawyers said that Jimmy would now plead the Fifth Amendment and refuse to testify in response to all questions.

For the prosecutors, the maneuver was in part purely tactical, a way of stepping up the pressure or, in Lubin's words, "orchestrating a climax to the investigation." Jimmy's lawyers tried repeatedly to meet with Lubin and Mendelson to find out why they had changed their position toward Jimmy, but the prosecutors refused, deliberately allowing the lawyers' anxiety to mount that other officials—even the company chairman—might also become targets. "They were dying to know what was going on," Lubin recalls with satisfaction.

The tactic seemed to work. Chairman McDonnell, the company's founder, who was now eighty years old, had consistently refused to provide any testimony. He'd taken the position that he had nothing to contribute to the investigation, since his position was far above the level at which such dealings occurred. He'd also broken his hip in a recent fall, making travel to the grand jury difficult. Now, however, in an effort to head off an indictment of his middle (and some say most loved) son, McDonnell, known to all as "Old Mac," agreed to be questioned if the prosecutors would come to his office in St. Louis. Lubin eagerly accepted.

Lubin arrived at McDonnell Douglas's St. Louis headquarters on a hot day in mid-July. McDonnell's office had a huge window looking out on to Lambert Field, St. Louis's international airport, where McDonnell could watch the planes he had helped design in action. In the office he had a scale model of every aircraft his company had ever designed and produced, from the old DC-3 to the company's most recent, the DC-10, one of which had just crashed after takeoff in Chicago in one of the country's worst aviation disasters.

Lubin and McDonnell were alone in the office; McDonnell's lawyers had agreed to be excluded, much to Lubin's surprise. But the tactic worked to McDonnell's advantage. Gradually, he wooed Lubin. He told him how, as a young man fresh out of MIT, he couldn't find a job and had to start his own aviation company. Later, he bought the Douglas Aircraft Company, one of the companies that had turned him down flat years before. They talked aeronautics, and McDonnell told of his love for the company and its employees. Lubin felt himself being won over.

Later, Lubin thought about his encounter with McDonnell when McDonnell's lawyer, the eminent Washington defense attorney Edward Bennett Williams, urged him not to indict the chairman. "Edward Bennett Williams told me he'd represented a client," Lubin recalls, "and he was going to be indicted. Williams warned the prosecutor that the indictment would kill him. And it did.

"You do think about these things," Lubin continues. "Old Mac was a remarkable man, a pioneer of American aviation. He had sixty thousand employees. You can't just ask yourself, 'Do I have the facts to indict this man?' You have to ask, 'Should I, given his age and health?' "

Lubin hadn't yet resolved that question by the time plea negotiations in the case accelerated rapidly.

Citing Jimmy McDonnell as a target had initially been a setback to settlement talks. But gradually, counsel for the various potential defendants again began calling Lubin and Mendelson, asking for more talks. The prosecutors' strategy was to "crack" one of the top three individual defendants—Pruitt, Forsyth, or Brizendine—in return for testimony implicating individuals even higher in the corporation. It is a common tactic in conspiracy cases, and prosecutors often succeed. Potential defendants recognize that the first to agree to plead in return for testimony is likely to receive the best deal—once one has given in, further offers for cooperation tend to disappear.

Though the prosecutors thought they were close to an agreement with Brizendine, those negotiations fell apart in a shouting match with Brizendine's lawyer. The main obstacle was that Lubin and Mendelson insisted on guilty pleas to felony charges. The targets' lawyers thought the prosecutors were bluffing—that they wouldn't ever succeed in getting indictments against individual defendants in a case so novel. So no plea agreements in the individual cases emerged.

The corporate plea bargain was another matter, however.

BY early August, Lubin and Mendelson thought the grand jury was nearing the end of its work on McDonnell Douglas. They met again with the review committee inside the Justice Department, which approved the prospect of individual indictments, but again strongly recommended that plea negotiations with the corporation be resumed.

The committee's goal was to present Heymann, the Assistant Attorney General, with two clear-cut options. The lawyers knew that the decision to indict individuals in the case wouldn't be an easy one— McDonnell Douglas would be the first investigation of overseas sales practices of an American corporation to result in criminal charges against individual employees and officers. But individual indictments was one option. If that was rejected, the prosecutors wanted an alternative that was more than a slap on the wrist to the company—a plea to a RICO charge.

On August 22, Lubin met with the company's defense team, which included Riddle from St. Louis and Washington lawyer and former

Defense Secretary Clark Clifford, one of the capital's foremost power brokers, who had grown up in St. Louis with Old Mac. For a young lawyer like Lubin, the McDonnell Douglas team seemed awesome. "Here I was a kid in my twenties," he says, "up against Clark Clifford."

Lubin was still personally uneasy about the prospect of a corporate plea, but he assured the defense lawyers that if a satisfactory agreement could be reached, including a guilty or nolo contendere plea to a RICO count, he would recommend a Westinghouse plea to Heymann and recommend that the individual prosecutions be dropped. He couldn't promise that Heymann would accept the terms, but the defense lawyers realized that it would be an unusual step for an Assistant Attorney General to overrule the trial prosecutors in such circumstances. Somewhat to Lubin's surprise, Clifford seemed reasonably amenable to his proposal.

Lubin agreed to send a draft of the proposed plea agreement to the defense lawyers, and they met again in September to discuss it and make a few revisions. By mid-September, it looked as if they had an agreement. All that remained was for the final papers to be sent to St. Louis for approval by the chairman and the top corporate officers.

Lubin was pleased with the course of the negotiations, and slightly surprised that they had gone so smoothly, especially after his failure with counsel for the potential individual defendants. At the same time, he felt some misgivings. Deep down, he knew that once McDonnell Douglas had agreed to a plea, his hopes for individual prosecutions would be dashed.

On September 26, at 4:30 in the afternoon, the McDonnell Douglas lawyers were scheduled to meet with Lubin and Mendelson to deliver the company's final response to the proposed plea. That morning, Lubin was at the grand jury, questioning the last scheduled witness in the McDonnell Douglas matter. Time was becoming a pressing consideration; on October 15, the statute of limitations—the period during which criminal charges can be brought by the government—was due to expire with respect to McDonnell Douglas. It had been one thing to get a second grand jury involved in the case. An extension of the statute of limitations was almost unthinkable.

During the lunch break, Lubin got word from another lawyer in the office that the meeting that afternoon had just taken on a new dimension. Clifford had called the department to report that in addition to the lawyers for McDonnell Douglas, Old Mac himself had insisted on coming to the meeting, despite his broken hip. Clifford said that he had tried to talk the chairman out of coming—anything the chairman said might be used against him or the company, just as if he were testifying without immunity—but Old Mac had rejected his lawyer's advice. He was, in fact, already en route to Washington on a company jet.

"We're meeting with the Old Mac," Lubin told Mendelson as soon as he got off the phone. Mendelson seemed unconcerned, but then, he hadn't met the redoubtable chairman. Lubin had misgivings. "He's a proud man," Lubin said, speculating that the plea negotiations might yet develop an unexpected twist. He wondered if they'd pushed too hard with the chairman's son. He knew the fierce loyalty Old Mac felt toward his family.

When they got back to their offices in the Justice Department building, the prosecutors met first with Clifford and the other lawyers for the company, warning them that they were concerned about meeting directly with the company chairman. But Clifford said that the chairman had insisted on coming to Washington so that he could personally deliver his reaction to the proposed plea agreement. It would be a terrible blow, he said, to deprive the elderly man of that opportunity now.

Old Mac was invited into the meeting. He walked slowly because of his injured hip and looked grave, but still managed to convey the commanding air that had so impressed Lubin in St. Louis. He took his place at the conference table, then Mendelson explained that he would have to give him Miranda warnings. He told him that his statements could be used against him if he became a defendant in the case, and that anything he said could be used against the corporation as well. Then the prosecutors left the room so that McDonnell's counsel could discuss the warnings with him and try to talk him out of speaking.

When they returned, Mendelson asked if Old Mac understood and, if so, if he still wanted to make a statement. Clifford said that the chairman understood the warnings and that he did wish to make a statement, although the only subject he would address was the proposed plea agreement.

"To make a long story short," the chairman began in a firm voice, gazing directly at the prosecutors, "McDonnell Douglas Corporation cannot make this settlement. I couldn't live with myself if I did." There was a moment's shocked silence, then he went on.

"This [McDonnell Douglas] is my baby, my little jewel. I cannot live with this settlement. I say 'I' for simplicity, but our company, our people can't. We have labored forty years . . . When I graduate to another phase of existence . . ." His voice wavered, and he seemed momentarily unable to proceed. But taking a deep breath, he continued, "I can't do it. I can't see my baby clobbered this way. I can't live with it. I can't die with this. After working on this with my associates all day yesterday . . . I couldn't sleep last night. A deep inner psyche says fight all the way. If we lose, fight on appeal. That's where it stands. That's where Old Mac stands."

The chairman bowed his head, wiping tears from his eyes. Then he rose slowly from his chair and walked by himself out of the room. No one spoke.

Lubin was stunned, and deeply moved. He had just seen the consequences to one of the country's most esteemed corporate titans of an investigation he, a young, relatively inexperienced prosecutor, had set in motion more than a year ago. It was a humbling experience. Even so, he knew something had to be done to salvage the negotiations.

He and the other prosecutors asked the defense counsel for an explanation. Was it just part of the plea proposal that McDonnell found so objectionable? Or was the very idea of a guilty plea anathema to him? Defense counsel indicated that the RICO charge, which would have branded McDonnell Douglas a "racketeer," with all its associations with organized crime, was most objectionable. Discussions quickly foundered, however, because the RICO charge was an aspect of the plea that the prosecutors weren't willing to negotiate. The lawyers decided to take a break.

During the interval, the prosecutors discussed how to proceed. They weren't sure whether McDonnell fully understood the consequences of rejecting the plea. Did he realize that individuals were likely to be indicted? If he was so concerned about his "baby," McDonnell Douglas, what about his real baby—his son Jimmy? But they opted not to discuss the consequences with McDonnell himself. They assumed that his lawyers had already explained them to him, and they also feared that such a discussion might later lead to charges that they tried to pressure him unfairly with threats of individual prosecution.

When they rejoined the McDonnell Douglas defense lawyers, they discussed whether to speak again to McDonnell. They said they were concerned that McDonnell's long, personal attachment to the company might have clouded his judgment and his understanding of the hardships a trial would impose on the company. Clifford agreed, and asked McDonnell to rejoin the meeting.

The effort was unavailing. The prosecutors explained the consequences of an indictment (without mentioning the possibility of individual indictments) and indicated that recent evidence in the case had been so strong that they were barely able to recommend the plea agreement that had been reached. It was, in other words, the company's last chance to escape a long, expensive, potentially damaging public trial.

Old Mac said he understood everything he was being told, but he remained adamant. "If this company that I've led is as rotten as you say, then I want to see it in court and all McDonnell Douglas people will have to take the consequences," he said. The meeting adjourned.

The next day, Lubin, Mendelson, and the other prosecutors present for the meeting met with the Deputy Assistant Attorney General for the Criminal Division, Jack Keeney, to report on the progress of the plea negotiations. They didn't expect Keeney to be pleased. The quintessential career administrator, Keeney seemed to prefer tidy plea bargains to public trials. Nonetheless, he could be counted on not to rock any boats.

What they had to report, of course, was a total breakdown of the plea negotiations. They had failed to avert what was a politically sensitive dilemma. If both the company and individual executives weren't indicted, then the administration might be criticized for softness on white-collar crime; if they were indicted, others would probably criticize the administration for unfairly indicting American business.

But Lubin's job was prosecution. As he explained to Keeney, as far as he was concerned, McDonnell Douglas had made the decision, and had relieved the administration of what was likely to be a difficult choice. There was no doubt in his mind now that the indictments should go forward. Keeney finally agreed, and authorized Lubin and Mendelson to proceed with drafting the indictments for presentation to the grand jury.

The defendants made one last attempt to reach a settlement. The day after the meeting with Keeney, the prosecutors called or sent letters tó the likely defendants, notifying them that indictments had been approved by the Deputy Assistant Attorney General. Jimmy McDonnell was told that no decision had yet been made in his case.

Clark Clifford immediately asked for another meeting, claiming he had some new information that the prosecutors should consider. He said that the McDonnell Douglas board of directors had been stunned to learn of the chairman's position, and were willing to override his objections and enter into the proposed plea that Old Mac had rejected. But even if the prosecutors had wanted to accept the plea now, it was too late. As they explained to Clifford, they couldn't accept the plea now that official letters had been issued to potential defendants notifying them that indictments had been authorized at the highest levels of the department. If they did, it would look as though the government had allowed McDonnell Douglas to "buy off" the individual indictments by rushing in with a plea only after it was obvious that the executives would be indicted.

Clifford seemed exasperated, and asked for a meeting with both the Assistant Attorney General himself, Heymann, and Keeney. They met the following day, on October 3, and Clifford charged that the prosecutors were now pursuing vengeance against the company and its officers because of Chairman McDonnell's intransigence at the meeting that was supposed to conclude the plea bargain.

The meeting made both Lubin and Mendelson nervous. They were present, but weren't supposed to speak. They hadn't had much contact with Heymann, and didn't know him well. Heymann had come to Washington as a Harvard Law School professor, and they worried how a professor's mind would respond to such real-life confrontation. Adding to their anxiety was the date—the expiration of the statute of limitations was only twelve days away. The grand jury term was expiring even sooner—on October 10.

Both at the meeting and by telephone the next day, Heymann rejected Clifford's suggestions and ruled out the possibility of the Westinghouse-type plea. But as Lubin had feared, Heymann wavered slightly, indicating that he might be willing to reopen negotiations if the problem with the statute of limitations could somehow be resolved.

Meanwhile, Lubin and Mendelson worked furiously on drafts of the indictments that would be submitted to the grand jury, a task that also posed some delicate problems.

Chief among them was what to do about the RICO charges that had proved to be the stumbling block for Chairman McDonnell. Lubin and Mendelson wanted to include them, in large part because they offered the potential for treble damages. They and others in the department recognized, however, that RICO charges against American companies that seemed far from the mainstream of organized crime were becoming increasingly controversial.

The problem was largely the language of the statute and its use of the word "racketeer." In the minds of most Americans, that meant the Mafia. Corporate defendants accused under the statute had been reaping a public-relations windfall by attacking the government for linking them unfairly to organized crime. In front of a jury, the statute also posed problems. How should prosecutors explain to juries that though the statute used the word "racketeer," it meant anyone who might have been involved in fraudulent activity?

The issue was such that Heymann himself had to become involved in the departmental discussions about how to phrase the charges. The Justice Department had RICO cases, hundreds of them, pending all over the country. Most of them were in areas such as narcotics that had direct or close ties to organized crime efforts. Nonetheless, there were already rumblings in Congress that the RICO statute was being abused by the government to indict respectable citizens. Heymann and the prosecutors knew already that the McDonnell Douglas case, being the first of its kind, would generate a storm of publicity. Risking further controversy by charging the defendants with racketeering, they decided, was too dangerous, even though legitimate under the law. Heymann made the final decision: the RICO charges would be dropped. If that decision had only been made earlier, Old Mac probably wouldn't have derailed the plea negotiations.

By now there were only days remaining before the grand jury deadline, and Lubin started drafting furiously, working from seven in the morning to midnight.

It was a daunting task. Out of the masses of documents and information presented to the grand jury, Lubin had to select those facts that added up to a clear violation of law, one that could be followed first by the grand jury and later, if the grand jury approved the indictments, by a trial jury. It was no use throwing in everything but the kitchen sink: that risked including weak allegations, which, when they become the focus of defense counsel at trial, can sometimes drag down an entire case.

Clearly, the Pakistan events would form the core of the indictments. But McDonnell Douglas had been bribing foreign officials in other countries too. Out of a laundry list of possibilities, Lubin settled on Pakistan, the Philippines, Korea, and Venezuela. The latter three were concededly less clear-cut and less egregious, but they demonstrated that the events in Pakistan weren't isolated—they were part of a worldwide pattern of behavior.

JoAnn Harris worked closely with both Lubin and Mendelson on the drafting and conceptualizing of the indictments, though she was distracted by the death of her father while the indictments were being prepared. So did Richard Shine, the department's expert on foreign payments.

Finally, during the first week in October, a finished draft was ready for review by senior lawyers in the department. The indictments named McDonnell Douglas and four individuals: Brizendine, the president of Douglas Aircraft and a member of the McDonnell Douglas board; Pruitt, the sales manager for Pakistan; Forsyth, the vice president for marketing; and finally, James McDonnell III, the chairman's son and a member of the corporation's board. The Pakistani participants, including Leslie Sequeira and Afsar Hussain, were described as "co-schemers."

The boldest aspect of the indictments would be the naming of Jimmy McDonnell, and the prosecutors wanted his involvement to be clear in the document in anticipation of the storm of protest and publicity that was likely to result. The draft alleged that Jimmy reviewed agreements and amendments to agreements with Sequeira Brothers, had phone and telex communications with Forsyth while the arrangement was being made, discussed the secret payments with Pruitt, received memoranda outlining the arrangement, and, ultimately, approved some agreements. Keeney had already approved the inclusion of McDonnell in the indictments (though Heymann hadn't yet reviewed it), and on October 5, McDonnell was notified officially that the decision had been made to seek his indictment.

Although detailed, the draft managed to condense the events of a multiyear period into twenty-one pages and eleven counts of fraud and conspiracy, including seventy-three "overt acts" committed in furtherance of the conspiracy.

The principal victims of the fraud: Pakistan and its state-owned airline, PIA. McDonnell Douglas had secretly taken $500,000 out of its proceeds from each DC-10 aircraft (each cost PIA more than $20 million) and paid it to Sequeira, Bhutto, and Mahmoud. PIA paid the money as a result of "false and fraudulent representations as to the identity of its sales agents and the amount of commission to be paid," the document charged.

In crafting the indictments, the prosecutors had been careful to skirt the issue of foreign payments subsequently made illegal by the Foreign Corrupt Practices Act. As crafted, the indictments didn't claim that the foreign bribes were the essence of the crime. Rather, it was the failure to disclose them that constituted crime.

All that remained was Heymann's approval. He was a nice guy, but could he make a decision? Was he such an intellectual that he was paralyzed? This impasse was exactly what Lubin feared when he learned that a Harvard professor was heading the Criminal Division. He kept flip-flopping on this case.

The day passed, and still no decision. The grand jury term was expiring the next day. Then Lubin learned from Keeney that Heymann couldn't decide. He didn't want to be rushed into a decision.

The morning of the tenth, Lubin arrived at the office at 7 A.M. to go over the final document and correct any typographical errors. By 9 A.M. he was ready to leave the office for the courthouse; he planned to present the indictments to the grand jury when its session began at 9:30 A.M.

By 9 there was still no word. "Heymann was agonizing," Lubin recalls, "and finally he just threw up his hands. I was so exasperated. I'd been in there the night before until midnight, in early that morning. The grand jury was about to expire, and it's terrible to have to re-present a case."

The prosecutors got on the phone to defense counsel. They indicated that there were some second thoughts within the department about the indictments, but that the expiration of the grand jury and the statute of limitations was weighing heavily on the decision. If they were held to those deadlines, the department might be forced into approving the indictments. If not . . . The implication was clearly that if given more time, the indictments might not be approved; plea negotiations might even be reopened.

Clark Clifford, sensing opportunity, proposed a thirty-day extension of both deadlines. Still, he had to obtain the approval of all the defendants that very day before the grand jury term expired without an extension. Lubin and Mendelson were on pins and needles waiting for news. Finally, late in the day, Clifford called them back. The defendants had all agreed to a thirty-day extension. Now all the prosecutors had to do was to win over their own boss.

During the next month, defense lawyers made strenuous efforts to dissuade Heymann from approving indictments. On several occasions, meeting alone and in various combinations, the defense lawyers made policy arguments and even submitted their own interview notes of potential witnesses to make their case. It was a measure of the legal and political sensitivity of the case that the head of the Criminal Division committed hours of his time to the exercise. Throughout the meetings, Lubin and Mendelson were present, and they weren't persuaded.

But several themes emerged. On policy grounds, the defense lawyers argued that it wasn't fair to single out McDonnell Douglas and some of its top officers in what was "a typical overseas payments case." They also raised issues of procedural fairness: they said they had been led to believe that the corporation would be allowed to plead guilty and the charges against individuals would be dropped. After Chairman McDonnell's statement, in what seemed like prosecutorial pique, that position had suddenly changed. And they argued that factually the government of Pakistan and PIA had never really been deceived—a member of the Bhutto family, the de facto government of the country, had even been involved in the alleged conspiracy.

Heymann too seemed unpersuaded by the defense arguments. He said he had fundamental problems with the notion of accepting a corporate guilty plea when it was individuals who were actually culpable. (The notion of corporate criminal liability has always posed such dilemmas since corporations are, after all, collections of people. But it has often proved a useful fiction that corporations, when they behave badly, have minds of their own.)

Heymann reminded the lawyers that the prosecutors had never promised them that a Westinghouse plea would be acceptable to the government. It was, at best, something that they could have recommended for Heymann's consideration. And he noted that just before and after Chairman McDonnell's statement, new facts had emerged that strengthened the government's case. The refusal to further consider the company's offers of a guilty plea, he said, had virtually nothing to do with the chairman's emotional outburst.

But Lubin could sense that Heymann was wavering once again. Heymann assured the defense lawyers that no indictments were imminent and that he would further consider their arguments.

During the first week in November, Lubin and Mendelson spent more time with Heymann than they had in the previous two years. They gave him copies of their prosecution memos for study, and spent hours each day going through the prospective evidence and considering the issues raised by the decision to prosecute this case. Heymann rarely sat in one place. He loved to pace his office, puffing on a pipe, as the prosecutors talked, or to take them outside for long walks around the Capitol mall. The technique forced the prosecutors to rely on their memories, and also made it difficult to take notes.

Although Attorney General Benjamin Civiletti was kept informed of progress in the investigation and of the issues raised, he didn't make any direct recommendations. By and large, the Attorney General stayed out of decisions to prosecute. As a political appointee and direct link to the White House, his participation might have been deemed excessively political in a process that, by its nature, was supposed to be as nonpartisan as possible. Crime is crime, whatever administration is in power, and the Carter administration wanted no suggestions that the powerful or well placed would receive different treatment than anyone else. Already, White House chief of staff Hamilton Jordan had been investigated for alleged cocaine use and Budget Director Bert Lance had been forced to resign after he was charged with criminal violations of the banking laws.

Once again, the decision came down to the wire. Lawyers for the company and the individual targets made lengthy written submissions, reiterating their arguments. On November 8, Heymann finally approved the draft indictments and formally rejected McDonnell Douglas's renewed offer to plead to RICO charges. The next morning Lubin and Mendelson appeared for the last time before the grand jury. The jurors voted for the indictments enthusiastically; several later said they had been hoping the government wouldn't let the individual officers off the hook after what they had heard in testimony.

The immediately ensuing events were traumatic for McDonnell Douglas and the individual defendants, who apparently had never really been able to accept the fact that their criminal indictments were a likelihood.

BEFORE presenting the proposed indictments to the grand jury, Lubin and Mendelson had contacted the U.S. Attorney in Los Angeles, near where all the individual defendants lived and worked, and asked him to have one of his assistants ready as soon as the indictments were approved. That way, FBI agents could move immediately to arrest those indicted and an Assistant U.S. Attorney could bring them into court for an arraignment, where they would be formally notified of the charges against them.

Speed was of the essence. The prosecutors knew that white-collar criminals are more likely to flee and go into hiding than other criminals, principally because they have the financial resources to make escape viable. What's more, one of the defendants—Pruitt—lived on a boat in Long Beach. He could easily pull up anchor and be beyond the U.S. territorial jurisdiction in a matter of hours, with his home intact. They also knew that Pruitt had a Swiss bank account, so getting money out of the country wouldn't be an obstacle for him.

They were so concerned about Pruitt that they had him placed under full-time surveillance. As soon as the indictments were approved by the grand jury, Lubin telexed arrest warrants to Los Angeles. The agents tailed Pruitt as he left his boat and drove to Douglas Aircraft's Long Beach plant.

The agents hoped to catch him before he got inside, but they were detained briefly by security guards. By the time they caught up to him, he was in the middle of the plant, in full view of his fellow employees. Pruitt was arrested on the spot and was read the customary Miranda warning that anything he said henceforth might be used against him in court. Worse, from his point of view, he was handcuffed and led out through the plant. It was a humiliating experience, and one that shocked many of his fellow employees, who had no idea that individual indictments were being considered, let alone imminent.

The defense lawyers were furious. Jack Bray, Pruitt's lawyer, called Lubin and screamed. Brizendine's lawyer, William Norris (now a judge on the Ninth Circuit Court of Appeals), called as soon as he heard of Pruitt's arrest, begging Lubin to reconsider indicting Brizendine. Lubin told him it was too late.

McDonnell Douglas was hit with an avalanche of press coverage. The blitz of adverse publicity that the company's lawyers had hoped to avoid had begun.

The reality of the indictments prompted another round of discussions with the defense lawyers. "We had constant meetings with defense counsel," Lubin recalls. "We ran from one set of defense attorneys to another. They all came in, trying to convince us to drop the prosecution or to let them plead to minor charges."

The prosecutors were most interested in talking to Pruitt and his lawyer, since they felt they still had some leverage with Pruitt. Although Pruitt was indicted for his conduct in the Pakistan bribery scheme, he hadn't been indicted for perjury. And although Pruitt was in some senses the one who had behaved most criminally, he was also the lowest ranking of the defendants. It might be worthwhile to let Pruitt plea bargain in order to obtain additional information from him and secure his role as a cooperative witness at trial.

"We wanted Sherman [Pruitt] to cooperate," Lubin recalls. "We thought he could probably further the investigation, especially on Forsyth. We kept hoping we could take this investigation higher, into the top ranks of the company.

"Typically," he explains, "you get a situation in a conspiracy where the whole thing collapses. The defendants break ranks. It's no secret that sometimes the first one to break can cut the best deal—maybe the only deal. We thought Pruitt would understand this."

Indeed, there was some indication that the loyalty the individuals felt toward McDonnell Douglas might be weakening. Several of their counsel had been furious at Chairman McDonnell's behavior prior to the indictments. They indicated to the prosecutors that the company was trying to make their clients the scapegoats just so Chairman McDonnell's sense of honor would be protected.

Against this backdrop, Lubin and Mendelson opted for a tough approach toward Pruitt. "We read him the riot act," Lubin recalls. "We confronted him for the first time with the fact that he'd committed perjury." And they did offer him a deal—they'd forget the perjury charges if Pruitt would plead to a felony fraud count.

But their efforts were in vain. Pruitt wouldn't plead to a felony, nor would he agree to talk. The prosecutors concluded he'd been "muzzled" by McDonnell Douglas, though they didn't know how. Their efforts to extract pleas from Brizendine and Forsyth, with whom they had less leverage than with Pruitt, were equally unsuccessful. Although Lubin and Mendelson felt they had real strengths as prosecutors, they were beginning to conclude that plea negotiating wasn't one of them.

But momentum, they felt, was on their side. Both the company and the individual defendants were still reeling from the shock of the indictments, and Lubin had an idea that would put them even more on the defensive. It was also a tactic that looked far ahead in the case, to the time when any convictions the prosecutors eventually obtained might be on appeal. When a criminal case is likely to be controversial, appeals from any convictions are a near certainty, and prosecutors have to measure everything they do by the standards likely to be applied by an appeals court.

In this instance, Lubin was worried by the role that McDonnell Douglas's lawyers had played during the investigation, since both the Bryan, Cave firm in St. Louis and Williams & Connolly in Washington had represented not only the company but some of the individuals as well. (It might also help explain how the defendants had maintained such a united front.)

Lubin's fear was that after being convicted the individual defendants would argue on appeal that they had been denied their right to independent counsel, since their lawyers were also representing McDonnell Douglas, which had different interests. The argument was all the more likely, Lubin thought, since it was the company's chairman who had scuttled settlement talks that, if successful, would have kept the individuals from being indicted.

Such arguments didn't seem all that likely to succeed. The individuals had chosen their own lawyers, fully aware that they were also representing the company. But Lubin didn't want to take any chances. Working with the appeals division of the Justice Department, he prepared a motion asking that the lawyers for McDonnell Douglas be disqualified.

He had to admit that the motion's appeal was as much tactical as anything else—filing it was the equivalent of lobbing a hand grenade into the enemy camp.

"We had them on the run with the indictments," Lubin gleefully recalls, "and then we filed the first motion. It was great tactically. My adrenaline was really flowing."

For Lubin and Mendelson, it was the high-water mark of both the prosecution and, as it turned out, their careers as prosecutors.

THE McDonnell Douglas cases, docketed in the federal District Court for the District of Columbia, were assigned to a relatively recent Carter appointee to the federal bench and a woman, Joyce Hens Green. Judge Green hadn't developed much of a reputation in complicated business cases, but the prosecutors were pleased nonetheless. They didn't fear that she would identify more with the defendants than with them, as might be the case with some judges who maintained strong Establishment ties.

When the judge asked for a hearing in the case, Lubin and Mendelson realized that they had underestimated the resources that such a major corporation could bring to bear in its defense. The two relatively young prosecutors sat alone at the large table reserved for the government lawyers. On the other side of the room, defense lawyers filled their table and spilled over into the spectator area, which was full. Several lawyers stood. Judge Green quipped that if she wanted to descend from the bench to talk with counsel she'd have no choice but to sit on the prosecution side of the courtroom.

"They had legions of people," Lubin recalls. "Every firm had two or three lawyers plus a team of paralegals. There were eight lead counsel, who could barely fit around the counsel table."

The prosecutors' hopes that their motion to disqualify defense counsel would embroil their opponents in responding were dashed. The defense had ample manpower to handle the disqualification motion at the same time they prepared their own counteroffensive. When it came it was massive, and it quickly put Lubin and Mendelson on the defensive, struggling to defend their own conduct at the same time they tried to keep the prosecution going forward.

When the defendants weighed in with their motions to dismiss the indictments, one major thrust of the arguments wasn't unexpected. Just as the prosecutors and Heymann had struggled with the appropriateness of what were concededly novel charges, the defendants seized on this aspect to argue that they had been denied due process of law.

The "due-process" clause of the Fifth Amendment to the Constitution—that no man shall be denied "life, liberty, or property, without due process of law"—is the wellspring of the body of jurisprudence that forms the core of American criminal law. Its principles have been applied in sometimes far-reaching ways; some of its applications have prompted attacks from law-and-order advocates, arguing that it has been distorted by judicial activists with excessive concern for the alleged rights of criminals.

The meaning of the clause has been largely defined by the judiciary, the Supreme Court in particular. One area it has addressed under the rubric of due process is the right of a defendant to advance notice that conduct may be criminal; in the words of the Supreme Court, "no man shall be held criminally responsible for conduct which he could not reasonably understand to be proscribed." That principle, in turn, has led courts to strike down countless statutes as too "vague" to provide adequate warning of what conduct is forbidden. Vagrancy and loitering statutes, in particular, have fallen afoul of this requirement.

Related to this notion is the more constitutionally explicit prohibition of ex post facto laws. While that provision of the Constitution applies to Congress, it has been applied to the judiciary as well through the due process clause.

McDonnell Douglas and the individual defendants seized on these basic principles:

> The indictments, although couched in terms of mail fraud, wire fraud, and conspiracy, are in fact based upon the payment of commissions to Pakistani nationals allegedly for the purpose of corruptly influencing the decision of Pakistan International Airlines and the Government of Pakistan with respect to the purchase of wide-bodied aircraft. At the time these payments are alleged to have been made, they were not prohibited by the criminal laws of the United States, nor had any American corporation or individual ever been prosecuted for such conduct. Defendants therefore had no fair warning that their conduct could subject them to penal liability.
>
> A fair reading of the indictment reveals that what is alleged in this case is the same kind of activity that formed the gist of the hundreds of similar pre–Foreign Corrupt Practices Act cases, which have been investigated and disposed of by the Department of Justice and the Securities and Exchange Commission without the indictment of a single corporation or a single individual.

The defendants also attacked the prosecutors for characterizing the case as fraud, using the proposed indictment that had been the basis for the failed plea negotiations to buttress their charge.

"In an effort to avoid the appearance of a retroactive application of the Foreign Corrupt Practices Act, the prosecutors sought in the indictment to shift the focus from the nature of the payments to their nondisclosure." They noted that, in the earlier proposed indictment they had seen, the prosecutors had used the language of the Foreign Corrupt Practices Act, talking of efforts to "corruptly influence" PIA's decision. In the indictment approved by the grand jury, this language was dropped. Instead, the offense was characterized not as bribery but as "nondisclosure."

"These alleged nondisclosures," the defendants continued, were "nothing more than an incidental concomitant of the commission payments themselves. The secrecy, nondisclosures, and deceit alleged in

58

this indictment are the necessary and almost universal features of any payments such as those alleged here." In other words, if bribery wasn't illegal until passage of the Foreign Corrupt Practices Act, and secrecy is part and parcel of bribery, then the secrecy that accompanies bribery couldn't have been criminal before bribery was.

The defendants were also filing their motion at an opportune time. Just a few months earlier, it was revealed that President Jimmy Carter's brother, Billy Carter, was working as an agent for the government of Libya, one of the world's most notorious havens for terrorists. The McDonnell Douglas lawyers were quick to point out that what their clients were being accused of wasn't so different from what the President's brother had been doing:

> William Quandt, a high-ranking official of the National Security Council and an expert on Middle East and North African affairs who had briefed Billy Carter's associate in 1979 [the defense lawyers wrote], commented that it was not surprising that the Libyans had selected the President's brother as agent:
> "In Middle East culture, you always have to have an intermediary to conduct business and blood ties are the closest ties there are. . . . For the Libyans to use the President's brother to try to improve diplomatic relations would be a simple, traditional Middle Eastern pattern."

In one sense, the prosecutors were relieved by the motion. It raised many of the same issues that had figured in their own discussions about whether to pursue the indictments, and it laid the crucial substantive law issues out on the table. They had known they would have to respond to such arguments. Now they could get a judicial resolution of these issues before trial. If the judge supported their legal positions, then they would go forward more confident that any convictions would be later sustained on appeal. If they lost, then at least they wouldn't have wasted the massive effort needed for a full trial.

But they had barely had time to absorb the arguments in the joint motion to dismiss the indictment when they received an entirely separate motion to dismiss filed by the individual defendants. This motion, unlike the first, made the prosecutors' own conduct the issue, charging that they had vindictively obtained the indictments against the individual defendants in retaliation for McDonnell Douglas's refusing to plead to the racketeering charge—a theme earlier sounded in talks with Clark Clifford.

The thrust of their argument was that in the course of plea bargaining, the prosecutors had never explained fully the consequences of rejecting the proposed plea. "Once the prosecutors did make clear the consequences of a rejection of the plea—by sending notices of intention to indict individuals—the corporation promptly authorized its counsel to conclude the agreement. Thus, once informed of its options . . . [McDonnell Douglas] immediately expressed its informed choice," the defendants wrote.

Furthermore, they charged, the indictments were sought out of vindictiveness, not out of a genuine belief that justice demanded criminal indictments. "The obvious prosecutorial interest in McDonnell Douglas's acceptance of the plea proposal, the haste with which the prosecutors acted after communication of Chairman McDonnell's objection to the racketeering language, and the final twist—a RICO threat but thereafter no RICO indictment—together create an unacceptable appearance of vindictiveness. Consequently, due process requires dismissal of the indictment as to the individual defendants."

Lubin and Mendelson were taken aback by the charges, particularly since they had never wanted McDonnell Douglas to plead. They hadn't "retaliated" for its failure to do so; they had been pleased when the company made it possible to prosecute the case the way they thought it should have been all along.

Nonetheless, they realized the motion raised some delicate issues which, since their behavior was at the center of them, would probably decide the fate of their careers. They also recognized that tactically it was a shrewd maneuver by the defense lawyers, the classic strategy of shifting the court's focus from the clients' allegedly criminal conduct to the conduct of someone else. Usually in criminal cases it is the police who become that focus; in this instance it was plainly going to be the prosecutors.

From a legal standpoint, Lubin and Mendelson weren't particularly worried, even though they recognized that the charges would lead the court into the relatively murky area of plea-bargaining law. Plea bargaining is an inherently difficult area of jurisprudence, since the concept is essentially in conflict with the basic notions of due process, yet seems to be essential if the criminal-justice system in this country is going to function.

After all, every plea bargain has an element of "retaliation" in it. The usually tacit bargain is that the prosecutor will recommend less serious charges or lighter sentences if the defendant spares the government the cost and time of putting him through a trial. Since every defendant is constitutionally guaranteed a trial by jury, he is essentially rewarded if he gives up that right and punished if he insists on exercising it.

In the leading case in the field, the Supreme Court tiptoed around this conundrum in the following manner:

> In the give-and-take of plea bargaining, there is no such element of punishment or retaliation so long as the accused is free to accept or reject the prosecution's offer. . . . While confronting a defendant with the risk of more severe punishment clearly may have a discouraging effect on the defendant's assertion of his trial rights, the imposition of these difficult choices is an inevitable—and permissible—attribute of any legitimate system which tolerates and encourages the negotiation of pleas.

As a result, courts have focused on the aspect of free choice in a defendant's decision to accept or reject a plea bargain, and one aspect of choice is whether the defendant has been told the consequences of his decision. The individual defendants in McDonnell Douglas, the lawyers argued, had not.

More worrisome to the prosecutors than these legal principles, however, was the factual aspect of the defense motions. The defense lawyers demanded a full-blown evidentiary hearing into the prosecutors' conduct during and after the plea negotiations with the corporation. Lubin and Mendelson knew they would be placed on the witness stand and subjected to grueling examination by the defense attorneys. They would probably need some kind of representation themselves. That could delay progress in what was already a complicated case for months, even years.

They decided to dig in and fight these diversionary tactics. During the summer of 1980, they again found themselves working weekends and twelve-hour days trying to answer the charges, prepare detailed accounts of the facts leading up to the indictments, and supervise the necessary legal research and drafting of briefs. It was an unusually warm summer, and during the evenings and on weekends, the air conditioning in the Justice Department building was turned off. Lubin bought five fans for his office alone; still, several papers were ruined by sweat dripping off his brow. He felt annoyed every time he drove by the air-conditioned offices of his adversaries. But by early October, nearly a year after the indictments were handed down, the papers were done and the government's answers filed with the court.

There were other reasons why the prospect of delay was so disquieting for Lubin and Mendelson. During the summer they were working on their reply papers to the defense motions, the 1980 presidential election campaign was heating up. By the time they filed their motions, it was increasingly obvious that Ronald Reagan was going to win and that there would be a change of administrations in Washington.

As career prosecutors and civil service employees, Lubin and Mendelson weren't concerned about the fate of their own jobs; neither of the two men is particularly political or ideological. And they weren't terribly worried about the McDonnell Douglas case, since the indictments had already been handed down. Once indictments are issued, it is nearly unheard of for a new administration to drop a prosecution altogether. Even civil cases tend to survive political changes in the White House.

Nonetheless, Lubin and Mendelson recognized that the rhetoric emanating from the Reagan camp wasn't sympathetic to the charges they were pursuing. President Carter's foreign policy was a constant subject of Republican derision, including what was deemed an excessive and "soft" concern for foreign morality at the expense of U.S. security and business interests. There had even been talk among Republicans about trying to repeal the Foreign Corrupt Practices Act. Lubin, in particular, wished the case was just a bit further along. It would have been helpful, for example, if Judge Green had ruled in their favor on the motions to dismiss, at least vindicating the legal positions they had taken and their conduct of the investigation.

A month after the reply briefs were filed, Reagan was elected in a Republican landslide. All of Washington shifted to a transitional frame of mind, as did the Justice Department; it was just as well that not much could happen anyway in the McDonnell Douglas case while the judge was considering the motions. Lubin and Mendelson considered whether now was the time to leave the department, but opted to stay, largely because of their close identification with the case. JoAnn Harris, their section chief, encouraged them. She was confident that, despite a change of administrations, the case would be vigorously pursued, and she thought Lubin and Mendelson were doing a fine job. She assured them that they'd have her backing.

And just before the presidential inauguration, their spirits got a big boost when Judge Green ruled on all the pending motions. Her decision was a sweeping victory for the prosecutors.

"There is no indication of prosecutorial misconduct warranting dismissal of the indictment," Judge Green wrote. "Although the prosecutors certainly were not obligated to reject McDonnell Douglas's change of heart regarding the proposed plea agreement, they had every right to do so. Especially with a statute of limitations about to expire, the prosecutors cannot be faulted for going ahead with the indictments after the plea agreement was rejected." She also made short shrift of the defendants' claims that the fraud charges masked a foreign bribery case. "The prosecutors have disclaimed any intent to prosecute the defendants for foreign bribery, and in fact have not indicted them for that offense."

Although the defendants appealed the decision, the appeals court upheld Judge Green's opinion, and did so with surprising speed. In little more than two months—by mid-March—the case was once again ready to proceed. Judge Green scheduled trial for May.

By the time the Court of Appeals upheld the ruling, the Reagan administration had installed its team at Justice: William French Smith as Attorney General; Edward Schmults as his deputy; Giuliani as Associate Attorney General, the number-three man in the department; and Jensen as the chief of the Criminal Division. Heymann, of course, was gone, but below that level, Lubin and Mendelson were still dealing with the same chain of command: Harris remained head of the fraud section, and Keeney was still deputy chief of the Criminal Division.

After taking office, Smith had asked for a routine review of major pending cases. Harris prepared a list for the fraud section and forwarded it to Jensen, who in turn passed it on to Giuliani. Among the cases singled out for further in-depth review was McDonnell Douglas.

Neither Harris nor Lubin and Mendelson were particularly surprised. Such reviews of important cases were standard, and the case was concededly complicated and politically controversial. Working with Harris, Lubin and Mendelson prepared a comprehensive, detailed analysis of the indictments and what had led up to them, based in part on the earlier memos they had prepared for the department review committee. They were pleased with the work, even though it took time and attention away from the case itself. If anything, they felt the case had grown stronger over time. And now the judge trying the case had accepted their legal theory of the case.

They received no immediate response from the upper levels of the department. Then the first inkling that there might be trouble reached them in a rather indirect way.

The Reagan campaign rhetoric criticizing the Foreign Corrupt Practices Act had quickly been translated into action after the new administration took power. Various legislative proposals were already circulating, intended to repeal or weaken the act. Potential sponsors of the bill had turned to the Justice Department for guidance and an assessment of the act and how it had worked.

Richard Shine, the fraud section lawyer who had worked so closely with Lubin and Mendelson when they were seeking approval to pursue the indictments against McDonnell Douglas, had almost single-handedly been the architect of the Carter administration's campaign against foreign bribery. He was the resident expert on the act and the various cases that had been brought under it. Yet he was excluded from departmental meetings with Jensen and Giuliani in which the act was discussed. "Their position," says one lawyer familiar with the situation, "was that Shine was obsessed with the act and the issue of foreign bribery. They were convinced that all he would try to do was sabotage the Reagan administration's efforts and be a political embarrassment to the department." Gradually, Shine was frozen out of other meetings on other topics too.

The obvious disfavor into which Shine had fallen cast a chill over the fraud section, including Lubin and Mendelson. Shine was a highly regarded lawyer, someone who had worked with dedication in a difficult area, but who was certainly not a political ideologue bent on embarrassing large multinational corporations. He wasn't a political appointee, yet the new administration was turning him into an outcast. Moreover, his exile within the department was a clear indication that administration feelings about the Foreign Corrupt Practices Act ran very high. Despite the careful wording of the indictment and the ruling by the federal court, the McDonnell Douglas case still looked like a foreign bribery case.

Then one day Lubin got a phone call from a friend of his who was a Senate staffer. In a Senate Foreign Relations Committee hearing, Senator John Danforth had asked for the release of some classified information related to foreign payments, and the staffer thought Lubin might be interested.

Lubin knew quite a bit about Danforth. He was a Republican senator from Missouri, McDonnell Douglas's home state. He was an heir to the Ralston Purina fortune, and his brother was chancellor of

Washington University in St. Louis. The McDonnell family and McDonnell Douglas were major benefactors of the university, as was the Danforth family, and Danforth's brother was a member of the McDonnell Douglas board of directors.

Lubin decided to call the senator's office, and he struck up a conversation with one of the senator's assistants. Lubin didn't like what he learned. Danforth was apparently trying to obtain information about other foreign payments cases for use by McDonnell Douglas. In fact, Danforth had written a letter to Senator Charles Percy, then head of the committee, saying explicitly that "it is my belief that the record [of a classified committee hearing into foreign payments] would be material to the preparation of McDonnell Douglas's defense." Lubin thought Danforth was acting more like a lawyer for the company than someone concerned with the public interest. The incidents also suggested the unusual degree of political influence that this defendant could command. "This whole thing made me a little nervous," Lubin recalls. He worked quietly to make sure that Danforth's request for information was denied.

These events took place in April. As May approached and top department officials still hadn't finished their review of pending cases, Lubin had to ask Judge Green for a postponement of the scheduled trial date. Judge Green had heard the administration's talk about the Foreign Corrupt Practices Act, and she wondered if that had implications for the prosecution of the case in her court. She called all the lawyers in the case into a closed, off-the-record session in her courtroom.

Judge Green was characteristically blunt. She said she was aware of sentiment against prosecutions for foreign bribery in the new administration. She didn't think it was fair for the defendants to be put through the time, energy, publicity, and anguish of a trial if the government then might drop the case. She also thought it a monumental waste of the judiciary's resources, including her own time. She told Lubin and Mendelson that she wanted a clear statement of prosecutorial intent from the new administration—a "clarion call"— before she rescheduled the case.

Once again, Lubin and Mendelson were forced to advocate the case within the Justice Department rather than in court.

Lubin and Mendelson went back to JoAnn Harris, who reassured them that the memos they had prepared explaining the case were excellent and would prove persuasive. She also assured them that, as head of the fraud section, she would take a position supporting continued prosecution of the case. She thought it was a terrible precedent to drop a case already under indictment for reasons that were essentially political. She thought it would be a terrible thing if a change in administration meant that criminal cases would be dropped. There had been no change in the facts or change in the law which suggested that McDonnell Douglas shouldn't be prosecuted. If this case were now abandoned, she foresaw endless lobbying efforts by every major corporate defendant charged with crime.

Harris scheduled a meeting with Lowell Jensen, the head of the Criminal Division, to discuss the judge's comments and the case. As usual, Jensen was thoroughly professional. He listened carefully, and assured the lawyers that he understood their position and the issues raised. He was also honest about where the final response would be made: in Associate Attorney General Giuliani's office rather than his. Lubin thought it was pathetic the way Giuliani had moved to seize power within the department, mostly at Jensen's expense. But he could see that Jensen didn't have the temperament for that kind of internal power struggle. Jensen assured the lawyers that he'd argue their position to Giuliani.

Lubin and Mendelson emerged from the meeting considerably cheered. Harris assured them that they could count on Jensen to make sure their position received a fair presentation. She also told them she was recommending them for a special commendation. Among other qualities they had come to respect in her, Harris was single-handedly propping up morale in an administration where her lawyers feared the rug would be pulled from under them at any time. Harris's glowing recommendation of Lubin read:

> I strongly recommend Michael Lubin, an attorney in the fraud section, for a Special Commendation Award. From the fall of 1977 through December 1978, Mr. Lubin was solely responsible for the conduct of the grand jury investigation of McDonnell Douglas Corp., a complex investigation of overseas bribery spanning that corporation's activities in approximately a dozen foreign countries for a ten-year period. In January 1979, joined by another fraud section prosecutor, Mr. Lubin continued the grand jury investigation, which led to the indictment of McDonnell Douglas, three of its officers and one salesman on charges of fraud and conspiracy in connection with the sale of DC-10s to Pakistan International Airlines. Additionally, the corporation was indicted for concealing and covering up material information from the Export-Import

Bank of the United States in connection with the financing of commercial aircraft sales in Pakistan, Zaire, Venezuela, Korea and the Philippines. As an outgrowth of that investigation and based directly upon Mr. Lubin's 1977 efforts in the grand jury, Mr. Lubin, along with another fraud section attorney, was responsible for the separate indictment of one of the McDonnell Douglas defendants in April of 1980 for perjury before the grand jury. Additionally, from the fall of 1977 to January 1980, Mr. Lubin began and completed the investigations of three other major American corporations (General Foods, Honeywell, and the Carnation Company) which were based upon possible violations of criminal law associated with overseas payments.

Mr. Lubin's achievements in connection with the McDonnell Douglas case are notable. With no previous grand jury experience and no similar investigation upon which to model his efforts, Mr. Lubin through tireless diligence and dedication completed the investigation with the help of two grand juries in 24 months before the statute of limitations barred prosecution. This was accomplished by a briskly paced jury presentation which some weeks included three or more days of grand jury testimony. In connection with this investigation he has taken the testimony of scores of hostile corporate witnesses, from the level of secretary to the Chairman of the Board, all of whom were represented by the same one or two law firms who were vigorously orchestrating the defense by engaging in the practice of multiple representation of corporate employees. During the investigation stage, he was responsible for successfully persuading more than half a dozen foreign witnesses to come to the United States from their home countries to be interviewed or give testimony before the grand jury, or both. Mr. Lubin's efforts included negotiating the cooperation of the Government of Pakistan (as well as that of other foreign governments) which led to the critical development of the heart of the charges brought by the grand jury. His investigative efforts included obtaining Swiss and other foreign bank records and tracing money throughout the world.

Since indictment, Mr. Lubin's efforts in furtherance of this prosecution have included extensive plea negotiations, preparing for trial, and responding to a barrage of defense actions from eight litigation law firms which have consumed an entire year and have ranged from motions for severance to motions to dismiss the indictment. To date, the Government has enjoyed a 100% rate of success repelling defense efforts to attack the indictment or gain tactical advantage.

Then came a phone call that changed Lubin's life.

It started innocently enough, a routine call about scheduling some pretrial discovery from one of the McDonnell Douglas defense attorneys. Lubin was about to end the conversation when he was electrified by a comment from the lawyer about the Associate Attorney General, Giuliani. It was something to the effect of "I understand Danforth's conversation with Rudi Giuliani went well," Lubin recalls.

Lubin was stunned. He wanted more information, but he also didn't want to let on to a defense lawyer that he knew nothing about any direct contact between Danforth and Giuliani. He mumbled something, pretending the reference to the meeting was no surprise. But the defense lawyer soon ended the conversation without giving more details.

Lubin rushed to Mendelson's nearby office. He was beside himself. What he had considered paranoid anxieties now seemed to be coming true. Giuliani was actually talking to Danforth about the case.

Mendelson agreed that they had to find out more facts by calling back the defense lawyer. They also decided to call other defense counsel, probing as discreetly as possible.

What they learned was that not only had Danforth apparently spoken with Giuliani about the case on the phone, but that a lawyer inside McDonnell Douglas, John Sant, had actually had a meeting with Giuliani and his top aide, Kenneth Caruso. The sole topic of discussion had been the McDonnell Douglas prosecution.

As far as the prosecutors were concerned, Giuliani's meeting with Sant was far worse than a meeting with Danforth. Lubin had thought seriously about naming Sant as an unindicted coconspirator in the case. Sant was actually named in the counts of the indictment. Was Sant fearful that evidence at trial would reveal the full extent of his own involvement, possibly the grounds for his criminal liability? As far as Lubin was concerned, Giuliani might as well have sat down with Jimmy McDonnell, or the chairman himself.

Lubin and Mendelson could draw only one conclusion from the fact that the meeting had taken place and they hadn't been told. "I thought the case was being fixed inside the Department of Justice," Lubin recalls. "What else could be going on? I felt we were in the middle of something very peculiar. It wasn't just this one event. It was the whole pattern that had been developing since the Reagan administration took power. Here we have an indicted case, and then there are high-level meetings we don't even know about.

"Why couldn't we hear what Sant had to say?" Lubin wondered. "How bad could it be? That Mendelson and I had been unfair to

McDonnell Douglas? We'd already heard that before, and we could sit through it again." Nor could the lawyers ascribe it to Giuliani's relative inexperience in Washington. He'd been a prosecutor in the Southern District of New York, where such practices were unheard of. And surely he knew how devastating such a meeting would be to the front-line lawyers handling the case. To the prosecutors, it looked ominously like a deliberate and secretive effort to get rid of the case.

Neither Mendelson nor Lubin could recall any precedent for the situation. Mendelson had worked for the U.S. Attorney in New Jersey, where such contacts were plainly forbidden. When Harris joined the department, she had warned against the practice of Justice Department lawyers talking too much with targets of investigations, a practice that had become common in prior administrations, but that Harris hoped to reduce. But actual defendants? The possibility had seemed so outrageous and unlikely that Harris hadn't even specifically addressed it. She simply assumed that it wouldn't happen.

One option was for the two prosecutors to do nothing. But "what if it was an out-and-out fix going on?" Lubin says. "Who were we supposed to go to in the department? What if the Attorney General himself was behind this? What if there was some kind of bribe?"

The issue was so potentially explosive that Lubin and Mendelson decided to involve no one else in their planning, not even Harris, whom they thought they could trust. "We didn't want to involve anyone else. We realized we were probably risking our careers" he says.

They decided to make their concerns public almost immediately, in the form of a letter to Giuliani. Working slowly and late into the night, they finally came up with a final draft.

> DEAR MR. GIULIANI:
> As the prosecutors who have worked on the McDonnell Douglas case for several years, we were shocked and dismayed to learn, after the fact, of your recent meeting with John Sant, General Counsel for the defendant McDonnell Douglas Corporation.
> Compoundng our concern is your conspicuous failure to inform us that you even met with Mr. Sant. We are concerned about the ramifications of your meeting and wish to share our concerns with you and with some of our colleagues in the Criminal Division. [The two prosecutors had already decided to provide copies of the letter to everyone in the fraud section.]
> We do not question the authority of senior-level Department of Jus-

tice officials to determine policy and ultimate litigative decisions on major cases. We do, however, question the wisdom and propriety of private meetings held during the pendency of a prosecution with defense counsel or, even more problematic, with someone so closely identified with a corporate defendant as a person who is both a member of its Board of Directors and its General Counsel. While we have no reason to believe that you intended to cause any harm, such private meetings undermine the morale of the prosecutors, agents and staff working on cases and have the potential of adversely affecting the Government's litigating or negotiating position. Your action creates an appearance that certain influential defendants have access to senior officials when other defendants or their attorneys do not. Most importantly, such meetings erode the public's confidence in the fair administration of justice.

As the letter continued, the prosecutors could barely contain their ire.

Had you inquired of us prior to your private meeting, we could have briefed you on the facts and history of this case; and, more specifically, as to the position of Mr. Sant vis-à-vis the conduct charged in the indictment, his role as a participant in significant meetings and discussions concerning some of the activites alleged in the indictment, and his status as a potential witness at trial. We could have told you, for example, that Mr. Sant's subordinate, the General Counsel of the Douglas Aircraft Company, has been named by the United States as an unindicted coconspirator in the prosecution because of his role and the significant role played by the internal legal staff at [McDonnell Douglas] in the conspiracy.

Additionally, we would have informed you that Mr. Sant was the author and recipient of many corporate documents which were subpoenaed but were withheld from the grand jury on an overbroad claim of attorney-client privilege, which is now being challenged by the United States. All of this information would have aided you in your evaluation of Mr. Sant's presentation.

It is sadly ironic that a corporation which has been charged by a grand jury in connection with the purchase of improper influence and under-the-table dealings in foreign countries should be permitted by the Department of Justice to engage in back door approaches presumably in an effort to dispose of this case. We would ask you to think back to your years as a federal prosecutor and contemplate your own reactions had former Congressman Podell or his lawyers lobbied senior Department of Justice officials without your knowledge while that case was awaiting trial.

This paragraph, in particular, Lubin thought, would hit its target with deadly accuracy. The prosecution of former New York Congressman Bertrum L. Podell for misuse of his government office had been Giuliani's greatest triumph as a young prosecutor, and it was a case that he still managed to cite on countless occasions to demonstrate his own tough approach to high-level crime. The analogy to McDonnell Douglas was too good for Lubin and Mendelson to resist.

> We believe that you would have reacted as we and some of our colleagues have reacted—with outrage and great personal and professional disappointment.
> We think that it is in the best interests of the United States in this criminal prosecution that you personally inform us of the substance of Mr. Sant's conversation with you in order that we can provide you with any appropriate evaluation or information responsive to his presentation. We further believe that it is in the interests of the United States that the prosecutors be present at any future meetings with representatives of the defense. Finally, we urge you to adopt a formal policy of not holding any meetings with representatives of criminal defendants on any case outside the presence and without the knowledge of the prosecutors. Sincerely . . ."

Boldly "cc'd" at the bottom of the two-page letter were D. Lowell Jensen, John C. Keeney, Mark M. Richards, like Keeney, a deputy assistant attorney general for the Criminal Division, JoAnn Harris, and "all fraud section attorneys."

They knew that giving copies of the letter to every lawyer in the fraud unit was like rubbing salt in a wound. But if they were going to take such a risk for a cause they believed in, they didn't want it hushed up inside the department. They had already seen another matter with political implications swept under the rug.

The matter had involved another fraud case, one involving alleged misuse of CETA funds. The target of the investigation was a well-known black leader. Although the person in question hadn't yet been indicted, the prosecutor working on the investigation was convinced that the man should be indicted and that he'd have no difficulty obtaining an indictment from a grand jury. But the target met with someone from the Reagan White House, and soon after, the prosecutor was told to drop the investigation—very quietly. Although some details of the matter spread within the fraud unit, causing a good deal of concern about prosecutorial policies in the new administration, no protests were lodged, nor was there ever any official explanation of what had happened.

Lubin and Mendelson didn't want to see the same thing happen again, this time with an even more egregious situation, since indictments had already been handed down.

After drafting the letter, Lubin and Mendelson decided to sleep on their decision. The next morning they again discussed their options. Inside the Justice Department there is a unit called the Office of Professional Responsibility, charged with investigating internal breaches of department regulations and ethics, but they quickly rejected any thought of filing a complaint against Giuliani there. "That office serves the administration," Lubin says. "If it's any kind of a political question, there's not going to be any action."

Keeney would have been the logical person to turn to, since they'd decided they didn't want to involve Harris. But "Keeney's a survivor—thirty-eight years with the department," explains Lubin. "He's not about to make any waves."

So late that afternoon, they decided to go ahead with the letter. They walked across the street from the building where the fraud section had its offices to the main Justice Department building where Giuliani occupied a large corner suite. Lubin felt concern and apprehension, but he drew confidence from the belief that he was doing the right thing. When they reached Giuliani's outer office, they discovered with a certain amount of relief that Giuliani was out of town that day, but was expected back that night.

ON the way out of the building, the two prosecutors stopped off at Jensen's office, leaving a copy of the letter with his secretary. Then they crossed back to their building, where they called on Harris.

They handed her the letter, sat down, and waited while she read through it. Her eyes widened in amazement—over both the details of Giuliani's meeting with Sant, which she knew nothing about, and the fact of the letter itself. She had, in fact, just hung up her phone after trying to reach Giuliani to ask him about progress in his review of the case. Judge Green had been pressing the department for its response to her earlier request.

Harris said very little to Lubin and Mendelson. She said only that while they had raised a serious and important issue, the manner in which they were pursuing it was "not commendable." She said she would discuss the matter with Jensen and Giuliani and talk to them the next morning. The two prosecutors left, and dropped copies of the letter on their colleagues' desks before going home for the night.

Harris's reaction was actually far more complicated. She was absolutely appalled at what Giuliani had done, if Lubin and Mendelson were correct in their allegations. She knew this would have a devastating impact on the fraud unit; she wondered how long she herself could stay under such conditions. But the manner in which the two prosecutors had chosen to air their concerns was bad, very bad. Distributing so many copies greatly increased the risk that the letter and its allegations would become public. She feared this would only increase the new administration's suspicions that many of the fraud unit lawyers were liberal ideologues out to embarrass the Reagan administration. Harris groaned inwardly. She foresaw a major storm developing.

The next morning, a Friday, Lubin expected his phone to be ringing off the hook with calls from colleagues wanting to discuss the letter. Oddly enough, there seemed to be no immediate response. Finally he called a friend. What letter? the friend wanted to know. Lubin made some more calls. It seemed that no one had gotten the letter! Finally he tracked down someone who had still been in his office when Lubin delivered the letter. He learned that after he had left, someone from internal Justice Department security had come around and collected all the copies.

Lubin was dumbfounded. Who could have ordered such a bizarre step? Harris or Jensen? Giuliani? He didn't even know whether Giuliani had read the letter yet. In any event, the attempt to suppress distribution of the letter failed. A few people had gotten it, and the copying machines were soon whirring. Within several hours, Lubin and Mendelson were causes célèbres within the fraud unit. Their allegations and response to them were sensational in and of themselves. But causing a nearly equal stir was the effort to remove the letters. As Lubin and Mendelson had seen so vividly in the cases they had worked on, the effort to cover up often backfires. That was yet another lesson they felt the Reagan Justice Department would have to learn the hard way.

As word and copies of the letter spread, other prosecutors started pouring into Lubin's and Mendelson's small offices. Many of their messages were congratulatory, to the effect that "I wish I had the guts to do something like this." And there was also a good deal of criticism.

"Many prosecutors tend to be very straight personalities," Lubin explains. "There are lines that are never crossed. In the eyes of many of our colleagues, we'd crossed that line. Our behavior wasn't acceptable to them." An informal poll would have produced the almost unanimous sentiment that the two prosecutors would be fired for their outspokenness.

But they weren't. In fact, the entire day passed without any word from Giuliani, Jensen, or Harris.

That night, while Lubin was at home, he wondered how long the silence would continue. Naturally curious, he was anxious to know what was going to happen, and the sooner the better. Then the phone rang.

Lubin turned pale as he listened to the caller. It was a reporter from *The New York Times* who said he had just gotten off the phone after talking with Jensen. He said Jensen had confirmed essential details about the letter and its contents, and he wondered if Lubin had any response.

Lubin was dismayed. He had wanted wide circulation of the letter within the department, it's true. But he had never wanted it to get to the press. Perhaps he'd been naïve. In any event, he told the reporter he had no comment and wouldn't comment on anything related to the McDonnell Douglas case.

The next morning he rushed out to check the Saturday *New York Times*; there wasn't any mention of the case. He called Mendelson, who said he'd been out the previous night and hadn't heard from or talked to any reporters. They spent a fitful weekend wondering what was going on.

Soon after they arrived at the office Monday morning, the expected call came from Harris: they should meet her at Jensen's office in fifteen minutes. They felt the axe was about to fall.

Jensen was calm. He didn't seem terribly angry—stern was more like it, Lubin thought. He lectured them about following proper channels. The letter, if they felt they had to write it, should have been given to Harris first, and then to him. "He chewed us out, but quietly," Lubin recalls. He and Mendelson thought it significant that no effort was made to refute the essential charges in the letter. Obviously, the meeting between Giuliani and Sant had taken place. Lubin wondered what Jensen would do with that information. Lubin thought Giuliani had treated Jensen so badly; he suspected Jensen might be able to use this mishap effectively to win back some of the authority that Giuliani had seized from him.

But then Jensen accused Lubin and Mendelson of leaking their letter to the press, and Lubin found he could no longer bite his tongue.

"That's a very interesting charge," Lubin told Jensen, "because Friday night, I received a phone call from a *New York Times* reporter who said he'd been talking to you. He said you had confirmed the fact that the letter had been sent and confirmed its contents."

The normally placid Jensen, Lubin recalls, turned red. He was embarrassed, especially in front of Harris. "He'd just dressed us down for doing exactly what he'd done," Lubin says. But he didn't deny talking to the reporter. And after taking a deep breath, Jensen calmed down. He dropped the subject of press leaks, and soon indicated that as far as he was concerned the matter was over.

When they got back to their office, Lubin and Mendelson found the long-awaited message from Giuliani. He wanted to meet with the two prosecutors at 11 A.M. They knew that this would be the real test, but they hardly knew what to expect. Neither knew Giuliani at all except by reputation.

They arrived promptly, about the same time as the federal director of prisons. Giuliani asked to see the director first, keeping the two prosecutors waiting for the duration of their meeting. Then the secretary told them to enter.

They walked the length of the large office as Giuliani and his assistant, Ken Caruso, watched silently. They sat down without handshakes. Then Giuliani started screaming.

"As far as I'm concerned, we were watching a madman," Lubin recalls. "It would have made a great video tape. I've never seen or heard anything like it, even in the movies. He ranted and raved for a full twenty minutes. He just went nuts. I've never seen a public official behave like this."

Other participants agree that Giuliani was angry with the two prosecutors and made it clear during the session. Caruso, however, says, "I wouldn't call it ranting and raving. I don't remember him raising his voice. He was professional, and I believe we handled it appropriately."

When Giuliani finally calmed down a bit, he told Lubin and Mendelson that he had asked Jensen for the file on the case before meeting with Sant, and that there was a memo from Caruso to Jensen to prove it. He hadn't gone into the meeting uninformed, he insisted.

The two prosecutors said nothing, but Lubin strongly suspected that Giuliani was lying about that. Lubin was, after all, a trained prosecutor, and Giuliani was acting just like a guilty suspect. Lubin told himself that he'd try to check Giuliani's story. In any event, he thought the explanation didn't justify Giuliani's meeting with counsel for an indicted defendant without them.

Lubin and Mendelson tried to ask Giuliani a few questions, but Giuliani cut them off. He said he'd be the one doing the questioning, and then he dismissed them.

Their heads were still spinning when they got out of the building. First of all, Giuliani hadn't fired them! It was obvious that he'd wanted to, but someone else must have stopped him; maybe Jensen. It might have looked too bad. And then there was Giuliani's bizarre behavior. It was simply an incredible performance. They were convinced that this man shouldn't be at the top of the nation's system of criminal prosecution. They didn't think they could work under him.

Their thoughts along those lines would soon become irrelevant. Giuliani wasted no time in counterattacking.

That night Lubin again received a call, this time from a United Press International reporter whom he considered a friend. She told Lubin that she had just been "leaked" a copy of an internal memo from Giuliani to Jensen that obviously represented Giuliani's official response to the charges in Lubin and Mendelson's letter. The memo came from Giuliani's office, she said.

Lubin was amazed by Giuliani's audacity. Obviously, the Associate Attorney General had decided to minimize the impact of the matter by going public with it himself, and this after rampaging about leaks to the press.

Lubin quickly arranged to obtain a copy of the memo. He wasn't surprised to find that it read like a press release, or that he and Mendelson were portrayed as the culprits in the matter—not Giuliani, or Sant, who represented the real defendant.

I am writing to formally bring to your attention the letter dated June 18, 1981, written to me by two trial attorneys in the fraud section, George J. Mendelson and Michael A. Lubin [the memo to Jensen began]. The letter in question contains an attack on the propriety of my meeting with Mr. Sant. Unfortunately, neither Mr. Mendelson nor Mr. Lubin made any attempt to learn the facts before writing. As a result, their letter is replete with claims that, while certainly sensational, are also wholly false.

As an example, Messrs. Mendelson and Lubin state several times that my meeting with Mr. Sant was "private," implying that just the two of us were present. In point of fact, my Special Assistant, Kenneth A. Caruso, was present at all times and duly memorialized the meeting for our files. In a related claim, Messrs. Mendelson and Lubin cite my "conspicuous failure" to inform them of the meeting. The fact is that, as soon as it became apparent that Mr. Sant had requested the meeting to discuss the criminal case against his company, I directed Mr. Caruso to ask you to have the Criminal Division review it. Such a request proved unnecessary because a Criminal Division review arrived at my office a few days later. At that time, Mr. Caruso apprised you, and later your deputy, John Keeney, that a meeting had taken place, that no decision as to how to proceed had been made and that a meeting with defense counsel would be scheduled after review of your office's report.

Since the letter has brought up the general topic of meetings between senior Department officials and defense counsel, let me state that I am aware of no statute, regulation, policy or canon of ethics preventing an attorney from presenting his views to government officials at any level on matters of mutual concern. Likewise, I am aware of no proscription preventing a government official from hearing those views.

To put the matter affirmatively, it has been and will continue to be my policy to afford attorneys a reasonable opportunity to present arguments as to why a case should not go forward.

The memo continued at some length about the benefits of such contacts, then turned into an attack on Lubin and Mendelson:

I must emphasize that, in writing their letter, Messrs. Lubin and Mendelson displayed a disrespect for the facts and an immature petulance that gives me pause as to the judgments they may have made during their period of service in the Department. It is dangerous, to say the least, for prosecutors to shoot from the hip without checking the accuracy of their charges. If either Mr. Mendelson or Mr. Lubin had made any attempt to verify their statements, they would have found that the very premises of their letter—that there was a private meeting and that it was somehow concealed from the Criminal Division—were untrue. Although the incident is regrettable, it does not in any way affect my view that the vast majority of prosecutors, including the fine professionals in this Department, seek to have decisions made on the merits rather than by attempting to apply pressure based upon widely circulated sensationalized claims of impropriety.

Lubin noticed that the date on the memo was June 23—the next day—meaning that copies were being "leaked" even before the memo supposedly had been written.

Sure enough, the next day papers carried accounts of the prosecutors' memo and Giuliani's response. And it looked as if Giuliani had, to a large degree, managed to control how the news was played and presented. *The New York Times*, for example, which Lubin knew had the story the previous week, carried it as a minor item under "Company News" in the Business Section. Both the Washington *Post* and the St. Louis *Post-Dispatch* gave it fuller coverage, but the prosecutors' charges were blunted by Giuliani's counterattack. The leads to the stories were of the "rift inside Justice Department" type, rather than "prosecutors charge impropriety." What Lubin and Mendelson believed to be a serious issue both in the McDonnell Douglas case and for the new administration's prosecution policies was reduced to a personality clash with two low-ranking prosecutors.

But in Lubin's and Mendelson's minds, serious questions remained. Foremost among them: Just what had happened among Danforth, Sant, and Giuliani?

Some clues emerged from the news accounts of the flap over the prosecutors' letter. Giuliani told the Washington *Post* that he hadn't acted improperly and said he hadn't known at the time of the meeting on May 14 that McDonnell Douglas was under indictment. "I feel kind of silly saying this," the *Post* quoted Giuliani, "but I didn't know McDonnell Douglas was under indictment. It was put on the schedule to discuss their problems or unfair treatment by the department. I thought it was going to be about civil rights or maybe an investigation. I knew the company was under investigation years ago." He added that he believed Lubin and Mendelson had only recently found out about the meeting and "automatically assumed the worst, and without checking, jumped to two or three conclusions."

Although Giuliani added that the matter was turned over to the Criminal Division for review, Lubin noticed that there was no reference to the alleged note Giuliani had said he had Caruso send to Jensen, notifying the division of the meeting. And there was a curious response from Jensen in the article. The Criminal Division chief said he couldn't remember whether he had learned of the meeting at the

time from Giuliani's office or in the context of the current controversy. Lubin made a mental note to check with Jensen himself.

The St. Louis *Post-Dispatch*, which had consistently covered the
case more aggressively than any other newspaper, had by far the most
thorough account, which it began on page one. The paper had managed to piece together the events leading up to the meeting by interviewing Senator Danforth and Caruso, Giuliani's aide.

According to Danforth, Sant had telephoned him to ask his help in
arranging a meeting with top Justice Department officials in the new
Reagan administration. "His [Sant's] basic position was that McDonnell Douglas was being unfairly treated by the Justice Department;
that it was being singled out for special treatment," the paper quoted
Danforth.

"Here was James S. McDonnell, eighty-one years old, and they
wanted him to enter a plea to a racketeering charge, and he felt it was
an insult to him and to his company," Danforth continued. "So what
should have been settled by negotiations never was.

"Sant said an inertia had developed, with very young litigators all
revved up to take the case to court. Sant felt the company was getting
a bum's rush to the courthouse." For that reason, Sant had specifically
requested that the two prosecutors be excluded from the meeting.

Danforth had then called Edward Schmults, Attorney General
Smith's deputy, who explained that both he and Smith had disqualified themselves from all consideration of the case because their former
law firms had represented McDonnell Douglas. Schmults said he
would have Giuliani, who was overseeing the case, get back to the
senator.

Danforth said that Giuliani had called him, and that they arranged
the meeting. The senator said he had explained to both Schmults and
Giuliani that the McDonnell Douglas criminal case was the reason for
the meeting, and that he wasn't asking the department to drop the
case, but simply to listen to Sant. "Here we have the largest employer
in the state of Missouri and one of the finest corporate citizens and a
family that has done more for St. Louis than any other family, and
they have been unfairly treated," Danforth concluded, justifying his
intervention.

The *Post-Dispatch*'s account also quoted Caruso as saying he didn't
mention the meeting to Jensen until a week later, when Jensen brought
up the status of the case in a phone call. Caruso said nothing about
being instructed by Giuliani to notify the Criminal Division.

That wasn't the only inconsistency between the *Post-Dispatch*'s version of events and Giuliani's explanations.

Lubin had found it hard to believe Giuliani's disclaimer that he hadn't known McDonnell Douglas was under criminal indictment when he agreed to meet with Sant. It was, after all, the most highly publicized criminal fraud case in recent memory, and had been repeatedly cited in recent congressional hearings on the Foreign Corrupt Practices Act. Furthermore, the reason that Sant was directed to speak with Giuliani was because both Smith and Schmults were disqualified. Surely Giuliani would have been aware of a case in which he had the final prosecutorial authority in the department. Now Lubin saw that Danforth had in fact made his intent to discuss the case quite clear both to Schmults and to Giuliani before the meeting.

HAD Lubin had access to Caruso's files on the matter, he would also have learned that Sant immediately made his purpose clear at the meeting, which could have been terminated had Giuliani or Caruso had any problems with the topic. In a "memo to the files," apparently written shortly after the meeting, Caruso noted that

> On Thursday, May 14, Rudy Giuliani and I met with John Sant, of McDonnell Douglas. Mr. Sant explained to us that McDonnell Douglas was under indictment in the District of Columbia. He wanted an opportunity to explain why he believed the case should not be prosecuted. Rudy attended the meeting for about 15 minutes. After he left, I continued with Mr. Sant for another 20 or 25 minutes.

Among the usual arguments the defense had repeatedly put forward for dropping the case, Sant had made two overtly political appeals.

> Mr. Sant also notes the bill introduced [in] the Senate by Senator Chafee, which seeks to amend the Foreign Corrupt Practices Act. He argues that continued prosecution would be inconsistent with the policy behind amending the Act to make it less stringent. Finally Mr. Sant notes that prosecution might well hurt our relations with Pakistan, which the State Department and the Administration have been trying to improve. Relations would be hurt because in its defense McDonnell Douglas would probably elicit much testimony, regarding the extensive

numbers and amounts of bribes and/or commissions paid to representatives of the Pakistan government by the airline industry over the years.

Nowhere in the memo did Caruso mention any of the countervailing arguments for continuing a prosecution of a case already under indictment.

Lubin also continued to have strong doubts about Giuliani's alleged instructions to Caruso to notify Jensen and the Criminal Division about the meeting. He later questioned Jensen about the matter, and couldn't get Jensen to confirm that any such communication had ever reached him. Lubin later made a Freedom of Information Act request for the alleged written note revealing the meeting; no such document was produced. Lubin is convinced it doesn't exist. Indeed, when questioned about the memo, Caruso says he doesn't recall writing it or being asked by Giuliani to do so.

Giuliani insists that he didn't know the purpose of the meeting. He notes that he was still relatively new in his position and hadn't studied the case closely since he had learned only just before the meeting that he was the senior official on the matter due to the disqualification of Smith and Schmults. He says he directed Caruso to notify the criminal division and, in any event, there was nothing secret about the meeting. He adds that he doesn't care whether Lubin and Mendelson believe he's telling the truth, since he believes "it's quite obvious from the way they conducted the case that they can't tell who tells the truth and who doesn't."

Lubin recognized that Giuliani was correct in his assertion that the meeting itself didn't violate any laws or Justice Department regulations. But that was, in part, because it went without saying that such meetings were bad policy. Heymann, the Criminal Division head who had approved the case and never met alone with defense counsel, says that "the system suffers badly when a top political official arranges a meeting with political appointees in the Justice Department without the career people even being notified. It creates suspicions. It is highly demoralizing because it places private counsel above government counsel and tells private counsel they can ignore what line attorneys say. And there is real risk of screwing up because the top officials are not well enough informed without consulting with the lawyers handling the case."

It was clear from Giuliani's statements to the press, however, that he was totally unrepentant. And Lubin was also convinced that he had lied to him and to the public about crucial details in the matter. In Lubin's mind, it confirmed what Lubin had heard about Giuliani's political character: that he would never admit publicly to being wrong, no matter what steps he had to take to maintain his position; and that nothing made him angrier than to be confronted with evidence that he had made a mistake. Lubin thought it a dangerous trait in a prosecutor, whose mistakes, if unacknowledged, risk sending innocent people to prison.

Lubin and Mendelson, however, were hardly in a position to have their views on such subjects considered. And events in the McDonnell Douglas case were rapidly moving forward, without the participation of the two prosecutors.

In fact, just the day before, there had been another meeting between defense lawyers in the case and Giuliani. This was a full-blown affair. Attending besides Giuliani, Sant, and Caruso were Jensen and lawyers for each of the four individual defendants. Conspicuously absent and uninvited were Lubin and Mendelson.

They were still nominally the chief prosecutors in the case. But that day, when they arrived at the office and learned of yet another important meeting from which they were excluded, they recognized that their effectiveness was at an end. If there was any chance at all for the McDonnell Douglas cases to go to trial, new prosecutors would have to take their places. Under the circumstances, they thought it unlikely that they would be given new assignments of any significance.

The previous week, the two prosecutors had drafted letters to Judge Green, announcing their intention to withdraw from prosecuting the case. Now they decided it might be time to leave the department altogether, even though neither had yet had time to line up another job. Lubin had never been sure he wanted a lifelong career as a prosecutor; this experience convinced him that he didn't. Mendelson had come to Washington from New Jersey to be a prosecutor, not a politician. He was uncomfortable in the environment of the Reagan Justice Department, and he didn't feel he had any kind of aptitude for shifting with political winds.

Lubin had thought about leaving the department months earlier, but the McDonnell Douglas case had held him. Now he doubted that anything he did would have any effect on the outcome. After the second meeting between Giuliani and Sant, Giuliani had said he hadn't yet made up his mind about continuing the prosecution, and that the decision was a "close call." But in conversations with the defense lawyers, Lubin could tell that they were confident of prevailing. They talked as though the case were already over.

And the end was, in fact, at hand. On Sept. 9, 1981, Giuliani announced that the case would be ended by a plea bargain in which the corporation would plead guilty to fraud and making false statements and pay a fine of $55,000 plus a civil penalty of $1.2 million. The indictments against the four individuals would be dropped. Chairman McDonnell, despite the dismay of his board of directors at his earlier outburst, had finally prevailed—posthumously. He had died the previous summer without the vindication he had sought. Some say the indictment killed him.

Despite his statement at the time that the case was a close call, Giuliani now says that "McDonnell Douglas was the clearest case I've ever seen. It was an easy decision. It was so clear the four individuals should never have been indicted. The corporation was a closer case."

Giuliani says he acted only out of the purest motives in ending the case with the Westinghouse plea that the defense had sought almost from the inception of the case. "Do the innocent ever get convicted? That is the nightmare of being a prosecutor," he says. "There are enough cases of clear criminality that we shouldn't waste a moment on a case when the individual might be innocent."

As for McDonnell Douglas, "I did think the conduct was wrong. But when they committed the misconduct, it wasn't clear what they did was illegal. A foreign bribe was not a clear violation of U.S. law. They couldn't have known they were violating the law."

And despite the rejection by both the trial court and the Court of Appeals of those same defense arguments, Giuliani embraces the defense's theory of the case even more fully. Of the decision to indict, following Chairman McDonnell's rejection of the plea, he says, "It was vindictive. It was a distortion of how the Department of Justice should operate. If the four individuals were political activists, there would have been screams. They would have been a cause célèbre."

Sherman Pruitt, alone among the defendants, wasn't entirely off the hook, since he still faced a separate indictment for perjury. In the face of incontrovertible evidence that he had lied under oath about, among other things, the existence of his Swiss bank account, the McDonnell Douglas sales manager did plead guilty in October to a reduced charge of "making a false statement."

When Lubin read the sentencing memo on Pruitt prepared by the Justice Department, he was disgusted. It was an encomium! It made

Pruitt sound like some kind of hero. He was, after all, an admitted felon. "For a man who has led an exemplary life," the memo read, "both as a private citizen and as a decorated war veteran, the personal grief, pain and suffering of seeing the later years of his life, including the retirement years, soiled by highly publicized indictments growing out of the investigation of the McDonnell Douglas Corp. is incalculable." The sentencing recommendation was barely a slap on the wrist: probation.

The judge in the case, in a rare example of imposing a more severe punishment than that requested by the prosecution, sentenced Pruitt to six months' probation, two hundred hours of community service, and a $40,000 fine. The McDonnell Douglas case was over, at least for the defendants.

On June 9, 1981, an otherwise dejected Lubin and Mendelson had received the first good news in what seemed like months. In the mail, each received a letter from Jensen announcing that they had been chosen to receive one of the Justice Department's highest honors, the Special Commendation Award. "It was my pleasure to approve for you a Special Commendation Award for your outstanding service to the Criminal Division," the letters read. "This award will be presented during the Attorney General's Annual Awards ceremony at 3 P.M. on July 2, 1981, in the Great Hall of the main Justice building." Signed by Jensen, the letters concluded, "Congratulations and thank you for your outstanding service."

Lubin, in particular, was genuinely thrilled. "It's a very impressive ceremony," he says. "I'd been to many of them, and I'd seen some awards for true heroism. I was honored I'd been selected, especially after what we'd been through."

Lubin and Mendelson assumed that they had Harris, the head of their section, to thank, but they were also impressed that it was Jensen who'd sent the letters and had apparently approved their selection. Since Giuliani, it seemed to them, had been seizing turf from Jensen at every opportunity, they assumed that if Giuliani had been able to, he would have blocked their being honored. It seemed inconceivable to them that someone who had been as angry at them as Giuliani was could now be singling them out for a high honor. They were impressed that, nonetheless, the department was giving them an award. It raised the already high esteem they felt for Jensen.

When they went in to thank Harris for her role in nominating them for the award, they all had a good laugh. She told them that, as a matter of fact, Giuliani had decided that he—and not Jensen—would personally be handing out the awards at the ceremony. "The irony was rich," Lubin recalls. "We were all laughing that Giuliani was going to have to give out the awards and read the commendation for our work on the McDonnell Douglas case in front of the entire world. It was a very satisfying prospect."

Their mirth was short-lived. Three weeks later, they received a terse letter from Jensen:

> Reference is made to my letter of June 9, 1981, in which I advised you that you would be presented a Departmental Special Commendation Award at a ceremony on July 2, 1981.
>
> I regret to inform you that the presentation of this award is being held in abeyance pending resolution of issues arising from your letter of June 18, 1981, to Associate Attorney General Giuliani with respect to the McDonnell Douglas prosecution.
>
> Sincerely,
> D. LOWELL JENSEN

The prosecutors were stunned. They'd already seen the printed programs for the ceremony with their names included. They soon learned that all those programs had been ordered destroyed and re-printed—at government expense. "This kind of retaliation was almost unbelievably petty," Lubin says.

As was the case with their earlier problems, Lubin and Mendelson went to their boss, Harris. She had tried consistently to act as a mediator between the two prosecutors and Giuliani, but she felt matters had now gone too far. She called Jensen to find out what was happening, but got nowhere. He wouldn't discuss or reconsider his decision, and it was clear that it wasn't really his—the decision had come from Giuliani. From his tone, Harris inferred that Jensen was embarrassed about the matter but wouldn't do anything.

The day they received the letter, Lubin and Mendelson made a desperate attempt to have the decision reversed. They wrote Jensen, charging in their letter that Giuliani's retaliation violated the government whistle-blower statute since it appeared they were being punished simply because they had criticized a senior official for what they believed was improper conduct.

Giuliani doesn't recall making any decision to deny Lubin and

Mendelson the award, but says they certainly didn't deserve one. "They are jerks," he says. "They had no perspective or judgment."

Not surprisingly, the letter produced no results. The awards ceremony was held the next day as scheduled, without the participation of either Lubin or Mendelson.

The experience was thoroughly disillusioning not only for the two prosecutors but for Harris. Not long after, she began to make plans to leave Washington. Lubin and Mendelson hurried up their own departure plans.

It was now clear to them, and to many others in the department at the time, that the man they were really working for was Giuliani. Smith knew little about criminal law and had delegated authority in the area. More and more, Jensen was being relegated to a position as little more than one of Giuliani's staff members, forced to report to Giuliani through his principal aide, Caruso. Giuliani had turned the Associate Attorney General position into the top job in criminal law enforcement. Jensen was a man whom Lubin, Mendelson, and Harris thought they could work for. Giuliani was not.

As events unfolded, some of their conclusions turned out to be, if not actually wrong at the time, premature. Perhaps they had underestimated the quiet resolve of Jensen. For within the next year, there were several telling developments.

Months after Lubin and Mendelson left the government to start their own law firm in Washington, they received a box from Jensen's office. When they opened it, they were startled to discover their Special Commendation Awards. Without any fanfare, the awards had been reinstated. Was Jensen in the ascendancy?

Moreover, their friends still working at Justice told them that Giuliani seemed to be growing frustrated. He was spending much of his time on purely administrative matters. Meanwhile, the biggest criminal case of the Reagan administration so far had just broken. It was the Hitachi sting operation—a daring undercover investigation that threatened major repercussions for Japanese-American relations. Giuliani had disqualified himself from any involvement in the case, because his former law firm was involved. Jensen was in charge.

THE HITACHI STING

JUNE 22, 1982, was a hot, dry, sunny day in Silicon Valley. By afternoon, the Great America amusement park in Santa Clara was thronged with visitors, mostly kids out of school for the summer. On nearby Bowers Avenue, an orange van pulled up in front of a small, nondescript two-story office complex. On the second floor, in Suite 229, were the offices of Glenmar Associates, one of hundreds of small computer and high-tech consulting firms that had sprung up south of San Francisco during the late seventies and eighties. Glenmar was one of the newest. It had rented its space a little more than a year before.

Inside the Glenmar offices, Alan Harrison, Glenmar's president, tightened his tie nervously as he gazed out the window. Suddenly he turned to Richard Kerrigan, Glenmar's lawyer. "Dick, they're here." He gestured for Mary, his secretary, to take her place at the receptionist's desk. Glenmar's biggest deal was about to be consummated.

Within moments, the door opened and two beaming Japanese businessmen entered with hands outstretched in greeting. Kenji Hayashi had been working with Glenmar for months—ever since the previous November, when he was first introduced to Harrison and Kerrigan in Las Vegas, and learned about Glenmar's extraordinary ability to procure secret information and equipment from International Business Machines Corporation. Hayashi and his colleague, Isao Ohnishi, were both executives with Hitachi Ltd., the Japanese conglomerate that is one of IBM's most formidable competitors worldwide.

Hayashi and Ohnishi looked elated as their eyes gazed over a treasure trove of sophisticated computer equipment and information, including the design workbooks for IBM's newest (and still unreleased), most powerful mainframe computer. Hayashi was convinced that acquisition of this information—for which Hitachi had already paid Glenmar more than $500,000—would be a coup of inestimable value to his career.

The Japanese wasted no time before hurrying to the equipment to ready it for transport to Japan.

"Take it off, the IBM signs," Hayashi said to Ohnishi, gesturing that he should pry off the IBM trademarks on the equipment.

Ohnishi glanced out the window. "They are waiting. Uh, Tom waiting. If, uh, it's available, he'll soon be back."

"Tom," Harrison recognized, must be Tom Yoshida, president of NCL Data, Inc., who had been acting as an intermediary in order to disguise payments from Hitachi to Glenmar. Harrison, for his own reasons, wanted Yoshida in the office.

"He's just gonna sit and wait?" he asked. The Japanese nodded.

"Why don't you tell him to come on up?" Kerrigan suggested.

Harrison gazed out the window again and spotted the orange van parked outside. "Oh, there's Tom's little truck. I see 'em."

Kerrigan renewed his suggestion: "Why don't you tell him to come on up?"

But Ohnishi and Hayashi were too busy poring over the materials, talking quickly between themselves.

Then the phone rang. "Let me catch this," Harrison said.

"Hold it a second," said Kerrigan.

"Mary'll catch it. Go ahead, Mary. Catch the phone," Harrison directed.

Hayashi took a pliers to the IBM equipment. "OK, I want to take off these . . ." The two Japanese succeeded in wrenching off the identification plates.

"I wouldn't ruin it, huh?" Harrison chided. "You got 'em off, huh?"

"IBM has been removed," Kerrigan confirmed. "It is now the property of Hitachi."

Hayashi looked delighted. Raising a plate, he said, "Uh, I'd like to have this for . . ."

"You want that as a souvenir?" Kerrigan continued.

". . . for my . . . for my Dr. Nakazawa's present," Hayashi finished. Dr. Kisaburo Nakazawa, Hayashi's boss, was general manager of one of Hitachi's largest computer works. Ohnishi burst into laughter at the prospect.

"A present for Dr. Nakazawa?" Kerrigan repeated.

"Yeah, uh-huh. OK?"

"Oh, I love to please," exclaimed Ohnishi, as he turned to the next piece of equipment.

"Jesus, you got your pliers, huh?" Harrison said, as Ohnishi pulled a pair out of his briefcase. "Well, we might as well do it then."

"Yeah, I think so," said Kerrigan.

There was a pause. Hayashi and Ohnishi continued to wrestle with a particularly stubborn IBM nameplate.

Then, in a louder voice, Harrison said, "Let's do it, because Thompson's out there."

But Hayashi paid no attention to Harrison's reference to the unknown Thompson. Exasperated, he urged Ohnishi to pull off the plate.

Now practically shouting, Harrison said again, "Let's go ahead and do it." And again: "Let's go ahead and do it then."

Harrison and Kerrigan both had only one thought: Where the hell was the Federal Bureau of Investigation?

ASSISTANT United States Attorney Gregory Ward, a lanky, sandy-haired thirty-five-year-old, tried to shift his weight in the crowded, cramped back room off the Glenmar office. With six FBI agents and himself in a room already crowded with audio and video equipment, including a television monitor trained on the proceedings outside, there was hardly room to breathe.

Ward had been in the Glenmar office since eight-thirty that morning waiting for this moment. Now his heart pounded with excitement as Ohnishi and Hayashi entered the outer room. They looked so smug and so on top of the world.

Ward was mesmerized by the sight on the TV screen of the two Japanese struggling to rip off the IBM labels. So much so that he hardly noticed when "Harrison"—in reality FBI undercover agent Alan Garretson—said for the first time, "Well, we might as well do it then."

The agent repeated the phrase. When Ward heard it the fourth time, its significance finally sank in. "Oh, my God!" he exclaimed to the agents. "It's the signal, the code word. Let's get the hell out of here." Ward could hardly believe it: a sophisticated year-long undercover operation jeopardized because they forgot the password!

Practically tripping over one another in their efforts to get out the small door, Ward and the six agents, including Kenneth Thompson, the FBI agent who had directed the operation, code named Pengem, burst into view in the outer room, suddenly becoming actors in their own video screen drama.

"Mr. Ohnishi?" Thompson asked the astounded-looking Japanese businessman.

"Uh-oh, Ken," Harrison said to Hayashi. "We got company."

"Mr. Ohnishi," Thompson continued, "this is the FBI. You're under arrest."

Ohnishi looked puzzled, pliers in hand. "Yeah?" he asked.

"FBI. You're under arrest, Mr. Ohnishi."

"OK," he said.

Thompson motioned for both men to move against the wall. "Come right over here. Step over here, please. Put your hands right here. Put your hands up against that wall." The two men were searched, then— an act of severe humiliation for the Japanese—handcuffed.

"You're being arrested for conspiracy, interstate transportation of stolen property," an agent intoned, then read Miranda warnings in both Japanese and English. With that, the Hitachi sting operation was sprung. And Ward embarked on what he thought would be the prosecution of a lifetime and the making of his career.

BY the spring of 1980, Assistant U.S. Attorney Greg Ward was feeling restless and frustrated. He had come back to San Jose, his hometown and the capital of California's burgeoning Silicon Valley, with visions of prosecuting glamorous high-tech crime. But nearly all of his time so far had been spent on far more mundane matters. As head of the San Jose office, Ward had more autonomy than most assistants, but he still reported to the San Francisco U.S. Attorney. Ward spent a good deal of time trying to persuade the U.S. Attorney there either to give him more manpower or to prosecute more of the cases out of San Francisco.

Some of the theft and burglary cases had also given Ward the impression that many of the crimes in Silicon Valley weren't routine.

Money often didn't seem to be involved. Instead, there were mysterious disappearances of papers, file drawers, software—all of which added up to industrial espionage. Much of what was stolen, Ward and his colleagues surmised, was destined for the Soviet Union or the Soviet bloc. But so far, none of the cases Ward had prosecuted had seemed to make a dent in this activity.

So when Kenneth Thompson, an FBI agent assigned to the San Jose office, dropped by to see Ward in his office one day that spring, Ward was immediately intrigued by the idea Thompson had in mind: a high-tech brokerage firm that would in reality be an undercover FBI operation to infiltrate industrial spy rings. The FBI had been gathering evidence for months, and had some promising leads, even some named suspects. But it hadn't been able to get enough evidence to ask Ward for any indictments, and it had become convinced the only way to do so was to get inside some of the operations. In short, Thompson told Ward, he wanted a sting operation.

The prospect of a sting made Ward simultaneously excited and nervous. Only two months before, what was arguably the most sensational—and controversial—sting operation ever, Abscam, had burst into public view. That undercover operation, in which FBI agents posed as Arab sheiks and offered bribes to U.S. congressmen (the name Abscam was a condensation of "Arab scam"), had resulted in the criminal convictions of a U.S. senator, six members of the House, and various municipal officials, businessmen, and lawyers.

And Abscam was only the most visible of what was a rapidly growing phenomenon. In 1976, Congress made the first appropriation specifically earmarked for undercover operations overseen by the Justice Department, and the following year the FBI conducted 53 operations. By 1981, two years after Abscam began, the number of undercover operations leaped to 463.

While undeniably successful as a law enforcement tool, Abscam triggered a storm of criticism from journalists, civil libertarians, scholars, and others. Gary Marx, a professor of sociology at the Massachusetts Institute of Technology, writing in the journal *Crime and Delinquency*, commented in light of Abscam that

> some of the new police undercover work has lost sight of the profound difference between carrying out an investigation to determine whether a suspect is, in fact, breaking the law, and carrying it out to determine if an individual can be induced to break the law . . . American society is

fragmented enough without the Government's adding a new layer of suspiciousness and distrust . . . Fake documents, lies, subterfuge, intrusive surveillance, and the creation of apparent reality are not generally associated with the United States law enforcement. However, we may be taking small but steady steps toward the paranoia and suspicion that characterizes many totalitarian countries.

Alan Dershowitz, professor of criminal law at Harvard and a noted defense lawyer who would help gain the acquittal of Claus von Bülow, chose *Penthouse* magazine as a forum for appealing to the public that "the Government cannot be allowed to select targets at will, expose them to all manner of temptation, and then pounce on those who succumb."

Ward was aware of these concerns, though philosophically he had always sided with those favoring strong law enforcement. While many of his classmates at Harvard Law School boycotted classes to protest the Vietnam War and the shootings at Kent State, Ward had joined both the student public defenders and district attorney organizations to get more firsthand exposure to criminal law. "I always wanted to practice criminal law," he says.

After he graduated, in 1972, he worked for a year for the Pennsylvania Crime Commission investigating organized crime, then joined the organized-crime section of the Department of Justice. He spent four years in Chicago, where for part of that time he ran an undercover fencing operation and learned a good deal about how to conduct an undercover investigation. He instinctively liked Thompson's proposal. "I figured the main difference from [Chicago] would be that we'd traffic in semiconductors instead of TV sets," he says.

Frequently the FBI comes to a U.S. Attorney only after an investigation is complete, when it wants an indictment. The Bureau, though under the aegis of the Department of Justice, is semiautonomous, a reaction to criticisms that the Bureau became too politicized during the Teapot Dome scandals of the Harding administration and a tradition firmly established after J. Edgar Hoover took charge in 1924. Curiously, in light of his strict law enforcement orientation, Hoover himself opposed using FBI agents for undercover operations and scams. He feared that such activities would require his agents to emulate the language, style, and values of the underworld in order to succeed, which he found distasteful and which he feared would cost the Bureau public support. He also feared that his agents would succumb to the temptations of money and narcotics inherent in under-cover work.

Hoover's strictures, however, weren't always observed. During the late sixties, some FBI agents infiltrated groups opposed to the Vietnam War, apparently without Hoover's knowledge. William C. Sullivan, assistant director for the FBI domestic intelligence division at the time, told a Senate committee that "some agents, especially some of the younger ones, infiltrated many of the groups in spite of Hoover's insisting to me that no agent should wear long hair, dress in jeans or wear a beard. I said 'the hell with it' and made the decision myself to go against Hoover's dogmatic ruling." After Hoover's death, in 1972, FBI agents began operating as undercover operatives more and more frequently. One agent infiltrated the Weather Underground and spent four years there, although the kind of fencing operation Ward worked on in Chicago was more typical, especially after political radicalism faded in the early seventies.

Partly in response to criticism arising from Abscam, Attorney General Smith issued new guidelines soon after he took office governing the conduct of FBI undercover operations. Particularly in order to avoid targeting any individuals or organizations for what might be deemed improper political reasons, major operations had to be approved in advance by a committee within the Justice Department. While FBI agents proposing such operations weren't required to obtain the consent of the U.S. Attorneys in their area, they were expected to consult with federal prosecutors and enlist their support for any prosecutions that might result.

At least in San Jose, FBI agents and the prosecutors in Ward's office worked closely together anyway; they typically invited each other to their office parties. (That isn't always the case, especially since prosecutors and FBI agents often jealously guard their turf. At the highest level, FBI Director William Webster was snubbed by not being given tickets to President Reagan's second inauguration. Webster had to obtain them through friends.) Ward already knew and liked Thompson; nonetheless, he felt it was his job to give the proposal independent scrutiny. "I studied the concept," he says. "My principal concern was whether we could generate usable evidence. We didn't want to gather evidence only to have it suppressed at trial. I thought if this were handled carefully, it could succeed. I gave my recommendation."

Thompson forwarded the proposal to Washington, where the Justice Department balked at first, citing the new guidelines, which provided that "an investigation may be opened when there are facts or circumstances that reasonably indicate a federal criminal violation has occurred, is occurring, or will occur. This standard . . . does require specific facts or circumstances indicating a violation." Thompson and Ward produced a fuller account of the suspected espionage in Silicon Valley. In April 1981, Operation Pengem—an acronym for Penetrate Gray Electronics Markets—was formally approved.

The following week, Ward arranged a top-secret meeting with the FBI undercover agents assigned to Operation Pengem. Thompson wouldn't be present—as the FBI agent coordinating the operation he would never be seen publicly with the agents posing as computer industry business people. For the site of the meeting, Ward chose the Marriott Hotel next to Great America, a popular amusement park in the San Jose area. He thought the hotel, thronged with tourists, would provide a good cover as he and the agents slipped into the building.

Ward introduced himself to the agents as they arrived: first Alan Garretson, who had been designated the principal undercover operative, and Mary Williams, who was also assigned to the operation full time. Two other agents attended who would play backup roles when necessary.

The nature of the operation had already been determined at the time approval was obtained from Washington: the agents were to go into business as a computer brokerage firm, operating under the name Glenmar Associates. An inconspicuous location in a nearby office complex had already been rented as the location of the business. A brokerage operation was selected because it enabled the agents to pose as both buyers and sellers of information, allowing them to insinuate themselves into a position where both the instigators and the recipients of espionage could be identified and ensnared. At the same time, the roles wouldn't require a vast amount of technical expertise.

Nonetheless, the agents had to know something about the computer industry, and they had to have plausible fictional employment backgrounds. As part of the proposal submitted to Washington, Thompson had suggested that International Business Machines Corporation, which had a large San Jose operation, be enlisted to provide the agents with technical training and false employment histories. Thompson had contacted IBM and IBM had assigned one of its employees to act as a liaison with the FBI, even though the corporation hadn't yet formally agreed to provide what the government wanted. Presumably, however, it had an incentive to do so—IBM was plainly one of the principal targets of the kind of crime the undercover operation was designed to detect.

Ward, however, wasn't so interested in the logistics of the scam. His goal at the meeting was to impress upon the agents the need to obtain evidence that would be admissible in a trial of any indictments that resulted from the operation. And that required the agents to understand the sometimes fine line between detecting crime and actually instigating it.

"We spent several hours going over this," Ward recalls. "I went over the issue in general terms, and we discussed various hypothetical examples of what could happen." The targets of the investigation, Ward emphasized, must be the ones to actually suggest the commission of a crime; on the other hand, the agents had to make it clear that they were interested in participating. "You have to act just like a sophisticated criminal," Ward told the agents. "Spread the word that you're interested, but don't plant any criminal intent in anyone's mind. Always seem interested, but don't make any requests that specifically ask that a crime be committed. Let the criminal mind figure out what should be done."

The thrust of Ward's admonitions made clear that his purpose was not only to obtain admissible evidence but to make sure that eventual defendants weren't acquitted on the grounds that they were entrapped by government agents.

Nonetheless, and not surprisingly, the agents had a hard time figuring out what they would and would not be allowed to say in the course of their new enterprise. Ward himself admits to a certain amount of confusion over just how investigators can shape their conduct so as to make sure they don't run into entrapment problems.

Entrapment is easily one of the most misunderstood of legal concepts—in part because the doctrine has been so inconsistently and confusingly applied by courts, including the Supreme Court, which created the doctrine in 1932.

As the Court ruled then and in subsequent cases, entrapment isn't a doctrine based on the Constitution—there is no constitutional right not to be entrapped, though some commentators have argued there should be. Rather, the Supreme Court held that Congress couldn't have intended "that its statutes were to be enforced by tempting innocent persons into violations," and found this concept to be implicit in every federal criminal statute. Thus, the Court reasoned, a defendant induced to commit a crime by a federal agent may be convicted only if he or she was "predisposed" to commit the crime. Hence, Ward's admonitions to let the targets of the investigation suggest the crime itself—presumably evidence of predisposition.

Though seemingly simple, the entrapment doctrine has led to a myriad of practical problems. Since it focuses primarily on a defendant's state of mind—predisposition—and not on the conduct of police or other investigators, inducements that produce acquittals in one case nonetheless produce convictions in instances where the defendants were "predisposed."

Nor does the notion of predisposition play any significant role in criminal cases where the person inducing the crime isn't a government agent. A person who commits a criminal act under duress—as Bernhard Goetz, for example, argued that he did when he shot four black youths in a New York subway—may be acquitted under other principles, such as self-defense or justification. But defendants who simply succumb to criminal temptation—even temptations so large that they would seem nearly impossible to resist (an offer of a million dollars to double-park, for example)—have no defense.

Furthermore, the notion that Congress didn't intend that certain enforcement tactics be employed is a fiction—Congress has never said anything of the sort. What seems the real, if largely unarticulated, reason for the defense is to curb what are deemed egregious police practices and the underlying fear of totalitarian tactics.

Unfortunately, the doctrine currently permits virtually any government conduct as long as the defendant was predisposed to commit a crime, which makes defendants with previous convictions particularly vulnerable.

Adding to the confusion is that most entrapment questions are settled by juries, not judges and courts. Who knows how juries interpret such elusive factors as a defendant's predisposition to commit crime and to what degree police tactics influence the outcome? Steven Brill, editor of the *American Lawyer* magazine, interviewed the jurors who acquitted former auto-maker John DeLorean on charges of cocaine dealing in 1984. They couldn't even agree among themselves whether or not entrapment was the grounds for their verdict, though several expressed disapproval of the government's tactics and its reliance on a particularly unsavory undercover agent who was himself an admitted criminal. Since there are no appeals from criminal acquittals, there will never be a judicial determination of whether DeLorean was or wasn't entrapped, or whether the government's conduct was improper.

Ward himself believes the standards are vague and confusing. "We try to take the most cautious approach consistent with having an effective operation. Obviously, at some point the only way to be certain you won't lose a case on entrapment grounds is not to have any undercover operations at all. Clearly, that's no solution." And as he had indicated in the proposal to Washington, Ward felt confident that Operation Pengem didn't pose serious entrapment risks. For one thing, it was being run by trustworthy career FBI people—not unsavory underworld types agreeing to cooperate in a scam in order to ward off prosecution themselves. And the targets were, for the most part, sophisticated business people, the type who wouldn't be expected to succumb to criminal temptation unless predisposed to do so.

Armed with Ward's admonitions, Garretson, Williams, and the other agents moved into the offices that served as Glenmar's headquarters. They were instructed to have no further contact with Ward unless they had specific questions about tactics or until their efforts produced evidence of a crime.

Ward heard nothing for six months. In November he received a call from agent Thompson and learned that during the intervening time Operation Pengem had made little progress. But IBM itself had apparently stumbled on to evidence of some high-tech criminal activity by an extraordinary and unexpected culprit. It wasn't the Soviet Union or a shadowy KGB agent, but Hitachi—one of Japan's most important and prestigious companies, and a fierce challenger to IBM.

Thompson told Ward that he had received a phone call during the last week in October from Richard Callahan, the IBM employee whom IBM had assigned to assist the FBI in Operation Pengem. Callahan worked as an investigator with the IBM general counsel's office; he was also a natural choice for the assignment since he is a former FBI agent himself, working in the Soviet counterintelligence section in New York City from 1954 to 1961. He also spent six years in the U.S. Bureau of Narcotics and Dangerous Drugs. Several Callahan-led undercover operations had previously led to prosecution of IBM competitors, and IBM had actively aided those investigations, providing witnesses and, in a few instances, cash to finance the investigations. Callahan also has the physical advantage of looking nothing like a spy: he is a quiet, graying, inconspicuous type who would look at home as the host of *Mr. Rogers' Neighborhood*, a children's television show.

Callahan had met a month earlier with several executives from a consulting firm in San Jose, Palyn Associates, staffed in part with former IBM employees. One of the services Palyn provided its clients was to monitor developments at IBM based on publicly available information. The service was in great demand by IBM's competitors, which, like Hitachi, manufactured "plug compatible" equipment—machines that could be connected to IBM products.

Palyn has always had curiously close ties to IBM, and there are those who believe it has served as IBM's own undercover operation. One of the Palyn executives, Maxwell Paley, is a former IBM engineer who maintained close contacts with the company. He told Callahan that he had just received an extraordinary telex from Kenji Hayashi, a senior engineer for Hitachi and one of Palyn's regular clients. Palyn had recently offered Hayashi a report discussing an addressing feature of IBM's new 3081 mainframe computer, but in the telex Hayashi replied that he already had much of that information. In what was, in retrospect, an incredibly indiscreet communication, Hayashi said that "we have already got Adirondack workbook that is similar to your covering." But the Japanese engineer said Hitachi didn't have a complete set of the multivolume workbook, adding, "If you have another vol., let me know. We consider again."

According to Callahan's account, Paley was stunned by the reference to the Adirondack books. From sources inside IBM, Paley knew that Adirondack was the code name the company had used to identify the top-secret program that developed the model 3081 computer. Even though he himself had never gotten copies, he understood that the books covered far more than the 3081 addressing feature, and that most of it was highly confidential.

Callahan told Thompson that he'd been intrigued by Paley's disclosure, and suggested that Palyn and IBM see if Hitachi could be tempted further. At Callahan's behest, Paley telexed Hayashi, telling him that he had established a contact inside IBM and "was told information you requested is under strict control but can be obtained," a statement that was, on its face, true. Paley also waved what should have been a red flag if Hitachi had come upon the books innocently: he urged that "no further reference should be made by telex in view of sensitive nature" and suggested they meet in Tokyo.

They did, on October 2. Unknown to Hayashi, Callahan was also along on the trip. Paley showed Hayashi a copy of the index to the latest version of the Adirondack workbook, the Alpine workbook, stamped "Do Not Copy," "Restricted," and "IBM Confidential," that had been given him by Callahan. Four days later, Hayashi returned the index, marking those portions that Hitachi wanted, at the same time providing copies of several of the books Hitachi had already received.

According to Callahan, there wasn't any doubt that Hayashi knew he was asking Paley to steal the additional information Hitachi wanted. At their meeting, Paley had warned Hayashi that Palyn wasn't in the business of acquiring confidential information; Hayashi had replied that Hitachi would pay a substantial premium for the books and would steer additional consulting contracts to the firm. And the books Hitachi had already received were plainly marked "Confidential." Furthermore, Hayashi had directed that the name Hitachi not be mentioned to any direct suppliers of the confidential books and proposed that the endeavor be mentioned only in code—"memory hierarchy study phase II" was one possibility.

Callahan told Thompson that he had verified that the Hitachi copies of the books were, in fact, volumes of IBM's top-secret Adirondack workbook by submitting them to the FBI lab in Washington. He suspected that Hitachi had already committed a crime and was prepared to go much further. Since Callahan was already involved in Operation Pengem, he said, why not turn the government's undercover operation to what appeared to be ongoing criminal conduct from one of Japan's largest corporations?

Thompson said he'd consider the proposal, discuss it with his colleagues in the Bureau, and talk to Ward, which he was doing now.

Although intrigued by Callahan's story, neither Thompson's nor Ward's first reaction to the idea was especially enthusiastic. Hitachi was not a named target in the proposal for Operation Pengem that had been approved in Washington, nor did IBM's disclosures seem likely to lead to any penetration of the alleged gray market in computer technology for which Operation Pengem had been designed.

Shifting the target of an investigation had also become more sensitive since Abscam, in which the government had been criticized for relying too heavily on untrustworthy informants, some of whom had personal motives for implicating congressmen and others. Indeed, *Penthouse* magazine publisher and businessman Bob Guccione became a target of the Abscam investigation even though agents had no evidence that any crime by him was in progress or that he was predisposed to commit a crime. The Senate committee reviewing Abscam ultimately concluded that "the Guccione events provide a chilling reminder of the risks imposed by lax procedures and inadequate supervision of an informant like [Melvin] Weinberg [the principal Abscam informant], by allowing him wide discretion in the targets he selects. . . ."

And Abscam had been specifically criticized for straying from the mandate it received when its proposal was approved, shifting from an investigation of property crimes to political corruption.

Callahan was hardly a Melvin Weinberg—a convicted felon whom the FBI had previously urged be terminated as an undercover operative because he had committed crimes while acting as an informant—but, by urging the operation be targeted at Hitachi, Callahan's role had shifted from that of a liaison with IBM to that of an informant. And both Ward and Thompson were fully aware that Hitachi was one of IBM's principal competitors, and Callahan had obvious motives for focusing suspicion on Hitachi.

Those concerns, however, were secondary to Ward. "The truth is, I didn't care," he says. "My sole concern was, should this be investigated? If so, using Operation Pengem was an ideal way to do it."

Both Ward's and Thompson's principal reservations focused on the nature of the alleged Hitachi crime and the likelihood that further investigation would lead to indictments. Based on Callahan's account, they weren't that optimistic. For all they knew, Hitachi had come into possession of the Adirondack books through some legitimate channel. There hadn't been any strong indications that Hitachi itself had stolen the materials, or that it had even induced someone else to steal them. Nonetheless, if Callahan's account could be believed—and they were somewhat skeptical, given IBM's interest in the matter—a Hitachi executive had shown a promising willingness to at least approach what would be criminal conduct.

Meanwhile, Callahan called back to report that negotiations with Hayashi were going forward, and that Paley had arranged to meet him again at a hotel in Las Vegas the following week. Callahan urged Thompson to send one of his Pengem agents along, to see for himself how eager the Japanese were to embark on a criminal conspiracy.

Ward and Thompson couldn't resist the opportunity to look in on the Palyn/Hitachi negotiations. Their concerns about Callahan's reliability could be alleviated by having their own agent present. Still, their expectations weren't all that great. "We didn't know if this would amount to anything," Ward says. "We were cautious. I figured that

Operation Pengem would continue its original efforts and then, if this panned out, fine. We'd see about getting involved." Without making a formal, long-term commitment, they arranged for agents Garretson and Williams to rendezvous with Callahan in Las Vegas the following week.

THE meeting in Las Vegas, in a room on the fourteenth floor of the Hilton Hotel, proved to be a turning point for Operation Pengem. When Ward reviewed the tapes of the session, this is what he heard.

Hayashi arrived at the room promptly, and was introduced to "Harrison," the president of Glenmar, and "Kerrigan," Glenmar's lawyer. He'd come with a veritable shopping list for IBM equipment and materials: he offered $10,000 for maintenance manuals and a "viewing" of one of IBM's newest mainframe computers; $50,000–$100,000 for mainframe operating programs; and $5,000 for two of the Adirondack books Hitachi didn't already have.

Garretson warned Hayashi that the person who had the books could "get in serious trouble" if he were caught. He "could be put in jail for stealing," Garretson said pointedly. Hayashi assured him of secrecy: he would arrange for what he called a "tunnel company" to make payments, and all references to the requests would be made in code. Garretson promised to arrange the viewing of the new mainframe, and the meeting ended on a cordial note.

As soon as Garretson returned from Las Vegas, he and Thompson arranged to meet with Ward. They were brimming with enthusiasm over what seemed to be Hitachi's positive eagerness to commit a crime, a factor that helped Ward overcome any lingering reservations about making Hitachi a focus of the investigation. Plainly, this was sufficient evidence of predisposition.

After hearing the tapes, Ward was quickly persuaded that efforts should continue to ensnare Hitachi in a criminal scheme to obtain trade secrets from IBM at the same time they searched for evidence that Hitachi had actually stolen the Adirondack books and possibly other confidential materials. But he didn't want the resources of Operation Pengem squandered on a relatively low-level executive like Hayashi, he told the agents. The operation should be more ambitious: how deep and how high into the Hitachi organization could the agents penetrate? The agents agreed, and set out to pursue the operation. For the next four months, Ward heard virtually nothing.

MEANWHILE, in the U.S. Attorney's office in San Francisco, a change of the guard was under way in the wake of President Reagan's election a year earlier. For the previous year, the office had been run by an acting U.S. Attorney who stepped in for the Carter appointee, who had resigned. San Francisco hadn't been high on the new President's priority for appointments, and a search committee operating under the auspices of California Republican Senator S. I. Hayakawa had taken a year to select a candidate for the post. During that time, Ward found that he was able to secure a high degree of autonomy for his own operation in San Jose.

The search committee's final choice was a San Francisco lawyer, Joseph Russoniello. From the Reagan administration's point of view, Russoniello was unusually well qualified. He'd joined the FBI as a special agent right after graduating from New York University Law School in 1967, and he was an experienced prosecutor: after the FBI, he spent six years in the office of the San Francisco District Attorney prosecuting business fraud cases. He'd run for District Attorney as a Republican and lost in 1979, and he'd been an active supporter of President Reagan in the 1980 campaign. Perhaps more importantly, he seemed to be on the same wavelength, ideologically, as President Reagan and top people in the Justice Department.

"What I knew about Bay Area prosecutors when I was nominated," says Russoniello, "was bad. Prosecution was lackluster. The focus was on white-collar crime—period. Street crime wasn't given the attention it needed. The reason being all this sociological stuff. The attitude was liberal—much too liberal. I felt strongly that this was wrong."

Russoniello was enthusiastic about the nomination—he'd always wanted to be a high-level prosecutor. And he was especially enthusiastic now that Reagan had taken office. "I knew Lowell Jensen—he'd been a very highly respected District Attorney. And I knew Rudi Giuliani. They're first-class people. The climate seemed right for prosecuting.

"I recently spoke to a prosecutor who was retiring, and he said his life had been a failure. Prosecuting during the Warren Court was futile. Fortunately, those attitudes have changed."

All during the time Russoniello's nomination was pending, he was told nothing about Hitachi, the most sensitive and secret investigation over which he would soon be presiding. Then, on November 15, the day after Russoniello was confirmed as U.S. Attorney by the Senate in Washington, Mark Richards at the Justice Department gave him an overview of Operation Pengem. Russoniello says he wasn't surprised that there was industrial espionage in Silicon Valley; he was more surprised that the culprits were Japanese rather than Soviet.

As soon as Russoniello returned to San Francisco, he met with Ward, who briefed him in detail on the progress of the investigation up to that point. Somewhat to Ward's dismay, Russoniello indicated that he didn't want preoccupation with Operation Pengem to interfere with Ward's work on more mundane matters. Consistent with his earlier pronouncements, white-collar crime was not to get top billing during the Russoniello term. And Russoniello also laid down reporting requirements that, Ward says, made him realize that his days of running a quasi-autonomous office were over.

During the next few months, Ward's and the San Jose office's case load was stepped up as a result of Russoniello's directives. "We were swamped," Ward recalls. "Every garden-variety federal crime imaginable. We had three attorneys and one-third of the case load in the district. Pengem was practically a memory."

Then Ward got another call from Thompson. The FBI was increasingly enthusiastic over the progress Garretson and Williams were making with Hitachi in their Glenmar Associates operation. Since Ward and Thompson's last conversation, the agents had told Hayashi that they had obtained a secret operating manual for IBM's model 3033 extensions, code named P-9, an item the Japanese had indicated was top priority and would demonstrate that Glenmar could deliver the kind of intelligence it had promised. In response, Hayashi wrote that "I am very glad to have heard you have completed P-9 study within our target. Our management would recognize your potential . . . As you know I like to visit Las Vegas with my hobby. If possible I would like to have same treatment with which I enjoyed very much last November."

The P-9 study had been handed over in Las Vegas (where Hayashi successfully pursued his "hobby"—blackjack), a payment channel had been established that routed money to Glenmar through an intermediary, and Garretson and Callahan—the latter still posing as a lawyer for Glenmar—tantalized Hayashi with the prospect that even more valuable information could be provided if they were allowed to meet with some more senior Hitachi executives to discuss it. Hayashi had agreed to try to set up such a meeting in Hawaii sometime in March.

Thompson told Ward that he thought the Hawaii meeting could be crucial to their efforts to penetrate further into Hitachi, and he said he wanted Ward to be there, if possible. Ostensibly, Thompson wanted Ward's presence because he thought the Hawaii meeting might yield some audio and video tapes that would be used as evidence, and he wanted to make sure that the agents elicited the most incriminating comments without crossing the line into entrapment. This meeting was initiated by Glenmar operatives, and they would be proposing a substantial escalation of the espionage operation against IBM.

Thompson also had another motive: he wanted to muster more enthusiasm for the operation within the U.S. Attorney's office. He'd sensed that Ward was being increasingly occupied by other matters, and knew that Russoniello hadn't indicated unbridled enthusiasm for the project. Perhaps if Ward could be persuaded to see the developing crime firsthand, Thompson would excite some determination that Hitachi be prosecuted.

Ward was delighted at the prospect of joining the agents in Hawaii. But he referred Thompson to Russoniello. "He's the one you have to persuade," he told the agent. Somewhat to Ward's surprise, the FBI seemed to have more clout in San Francisco than he did. The U.S. Attorney agreed to send Ward to Hawaii.

IN mid-March, Ward flew to Honolulu, and met Garretson, Williams, and, for the first time, Callahan, at the Colony Surf Hotel, an aging pink-stucco resort hotel on Waikiki Beach. A feature that set the Colony Surf apart from other such hotels was the fact that its penthouse suite had been thoroughly wired for sound by the FBI. The site was rumored to have been used previously by CIA operatives in Honolulu.

Soon after arriving, Ward asked one of the video technicians where the television monitor was hidden. "In the bedroom," the technician replied, leading Ward into an adjoining bedroom stuffed with technical equipment and the television monitor. Ward was aghast. "I said, 'This is a joke!'" Ward recalls. "I mean, where is the first place you'd look if you were worried about surveillance? I was very concerned the Japanese would want to come in here. When I was doing this kind of thing with Mafia types in Chicago, the first thing they'd do was to check all the rooms for bugs."

Garretson reassured Ward that if the door was closed they'd be safe. It was contrary to the Japanese character to inspect the premises, he explained, since it would have implied a lack of trust, a serious breach of business etiquette in Japan.

Garretson's knowledge of Japanese customs helped the technicians place their cameras and video recording equipment. Because the Japanese customarily choose seats based on rank, with the highest-ranking person at the center, the agents could predict exactly where their guest would sit, and train the cameras accordingly.

Ward took up his position with the technicians in front of the bedroom monitor shortly before their guest was expected.

Katsuhiko Kato arrived punctually. Ward, though familiar with many of the participants in the scheme, knew little about Kato. As a department manager in Hitachi's Odawara computer works, Kato was a key link to higher executives, but the scope of his involvement wasn't clear. Garretson introduced himself and the others in the roles they had become accustomed to playing: himself as Alan Harrison, president of Glenmar; Mary Williams as his secretary; and Richard Callahan as Richard Kerrigan, Glenmar's lawyer.

After some initial pleasantries, Garretson asked Kato if he knew Jun Naruse, the engineer from the Odawara works who'd met with Garretson in Hartford to view the Pratt & Whitney computer. Kato nodded and said yes.

Periodically, Williams would leave the room and join Ward in the bedroom, ostensibly getting supplies, or documents, or whatnot. On those visits, Ward gave Williams messages to take back to the other agents. Ward, having read Edwin Reischauer's classic study of Japanese behavior, was worried that language ambiguities might spoil the tapes as evidence. "Saying yes, to the Japanese, doesn't necessarily mean agreement," he explains. "It's just a polite expression. So 'yes,' by itself, that wasn't enough on tape. I kept telling the agents to interrupt frequently, asking if the Japanese understood. Then if the Japanese answered yes, we knew they understood us."

So Garretson pressed Kato for fuller responses, though Kato didn't seem very garrulous. Kato acknowledged that Odawara had received various documents and equipment from Glenmar and that they had been helpful; he also asked for more. Without any prompting by the agents, he offered $20,000 for the source microdes for two of IBM's new computers, and another $20,000 for the automated logic diagrams for the same machines.

On one of her trips to the bedroom, Williams was asked by Ward to pursue the source of the funds. Did Kato have the authority to make such payments, or might it be necessary for someone higher up in the organization to approve them? Kato, however, seemed cautious about mentioning other names, and said he did have the authority to approve the payments.

Ward's fears that the Japanese businessman would search the penthouse proved unfounded. In fact, Kato didn't behave anything like the criminals Ward had come to know in Chicago, or anywhere else, for that matter. At the end of the meeting, Kato admired the view and mentioned that he'd like to have a snapshot to memorialize the occasion. Garretson quickly volunteered to help, and positioned him on the balcony. Soon after, he sent Kato copies of the photo, with the Hitachi executive's smiling face against the backdrop of Diamond Head and the Pacific Ocean.

THE FBI was disappointed by Kato's performance. He had been laconic and he hadn't led them any deeper into the Hitachi organization. The transcript of the video tape was studded with "Uh-hmms," pauses, and nods. But the experience had its intended effect on Ward. Having seen the undercover agents and a high-ranking official from Hitachi, he was, in his words, "enthused. My adrenaline had really gotten moving. I felt committed, and started spending nearly full time on the operation."

As soon as he returned to San Jose, Ward met with Thompson to map strategy. Thompson was getting concerned about the materials being turned over to the Odawara works. So far, nothing of any great importance to IBM had been handed over, but Hitachi was becoming more sophisticated and demanding in its requests. IBM would soon be faced with the need to produce extremely sensitive, competitively damaging materials. Meanwhile, the operation hadn't succeeded in getting beyond Kato into the Hitachi organization.

Thompson proposed an end run: an entirely new proposal involving high-level IBM executives who might "consult"—i.e., spy—for Hitachi, but only if their security was guaranteed by comparably high-level Hitachi executives. Given Japanese business customs, Ward and Thompson thought it likely that if Hitachi could be interested in the idea, the company would produce high-level executives for the negotiations. In Japan, executives tend to deal directly only with other businessmen with similar rank.

Three days later, Garretson called Hayashi and complained about Kato. Couldn't he be assigned someone else within the Odawara works? Anxious to please, Hayashi promised to find another liaison. The negotiations over the private consultant arrangement looked as if they might be even more productive: Hayashi volunteered that the general manager of the Kanagawa works, Dr. Kisaburo Nakazawa, knew about the work Glenmar was doing and might be the person who would negotiate.

By this point, Hitachi was no longer the sole target of Operation Pengem, although the focus of the investigation had shifted entirely to the Japanese. Palyn Associates had other Japanese clients, and one of them, Mitsubishi, had expressed a similar interest in confidential material obtained from IBM. So Palyn, as it had with Hitachi, arranged for Mitsubishi to meet with Glenmar personnel. Negotiations began, though the other Japanese didn't seem to be taking the bait nearly as fast as Hitachi.

And the Hitachi operation soon began accelerating. A few days after their previous conversation, Hayashi called to confirm that he'd arranged for Garretson to meet with Nakazawa, the Kanagawa works manager, when he was in San Francisco later that month.

Ward was excited by the development—Nakazawa was the highest-ranking executive to date to become ensnared. Ward urged the agents to probe the scope of Nakazawa's involvement and to press him for the names of even higher-level executives. The undercover team met with Nakazawa April 23 in the penthouse of the St. Francis Hotel, on Union Square in San Francisco. Ward and the audio and video technicians were again hidden in a bedroom off the main room, listening and watching closely as Nakazawa was ushered in.

The executive proved maddeningly monosyllabic, but indicated he was fully aware not only of the proposed consulting arrangement but also of the transactions involving the Odawara works.

"Do you know how the payments are made now to us?" Callahan asked Nakazawa. "Through Mr. Shirai and Mr. O?" Garretson added.

"Shirai," Nakazawa answered.

"NCL Data?" Garretson asked, to see if Nakazawa was familiar with the company acting as a payment intermediary.

"NCL Data . . . no, no," Nakazawa said.

Callahan and Garretson explained the secret payment channel in some detail, then elicited an acknowledgment that Nakazawa knew Hitachi was the source of the funds.

"Hitachi pays Nissei [another intermediary]?" Garretson asked.

"Yes, Hitachi pay Nissei and Nissei pay, oh, NCL?" Nakazawa answered.

"NCL," Garretson confirmed, "and then NCL pays us."

"Um-hmm, um-hmm," Nakazawa murmured, nodding his head in agreement.

The agents also wanted to establish that Nakazawa knew he was receiving highly confidential information and that the process had to be shrouded in secrecy. Seeking assurances that the identities of the "consultants" would be kept secret also provided a vehicle to probe for higher-level involvement inside Hitachi.

"There are not many people who will be in a position to provide the kind of information that you're asking us to get, so if it [IBM] becomes aware that that information has gotten to Hitachi, IBM will start its investigations," Callahan said.

"Yes, yes, I understand," said Nakazawa.

"You understand?" Garretson added for good measure.

"Yes, yes," replied Nakazawa. In a talkative burst, Nakazawa assured them that access to the materials was tightly restricted, and that only one engineer would be permitted to study them. "We are very confident that the . . . ah . . . secrecy of this document may be keeps in this whole person and authorized secret engineer."

"This is a very risky business," Callahan emphasized. "We have to be very, very careful to protect everybody involved."

"Yes, yes, I understand, yes. May be difficult, I see," Nakazawa answered, looking concerned.

"I'd like you to, you know, give me your best counsel and advice and guarantee where you can give them," Callahan continued, "and if you can't give me the guarantees on behalf of everybody, make arrangements for us to meet the people who can.

"Uh-hm."

"The approvals of the past business that we have done and the money approvals have all been made by their top management."

"Uh-hm."

"I need those assurances before I can really move forward. I really do because I'm not gonna put my people at risk, uh, until I have those assurances from top management."

"Uh-hm."

"How do you suggest we proceed from here? You will go back to Japan?"

"Yes."

"And then, uh, what? Be in touch with us?"

Suggesting the precariousness of the English-language dialogue, Nakazawa suddenly looked troubled. "What do you mean by touches?" he asked.

"Well, touches in American . . ." Callahan began, then Garretson interjected "Contact."

"Contact," Callahan repeated, seizing the definition with relief. "Let us know the results of your discussions."

Events, however, were moving more quickly than Ward and the other agents wanted. Hitachi was pressing for the model 3081 design document and said it wanted them by the end of May. IBM, however, was about to draw the line: it did not want those materials in the hands of a Japanese competitor. Although Garretson stalled by haggling over the exact price terms, on May 18 he received a telex from Hayashi saying Hitachi accepted the $525,000 price Garretson had been demanding. Hitachi also sent a good-faith down payment of $30,000. There was little maneuvering room left before the materials had to be delivered or the operation abandoned.

Ward, Thompson, and the agents gathered at the Glenmar headquarters and reluctantly reached the conclusion that the operation should be collapsed. It was getting harder and harder to move deeper inside Hitachi at the same time the company's demands were mounting. So they devised what they called a "closing scenario."

Ward, in particular, was worried about several legal issues that would affect prosecution of the case. One was extradition. Given the nature of the undercover operation and the embarrassing publicity it would generate for the Japanese, it seemed unlikely that successful prosecutions could be mounted against any of the defendants who were in Japan at the time of the arrests. Japan outlaws undercover operations except in drug cases, so it was unlikely to recognize the Hitachi arrests as legitimate. How could as many of the Japanese conspirators as possible be brought together on American soil?

They concluded that a physical exchange of the IBM equipment and plans Hitachi had requested might provide the opportunity. The agents would insist that Hitachi send higher management representatives to verify that the materials being delivered were what the company had requested. If they succeeded in luring enough Hitachi personnel, the trap could be sprung as the delivery was taking place.

Accordingly, Callahan wrote a letter on Glenmar stationery to Nakazawa:

We will be prepared to deliver these materials by the agreed date, 6/21/82. I must ask you for the following additional assurances:

1. The entire amount of money agreed ($545K) be in our hands in either currency form or by wire transfer to an identified bank account before information is delivered.

2. We will make all five items requested available for examination by your staff before any fund transfers are completed to insure that Hitachi is fully satisfied with what we deliver. In this regard, I would suggest that you have available here on that date enough competent staff to insure that that product expected is the product delivered. We have had many past problems in this area, and I strongly suggest you send enough competent staff in June to avoid these problems . . .

Warm regards,
R. KERRIGAN

But the Japanese proved obstinate, agreeing to send only Hayashi, Ohnishi, and a representative of the Odawara works, a man named Nakagoshi. Then Hayashi announced that Nakagoshi's daughter had become ill, and only he and Ohnishi would come.

Callahan was furious. He called Ohnishi.

"This is a very sensitive deal, and I, I want it to be done very, very well and very cleanly, but I have to have somebody from Odawara who can look at this stuff and say yes, that's exactly what we asked for, so that the payment can be made . . ."

"Ken will learn . . ." Ohnishi replied, suggesting that Hayashi was competent to evaluate the material.

"Ken will not learn," Callahan insisted. "Ken knows nothing about Odawara. He's told me that fifty times."

Ohnishi laughed. "It's impossible."

"Well, if it's impossible then we have serious problems."

"But . . . ah . . . they . . . how shall I say . . . Mr. Nakagoshi's daughter got sick, very serious sick . . ."

"Yeah," Callahan interrupted, "I mean, that's too bad . . . but Mr.

Kato's daughter is not sick. Mr. Naruse's daughter is not sick . . . I mean, we want somebody from Odawara here. Ken cannot do it."

"Ken can do that," Ohnishi insisted, repeating that it was "impossible" for anyone else to come.

Callahan boiled over. "Why is everything such a problem with you folks? This is what I have guaranteed to my clients who are producing all this stuff, and, as I say, that's the agreement, and you call Ken or Nakazawa or whomever you have to call, and just tell them that that's the way it is." He slammed down the phone.

Later Hayashi called Garretson, saying they might send Naruse from Japan to represent the Odawara works, but weren't happy about it.

"You're ready to send Mr. Naruse?" Garretson asked.

"Yes . . . uh . . . if . . . uh . . . Dick [Callahan] want to see another persons, uh . . . but I and . . . uh . . . Mr. Nakagoshi and Mr. Kawano don't like it and . . . uh . . . we think Dick is . . . uh . . . thickheaded person." Hayashi broke into laughter.

Garretson said he thought Naruse would be acceptable, but then Hayashi said something alarming about Naruse: "He . . . uh . . . he's afraid now to do such the business."

"He's afraid?" Garretson asked quickly. Hayashi laughed again nervously.

"Why? Why is he afraid?"

"He . . . uh . . . he afraid of the business," Hayashi said.

When Ward learned of the conversation later that day, he was concerned. What they didn't need was some high-level Hitachi official getting cold feet, possibly scrapping the whole operation. The prospect was like landing a big fish only to see it slither off the hook just before reeling it on deck. The agents decided to drop the demand that someone from Odawara be present and to settle for Ohnishi.

On June 21, 1982, Hitachi wired $500,000 into the Glenmar account. The next day, Hayashi and Ohnishi arrived at the Glenmar offices, and minutes later, the trap snapped shut.

THE arrests of Hayashi and Ohnishi touched off a barrage of publicity in both the United States and Japan. For the most part, the Japanese, though shamed by the allegations, were indignant. A Japanese Cabinet official said Japan had been "slapped in the face" by the sting.

The sudden worldwide media attention subjected Ward to intense pressure. Immediately after the arrests, he conferred with Russoniello, then set about drafting indictments in the case. At Russoniello's urging, he also conferred with Justice Department officials in Washington. Jay Stephens, the Justice Department lawyer who oversaw the case, was worried about the legal grounds for criminally indicting a corporation, especially since the case was bound to exacerbate trade relations between the U.S. and Japan.

Given the complexity of the undercover operation, Ward's indictment was surprisingly simple. It charged a single violation of the U.S. Criminal Code: conspiracy to transport stolen property across interstate lines. In the pantheon of federal crimes, it doesn't rate very highly, carrying as it does a maximum sentence of five years in prison and a $10,000 fine.

But Ward didn't have much choice. In purely legal terms, the outcome of the operation was something of a disappointment. At the outset, the FBI had thought it might discover that Hitachi had stolen the Adirondack books that triggered the investigation, or that Hitachi had stolen other materials from IBM or other U.S. competitors. Despite repeated questioning by the undercover agents, no evidence of that had developed.

On July 27, the four individual defendants in the U.S. appeared and entered formal pleas of not guilty, as did representatives of Hitachi itself. Nine of the defendants—including Nakazawa and Kato—failed to appear, thereby becoming fugitives in Japan. With the case formally begun, Ward says, "I braced myself for an avalanche of paper."

But what he got at first was an avalanche of phone calls from defense counsel trying to feel out the propsects of a quick settlement. As far as Ward was concerned, he says, they were wasting their breath. "They didn't have a leg to stand on. I said if they wanted to come in and plead guilty, fine. That was the extent of my negotiating."

Ward acknowledges that he may have been a little abrupt with the defense counsel—he says he found them, at times, insulting and condescending—and says they complained constantly that he wasn't being reasonable. "I said if you don't like it, go to Russoniello," Ward recalls. "I'm not going to sit here and listen to you whine." Defense counsel did complain—loudly—to Russoniello.

Ward couldn't even charge Hitachi and its executives with actually transporting stolen property. Hitachi itself hadn't stolen it, and, in any event, theft is a state—not federal—crime. So is solicitation to commit a theft, which, arguably, is a crime with which Hitachi could have been charged. But in the ever-present rivalry between federal and state prosecutors, there had never been serious consideration of bringing local prosecutors into the operation. "We didn't feel they'd be able to bring any charges that were substantially stronger than our federal ones," Ward says.

Within a week, Ward went before the grand jury, showed its members excerpts from the audio and video tapes, and obtained indictments against Hitachi and fourteen individuals involved in the scheme. The indictment read: "Defendants did knowingly and willfully conspire together to commit an offense against the United States, that is, they did conspire to transport in interstate and foreign commerce goods, wares and merchandise valued in excess of $5,000, knowing that these goods, wares and merchandise had been stolen and converted, in violation of Title 1B, United States Code, Section 2314." And it recited fifteen "overt acts" of the conspiracy, beginning with Hayashi's meeting with the undercover agents in Las Vegas.

Soon after the filing of the indictment, Ward realized that he wouldn't be facing the usual local defense lawyers. Hitachi and the individual defendants amassed a defense team of some of the top criminal lawyers in San Francisco and New York. The corporation alone hired two large New York firms—Paul, Weiss, Rifkind, Wharton & Garrison and Curtis, Mallet-Prevost, Colt & Mosle—and Graham & James, a prominent San Francisco firm.

It was a situation that also caused some concern in the U.S. Attorney's office in San Francisco. Russoniello worried that the case would need more than one lawyer working on it full time. And he had some reservations about Ward's experience and judgment given the publicity the case was receiving. Since becoming U.S. Attorney, Russoniello hadn't been getting along all that well with Ward, who had continued to chafe at what he saw as a curbing of his autonomy in San Jose.

Russoniello thought about taking over the prosecution of the case himself. One reason lawyers with political ambitions seek the U.S. Attorney post is because of the unparalleled opportunity for media exposure, and Hitachi was plainly the biggest case in the office from a media standpoint, with the possible exception of some cases arising from the Peoples Temple massacre in Jonestown, Guyana. Russoniello was already handling those himself.

But Russoniello passed on Hitachi. "It would have been grandstanding," he says. "Besides, I don't like to intrude on the assistants when they're enthusiastic to try a case. I take the cases that no one else wants, the tough cases to win, the ones that require a lot of preparation."

Others, however, say Russoniello's motives may not have been quite so noble. They argue that the political risks in Hitachi were significant: if the case was lost, there would be howls from the Japanese government, intense pressure from the State Department in Washington, and demands for accountability. They say too that Russoniello was aware that Hitachi could bring enormous resources to bear in its defense. It was likely to be a "tough" case.

And in any event, Russoniello demonstrated little regard for the feelings and enthusiasm of Ward in deciding how the case should be handled. Although he decided that he, personally, wouldn't take charge of the case, he assigned another, more senior prosecutor, giving him a mandate to take charge and moving the litigation headquarters out of San Jose and into San Francisco. Ward was, for all practical purposes, dumped.

"It hurt terribly," Ward says. "I knew I couldn't do the case all by myself. I'd discussed this with Russoniello, and he knew I wanted help. But this case had practically been my whole life for months. I knew it inside and out; I was committed to it. It was taken away from me, and I wasn't even consulted in advance. Maybe that's what hurt the most."

Ward was still on the case in a secondary capacity, and he was left in charge of the Mitsubishi indictment. But it was obvious he'd lost control, and it caused bad feelings that later spilled over into the press.

Some time later, Ward received a call from David Wilman, a reporter for the San Jose *Mercury-News*, asking to interview him for a profile. Ward had been deluged with calls from the press since the news of the operation had broken, and had said very little. But like most prosecutors, Ward has an ego. He was intrigued by the possibility of a profile, especially since the reporter agreed not to ask him about the details of the Hitachi case.

In the course of the interview, however, Ward couldn't resist criticizing Russoniello and the San Francisco office, particularly one of Russoniello's pet projects—the creation of a task force that would concentrate exclusively on high-tech crime. Ward complained that Russoniello had, in fact, slighted the prosecution of high-tech crime in Silicon Valley by assigning only three prosecutors to Ward's office.

Ward says he was horrified when the article appeared. Far from a profile of him, he saw it as an exposé, focusing on his unhappiness with Russoniello. And he says he was misquoted—he claimed he supported the high-tech task force. "I'd had problems with the paper," Ward says of the *Mercury-News*. "I'd refused to talk to a reporter about the Hitachi case, and she was upset. I don't know what happened, exactly. In the past I'd always had good relations with the press."

The reporter who wrote the story, David Wilman, has an entirely different recollection of the affair. "I did go to do a profile of him," Wilman recalls. "We wondered why the San Jose office was being passed over in so many high-tech crime cases, when Russoniello had said San Jose would be his 'beachhead' against high-tech crime. Anyway," Wilman continues, "in the interview Ward started saying these stunning things—how he felt spurned and excluded. I couldn't ignore that."

Wilman denies that Ward was misquoted. "After the interview, he called and asked me not to print some of the things he'd said. But it was all on the record. I thought about it, but we went ahead and published it. I taped our conversation, and I still have the tape, so there's really no doubt in my mind."

Russoniello, for one, didn't accept Ward's explanation that he was misquoted. When interviewed by Wilman and told of the comments, he said, on the record, "I'm very disappointed in Greg." Russoniello took Ward's remarks as a personal affront, and interpreted them as an indication of bad judgment and lack of maturity—just as Ward was working on the highest-profile and most sensitive case in the office. And the incident left a bad impression with the press. "We thought of Ward as a whining wimp," says one local reporter.

Despite that image, defense lawyers say—as does Ward himself— that he was, in fact, the toughest of the prosecutors, the one who staked out the hard-line positions and wouldn't budge. "Maybe I was too intense," Ward says. "Maybe I was too close to the case, maybe I cared too much. But I don't think so."

ASSISTANT U.S. Attorney Herbert Hoffman, then in his early forties, was anything but a wimp. A tough Jewish kid who grew up on the streets of Chicago, a high-school athletic star, and a veteran of hard-core murder and rape prosecutions in Washington, D.C., Hoffman's main problem in California was that he was too aggressive for local juries. "I was in the middle of a closing argument in San Diego," he says, "when one of the women on the jury put her hands over her ears. She wanted me to stop screaming. I had to learn that the tactics I used in Washington were sometimes a little too bold and brash for California."

At the time Russoniello's disenchantment with Ward was reaching its peak over the article, Hoffman was on hand in San Francisco, available for another case assignment. Although he worked in the San Diego U.S. Attorney's office, he'd been in San Francisco conducting a grand jury investigation of steel dumping allegations against another large Japanese conglomerate, Mitsui. That had just culminated in Mitsui pleading guilty to twenty-one criminal counts and paying $11 million in civil penalties.

So Hoffman was available and he'd just spent months dealing with Japanese defendants. He was a natural choice for the Hitachi case, and the San Diego U.S. Attorney granted Russoniello's request to keep Hoffman on in San Francisco for a while.

For Hoffman, the assignment was the pinnacle of a prosecutorial career that had advanced fitfully. When he was twenty-four years old, still in law school, Hoffman had gone to observe an offshoot of the Jimmy Hoffa prosecution in Chicago. "I saw the Department of Justice lawyers under Bobby Kennedy, and I was awestruck," he recalls. "I thought that would be the greatest job in the world."

After graduation, Hoffman went to Washington, D.C., joined the Justice Department, and became an Assistant U.S. Attorney in 1969. He lost his first case, a bid-rigging case involving Anthony DiAngelis, the so-called salad-oil king. Then for four years he prosecuted serious crimes like rape and murder (because of the District of Columbia's peculiar status in the federal system, federal prosecutors there handle crimes that in the states are handled by state prosecutors).

Those years took their toll. "My job was always the same—to convict," Hoffman says. "I'd frequently ask for the death penalty. There's a lot of soul-searching in that—you're asking for a person's death."

Hoffman decided to try private practice, and joined a firm with a large divorce practice and little interest in criminal defense work. The experiment lasted a year; Hoffman finally boiled over, told the senior partner he had more trial experience than anybody else in the firm, and walked out. When offered a chance to relocate in California and work in the San Diego U.S. Attorney's office, he took it, even though it meant starting at the bottom again. But by 1980, his trial success was such that he was designated by the Justice Department a senior litigation counsel—one of about thirty in the country.

Hoffman was delighted by the Hitachi assignment. "It was tremendously high profile, and I was impressed by the caliber of the defense counsel." Ward he handled gingerly. "I would have been disappointed too," he says.

Shortly after, defense lawyers had their first meeting with the prosecutors to discuss disposing of the case. Their Japanese clients, horrified as much by the barrage of adverse publicity as by the potential sentences, were eager to avoid a lengthy trial, along with a showing of the incriminating video tapes. Speaking for the defendants, New York lawyer Peter Fleming indicated that Hitachi might be willing to enter a plea of nolo contendere if charges against the individual defendants were dismissed, a stance similar to the one McDonnell Douglas had first taken.

Russoniello staked out the government's initial position: if Hitachi and the individual defendants pleaded guilty, the prosecution wouldn't ask for prison terms—it would seek only probation.

The meeting didn't last long, since Russoniello and Hoffman considered the defense proposition totally unacceptable. For one thing, the Department of Justice has a policy forbidding the acceptance of nolo pleas, in which a defendant neither admits nor denies the charges in the indictment but agrees to submit to sentencing. The policy had been conspicuously violated when former Vice President Spiro Agnew was allowed to plead nolo in 1973, but those were unusual circumstances and the barrage of unfavorable publicity subsequently weathered by the Justice Department only increased its determination not to make such exceptions.

Secondly, Hoffman emphasized to Russoniello, Hitachi, as a corporation, was hardly the most culpable—if anyone deserved a prison term, it was Hayashi, the major actor in the scheme. Dismissal of the charges against Hayashi, Hoffman told the defense lawyers, was completely out of the question.

Nor did Fleming find the government's offer appealing. He warned the prosecutors that extracting a guilty plea from the Japanese would be excruciatingly difficult and probably impossible. There were strong Japanese cultural and political prohibitions against making such public admissions of guilt.

Privately, however, Fleming felt he had emerged on top from the first bargaining round. He hadn't expected Russoniello to capitulate so readily on the question of jail sentences.

Fleming wasn't the only one surprised by Russoniello's initial bargaining position. Ward, for one, who hadn't even been present for the initial negotiating, was incensed. "He [Russoniello] just gave away the store. The concession came too early—it wasn't even made a negotiating point. Once the possibility of jail was gone, we didn't have much left to bargain with—just probation and fines. If I'd been asked, I would have said this was pulling the rug out from under the whole effort. But Joe just made up his mind, and that was it."

Nor was the Justice Department happy. In Washington, Assistant Attorney General Lowell Jensen got on the phone personally to Russoniello, chastising him for capitulating on the prison issue. And Jensen wasn't upset simply because a bargaining chip had been lost: there was strong feeling in Washington that if the Hitachi case was to serve as an effective deterrent, someone involved should be sentenced to prison.

At this juncture, however, there was little that could be done. "Practically speaking," Hoffman says, "once you've offered probation it's very hard to retract. Any sentencing judge would wonder why the government had made such an offer in the first place and then felt a stiffer punishment was necessary."

Russoniello cites several reasons for his decision to make such a generous first offer. The prosecution for conspiracy to transport stolen property was the first of its type, and he felt lesser sentences are appropriate in such situations. He also thought that the issue of the defendants' criminal state of mind was clouded by the differing cultural and ethical norms of the Japanese. Finally, there was language: had the Japanese really understood that their conduct was criminal?

Russoniello says that he also thought the offer might lead to a quick settlement of the case. "I was aware of the enormous impact this might have on U.S.–Japanese relations," he says. "This was a time of intense concern and tension between the Americans and the Japanese." He says, however, that he received no pressure from anyone in Washington to settle the case quickly, although he acknowledges that the State Department did bring the Japanese government's concerns to his attention and to the Justice Department, along with its hopes for a speedy resolution of the matter.

Russoniello's hopes for a quick settlement were dashed as the defense lawyers' strategy emerged. The cases stemming from the undercover operation had been divided into three groups: Hitachi, Mitsubishi, and a smaller case against those responsible for the original theft of the Adirondack books: Raymond Cadet and Barry Saffaei.

Early in the investigation, agent Garretson had pressed Hayashi for an explanation of how Hitachi had obtained the volumes of the Adirondack workbook that triggered the operation, suggesting that the information might help Garretson obtain the remaining volumes that Hitachi wanted. Hayashi gave him the name of an engineer at National Advanced Systems with whom Hitachi did business. The name sounded vaguely Middle Eastern. No one by that name, however, was employed at the company.

Soon after, the FBI lab's analysis of the books Callahan brought back from Japan enabled the agents to trace the original books to Raymond Cadet, a former IBM employee with access to the books who was now employed at National Advanced Systems. And he worked closely with a Dr. Saffaei—a name close to that provided by Hayashi. Cadet and Saffaei were arrested the same day that the undercover operation was sprung.

Lawyers for Cadet and Saffaei promptly made discovery motions, asking for a broad array of information presumably in the government's possession. In particular, they wanted everything bearing on the "past and present" relationship of IBM, Palyn Associates, and the U.S. government. Presiding judge Robert Aguilar granted their request, agreeing with the defendants that the information might be crucial to their claims of entrapment and government misconduct. Ties between IBM and the government, it developed, were an extremely sensitive subject.

Two weeks later, Ward asked the judge to modify his discovery order. Ward produced a copy of the written agreement between the FBI and IBM entered into after the first Las Vegas meeting with Hayashi, and argued that that should be enough. The judge refused.

Ward faced a quandary. In discussions with Hoffman and others in the U.S. Attorney's office, it had already been decided that the government would refuse to disclose any additional information about the government's ties to IBM and Palyn Associates. The prosecutors say they felt the information had no bearing on the case, and, furthermore, they were advised by the FBI that to make such disclosures might threaten other ongoing investigations. So Ward did nothing in response to the judge's order.

The defendants were quick to exploit Ward's inaction, and filed motions to dismiss the indictments on the ground that Ward was defying the judge's discovery orders. At the hearing on those motions, the judge was predictably furious. Few matters are likely to produce greater outrage in a federal judge than willful defiance, whether by government prosecutors or defense lawyers.

Judge Aguilar began the hearing by threatening to jail Ward until the government complied with his order. He was even angrier than he would otherwise have been, he noted, because Ward hadn't cleared the decision not to comply with Assistant Attorney General Jensen in Washington, a departmental requirement. Ward seemed stunned by the judge's threat to jail him, and nearly broke into tears as he tried to justify his decision, observers say. A defense lawyer, Paul Meltzer, had to come to his rescue, urging the judge to dismiss the indictments rather than punish Ward. "I was shaking," Ward acknowledges. "The judge wouldn't even let me sit at counsel's table."

Ward says he feels the judge's reaction was unjustified. He says he did ask Washington to approve his decision, but the Justice Department hadn't yet responded when the judge called the hearing.

The experience was traumatic for Ward, and his conduct was deemed a disgrace by some within the U.S. Attorney's office in San Francisco. It was a humiliating incident for the entire office.

The outcome of the proceeding was also disastrous for the government. Judge Aguilar adopted Meltzer's suggestion and threw out the indictments. Suddenly, all the cases growing out of the undercover operation, including Hitachi, were in jeopardy.

Precisely why the government refused to turn over the materials, even at the risk of losing the cases, remains a mystery. It was not done on a whim by Ward—eventually Jensen agreed that Ward had properly refused to comply with the judge's order. Hoffman insists that it was solely because the defendants' request was too broad and the materials called for were irrelevant to the case against the defendants. But that explanation hardly seems plausible.

Others involved say there were ongoing operations involving IBM that had to be protected. Since then, however, no such investigations have been made public. Perhaps they continue.

Ward says he won't confirm or deny that IBM was cooperating in other undercover activities at the time, but says that, in general, the government wanted to reveal as little about Operation Pengem and the Glenmar activities as possible. "We didn't want to make public how we operate," he says.

Whatever the reasons, other defense lawyers were quick to pick up on the prospect that they had stumbled on an Achilles' heel in the prosecution.

On October 8, the Hitachi defendants submitted their own lengthy motion to dismiss the indictments on grounds of due process and selective prosecution. But the theme that ran through all their arguments was similar to that in the Cadet dismissal: the notion that IBM had improperly infiltrated the executive branch of the U.S. government.

> Since their appearances in this Court on August 3, 1982 [the lawyers said in their motion], defense counsel have engaged in a preliminary but intense investigation of facts relevant to a fair determination of this case. This preliminary investigation, conducted without a subpoena power, has developed substantial evidence to substantiate the conclusion that IBM, for its own anticompetitive and economic purposes, improperly and unlawfully took control of a federal national security undercover operation, which IBM itself had volunteered to help establish, and used that undercover investigation to target and damage Hitachi and other Japanese competitors in the worldwide computer market.

The defense lawyers played up the impact of the case for U.S. trade relations:

> IBM's selective targeting of Japanese competition is consistent with public knowledge that other major segments of American industry have been increasingly upset about strong competition from other Japanese manufacturers. Trade and technology competition between Japan and the United States has, in the recent past, persistently been referred to in terms ordinarily reserved for military warfare.

And the papers included a statement from an IBM engineer who unwittingly told a correspondent for a Japanese newspaper:

> Guess you've been reading what IBM did to those Japs in California. We sure got them good. It took a little time, but we made sure they knew who was boss . . . those guys at Mitsubishi and Hitachi were set up so that they would learn an important lesson . . . the FBI worked

very closely with IBM because in a sense we are at war with Japan all over again. This time it's an economic war but it's still a war. Our side has to win. There are little ethics involved in war.

James Brosnahan, a former Assistant U.S. Attorney, now a partner at Morrison & Foerster in San Francisco, who represented Hayashi, says, "We believed then, and I still do now, that the government basically rented out the investigative process to IBM. This violated all the Justice Department guidelines. I'm also convinced," Brosnahan continues, "that the antitrust case against IBM [the government had sued IBM for antitrust violations in a massive case that spanned more than a decade] and the Hitachi matter were linked. The case against IBM was dropped by the Justice Department in January 1982. Within the same year, IBM is helping the Justice Department set up a major undercover operation. I can't prove it, but they're linked."

(Brosnahan's claim, superficially appealing though it is, doesn't seem plausible. IBM certainly benefited from the antitrust settlement and, according to the defendants' own arguments, it benefited from the Hitachi prosecution. That seems to belie any quid pro quo involving IBM cooperation in return for dropping the antitrust suit. Nonetheless, the decision to drop the antitrust case may have generated good-will that, in general, fostered closer ties between IBM and the government.)

To substantiate their claims and suspicions, the defendants demanded exhaustive discovery into the relationship between IBM and the government; the backgrounds of the undercover operatives, especially Callahan, who they claimed had CIA connections and had operated clandestine missions in the Middle East; and details of the Justice Department's handling of the case.

Hoffman, Ward, and Russoniello were, to varying degrees, angered by the defense position. "I didn't like the defense lawyers at all anyway," says Ward. "I couldn't seem to deal with them, partly because we had a rock-solid case and I just didn't see any reason to make concessions to them, especially after they leveled these charges. They were ridiculous, and they weren't true."

"I decided after they made that motion that we'd dig in and go to trial," Hoffman says. "I felt we had to clear the air. They made serious allegations of impropriety, and they were unfounded. I felt we could demonstrate this."

No sooner had Hoffman absorbed the motion papers than he was further annoyed by word from Washington that Fleming and the other defense counsel had gone above his head and made an appointment to talk to Assistant Attorney General Jensen about a nolo plea. "Not everyone can get that kind of audience," Hoffman says. "This is how people like Fleming earn their fees. He's a well-known former prosecutor; someone like him, or Harold Tyler [former Deputy Attorney General, now a partner at a New York law firm] have that kind of access." Unlike Giuliani with Lubin, Jensen made sure that Hoffman attended. At the meeting, Hoffman says, he said very little. He didn't need to, since Fleming already knew he opposed nolo pleas, and Hoffman knew that, if anything, Jensen was even more determined to prosecute the case, given his reaction to giving up the possibility of prison sentences. Fleming got nowhere with Jensen, but Hoffman thought the meeting might work to the prosecution's advantage in another way: the Japanese, once they learned they'd been rebuffed at the highest level of the government, might be more willing to enter a guilty plea on the government's original terms.

To test that theory, Hoffman called Fleming not long after and urged that settlement discussions resume before either the government or the defendants had to pursue expensive discovery campaigns in Japan. And to increase the pressure, he pushed for an early hearing date on IBM's motion of government misconduct.

The effort seemed to be working. Fleming and the other New York lawyers came out to San Francisco and discussions intensified. For the first time, Fleming showed a willingness to at least entertain the possibility of some guilty pleas. Hoffman pressed to have some of the Japanese fugitives submit to the U.S. courts and enter pleas. He realized that a formal extradition effort was bound to fail. Since Japanese law forbids undercover operations except in drug cases, Japan almost certainly wouldn't recognize the Hitachi arrests as legitimate.

To further heighten the pressure, Hoffman made what he calls a "tactical maneuver." He severed what he believed to be the two weakest cases, those of Kunimasa Inoue and Keizo Shirai, from those of the two other Hitachi defendants who were in the U.S. Not only had both men played small roles in the scheme, but neither spoke English. On one of the tapes, an undercover agent even said, "Don't tell Shirai anything." There was serious doubt they ever understood the scheme; Hoffman concedes that, once severed, the likelihood of their being brought to trial was minuscule. Eventually, the government withdrew their indictments.

As Hoffman explains, "You go in strong, against defendants you'll convict. Weak defendants detract from the whole case—they undermine your credibility with a jury. The defense lawyers understood that without those two defendents our case was stronger."

A week before the first hearing on the the motions to dismiss, the terms of a settlement were reached. In return for promises that no prison terms would be sought, Hitachi, Ohnishi, and Hayashi agreed to plead guilty. Tom Yoshida, the driver of the orange van who was arrested the same day, held out and refused to plead. And Hoffman gave up his demands that the other defendants be delivered from Japan.

Fleming flew to Tokyo to get the approval of the Hitachi board of directors, then returned to San Francisco. Hoffman too obtained approval of the settlement terms from Russoniello and from Jensen in Washington. By including individual pleas, the department achieved much of what it had sought in McDonnell Douglas. IBM had earlier communicated with the Justice Department in Washington—considered proper in this instance since IBM was the "victim," and, increasingly, prosecutors are trying to take into account the feelings of victims. IBM had urged the department not to be vindictive and to accept a reasonable plea. Hitachi was, after all, a customer as well as competitor.

The settlement papers were prepared, and Fleming, Brosnahan, and other defense lawyers met with Hoffman to sign them.

Then the agreement nearly fell apart. Brosnahan, who is naturally combative and had insisted that he could win if Hayashi's case went to trial, decided to needle Hoffman. "You'd better sign those papers or you'll lose at trial," he taunted.

Hoffman exploded. "Fuck you," he said, grabbing the papers and storming out of the room.

Hoffman says he may have overreacted, but that Brosnahan touched a raw nerve by suggesting that he was signing the papers only to avoid a courtroom loss. And what really bothered him, he says, wasn't the suggestion that he would lose—it was the implication that winning or losing was all that he cared about.

"I don't live or die over these cases, winning or losing them," he says. "You can't—not if you've been a prosecutor as long as I have. My financial remuneration doesn't depend on whether I win or lose a case, or on whether I get a lot of favorable or unfavorable publicity.

I work hard but I sleep well at night. Tomorrow there will always be another case.

"Brosnahan, Fleming," he continues, "these people agonize over winning and losing. They have to. But I see myself as a public servant. There are more important goals than winning or losing any particular case. I didn't have to sit there and be insulted."

Fleming rushed after Hoffman into the hallway, and managed to coax him back into the room. The Hitachi case, or most of it, was settled.

AFTER the settlement, both prosecutors and defense lawyers traded potshots. Defense lawyers claimed the government settled so the claims in their motion to dismiss involving the government's relationship to IBM would never be resolved against them. Prosecutors made the same claim in reverse—that the Japanese pleaded guilty so that the government couldn't disprove those allegations.

The timing of the settlement did seem curious. But both sides had strong motives for settling. Given the dismissals of the Saffaei and Cadet indictments after a similar hearing, the Japanese seemed to be in a strong bargaining position. Government prosecutors didn't want another such setback, which would likely generate even more unfavorable publicity. And the Japanese were eager to put the episode behind them and avoid the public airing of the damaging video tapes. Defense lawyers say the prosecutors never seemed to realize how horrified the Japanese were by the prospect of the tapes being aired on American and Japanese television.

Except for the pleas and the public humiliation, the defendants emerged nearly unscathed: Hitachi was fined $10,000, the maximum, but a pittance for such a major corporation. Hayashi was fined $10,000 and given five years' probation, though he was allowed to return to Japan, where he was reassigned to Hitachi's personal computer operations. Ohnishi was fined $4,000 and was sentenced to two years of probation.

Fleming says he believes the settlement was a good one for his client. "Brosnahan and I wanted desperately to try this," Fleming says. "We could have hurt IBM. And we probably would have lost. They had forty-eight hours of video tape—it looked like old World War II movies. Very embarrassing. They would have been a public relations disaster for the Japanese. The U.S. was in a serious recession. The Japanese were being blamed for all our economic problems. These tapes would have been on TV making things worse. As it is, Hitachi suffered minimal damage."

IBM may, indeed, have been the greatest beneficiary of the prosecution: soon after the guilty pleas, the company settled its civil charges against Hitachi arising from the same operation.

The terms of the secret settlement called for Hitachi to pay IBM approximately $300 million over a period of several years.

Meanwhile, Hoffman and Ward turned their attention to those cases that hadn't been settled. Ward was determined to extract greater concessions from Mitsubishi than Hoffman had gotten from Hitachi. That goal, like many he had had in the course of the prosecution, was frustrated. Despite Ward's vigorous opposition, in late 1983 the judge accepted a plea of nolo contendere from Mitsubishi. Two individual defendants pleaded guilty and received the maximum fines and probation. Ward proudly points out that the individual Hitachi defendants didn't receive the maximum penalties across the board.

Despite the small satisfaction he derives from that, the greatest case of his career left Ward bitter and disillusioned. "I was firmly opposed to the Hitachi settlement," he says. "We gave away too much—far more than we had to. From the outset, the emphasis was on settlement. Yet here was a case that, with the tapes, was a prosecutor's dream."

For Ward, the case left him crippled within the U.S. Attorney's office, his reputation with Russoniello in tatters. Eventually the Ninth Circuit Court of Appeals reversed Judge Aguilar's dismissal of the Cadet and Saffaei indictments, saying such a drastic remedy wasn't necessary. Ward felt vindicated by the opinion. But the court had some harsh words for Ward:

> We close our review of this matter . . . with the strong sense that this unfortunate contretemps could have been avoided had the United States Attorney's office been willing to produce . . . material in a timely manner and to submit material as to which there was any doubt for in camera review. While the discovery order was overbroad in some respects, it appears to us that the United States Attorney was more concerned with forcing an appellate confrontation in this matter than attempting to effect a reasonable accommodation with the district court's earnest efforts to protect each defendant's right to inspect discoverable materials.

Not surprisingly, Ward resigned from the office soon after the Hitachi and Mitsubishi cases were settled. Following a time-honored tradition, he is now a defense lawyer with a law firm in Palo Alto, representing defendants accused in both civil and criminal cases of stealing trade secrets.

Ward acknowledges that, after a lifetime of prosecution, he isn't entirely comfortable with the prospect of defending the kinds of people he would once have charged with crime. "I haven't been at this very long," he says, "and I haven't defended that many trade-secret cases. I prefer representing plaintiffs in civil trade-secret cases, where I'm in a quasi-prosecutorial role. As a prosecutor, your goal is to do justice. In the private sector, your duty is to represent a client. I'd like to think I can do justice and represent a client. Maybe that means I'll never be much of a criminal defense lawyer."

Ward says that even without the problems that sprang up in the Hitachi case, he probably would have quit to go into private practice. "There's a burnout factor about three or four years down the road. You do have a lot of power and discretion, and it can be very exciting. But there's something wearing, numbing about it. You have to be a peculiar type to stay much longer."

Herb Hoffman wrapped up the remnants of the cases. Tom Yoshida pleaded guilty, as did Saffaei and Cadet (their dismissed indictments having been reinstated by the Court of Appeals), during the summer of 1985. The other individual defendants are still in Japan, and technically are fugitives. No serious effort has been made to extradite them.

Hoffman returned to his post in San Diego. He says he would have liked to have tried the Hitachi case and would have enjoyed the attention and publicity it would have generated. But he conceded he probably wouldn't have loved the trial as much now as he would have ten years ago.

"More prosecutors would stay on the job if the government let you retire after twenty years of service, like the military. I love the job. But sixteen years in, you begin to think, What am I going to be doing in five to ten years? Trying a lot of criminal cases when I'm fifty years old? The prospect is pretty exhausting. Maybe I should become a judge. That's my long-range goal." Indeed, not long after this conversation, Hoffman was named a California Superior Court judge.

Nor did Hitachi prove to be the triumph that Russoniello had envisioned. Though ostensibly pleased by the pleas, the Justice Department's relations with Russoniello cooled. The principal way in which the department indicates the regard it has for U.S. Attorneys is through the appropriation and budget process. And when Russoniello sought funding for his cherished high-tech task force, his request was denied.

E V E N though Jensen hadn't been entirely happy with the outcome of the Hitachi case, his superiors seemed delighted by the results and by the accompanying media attention that showed the administration in simultaneous blows against white-collar crime and the Japanese trade threat. During and immediately after the case, other lawyers in the Justice Department say that Jensen's stature seemed to increase. Since Giuliani had been disqualified from the case, they turned directly to Jensen with their questions. Jensen's views of Hitachi and other criminal matters seemed to be treated with new respect and deference.

At the same time, Giuliani seemed increasingly restless. Although the process took two and a half years, he had finally completed the task of replacing the U.S. Attorneys with a victory over the most recalcitrant of the Democratic holdovers, Iowa's James Reynolds.

In many ways, Reynolds's replacement symbolized the degree to which the appointment of U.S. Attorneys had been politicized in the Reagan administration.

Reynolds himself had never been so naïve to believe that politics played no role in his own selection. Although his appointment five years earlier had been the result of an extensive "merit" search, he knew his candidacy had been enhanced by the fact that he was an early Carter supporter in Iowa, a pivotal state in Carter's election. Reynolds's wife had worked hard for Carter in the Iowa caucuses—the first political test for presidential aspirants back in 1975—and Reynolds and his wife had had Jimmy and Rosalynn as guests in their Dubuque, Iowa home.

Reynolds had met Giuliani at the U.S. Attorneys' meeting back in October 1982, where he found himself to be nearly the sole liberal Democrat in a sea of Republicans. He'd met Jensen there too. Reynolds had brought his mother to the meeting in lieu of his wife, who couldn't bring herself to attend a Reagan administration function. Reynolds's mother, a spry, vivacious woman who was Dubuque's version of Auntie Mame, accidentally poured a martini down Jensen's trouser leg at one of the cocktail parties.

At that and other events, Reynolds found himself to be the subject of considerable interest. Nearly alone among the U.S. Attorneys from the Carter administration, Reynolds was fighting to hold on to his job.

Reynolds says he wasn't simply trying to hang on to one of the best jobs in Iowa. Rather, he says he fought because he had bipartisan support for remaining in office and because his designated successor wasn't qualified.

Reynolds did, in fact, have bipartisan support. His efforts to investigate allegedly unlawful campaign contributions by agents of South Africa had impressed a number of senators interested in the issue, especially Orrin Hatch, Utah Republician, and Dennis DeConcini, Democrat of Arizona. The two senators had even urged the Reagan administration to name Reynolds to the high-level position now held by Giuliani. But when Iowa's new Republican senator Charles Grassley got wind of the plan, he was outraged. He told Reynolds that not only wouldn't he support him for a Justice Department post, but he'd unseat him as Iowa's U.S. Attorney.

Grassley's candidate to replace Reynolds was none other than Evan Hultmann, Reynolds's predecessor in the job, a choice that shocked Reynolds, for Hultmann himself was a subject of Reynolds's grand jury probe into the South Africa payments. Moreover, Reynolds was investigating allegations that Hultmann lied in his appearance before a Senate committee investigating South African campaign contributions. (Hultmann denied those charges and no action was ever taken against him.)

Giuliani says the charges involving Hultmann were politically motivated and that Reynolds was just trying to save his own skin. Still, Reynolds proved a surprisingly tenacious foe. Hultmann's nomination had been stalled in the Senate by Reynolds's allegations and the White House wasn't doing much to press for his confirmation. Grassley, who opposed the administration's efforts to sell AWAC planes to Saudi Arabia, said publicly that Hultmann's nomination was being held up as a means to pressure him to support the administration on the AWACs' sale.

Giuliani and his staff stepped up the pressure on Reynolds to resign, threatening to launch an investigation of Reynolds himself for alleged improprieties. "I dared them to do it," Reynolds says. "I had nothing to hide. They finally dropped it." (Giuliani says he doesn't recall threatening Reynolds, or any of the details about how Reynolds was persuaded to resign. "He was recalcitrant," Giuliani says of

Reynolds.) But once the Senate cleared the AWACs' sale, pressure on Grassley let up. Hultmann was soon confirmed, and in May 1983, Reynolds left office and returned to his father's law office in Dubuque.

"When I left," Reynolds says, "I was the senior U.S. Attorney in the country. Everyone had been swept out. This was unprecedented. I had been keeping track of all the U.S. Attorneys. I was horrified to watch my friends going down like dominoes."

Giuliani denies that it was politics alone that motivated the changes. "I demanded a new way of looking at the job," he says. "I wanted people in tune with their local constituencies. I didn't want them talking just to other law enforcement people. That had been a problem in the past, contributing to an air of unreality. I needed people who would listen. This was something that most of the holdovers simply couldn't adapt to."

Giuliani's housecleaning was no small achievement. But when the transition was nearly complete, Giuliani began to wonder about his own future. A purely administrative job wasn't what he had in mind. In February 1983, the U.S. Attorney for the Southern District of New York, John Martin, Jr., had stopped by to visit Giuliani in Washington. Martin told him that he was planning to resign, and wanted the department to have a few months' notice so it could find a successor.

Martin's decision to leave was good news to the administration, and Justice Department officials were relieved that he wasn't making a fuss like Reynolds in Iowa. Martin still had a year to serve in the U.S. Attorney's traditional four-year term. Blatant politicking to replace Martin with a Reagan loyalist would have looked bad, since the Manhattan U.S. Attorney was traditionally one of the most nonpartisan of the U.S. Attorney positions. Indeed, Martin, a former Assistant U.S. Attorney, had been chosen by a merit selection committee appointed by New York's Democratic senator, Daniel Patrick Moynihan. Though he had been an Assistant Solicitor General in the Johnson administration, he hadn't been active in partisan politics.

But subtler tactics to replace him had apparently worked. The Reagan administration had largely ignored him. The Attorney General's advisory committee of U.S. Attorneys often included the U.S. Attorney for the Southern District of New York, given the importance of the position. But Martin hadn't been invited by Smith to join the group.

After the visit from Martin, Giuliani scheduled a meeting with

New York Republican Senator Alfonse D'Amato to discuss a replacement for Martin. D'Amato, as a new senator currying favor with the Reagan administration, could be counted on to respect the administration's views about who should be named. "During our conversation," Giuliani recalls, "he said to me, 'Would you like to be the U.S. Attorney?' I thought he was kidding. That was my first reaction."

But the idea stuck. "I'd been an assistant in New York," Giuliani says. "Those are some of my best memories. From the time I first became aware of that office, I've had tremendous affection for it." Giuliani raised the possibility with his mother. "She said, 'You can't, it would be a demotion.' " Then he took the idea to his fiancée, Donna Hanover, a Miami television anchorwoman at the time. She said, "That's what you've always wanted," he recalls. Moreover, it would enable the two to consolidate their careers in New York. "I started to get excited," he says. "It was a job I knew I could do well."

Giuliani says he was afraid the Reagan administration wouldn't let him do it, given his importance in Washington. He first broached the possibility to Deputy Attorney General Edward Schmults, Smith's top aide. Giuliani was surprised that his response was so positive: "I knew that this would be what you wanted to do," he recalls Schmults telling him. The Attorney General too was supportive.

In fact, according to lawyers close to both men, the top administration people in the department were delighted that Giuliani, with a minimum of encouragement, had decided to leave Washington. Many lawyers in the department at the time believe that D'Amato's seemingly spontaneous suggestion that Giuliani take the job was orchestrated from above.

Lawyers in the department trace Giuliani's growing estrangement from the top officials to a variety of causes. For one, Giuliani didn't fit the mold of the Reagan administration. He was brash, aggressive, street smart, fast-talking, occasionally a bit rough at the edges. He had none of the relaxed, upper-middle-class western aura of the top Reagan appointees. His handling of the McDonnell Douglas case had done lasting damage.

His personal life too caused acute discomfort in the upper ranks of the department, where rectitude was the order of the day. Giuliani had divorced his wife shortly after being appointed. Then he had begun dating his secretary in the department, a subject of much gossip. He was now engaged to a television personality. By contemporary standards, it was pretty innocuous stuff. But it deepened the gulf between him and his more staid superiors. "Smith worried that Rudi was out of control," recalls one of the Attorney General's aides at the time. "He thought that Giuliani was going through some kind of mid-life crisis."

Giuliani says he never had the slightest indication from any of his superiors that his personal life was the cause of any concern. He confirms that he dated his secretary, as well as other women, during the three years between his divorce and his engagement.

Most damaging of all, probably, was Giuliani's media exposure. His becoming engaged to a television personality was, some felt, simply one indication of what they considered Giuliani's obsession with the media. Since coming to Washington, he had indeed become a tireless spokesman for the Justice Department and the Reagan administration's policies, whatever the subject at hand. He appeared on the *MacNeil/Lehrer Report* (whose producer was a friend of Giuliani's secretary) so often that some staffers called it the "Giuliani Report." He was a regular on ABC's *Nightline*. "Rudi is a media hound, and that didn't sit well in the department," recalls one lawyer there at the time.

On one occasion, Giuliani issued a televised appeal for an additional $3 billion appropriation for prisons. The same day, Meese gave a speech calling for more law enforcement with less money, in keeping with the President's budget-cutting efforts. When Meese learned of Giuliani's remarks, he was furious, and called the Justice Department to complain.

Giuliani did have some real successes. He effectively merged the Drug Enforcement Administration with the Federal Bureau of Investigation, greatly increasing the investigative capacity in the drug area. He lobbied for the use of AWAC planes in the war against drug trafficking, an imaginative idea that was given a brief test. He launched a major crackdown on drug smuggling in the Miami area, which was sufficiently successful that it at least diverted much of the smuggling to North Carolina. Still, even with the successes, Giuliani often felt frustration. He was annoyed when Vice President George Bush intervened in the Miami crackdown, grabbing credit for much of what had happened. And he was constantly wrestling with the Miami U.S. Attorney.

Giuliani wasn't forced out of Washington, and he would never have been asked to leave, Justice Department lawyers say. But by mid-1983, the top officials undoubtedly realized that such drastic action wouldn't be necessary, with the right lure. It wouldn't take much to induce Giuliani to make the decision for himself. The Southern District U.S. Attorney's office proved to be exactly the right bait.

Giuliani left Washington in a flourish. The department held a large farewell party, the highlight of which was Giuliani's speech. The planners had expected a modest list of thank-yous and a few brief remarks. Instead Giuliani, true to form, delivered a thirty-minute oration, including effusive but genuine praise for his mother. Afterward, a standard opening line among speakers at Justice Department gatherings was "I'm no Rudi. I'll keep this short."

Giuliani's decision to forsake Washington was probably the shrewdest he'd ever made. In New York, he and he alone was in charge. In no time at all he was in front of the TV cameras in a type of case that would bring him greater fame than anything he had achieved in Washington: insider trading, the quintessential crime of Wall Street. The Newman case, the largest and most intriguing insider trading case ever filed at the time, was well under way by the time Giuliani arrived in New York. But he quickly seized control—and credit.

INSIDER TRADING AT
MORGAN STANLEY

FOR a man who had just been fired from Morgan Stanley & Company, one of Wall Street's most prestigious investment banking firms, Adrian Antoniu looked remarkably confident and unconcerned as he pushed his way through the double doors into the grill room of New York City's Harvard Club.

It was March 1976, a fire blazed in the fireplace, and the dark-paneled room was filled with a crowd. At least a few heads—mostly female—turned as Antoniu moved across the room and chose one of the backgammon tables at the far side.

Though he recognized no one at the club, Antoniu was accustomed to such admiring glances. He was handsome in a way that hinted at his Rumanian origins and distinguished him from most of his blander investment colleagues. In his early thirties, he exercised to maintain a trim but muscular physique. He dressed expensively but conservatively, and he had charm—in abundance, say most people who knew him.

Antoniu asked the waiter for Scotch and a set of chess pieces. Shortly after, he was joined at the game table by a Harvard Business School classmate who had worked with him at Morgan Stanley, Jacques Courtois. Though he lacked Antoniu's style, Courtois had thrived at Morgan Stanley and was playing an increasingly important role in some of the mergers and acquisitions deals that Morgan Stanley handled.

The two men began their chess match, but a close observer would have noticed that their attention to the game quickly faded. Pieces were seemingly moved at random. For long intervals of conversation they ignored the game entirely. Nonetheless, Antoniu displayed the wits, charm, and guile of a chess master to achieve his objective. Courtois finally uttered three fateful words: "Pan Ocean Oil."

Antoniu was, in fact, a thief, and at that moment Pan Ocean Oil became his latest bounty. On Wall Street that March, Pan Ocean Oil represented information—a commodity more precious than gold, jewelry, or cash, as Antoniu and Courtois would soon demonstrate.

As the two men stepped out of the Harvard Club onto 44th Street that night, they shook hands on a scheme that seemed to have all the elements of the perfect crime. Much later, after their case rocked the financial world, went to the Supreme Court, and entangled the Justice and State departments, only Antoniu's and Courtois's prosecutors knew just how close to perfect the crime had been.

NEARLY three years later, Assistant United States Attorney Lawrence Pedowitz put aside his copy of that day's *Wall Street Journal* in disgust and gazed out the window of his office at One St. Andrew's Plaza in lower Manhattan. Pedowitz had been with the Southern District U.S. Attorney's office since 1974, following a brilliant career at New York University Law School and a Supreme Court clerkship, and now he'd been assigned to the office's securities fraud unit. It wasn't exactly where the action was in the Southern District. In fact, there weren't any securities fraud cases at the moment for him to work on.

Inactivity wasn't why Pedowitz had sought a job with the Southern District U.S. Attorney, then Robert Fiske. Nor was money—he was earning $30,000 a year, a fraction of what he could have made at a large Wall Street law firm. Like most of his colleagues in the office, he came for trial experience on some of the most important cases in the country, against some of the top defense lawyers. During his first year, when he, like all new Assistant U.S. Attorneys, was tossed into the general crimes unit, handling a myriad of standard crimes like bank robberies, drugs, and bad-check schemes, he had gotten more trial experience than some Wall Street litigators get in a lifetime.

Pedowitz had also chosen the Southern District because of its reputation as the premiere U.S. Attorney's office in the country. Manhattan's position at the vortex of finance and international trade guarantees that some of the most important crimes will occur within the Southern District jurisdiction (it also covers the Bronx, but not Brooklyn or Queens), and historically, its U.S. Attorneys have gone on to illustrious careers at the bar or in politics: Thomas E. Dewey, Edward Lumbar, Robert Morgenthau. They attracted the best and the brightest young lawyers. At many times, there have been more former U.S. Supreme Court clerks working as Assistant U.S. Attorneys in the Southern District than in any other government office or private law firm.

But prestige didn't fill Pedowitz's day. He had tried to get on the one major securities fraud case going on in the office, involving a financial printer named Chiarella, but he had to withdraw due to a conflict of interest. Before coming to the U.S. Attorney's office, he'd gotten a job offer from a law firm involved in the case.

But he knew there were other securities crimes going on. Each day, he scoured data in the *The Wall Street Journal* for bursts in the trading volume of particular stocks. Then he watched for news developments that affected the prices of those stocks. As often as not, he found them. Some people, he concluded, were making money—a lot of it— by trading on market-sensitive information before it was made available to the public. In the lexicon of securities fraud, such activity is called insider trading, and Pedowitz thought it was a practice so unfair as to be criminal. Nonetheless, there had never been a criminal conviction for insider trading.

Pedowitz had mentioned his interest in insider trading to some of the Securities and Exchange Commission agents who dropped by his office from time to time, and occasionally they mentioned a possible target. But none of those possible cases panned out. Usually the amount of money involved was too small or it wasn't clear that the target of the investigation realized that what he was doing was wrong. Pedowitz knew that probably the most important decision he'd make was which case, or cases, to prosecute. Insider trading wouldn't be an easy charge to make stick.

Just when Pedowitz was beginning to despair, SEC agent Lance Clifton dropped by Pedowitz's office and told him that he'd run into something he thought might interest Pedowitz. Pedowitz liked working with Clifton, a lanky, easygoing type modeled more on Columbo than Sam Spade, and he was intrigued by Clifton's information. According to Clifton, the Securities and Exchange Commission, which has civil jurisdiction over insider trading, was investigating a peculiar pattern of stock trading that appeared to be centered in Great Neck, New York, a prosperous Long Island suburb of New York City. For that reason, it had become known around the SEC as the "Great Neck" case. It was unusual in that the many threads didn't lead to any major investor or company "insider," and a great number of stock trades seemed to be involved.

Pedowitz and Clifton headed across Foley Square to the Manhattan offices of the SEC, where SEC investigators laid out the results of their efforts. The case had begun, they explained, in the "stock watch" office of the New York Stock Exchange, a group that does nothing except monitor the trading volumes of particular stocks for signs of unusual surges. When they spot them, the group contacts major brokers to get copies of their "blue sheets"—records of a particular day's transactions that identify the purchasers of shares.

Over the past year, the stock watch group had begun to notice the same names showing up on the blue sheets, an unusual occurrence because insider trading usually involves an insider—a corporate officer, for example—who knows information in advance about only one company. Here was a pattern that suggested a large number of people were receiving advance information about numerous targets of takeover attempts.

The stock watch group turned its information over to SEC investigators, who began to analyze the names. But by the time Pedowitz made his visit, they had come up with very little beyond the fact that most of those in question lived in Great Neck, and a large number of them were doctors and dentists. To attempt to clarify matters, the SEC investigators had begun trying to construct a chart based on known relationships between the various people whose names had been obtained. The links began to suggest a pyramid—not surprising in a large-scale insider trading scheme—but it was clear that these people were near the base. Doctors and dentists simply weren't the kinds of people to have regular access to closely guarded corporate secrets.

But Pedowitz was excited by what he saw. "This was big money and massive trading," he recalls. "And they were hitting the jackpot every time." Pedowitz realized that the individual doctors and dentists wouldn't make particularly appealing targets for prosecution—they were probably too far down the pyramid, and they were too small-time. But the missing top of the pyramid was what intrigued him. "It almost had to be a prominent source for the information," he says. "I expected a major law firm or a major investment bank with regular access to this kind of information." This would be the kind of powerful defendant that would justify bringing the full resources of the government to bear, Pedowitz thought.

The SEC investigators were only too happy to turn the case over to Pedowitz, because their efforts had in fact reached a dead end. They had tried to interview most of the names on their chart, and virtually every one had invoked the Fifth Amendment and refused to answer or said they knew nothing. The SEC, unlike the U.S. Attorney, doesn't have the power to immunize a potential witness from prosecution, thereby eliminating the need to invoke the Fifth Amendment. By doing so, Pedowitz thought, he might be able to make some progress beyond what the SEC had done.

Pedowitz returned triumphantly from his visit to the SEC, but his colleagues and superiors at the office were not as enthusiastic. The chief of the securities division, Jed Rakoff, backed him, but said the case looked like a long shot. Some of his fellow assistants began referring to it as his "doctors and dentists case," implying that he was dealing with small-time operators. But Pedowitz, working with Clifton, plunged into the case with undaunted enthusiasm.

He and Clifton began by scrutinizing the pyramid chart, deciding to focus first on those names that seemed to fall in the middle. They made phone calls; in some cases they persuaded people to come into the U.S. Attorney's office. A few named the sources of their information, but most of those names were already on the chart and there wasn't any consistent pattern. Clifton was dispatched to Great Neck, but found no unusual geographic or social ties among those named in the chart. After about a month, Pedowitz had to admit that he hadn't gotten much farther than the SEC investigators, but he still hadn't used the power of immunity.

"I didn't want to immunize," Pedowitz recalls. "After all, our job is to convict criminals, not protect them from prosecution. But I was reaching a high level of frustration. I couldn't crack the scheme."

For a change of pace, Pedowitz began to concentrate on a name that fell totally outside the chart, someone who lived in California. Yet Bruce Steinberg, a California businessman, had no links to any of the other names, as far as Clifton and Pedowitz could discern. No one had identified him as a source of information.

So far Steinberg had been totally uncooperative. He'd invoked the

Fifth Amendment when SEC investigators tried to interview him; he'd done the same when Pedowitz called. It was a gamble, but Pedowitz thought Steinberg might make a good candidate for immunization.

Pedowitz made his case for immunization to Rakoff, who tentatively approved, but all such requests must be referred to the Justice Department. Philip Heymann, then still Assistant Attorney General, gave his assent, and Pedowitz asked Steinberg and his lawyer to fly to New York.

The three spent a full day at Pedowitz's office in negotiation, during which Pedowitz tried to get assurances that, if immunized, Steinberg would have something useful to say. "It was a delicate cat-and-mouse kind of thing," Pedowitz says, "since Steinberg couldn't afford to say very much." And not until he received a letter of immunization, including the unusual language that the government wasn't "presently possessed of information that Bruce Steinberg has committed a crime," would Steinberg talk in any detail. Pedowitz finally gave him the letter, hoping Steinberg's information would be worth the cost.

It was a shrewd gamble, for Steinberg led Pedowitz to James Newman.

James Newman worked in a small stock brokerage firm and was Steinberg's stockbroker in New York. Steinberg was, in turn, one of Newman's most active customers. As Steinberg told the story to Pedowitz, in early 1975 he had become impressed with Newman's uncanny ability to pick "winners" and proposed that Newman take 20 percent of the profits in Steinberg's account in return for acting as Steinberg's "eyes and ears on Wall Street." Newman was so successful that Steinberg stepped up the commission to a third. In the next three years, Newman made about $180,000 off Steinberg's trades alone.

Recently, Steinberg told Pedowitz, the relationship with Newman had come to an end in circumstances that Steinberg seemed reluctant to describe. But he finally confessed the details.

Toward the end of 1976, Steinberg said, Newman had advised Steinberg to make a substantial purchase of shares of Deseret Pharmaceutical Company. The day after the purchase, Steinberg noticed, trading in Deseret stock had been halted on the New York Stock Exchange. Steinberg called Newman and said he wanted to know why. Newman, Steinberg said, told him not to worry; that Warner-Lambert Company was planning to make a "run" for Deseret, driving up the share price. Trading was halted pending a public announcement. Steinberg hung up the phone and learned the next day that Newman had been correct in his forecast.

This time, however, Steinberg wasn't willing to accept the Deseret development as happy coincidence. He called Newman and asked him how he knew that Warner-Lambert would be making the bid. Newman, who had carefully avoided ever hinting to Steinberg how he managed to pick stocks so successfully, blurted out "Morgan Stanley."

Pedowitz, who had been scribbling notes furiously, halted abruptly. Morgan Stanley! Was this the top of the pyramid he had suspected upon learning of the Great Neck case? If so, it might prove to be even bigger than he expected. Morgan Stanley was one of the most powerful, and to many the most prestigious, of the country's investment banking firms.

But Steinberg rushed on with his disclosures. Soon after the Deseret incident, Newman called him with another tip. Under questioning from Steinberg, Newman had admitted that the company was a take-over target and that he had again gotten the information from Morgan Stanley. Steinberg bought the stock, but he was sufficiently worried that he consulted his lawyer, Neil Baron. Baron was unequivocal. He advised Steinberg in a letter that while it wasn't certain that his investments were unlawful, the "SEC has taken a very clear position against trading on nonpublic, material market information" and told him not to trade through Newman based on either "nonpublic market or inside information." In an all-too-rare display of professional responsibility, Baron warned Steinberg that if he persisted in such activity with Newman he would resign as his lawyer.

Shortly after, Newman called Steinberg again, urging him to purchase Gerber Products. He again confessed that Gerber was an undisclosed take-over target and that he had obtained the information from Morgan Stanley. Steinberg told Pedowitz that this time he drew the line, refusing to buy Gerber, and warned Newman that his behavior might be illegal. That, Steinberg concluded, had ended his relationship with Newman.

AFTER showing Steinberg out of his office, Pedowitz felt ecstatic. Steinberg had proved to be the first major break in the investigation. Pedowitz took the SEC's chart and wrote in James Newman—a name that hadn't yet been encountered—close to the top of the pyramid. Newman, as a New York–area broker, could easily prove to be the link between Steinberg and the Great Neck crowd, Pedowitz thought. But above Newman, blanks remained. Pedowitz assumed Newman had a source at Morgan Stanley, but he didn't know who it was. Steinberg had never been told the name of the person at Morgan Stanley who provided Newman with his information.

Working closely with Clifton, Pedowitz plunged into intensive detective work. Newman refused to talk, but word went out that government investigations wanted to know everything about him. Working with some of the SEC investigators, Pedowitz obtained a copy of Newman's college application, his high-school record. The investigators subpoenaed his bank records. They got copies of all his telephone records for the previous four years. They called the numbers on the phone records to see who answered.

In one of these calls, an SEC investigator, Thomas Valery, reached a man who said his name was Adrian Antoniu. Valery asked Antoniu who he was and what he did for a living. Antoniu said he was an investment banker at Lehman Brothers Kuhn Loeb, a prominent investment banking firm since merged into Shearson Lehman/American Express. This disclosure made no special impression on Valery, since Lehman Brothers Kuhn Loeb didn't figure in the investigation. Valery asked Antoniu about his ties to Newman, and Antoniu seemed cooperative. He said he hardly knew the man; that Newman had tried to become his investment adviser, and that Newman had suggested some of the stocks that Valery mentioned the SEC was interested in. But the relationship had gone nowhere, Antoniu said. Valery filed his report along with hundreds of others derived from Newman's phone records, and Antoniu was forgotten.

The sift through the data did turn up some interesting links in the pyramid—for example, Norman Gomberg, a Long Island accountant who was a client of Newman's and who looked as if he might be the source for the Great Neck crowd. But Pedowitz and Clifton spent most of their time concentrating on the Morgan Stanley aspect of the case, where they expected to find the key source of information for the entire scheme.

But the Morgan Stanley information provided by Steinberg didn't prove to be as immediately valuable as Pedowitz had hoped. When he first called Morgan Stanley's general counsel, the response was coldly formal: he would consult with Morgan Stanley's lawyers, the prominent Wall Street law firm of Davis, Polk & Wardwell. There was no immediate promise of cooperation. Though Pedowitz didn't want to get into a fight with an institution that could be extremely important in cracking the case, he warned that he did have the power to subpoena documents and witnesses from the firm.

At Morgan Stanley, Pedowitz's bombshell had the potential for terrible ramifications. Nothing was more important to the firm than its prestigious reputation carefully groomed over more than fifty years. Part of that reputation was the ability to keep tremendously valuable and sensitive secrets. Pedowitz was suggesting not only that someone highly placed at Morgan Stanley had violated client confidences, but that extremely sensitive client documents and information related to the various take-overs that were the subject of the inquiry might be dragged into public view in the course of a trial. It was an investment banker's nightmare.

But Christopher Crowley, the Davis, Polk lawyer designated to handle the matter, warned his client that it had little to gain by resisting Pedowitz's inquiry. The firm decided to allow Pedowitz to question employees on a strictly confidential basis and to provide information other than clients' business secrets and strategies as a first line of defense, hoping that perhaps the Morgan Stanley lead might prove a red herring.

Over the next several months, Pedowitz began worrying that the Morgan Stanley angle might be just that. To begin with, Morgan Stanley had hundreds of employees. He narrowed the number of suspects to those working in the mergers and acquisitions group and to the the few others who had access to the group's information, and began lengthy and detailed interviews.

They led nowhere; in fact, they only seemed to deepen the mystery. Pedowitz learned that even other members of the mergers and acquisitions group didn't know the identity of acquisition targets in deals in which they weren't directly involved. And there wasn't a single person at Morgan Stanley who had been involved in all the deals in which there was suspect trading. It was baffling.

Almost a full, frustrating year passed before Pedowitz concluded he was getting nowhere by pursuing the Morgan Stanley sources. So he pushed aside all the files on the Morgan Stanley people and went back to Newman, the one name he was sure was close to the top of the pyramid, and re-examined the files the SEC investigators had compiled from their phone efforts. In doing so, he stumbled on Antoniu.

Pedowitz looked quickly through Valery's notes, then reread them carefully. He couldn't say what about them made him suspicious, but Antoniu was an investment banker, which at least distinguished him from the doctors and dentists who couldn't possibly have regular access to corporate secrets. But the Lehman Brothers Kuhn Loeb connection—it just didn't make sense.

Almost on impulse, Pedowitz asked Clifton to go over the Morgan Stanley personnel lists. There they found their man: Adrian Antoniu had been employed at Morgan Stanley, in the mergers and acquisitions department, until he was fired in December of 1974. It was an intriguing discovery, even if much of the mystery remained, for most of the trading being scrutinized involved Morgan Stanley deals that took place after December 1974, when Antoniu left the firm and joined Kuhn Loeb.

But it was the best—indeed, the only—hard lead Pedowitz had to go on. He decided it was time for a personal visit with Antoniu, and he called him at Kuhn Loeb and asked him to stop by the office. Antoniu agreed without any sign of hesitation or anxiety.

Pedowitz met Antoniu for the first time in March 1978. He was struck, first of all, by the fact that Antoniu had come to his office by himself, without an attorney. That was curious, since most people invited to visit St. Andrew's Plaza realized it wasn't a social occasion. Most brought lawyers, whatever their thoughts about their own guilt or innocence. Was Antoniu naïvely innocent, unaware that he might need the advice of an attorney? Or was he extremely shrewd, trying to suggest he had nothing to hide? Pedowitz wondered.

NOTHING else about Antoniu's appearance came as a particular surprise. He was handsome, well built, well dressed: Pedowitz had expected as much from what he'd already heard about Antoniu. He knew too from acquaintances of Antoniu's that he was aggressive, considered a social climber, frequented exclusive clubs and stylish restaurants, drove an expensive BMW. He was charming, poised, relaxed, possibly a bit too much so under the circumstances, Pedowitz thought.

Pedowitz asked Antoniu a bit about his work at Lehman Brothers Kuhn Loeb, then turned to Newman. Who was he? How did Antoniu know him? What was the nature of their relationship? Why was he on Newman's phone records?

Antoniu's answers were the same as those he had given the SEC investigator. He characterized Newman as a very minor acquaintance, someone who had tried to give him some stock tips. He said he barely knew the man. Pedowitz scrutinized Antoniu closely, because he was almost certain those statements were lies. His research later revealed that Antoniu and Newman attended New York University together and, in fact, belonged to the same fraternity. During one summer, they had both worked at Bell Labs. It was highly incredible that their relationship was as distant and recent as Antoniu indicated. Why would Antoniu lie about his relationship to Newman if he weren't deeply implicated? It was the fact of the lies that fascinated Pedowitz far more than their substance.

"YOU develop an instinct about these interviews," Pedowitz says. "And I became very suspicious." Pedowitz pressed Antoniu a bit, but he stood by his story. Then Antoniu displayed the first hint of anxiety. He said that he was anxious to clear up the Newman matter with Pedowitz because he was about to get married. "Who?" Pedowitz asked, genuinely sympathetic. "Francesca Stanfill," Antoniu replied.

The name meant nothing to Pedowitz, but the disclosure troubled him as he ushered Antoniu out of his office, for he felt very strongly that Antoniu was one of the men, if not the man, he was searching for. He knew that at the very least he was going to have to go to Antoniu's employer for further information, requiring an explanation of why he wanted the information about Antoniu. The next several days could be devastating for Antoniu and his career on Wall Street. "It made me feel very bad," Pedowitz recalls. "I knew I was about to take a major step, and I might ruin his life. It's not easy. I'm human, and I felt bad."

The next day, after sleeping on his suspicions, Pedowitz called and arranged a visit with Lehman Brothers Kuhn Loeb's general counsel. At the meeting, Pedowitz said he wanted access to the firm's personnel files and other documents, and explained that Antoniu was a target of his suspicions in a wide-ranging insider trading scheme. "I was very nervous," Pedowitz recalls. "I didn't want to ruin the guy's life. I emphasized that I wasn't sure I had the right man, and I didn't want to say too much."

Buf if the reaction at Morgan Stanley to the suggestion that one of its investment bankers was the mastermind of an insider trading scheme was severe, it was mild compared to that of Kuhn Loeb's. Lehman's general counsel was aghast, and told Pedowitz that it would be impossible for him to keep the U.S. Attorney's inquiries in total confidence. He would have to tell one of the firm's clients. Not just any client, but the firm's most important client—Twentieth Century-Fox Film Corporation.

Why? Pedowitz wanted to know, feeling panicky that the investigation was about to spin out of his control. "Because Dennis Stanfill is the chairman of Twentieth Century-Fox," the general counsel began, and didn't need to finish the explanation. It suddenly dawned on Pedowitz that Francesca Stanfill, Antoniu's fiancée, was Dennis Stanfill's daughter.

"I was worried," Pedowitz says. "The information was now out of my hands."

INDEED it was. Lehman's general counsel immediately called Eric Gleacher, and the head of the Kuhn Loeb mergers and acquisitions department, to report his interview with Pedowitz. Gleacher, he says, was astounded, first because Antoniu had failed to tell him about his interview with the U.S. Attorney, as required by firm rules, and second because Antoniu's marriage to Francesca Stanfill was imminent. The marriage suddenly had the portents of disaster. Dennis Stanfill was an extremely important client, and he had many friends at the firm. He had once worked there himself.

Gleacher summoned Antoniu to his office and demanded an explanation. He wasn't reassured. Antoniu told him that there was "nothing" to the federal inquiry, so there wasn't any point in bothering either the firm or the Stanfills about it. Gleacher was dubious. Anyone in the securities business knew a federal probe was a serious matter. Gleacher insisted that Antoniu inform his future father-in-law, arguing that if there was nothing to the probe, then the Stanfills would back him up. Antoniu agreed.

Privately, however, Antoniu apparently determined that he would stall as long as possible. His greatest fear, he later informed his lawyer, was that his marriage to Francesca would be halted.

The attitude was consistent with Antoniu's background and deepest aspirations. Born in Rumania, he had emigrated with his parents to the U.S. in 1965. His father died shortly after, and the family was left with few financial resources. Nonetheless, Antoniu had always seemed dazzled by the seemingly limitless possibilities in America. At Bell Labs, he had felt socially limited, confined, recognizing that a foreign-born engineer was unlikely to rise from the middle class. Harvard Business School had changed those perceptions, opening up new vistas. Marriage to Francesca Stanfill, a beautiful woman who moved in glittering social circles and was the daughter of a captain of American industry, was the fulfillment of a lifetime of dreams.

By June 28, Antoniu had managed to stave off what had seemed certain disaster. His wedding was slated for July 1 in Venice, Italy—an extravagant affair with guests from all over the world—and he and Francesca had arrived early to complete arrangements for the Italian civil service that would precede the church ceremony. But that night, Antoniu received a disturbing call from Gleacher, demanding to know whether Antoniu had yet informed the Stanfills. When he admitted he hadn't, and had in fact defied Gleacher's earlier request, Gleacher said that he was calling Dennis Stanfill himself. Antoniu hung up the phone, then turned to Francesca and confessed.

Two days later, the historic Basilica di San Pietro di Costello in Venice—a church that had been saved from ruin in part by the fund-raising efforts of Francesca's mother—was packed with a glittering crowd of wedding guests. A congratulatory message was read from the cardinal of Venice, the future Pope John Paul I. After the ceremony, the storybook couple—Antoniu and Francesca—glided away in a gleaming white gondola.

It was the end of Antoniu's dream. Within two days, Antoniu's office at Kuhn Loeb was empty, his desk cleaned out and its contents impounded. His marriage lasted a week before it was formally annulled. And Francesca turned against him, later becoming the most potent potential witness in the prosecution's arsenal.

Back in New York, when he heard from Kuhn Loeb that Antoniu had been fired while on his honeymoon, Larry Pedowitz hoped desperately that he'd been right.

LATER that summer, when much of New York City seemed to be on its August vacation, Pedowitz insisted on poring over more and more of the documentary evidence. He obtained Antoniu's telephone records; he subpoenaed his bank records. He studied the chart. Then he obtained some information that reinforced his suspicions that

Antoniu had in fact been lying about the closeness of his relationship to Newman. Newman, it turned out, had written a recommendation for Antoniu's application to the Harvard Business School. Later, the two men had shared a ski house. And Pedowitz's efforts uncovered other evidence. He spotted a canceled check from someone named Frank Carniol. The name rang a bell. He looked at the chart, and there it was. Carniol's name hadn't yet been precisely located in the pyramid but it was on the chart. He appeared to be a European, trading through European accounts.

Pedowitz included Carniol's name adjacent to Newman's. Then, increasingly confident that he'd gotten a step closer to the top of the pyramid, he mentally entered Antoniu's name above both of them. It was some progress.

But Pedowitz had now been working on the case for more than two years. He'd been a detective, not the trial lawyer he thought he'd be. Nonetheless, it looked as if he had identified the principal culprit. So why didn't he feel more elated?

"I kept thinking about Antoniu," Pedowitz recalls, "and I knew this was a tragedy for him. He suffered. I don't know if he really loved Francesca or not, but I knew that what I'd done had to affect the relationship. I was about his age, so I could put myself in his position. The power to accuse is really pretty awesome.

"I think the best prosecutors are pretty sensitive people. I know I often feel bad even convicting people who are guilty. There's a sense of triumph of justice done, but you know this person is hurting. You see it. I saw it in Antoniu's eyes.

"Whether to bring a case is the hardest thing. Totally innocent people are deeply affected—the family, for example. Once I tried a defendant with an anorectic daughter. I think it's probably easier to defend—your duties are clearer. As a prosecutor you have to do justice. What is it? It can be surprisingly amorphous.

"I tell people they should get out of prosecution after a few years. You come in as a young lawyer, and you're impressionable, idealistic, principled. You don't want people to become hardened to all the suffering, because you see it all the time."

Shortly after adding Antoniu's name to the chart, Pedowitz took his own advice. He left the U.S. Attorney's office and joined the New York law firm of Wachtell, Lipton, Rosen & Katz, a firm known nationally for civil litigation in the mergers and acquisitions area.

147

Neither Antoniu nor Newman nor anyone else, for that matter, had yet been accused of a crime.

IN the autumn of 1979, Jed Rakoff, Pedowitz's superior in the securities fraud division, bumped into Lee Richards in a hallway of the U.S. Attorney's offices at St. Andrew's Plaza. Seemingly on impulse, he called Richards into his office and said he wanted him on the "doctors and dentists case," as it was still being described in the office.

Richards wasn't sure how to react. He'd been looking for a new assignment, but he knew little about the case. Still, he felt it was bound to be an improvement. After an exhilarating year in the general crimes unit, he'd been assigned to the corruption unit, which he had found to be a frustrating assignment. Although political corruption cases are sometimes among the most important and visible cases in the office, Richards had worked on only one important case, and that one the government lost. It was demoralizing.

"Corruption is the most frustrating slot in the office," Richards says. "You spend most of your time on investigations and grand jury work, because you can't indict a political figure without a very strong case." Indeed, defense lawyers say that political defendants are the only ones truly accorded the presumption of innocence by most juries. Defense lawyers can often make a prosecution look like some kind of political vendetta.

So Richards, who looked more like a young corporate lawyer with his wire-rim glasses, neatly trimmed hair, and dark suits, and who had no special interest in criminal law at all, asked to get into the securities fraud unit. "They had the most complex cases, with high-quality defense lawyers," he says. Richards also wanted trial experience, and maybe "doctors and dentists" would be a case on which he could get into court. Rakoff told him that a good deal of the investigation had already been completed by Pedowitz before he left, and Richards agreed to work on the case.

He called in Lance Clifton and a more senior Assistant U.S. Attorney who had succeeded Pedowitz on the case, and they began poring over the raw data that had been accumulated, Steinberg's disclosures, and Pedowitz's other discoveries about the case.

In Richards's view, there were two major problem areas. First, there was Antoniu. He was pretty sure that Antoniu was guilty of a crime. Like Pedowitz, he was particularly struck by Antoniu's lie about his friendship with Newman. And Antoniu's behavior after the interview with Pedowitz had been suspicious, including his sudden departure from Kuhn Loeb. But was that really evidence of insider trading? If Antoniu could otherwise be believed, Newman was the source of the inside information and not vice versa. Richards wasn't yet satisfied that they had a case against Antoniu.

The other major problem—an even more glaring weakness—was the mystery of the Morgan Stanley source. They still hadn't reached the name at the very top of the pyramid. Richards thought it would be foolhardy to seek indictments against either Antoniu or Newman before they had figured out the full scope of the conspiracy.

Like Pedowitz before him, Richards began to be drawn into the perplexing mystery of the case, almost as though it were a Rubik's cube. Like Pedowitz, he scrutinized the personnel records and data on Morgan Stanley employees on the assumption that the tipper had to be inside Morgan Stanley. But again, that produced no obvious leads. He too was puzzled by the fact that none of the people in mergers and acquisitions had worked on all the suspect deals, or even a major percentage of them.

So Richards went back to the blue sheets compiled by Clifton, showing the source of the trading activity. He was struck by how out of control the information had become. In fact, direct trading by Newman and Antoniu obviously made up only a small portion of the trading. It reminded Richards of some of the heroin cases he had worked on. Users couldn't resist passing their habit on to others. Then there were the unnamed trading accounts in foreign banks: massive trading by an account at the Bank of Bermuda, the Banque de Paris, groups of banks in Luxembourg and Switzerland.

Steinberg had already told the prosecutors about the Bank of Bermuda connection, and it suggested to Richards the cunning and lengths to which the targets of the investigations would go to conceal their activity. According to Steinberg, at Newman's suggestion he had created a trust with the Bank of Bermuda. Newman would typically call Steinberg with a stock tip, Steinberg would pass on the tip to the trustees at the Bank of Bermuda, who would in turn place an order with New York stockbrokers who traded in an account identified only as the Bank of Bermuda.

When a transaction was complete, the bank would allocate the proceeds to the trust it held for Newman and Steinberg. Carniol's location on the chart suggested that he too might have had a similar relationship. Might Newman or Antoniu have concocted similar arrangements with other recipients of their stock tips? Richards wondered. Several foreign names floating on the chart looked suspicious: Marcello Leon, Fariborz Ghadar, Constantine Spyropoulos. But there were no known links between any of them and Antoniu and Newman. And they couldn't be questioned easily, since they resided outside the U.S.

Richards reluctantly turned back to the Morgan Stanley angle, and suddenly he had an inspiration. Up until now, they'd been stymied by the fact that no one at Morgan Stanley had worked on all the deals under investigation. So their focus had been on the Morgan Stanley employees who had worked on at least several of those deals. During Pedowitz's last summer on the case, all members of Morgan Stanley's mergers and acquisitions department had come in for interviews, but nothing suspicious had emerged.

Now Richards decided to take an entirely different approach: was there anyone in Morgan Stanley's m&a area who had worked on *none* of the deals? He and Clifton pored over their data, crossing out names, and the exercise produced an interesting result: only one person in the m&a group hadn't worked on any of the suspect deals. His name was Jacques Courtois.

Richards went back to the files of Pedowitz's interview notes. Pedowitz had spoken to Courtois about two weeks after his interview with Antoniu, when he first called in all the Morgan Stanley m&a people. There was little to distinguish Courtois's answers from those of his Morgan Stanley colleagues, except for one thing: he mentioned that he and Antoniu had jointly financed a T-shirt silk-screening business for a mutual friend. Each had invested $5,000, he said, but the venture had failed and the money was lost. Otherwise, he minimized his relationship with Antoniu.

In February 1979, Courtois abruptly resigned from Morgan Stanley and his promising career there, saying he would join a computer business in Washington, D.C. Actually, he traveled much farther, taking up residence in Bogotá, Colombia.

But even that otherwise suspicious maneuver had a possibly innocent explanation. When Richards made inquiries, he learned that Courtois had just married a prominent Colombian woman he had met at Harvard Business School. She was then the comptroller of Bogotá, and her uncle was the president of Colombia. Later asked for an explanation, Courtois said simply that he'd "fallen in love." Richards found it a plausible explanation, particularly since Courtois hadn't left at a point where any action against him was imminent. No one had been indicted, nor had Courtois yet been singled out as a target of the investigation. In Richards's experience, people didn't throw over their careers and flee the country until the heat was pretty intense. He felt discouraged.

But Richards had no other good leads to pursue. He called Crowley, the lawyer at Davis, Polk, and said he'd like to see Courtois again. Crowley wasn't particularly pleased; he'd been hoping that the interest in Morgan Stanley had faded, but he agreed to produce Courtois. Shorty after, Richards ran into Robert Fiske, who had by now been replaced as U.S. Attorney in the Southern District by John Martin and who had returned to private practice at Davis, Polk. Fiske jokingly told Richards that he, Richards, was viewed as a nemesis at Morgan Stanley.

Courtois returned from Colombia for one interview with Richards. It was a disappointment. Courtois stuck by his story, and Richards had the impression that he was a cool, tough, bright character. He found Courtois convincing, but there were nagging suspicions. "I just had the feeling he had ice in his veins," Richards recalls. Courtois flew back to Bogotá.

Meanwhile, there was a legal bombshell that threatened the whole case.

In the spring of 1980, the Supreme Court issued an opinion reversing the conviction of Vincent Chiarella for insider trading. Chiarella was a financial printer who learned from confidential documents submitted for printing that certain companies were going to be targets of take-over bids. He used the information to trade in the stocks, and made substantial profits. Chiarella had been successfully prosecuted by the Southern District U.S. Attorney's office; in fact, it was the case on which Pedowitz had hoped to work before he began his pursuit of Newman and Antoniu. The office was stunned by the loss, none more so than Richards.

Richards thought he might as well throw all the work on his case out the window, for what the Supreme Court had just ruled was not a crime was very close to what Newman and Antoniu had allegedly done.

When Richards obtained a copy of the Supreme Court's opinion it provided little comfort. The theory of the Chiarella case, and the theory on which Richards had been working, was that insider trading is a fraud whose victims are those who sell their securities to someone who knew before any public announcement that a take-over was imminent. Chiarella was also the first criminal case ever based on the alleged misuse of inside information.

Now, much to Richards's dismay, the Supreme Court had dashed that approach. It rejected the notion that a purchaser of stock in the market has any duty of disclosure to the sellers (a notion that was, admittedly, probably impractical). And it distinguished Chiarella from traditional "insiders," such as corporate officers, who are bound by various rules governing disclosure of information about the companies where they are employed. Chiarella, as a financial printer, had simply stumbled upon secrets about other companies. He wasn't an "insider."

"I thought this just blew us away," Richards recalls. "We had to confront the question of whether to drop the case. After all, a lot of the people we'd questioned were experiencing anxiety, and we had an obligation to let them know if this wasn't going to go anywhere." Richards went to Rakoff, the head of the securities section, sought the opinions of other assistants, and finally the matter had to be taken to Martin.

Despite the Supreme Court's seemingly unequivocal opinion, and after his initial shock wore off, Richards was reluctant to throw in the towel. Something told him that the Newman and Antoniu cases were different from Chiarella's. For one thing, he thought, they'd be easier defendants to convict. Chiarella was a struggling workingman who hadn't launched a worldwide, sophisticated conspiracy to profit from his information. Newman and Antoniu were well educated, affluent, and greedy.

And then there was the theory of the case itself. Richards was inclined to agree that it was hard to characterize a seller of stock as a "victim" in the traditional sense. After all, anyone who sells stock does so knowing that the price of the stock might rise after the sale. He thought for a while about the notion of a victim, and asked himself who had been hurt the most by Antoniu's behavior. The answer, it seemed obvious, was Morgan Stanley and Lehman Brothers Kuhn Loeb. They had certainly been the most distressed, and their reputations were at stake. Perhaps the crime wasn't the misuse of inside information per se, but the "theft" of that information in the first place from the institutions to which it had been entrusted.

The Supreme Court's opinion in Chiarella did provide some encouragement for that approach. In the appeal of that case, the government had argued a similar theory—that Chiarella had committed a fraud against his employer by using the confidential information to trade in stocks. But the jury that delivered the guilty verdict hadn't been given that theory as a basis for finding him guilty. So the Supreme Court didn't consider the approach. It wrote instead that it wouldn't "speculate" on whether, as a matter of law, Chiarella had been guilty of such a crime. Richards thought that left an opening for a case carefully crafted along those lines.

STILL, there were some obvious problems. Richards would have to convince a jury that Antoniu had "stolen" information. And that only underscored that the case was weak even without the added burden of Chiarella, since he still didn't know how Antoniu got most of his tips. Courtois was still nothing but a suspicion, and now he was in South America.

Soon after, Richards learned from colleagues at Lehman Brothers Kuhn Loeb that Antoniu too had eluded prosecution by joining an investment concern in Milan, Italy. "I was deeply discouraged," Richards recalls, over the knowledge that his principal suspects had vanished.

He didn't let on, however, to Audrey Strauss, who had replaced Rakoff as head of the securities unit under Martin. The Newman case could prove a massive waste of government resources, and Strauss never gave Richards the formal go-ahead he wanted. But she quietly supported him. She didn't put a stop to the case, and she didn't assign Richards to another matter. He wasn't about to stop. "This case had turned into a classic whodunit," he recalls, "and it was driving me nuts."

Having exhausted every approach he could think of, Richards decided it was time for decisive action with respect to Antoniu. He now felt that he needed to turn Antoniu into a cooperative witness—he was the one person, apparently, who could provide a positive identification of the top of the pyramid. Although the idea appalled him in many ways, Richards recognized that Antoniu's testimony would be so valuable that he might have to immunize him in order to get it.

But first he'd try in other ways to increase the pressure on Antoniu to cooperate, particularly by convening a grand jury and calling in for sworn testimony people very close to Antoniu—people who would in turn put pressure on Antoniu to cooperate and thereby bring the investigation to a halt.

The grand jury, a relic of English medieval law, is often an effective weapon in a prosecutor's arsenal. Ostensibly, the grand jury exists to protect citizens from prosecution that has no evidentiary basis. The grand jury reviews the evidence a prosecutor has amassed, and then decides if a formal prosecution seems warranted.

In practice, defense lawyers note, the grand jury is more of a boon than a bane to prosecutors. Its proceedings are entirely secret—it is, in fact, illegal for a prosecutor to divulge what happens before a grand jury. The accused isn't represented by counsel. As a result, there is virtually no check on a prosecutor's conduct before the grand jury, and in practice, the grand jury rarely fails to deliver the result a prosecutor wants.

Use of the grand jury can also be valuable in cases like Richards's— cases that are still under investigation. A witness testifies before the grand jury under oath; the procedure is far more solemn than a visit to a prosecutor's office. The target of a grand jury is also identified, and usually learns that a grand jury investigation is under way as friends and acquaintances are called to testify. It often proves to be an effective means of increasing the pressure on a potential defendant.

Richards systematically combed through the records and began to call anyone who looked like a close friend or business associate of Antoniu's. Naturally, one of his first calls was to Francesca Stanfill, now working as a reporter for *The New York Times Magazine*. She had just published a much talked about article about Oscar de la Renta, the fashion designer, and his wife entitled "Living Well Is the Best Revenge." It isn't, Richards soon learned. For Francesca Stanfill, bitter and humiliated by her abortive marriage, revenge was still the best revenge.

MANHATTAN lawyer Cornelius Ahearn was used to meeting clients in trouble. As an international lawyer specializing in securities, tax, and criminal matters, he'd encountered a wide range of alleged wrongdoers, such as financier Robert Vesco, one of Ahearn's clients who has so far evaded prosecution for tax and securities fraud and is currently believed living in Cuba. When Adrian Antoniu walked into Ahearn's office for the first time, Ahearn knew he was dealing with another person in trouble.

Ahearn recalls that Antoniu was nearly distraught, barely able to tell his story. He had just returned from his honeymoon, which had been a nightmare, he said, and now his wife was suing him for divorce. Finally he revealed the background to the wedding and divorce, including the investigation by the U.S. Attorney's office. Ahearn was alarmed. Antoniu was in more trouble than he realized.

Ahearn's advice to leave the country as soon as possible seemed to stun Antoniu. Only weeks ago, he seemed to be near the pinnacle of social and financial success. Suddenly he was being asked to give up practically everything—the BMW, the Park Avenue cooperative apartment, the membership at Doubles, a posh Manhattan social club—for an uncertain future in another country.

Antoniu protested, telling Ahearn that he had emigrated to the U.S. as a teen-ager from Rumania, that his widowed mother in Queens needed him for support. "He had an immigrant mentality, an almost irrational pride in being an American," Ahearn recalls. Finally the lawyer told Antoniu that his stay outside the country might only be temporary. "Ride this out in Europe," Ahearn told Antoniu, and maybe the case would be abandoned. If nothing else, Ahearn thought, Antoniu would have more bargaining power if he was out of reach of a U.S. subpoena.

Antoniu managed to find a job with an investment firm in Milan, and Ahearn met with him on his own periodic trips to Italy. For a while, the pressure on Antoniu seemed to ease, particularly since there were no signs emanating from the U.S. Attorney's office that the investigation was making any progress. But the divorce negotiations with Francesca weren't going well at all. Much to Antoniu's dismay, she was demanding substantial alimony, claiming that she was the wronged partner in the marriage. Ahearn thought she was being vindictive, given their relative financial positions and the expenses Antoniu faced.

On one of those trips, Ahearn was able to give Antoniu the first piece of good news he'd heard in months: the Chiarella case had been decided in favor of the defendant. Antoniu was exultant, wanting to know if it meant he could return to the U.S. almost immediately and resume his career. But Ahearn wasn't nearly so sanguine. He had retained Peter Leisure, now a federal judge but then in private practice who was an expert in securities law, and together they'd done an extensive analysis of the Chiarella case. Ahearn was worried that Antoniu, a Lehman Brothers Kuhn Loeb vice president, would be held to a far higher standard of conduct than a financial printer. And Leisure seized upon the ambiguous language in the Supreme Court opinion hinting that a different theory of the offense might support a conviction. They had, in fact, shrewdly anticipated Richards's own thinking about the case, so they urged Antoniu to stay in Europe with a wait-and-see attitude.

Then came an ominous development. Antoniu was notified that his bank records had been subpoenaed and that the bank had turned them over. Soon came word that friends and acquaintances were being called in not only to the U.S. Attorney's office but before the grand jury. Antoniu later confided that the impact of these disclosures was devastating, since his hopes had been flourishing and now were dashed. But even that was mild compared to his reaction to reports that Francesca was going before the grand jury.

Ahearn too was deeply concerned by that development. "Her demands about the divorce were appalling. And Peter [Leisure] and I both felt that if that was the way she felt about the divorce, then she was a major risk for Adrian as a witness. Adrian said he thought he could trust most of his friends, but Francesca was a wild card." Ahearn also knew that although Francesca had virtually no firsthand evidence of the scheme, she had plenty of hearsay testimony to offer. Antoniu had told him that he confessed the scheme to Francesca just before the wedding, and then spent much of the honeymoon on the telephone to his coconspirators, often within earshot of Francesca.

Ahearn made an attempt to find out from Richards just what he had gotten out of Francesca, but Richards couldn't tell him anything because of the secrecy that surrounds grand jury proceedings. Nonetheless, Ahearn says, "I was confident from the tone of the discussion that she had betrayed him totally." (Francesca declined comment.)

Richards's plan to step up the pressure on Antoniu was working as planned. As Antoniu seemed to become more distraught in Italy, Ahearn and Leisure concluded that his future had to be resolved. At one point Antoniu talked of suicide, and Ahearn says he took him seriously.

In September, Ahearn, Leisure, and several of their associates met with Antoniu at the luxurious Principe e Savoie hotel in Milan. The purpose of the gathering, which lasted for five full days of intense discussion, was to determine strategy for what was clearly a mounting campaign by Richards to snare Antoniu.

Ahearn explained that Antoniu had three options: he could remain a fugitive, he could return to the U.S. and fight the expected charges, or he could plea bargain.

The first option, to remain a fugitive, was only superficially appealing. Antoniu's U.S. passport was about to expire, and his movement would be restricted. It wouldn't be easy to find another nationality. Under the circumstances, there was only a handful of comparatively undesirable countries that would grant him citizenship. Ahearn pointed out that even Robert Vesco, with his enormous financial resources, had led a nomadic existence and had ended up in Cuba. Besides, he noted, the life of a fugitive can be lonely.

Antoniu rejected that option relatively quickly, mostly because he didn't want to lose his American citizenship. That left the other two options. The lawyers told Antoniu that given the unsettled nature of the law on insider trading, he might, like Chiarella, and after a long and expensive trial, ultimately win his case. But they also emphasized what they thought were the weaknesses in his defense. Leisure, in particular, says he thought that Antoniu's conduct was so plainly wrong—far worse than Chiarella's—that a way would be found to hold him criminally accountable. In any event, the legal uncertainty hadn't seemed to deter Richards from pressing forward with the investigation. If the government was going to drop the investigation because of Chiarella, they felt, it would already have done so.

That left the third option—a plea bargain. Ahearn couldn't be certain, but he suspected Richards would be receptive to an approach from Antoniu hinting at cooperation. Several factors worked in Antoniu's favor. First, he was in Europe and hard to reach. Extradition would be expensive and might not be successful. Second, as far as Ahearn could tell, Antoniu was the only person who could implicate Courtois with direct testimony. Newman, for example, had never been told the name of Antoniu's source at Morgan Stanley. Ahearn thought Antoniu had the kind of information worth bargaining for.

By the end of the meeting, no firm decision had been reached, but Antoniu authorized Ahearn to approach Richards for an indication of what kind of bargain might be worked out. Ahearn knew it wouldn't be an easy task. He had to convince Richards that Antoniu knew so much he was an indispensable witness, while at the same time he tried to minimize his culpability in order to get reduced charges. And he sensed that he wouldn't have much time, that the plea-bargaining "window of opportunity," as he calls it, wouldn't last long. For in a case like Antoniu's, only one major defendant can usually expect to strike a plea bargain. If Newman, for example, were to get to Richards first, Antoniu's chances of pleading to reduced charges would be practically nil.

LATE that October came the break that Richards had been desperately hoping for—the call from Ahearn and Leisure. "I figured Antoniu was weakening," Richards recalls. "A long investigation can be very tough on people. We kept getting people closer and closer to Antoniu. We knew they'd contact him, and usually a phone call is all it takes to keep the pressure on."

But Richards as well as Ahearn and Antoniu was now in a difficult position. By and large, Richards didn't like the idea of plea bargaining. By its very nature, it lets criminals plead to lesser offenses than they have usually committed. And often, the only bargain is one of judicial economy—prosecutors have to bargain because they and the courts would be overwhelmed if every criminal case actually went to trial. Such pleas have understandably often prompted public outrage.

But in Antoniu's case, there would at least be a real bargain—without his testimony and cooperation, Richards had reluctantly concluded, there might not be any convictions at all. The big questions on Richards's mind now were: what kind of information could he get from Antoniu? and at what price?

The negotiations between Richards and Antoniu's lawyers started slowly—Leisure and Ahearn wanted some indication of lenience just for bringing Antoniu back into the country. Richards was reluctant to make any kind of commitment until he had a reasonably good idea of the value of Antoniu's testimony. Finally they reached a compromise: Antoniu would return to New York and spend a day being questioned by Richards. If his testimony was as valuable as Ahearn said it would be, Antoniu would agree to cooperate with the prosecutors. In return, he would be allowed to plead guilty to two counts of criminal violations of securities Rule 10-b-5 and would be immunized from further prosecution. If Richards didn't want to go forward with the deal, Antoniu would be given forty-eight hours to leave the country.

Richards thought he'd struck a good bargain, but there were aspects that also appealed to Ahearn. "I trusted Richards to honor the spirit of the agreement," Ahearn says. "In other words, I didn't think he'd use the interview to squeeze the information out of Antoniu and then turn his back on our deal. The Southern District has a very strong reputation for honoring its word."

And Ahearn had other reasons for believing the arrangement would work. It was one thing for Richards to know what Antoniu had to tell; it was another to produce a witness who could testify in court. If Antoniu returned to Europe, Richards's most important witness would again be unavailable. And the potential plea itself had an important advantage. The 10-b-5 charges to which Antoniu would plead were the same as those struck down by the Supreme Court in Chiarella. If prosecution of Antoniu's coconspirators resulted in a similar ruling, Ahearn thought it might be possible to reopen Antoniu's plea. Finally, there was the promise of immunization. Ahearn knew, but didn't know whether Richards knew, that Antoniu's use of inside information hadn't been confined to Courtois and Newman.

In late October, Antoniu arrived for his interview, meeting Richards, the mysterious prosecutor he had come to view as a personal nemesis, for the first time. The two began a wary mating game, with Richards asking a number of relatively innocuous questions designed to test Antoniu's memory.

"This process is very difficult," Richards says. "I had been the enemy, and now, suddenly, I had to get close to him." Richards found Antoniu bright, articulate, and very charming, qualities that actually made his task more difficult. "It's easier to deal with an out-and-out criminal," Richards says. "Antoniu was a swindler—smooth and devious."

At first Richards wasn't satisfied that Antoniu was telling all he knew—he wanted detail, on nearly a day-by-day basis. But after several not so subtle suggestions that Antoniu might have to return to Italy, Antoniu seemed to open up. And as his disclosures mounted, Richards tried to control his excitement.

Antoniu was, in fact, at the center of the conspiracy. By mid-1974, he told Richards, he and Newman, who hadn't been close while Antoniu was at Harvard, were seeing each other socially at least once a week, and talking on the phone even more often. Antoniu complained about the large student loans he was trying to pay, and his mother's financial problems, stemming from the fact that her fabric business in Queens wasn't going well. Out of a series of those discussions was born the idea to trade on inside information Antoniu learned at Morgan Stanley. In return for sharing that information, Newman contributed the start-up capital and handled the trading. The two would then divide the profits in half. They agreed to tell no one else about the inside information and to strictly limit their trading.

The arrangement was more lucrative than either had anticipated. On one deal alone, based on Antoniu's advance knowledge of a takeover bid for Magnavox by North American Philips, the two made $50,000 in profits each. But both were aware that trading volume was monitored by the SEC, and Antoniu worried that their activity might be detected, especially as profits mounted.

He recalled that one day he showed Newman an article in *The Wall Street Journal* about another insider trading case to illustrate his concern, but Newman didn't seem worried. "Well, you see the worst that could happen in a case like this, they ask you for your money back and they give you a slap on the hand," Antoniu said Newman told him. Newman was gloating over their success, saying that most people "have to steal or kill for this kind of money."

What Newman didn't know was that Antoniu had already broken their solemn pledge to confine the use of the inside information to their own trading. Antoniu, seeing the success of the arrangement with Newman, had decided to multiply his own profits by entering into similar arrangements with others, specifically Carniol and Spyropoulos, both Harvard Business School classmates who now lived in Europe.

Their trading volume increased the risk of detection by the SEC, but Antoniu thought they couldn't be traced since their accounts were outside the U.S. He wanted a similar arrangement for his trading with Newman, and persuaded him to move their trading offshore. They established a trust at a Bahamas bank, trading through New York brokerage accounts in the bank's name.

But just as that operation got under way, they suffered a setback. Antoniu was called in by partners at Morgan Stanley and told to look for another job. His firing had nothing to do with any information leaks, but rather was part of a weeding-out process that most new investment bankers undergo at the firm. Antoniu recognized immediately that he would be cut off from inside information, the linchpin of the scheme.

He promptly launched a campaign to win over another source at Morgan Stanley. His name, Antoniu told Richards, was Jacques Courtois.

Richards was electrified. At last he had learned the name at the top of the pyramid, and it was, indeed, someone he had suspected. But Antoniu, and, apparently, only Antoniu, could provide a direct identification in court. Richards listened intently as Antoniu continued his narrative.

He chose Courtois, Antoniu explained, because he too was a Harvard Business School classmate. The two men had become close friends in Cambridge, and Courtois had introduced Antoniu to a glamorous circle of friends. Courtois himself represented many of Antoniu's own aspirations: he came from a wealthy and socially prominent Montreal family. Courtois's career at Morgan Stanley had flourished; in fact, he was moving into the mergers and acquisitions area.

Antoniu's effort succeeded. Courtois's participation was confirmed over the chess match at the Harvard Club, when, as proof of his good faith, Courtois offered Antoniu Pan Ocean Oil.

Pan Ocean Oil was subsequently acquired by Marathon Oil, as Courtois had told Antoniu it would be, and the group reaped substantial profits. Antoniu went to Newman and explained that the profits now had to be split three ways because there was another Morgan Stanley conspirator, though he never told Newman Courtois's name.

And then Antoniu got the job at Kuhn Loeb, which soon merged with Lehman Brothers, and was assigned to mergers and acquisitions himself. Though not as fertile a source of lucrative information as Morgan Stanley, it opened up additional avenues for trading. And as profits boomed, the scheme became increasingly complex in order to ward off detection.

For example, Antoniu explained, in order to increase the buying power of the offshore trusts, the conspirators purchased U.S. Treasury notes, which wouldn't identify their owners, and used them as collateral for loans from the various Caribbean banks where they had trust accounts. Then they started buying options written to the Banque de Paris, one of Carniol's banks. When the options were profitably liquidated, the proceeds were deposited in Carniol's account, then routed back to Courtois, Antoniu, and Newman through Spyropoulos's Swiss bank accounts.

Then, in the spring of 1977, came the call from the SEC investigator to Antoniu. Antoniu admitted that he had lied instinctively, then said he immediately called Newman. They agreed that if questioned further each would tell the same false story—that Newman was offering tips to Antoniu and urging him to become a client. But particularly at Antoniu's insistence, he said, they agreed that it was too risky to keep trading on inside information. That strategy seemed to work—Antoniu heard nothing more for a year.

Then came the call from Pedowitz, and the interview at the U.S. Attorney's office, where Antoniu repeated the same story. Despite the calm he tried to exhibit, Antoniu said he had in fact felt panicky, especially because of his upcoming wedding to Francesca. He insisted on meeting Newman clandestinely in Central Park that night. Although Antoniu was now moving in much loftier social circles than Newman and they had few friends in common, Antoniu was worried about one mutual friend dating from their days at NYU, Mike Negoescu, and he told Newman that he wanted Negoescu to leave the country so he wouldn't tell investigators that Newman and Antoniu were in fact close friends. Newman argued that Antoniu was overreacting and would only draw more attention to them. But Antoniu did go to Negoescu, and persuaded him to take a European vacation.

Next, Antoniu went to Courtois's apartment, and Courtois told him that he was concerned that Newman might not hold up under the pressure of an investigation. But Courtois was also reassuring, pointing out that what was clear to them wouldn't be nearly as obvious to outsiders.

But Antoniu continued to be upset, especially after his wedding trip to Italy when he saw his marriage crumble almost as soon as it occurred. He spent much of the honeymoon making calls to coconspirators, worrying about the progress of the investigation. Antoniu recalled that in one call to Courtois, Courtois became angry with him, cutting him off, saying that "everything was under control" and would be straightened out when Antoniu returned to New York.

But it wasn't. Antoniu returned to find his life in a shambles. He separated immediately from Francesca. He'd been thrown out of Lehman Brothers Kuhn Loeb, and he was convinced his irate father-in-law, Dennis Stanfill, would see to it that he never worked in investment banking again.

Soon after, Antoniu made his appointment with Ahearn, then fled to Milan. Richards knew the rest of the story.

Richards had now heard enough to know that he'd go through with the Antoniu plea, but he pressed for more details, asking Antoniu to cover some of the same ground again, and asking particularly if anyone else had been involved or had been given his tips. Antoniu said he'd told him everything.

By the end of the session, Richards was exhausted but elated. For the first time, he began to see a real possibility of convictions in the case. But they still weren't a sure thing. Antoniu might be a star witness, but he was now an admitted criminal and, as a result, inherently untrustworthy to a jury. Richards would have to find some corroborating evidence or testimony.

The next day, Antoniu and his lawyers formally entered Antoniu's guilty plea and Antoniu agreed to cooperate, but there was no public announcement. The plea was filed in federal court under seal, since Richards didn't want any of the other suspects to know that Antoniu had crossed into the government camp.

The most obvious corroborator of Antoniu's testimony was Newman, and Richards put in a call to Newman's lawyer, Frank Velie, now a partner at the Manhattan firm of Christie & Viener. Despite Courtois's earlier fears that Newman would be the one to break down under the pressure of the investigation, he had remained stalwartly uncooperative. When Richards called this time, he upped the ante, making it clear that he wanted nothing less than a guilty plea to criminal charges. Velie told Richards that he wasn't interested in negotiating and, if subpoenaed, would invoke the Fifth Amendment. The other likely candidates—Courtois, Carniol, and Spyropoulos—were out of the country, and it would require elaborate legal mechanisms and approval from Washington to reach them.

But two other ideas occurred to him. One involved Antoniu's description of the funding of the offshore trading accounts. Antoniu had seemed confident that by using unregistered U.S. Treasury bills, the conspirators could escape detection—there would be no "paper trail" of the funds from one of their accounts to another. But Richards wasn't so sure. He asked Clifton to check into the matter, and the detective made a useful discovery. He called Richards on Christmas Eve to report that although the notes themselves aren't formally registered, banks keep a record containing names of purchasers and the serial numbers of the notes purchased. Richards and Clifton immediately set to work obtaining the records, and then matching the serial numbers with those of the notes deposited in the Caribbean banks.

During Antoniu's statement, Richards had also been struck by the number of people involved who had attended the Harvard Business School, and the intensity of their loyalty and friendship to one another. So he went to the public library for a copy of Antoniu's business school yearbook. As expected, he found pictures of a number of

Antoniu's classmates he'd never met—Carniol, Spyropoulos—and a picture of Courtois, several years younger, of course. But as he combed through the pages, two other names from the class struck him as familiar: Marc Glassman and Fariborz Ghadar. When he checked back, he found their names on the original pyramid of suspected inside traders. Richards wished he'd consulted the yearbook sooner.

Ghadar, it turned out, was an Iranian national but had returned to the U.S. after the collapse of the Shah's government. He hadn't co-operated, and again declined to answer questions. But he hinted that he had useful information, particularly about Courtois, and said he'd talk if granted immunity from prosecution. Since he hadn't been men-tioned by Antoniu, Richards assumed he wasn't a major figure in the scheme, and he didn't have many other possibilities for corroborating testimony. He decided to immunize him.

Ghadar told Richards that he'd known Courtois socially at Harvard, and had stayed in Cambridge for three years after graduation to work on a doctorate. Then he had been tapped by the Shah to become Iran's assistant vice minister of finance, with responsibility for invest-ing the country's vast oil profits.

Just before returning to Iran in 1975, he'd run into Courtois by accident in Harvard Business School's Baker Library, and Courtois, now at Morgan Stanley, seemed fascinated by the news that Ghadar would soon be one of the world's major investors. At a going-away party for Ghadar, Courtois pressed some stock tips on Ghadar, trying to impress his investment expertise on his former classmate. Ghadar followed Courtois's advice, and made money—the tips were, in fact, stocks of take-over candidates. During the next year, Courtois passed on more tips to Ghadar, dropping the pretense that they were simply shrewd market analysis. Ghadar said he knew he was receiving inside information from Morgan Stanley.

Although Courtois didn't share in Ghadar's profits (Ghadar, in turn, passed many of the tips on to members of his family), Courtois's motive soon became apparent. In late 1976, Ghadar lost his position in the Iranian government, and Courtois cut off the flow of tips. Ghadar said Courtois told him that he was "now in the policy section of Morgan Stanley" and "doesn't have anything to do with those any more." Ghadar said he hadn't had any contact with Antoniu. None-theless, Richards was pleased that he could corroborate Antoniu's identification of Courtois as the source at Morgan Stanley.

Richards's interview with Marc Glassman proved to be far more disturbing. Glassman too had to be immunized, but Richards was now satisfied that those most culpable in the scheme were Antoniu, Courtois, and Newman. Glassman told Richards that he was receiving tips from Antoniu and had been an active participant in the trading. In fact, he'd contributed about $80,000 to help Antoniu purchase the Treasury notes to fund the Caribbean bank trading accounts. Richards was amazed by the spread of the information. Despite Antoniu and Newman's mutual pledge to keep the information to themselves, by Richard's calculation at least seventy-five people were regularly receiving the inside information.

But Glassman's disclosure posed a serious problem for Antoniu, Richards's projected star witness. During his interrogation, Antoniu had never mentioned Glassman's name. It was obvious that Antoniu had lied when he said that no one else had been part of the scheme. Under the terms of Antoniu's plea bargain, a lie, or withholding information, was grounds for revoking the deal.

Richards was livid, and he now faced a hard decision. It was clear that he hadn't yet secured the full cooperation of Antoniu, who apparently still thought he could outsmart the prosecutors. And he knew that a good defense lawyer would use this to rip Antoniu apart on cross-examination, by demonstrating that he lied even after having been granted immunity. This could have a devastating effect on the jury, Richards feared. But the alternative was to abrogate the plea bargain and lose Antoniu altogether.

Richards called Ahearn and told him that Antoniu had lied and had withheld information, that he wanted him to appear for another interview, and that he was thinking of rescinding the plea bargain. Ahearn was concerned. Antoniu hadn't told him anything about Glassman, either. When Ahearn confronted his client, Antoniu acknowledged Glassman's role in the scheme, but said he couldn't bring himself to betray a close friend who, as far as he knew, wasn't under suspicion. "It was terribly difficult for Antoniu to provide testimony against his friends," Ahearn says, "especially people whom he himself had brought into the scheme." But Ahearn lectured Antoniu that his new status meant those concerns had to be banished.

But Ahearn didn't think Antoniu was in any real danger of losing his plea bargain as long as there were no repetitions of the Glassman incident. He argued to Richards that the omission had been inadvertent and, that in the scheme of things, it really wasn't that important. "Richards was very upset, but I was confident that Antoniu was critical to his case. In my experience, if the government was really upset they would have reneged immediately on the plea agreement. It's not something they'd talk about."

"I had a very tense session with Antoniu and his lawyer," Richards recalls. "We could have breached the agreement; we could have asked for a plea to more counts. But I decided not to. I thought what he did was understandable—he was trying to protect others, not himself, and let's face it: we needed him."

With the corroborating testimony from Ghadar and Glassman, and the document trail left by the Treasury bill purchases, Richards concluded it was time to draft indictments to present to the grand jury. In most criminal cases, the wording of an indictment is standard. This one wasn't. The one model—Chiarella—had already failed Supreme Court scrutiny.

So with copies of the Chiarella opinion beside him, Richards worked on drafts of the indictment that would reflect a legal theory that he thought could pass muster. Since the Supreme Court had sidestepped the question of whether securities fraud might be alleged on the basis of a breach of duty to one's employer, that became the centerpiece of the indictment. Richards alleged that Antoniu had, in effect, stolen confidential information from Morgan Stanley, conduct for which his coconspirators were equally liable. Richards recognized that the indictment would break new ground—it would be the first securities fraud case in which the "victim" of the alleged crime wasn't a buyer or seller of stock. As a result, the drafts had to be reviewed both by Strauss, the head of the fraud division, and by U.S. Attorney John Martin. After much debate and consideration, approval was granted. In February 1981—seven years after Pedowitz launched his investigation—Newman, Courtois, Carniol, and Spyropoulos were indicted by a Manhattan grand jury on multiple accounts of mail and wire fraud in addition to criminal violations of Rule 10-b-5. At the same time, Antoniu's plea was unveiled.

The announcement of the indictments triggered a wave of publicity. In a highly unusual move, Morgan Stanley issued a press release even before the U.S. Attorney's office did, attempting to portray the investment banking firm as a victim of the alleged crime and to shore up confidence in the firm's integrity.

Newman was arrested and pleaded not guilty. Carniol, Spyropoulos, and Courtois didn't answer the charges, making clear their intention to remain fugitives. Richards, working with a special unit of the Justice Department in Washington, launched extradition proceedings in Luxembourg, Switzerland, and Colombia, their respective refuges. But extradition can be an agonizingly slow process, so he decided to proceed with Newman's case.

Newman's defensive response was swift. His lawyer, Frank Velie, filed a motion to dismiss the charges. Predictably, he zeroed in on the legal weakness that Richards had tried to anticipate. And he tried to characterize Newman as the real victim of prosecutorial zeal.

"This is a test case," Velie said at the outset of his motion to dismiss, arguing that the government charged Newman with conduct "never before held to be a crime" using theories "never before judicially approved."

Like many white-collar criminal defense lawyers in New York, Velie is a former Assistant U.S. Attorney in the Southern District. "I thought Newman's indictment was barbarous," Velie says, unusually strong words even for a defense lawyer. "When I was in the office, there were guidelines that had to be met before we'd sign an indictment. We didn't try to use a novel theory in a criminal case. For someone to be a criminal, he must have chosen criminal behavior. He must have known that what he was doing was wrong. But in their zeal to pursue insider trading, they've just thrown the rule book out the window."

Richards recalls that "Velie was genuinely angry with me, and felt we were overreaching. I just don't agree. Newman's and Antoniu's behavior cried out for criminal sanctions. And I didn't have any doubts at all that they knew what they were doing."

The two lawyers soon got the chance to argue their competing views of the case. The judge assigned to the case, federal District Judge Charles S. Haight, Jr., asked for oral argument on Newman's motion to dismiss. It came several weeks later, late in the day, and lasted for more than an hour and a half of intense debate as both Richards and Velie pressed their positions on the judge. Richards thought it had gone well, but at its conclusion Judge Haight delivered a "preliminary impression" that the government's conduct had been "fundamentally unfair." "I felt as if I'd been shot between the eyes," Richards recalls. The scene in the courtroom made him feel even worse. Newman was there, hugging and kissing his wife and family. Soon after, Judge Haight followed through on his impression and dismissed the indictment on the grounds that the defendants hadn't had adequate knowledge that their conduct would be deemed criminal. For Richards, it was the low point of his career as a prosecutor.

The decision was a blow to Richards's case in other ways too. Antoniu immediately stopped cooperating. "This put me in a peculiar position," Ahearn, Antoniu's lawyer, says. "Antoniu had pleaded guilty to something that now looked like it wasn't a crime. I started to think that Newman had been right to fight the charge." Velie argued vigorously, both to Richards and Martin, that the charges against Newman should now be dropped.

But Richards wasn't about to let years of work go down the drain because of one opinion. He argued that Martin should keep the case alive by seeking an expedited appeal to the Second Circuit. Such a decision, however, couldn't be made by Martin alone, especially since he was now a lame-duck U.S. Attorney, already a half year into the Reagan presidency. And in any event, the decision to appeal the dismissal of an indictment had to be made in Washington.

This prospect worried Richards. Currently on appeal to the Supreme Court was another insider trading case involving a stock analyst named Raymond Dirks. Dirks had been instrumental in uncovering the Equity Funding scandal, but had tipped clients to his disclosures before he made them. Equity Funding went into receivership as a result of the fraud allegations made by Dirks, and Dirks was subsequently charged by the SEC with violations of Rule 10-b-5. (He was never charged with criminal violations, however.) What alarmed Richards about the case was that Solicitor General Rex E. Lee, appointed by President Reagan, had done an about-face and repudiated the Justice Department's previous policy of supporting the SEC in the case. Instead, the Justice Department filed a brief supporting Dirks, and the SEC, ordinarily represented in the Supreme Court by the Justice Department, had to send its own counsel to argue the case. The SEC lawyers had been outraged.

"Rex Lee was certainly no friend of insider prosecution," Richards says. And, despite the law-and-order rhetoric of the Reagan administration, "We did not find him to be very pro–law enforcement, especially in white-collar crime cases." And Lee's office would have to sign off on any appeal in the Newman case.

In order to counteract what was believed would be hostility to the appeal from Lee, Martin made sure that Jensen, the head of the Criminal Division, and the SEC knew about the case and its dismissal at the district court level. According to the Assistant Solicitor General who eventually handled the case, the issue of whether to appeal came up at one of the Attorney General's morning meetings. "This is pretty unusual—only if a case raises significant policy issues does the Attorney General get involved," he recalls. The SEC presented its "keen interest" in the case—the chief of SEC enforcement had publicly announced his interest in curbing insider trading—and Jensen was anxious to avoid the unfavorable publicity that had followed the Justice Department's position in Dirks. In addition, there were very real differences between the Dirks and Newman cases. Dirks hadn't personally traded based on his information, nor had he directly profited from it. Jensen supported the appeal. If Solicitor General Lee had any real opposition to the appeal, he didn't have a chance to press his position before the decision was essentially made to approve the appeal. Shortly after, word reached Martin that the Justice Department had given the green light, and would support Richards's theory of the case, to the Supreme Court if necessary.

Within a month and a half, the oral argument was repeated before a packed courtroom and a panel of Second Circuit judges. But this time, Richards wasn't allowed to argue the case. He was deeply disappointed, since he was desperately anxious to vindicate his earlier performance. But he had acceded to Martin's insistence that the highly visible case required his personal attention. At least, Richards reasoned, the case was being taken seriously in the office and was deemed important in Washington.

The appellate judges gave no indication of their sentiments the day of the argument; if anything, Richards thought they had been fairly tough in their questioning of Martin. Several weeks later, Richards was questioning an important witness in another case in his office when the phone rang. It was the appellate court clerk with the news that the Second Circuit had reversed Judge Haight, reinstating Richards's indictment. "I leaped. I screamed. Then I asked her to repeat the message," Richards recalls. "The witness must have thought I was crazy."

When Richards received a copy of the court's full opinion, he felt completely vindicated. "We need spend little time on the issue of fraud and deceit," the court wrote, noting that the defendant "misappropriated—stole to put it bluntly—valuable nonpublic information entrusted to him in the utmost confidence." The court added that Rule 10-b-5's proscription of "fraudulent and deceptive practices upon any person in connection with the purchase or sale of a security provided clear notice to appellee that this fraudulent conduct was unlawful." The only roadblock to trial now was a possible petition for certiorari to the Supreme Court. But Newman's lawyer decided against it—he didn't want to risk an adverse opinion at a time when the Supreme Court would have to assume that the facts the government alleged were true.

Richards plunged into preparation for trial. Unlike large law firms, where teams of attorneys prepare a case for trial, Richards had only himself and Clifton, his chief investigator. And it was a factually complex case, requiring detailed information about nineteen separate, complicated take-over deals. "It was an awesome task," Richards recalls, "and I worried that I didn't know enough."

The trial itself began in April and lasted five weeks, almost all of it the government's case. Richards began with a witness from Morgan Stanley, Joseph Fogg, the distinguished head of the firm's mergers and acquisitions area. Richards felt shaky, and says "the pressure seemed overwhelming." But Fogg did much of his work for him, outraged by the defense cross-examination, which tried to make the point that investment bankers routinely leak highly confidential information to their most important clients.

Steinberg, the first of those involved in the scheme to be immunized, was an early witness, and Richards found him to be difficult. Richards feels that "he was cooperating more with Newman than he was with the government." After all, Newman had generated enormous profits for Steinberg.

Finally came Richards's star witness, Antoniu, freshly chastened and once again cooperative as a result of the Second Circuit's reversal. Richards's principal challenge with Antoniu was to establish his credibility. To do so, he engaged in a maneuver that prosecutors call "pulling the teeth" of the defense case. Richards himself questioned Antoniu about his failure to divulge the names of everyone he tipped even after having been granted immunity, trying to put it in the best possible light, letting Antoniu say that he was just being loyal to a friend. Richards thought Antoniu seemed calm and collected; he occasionally had to be asked to raise his voice so the jury could hear.

But Antoniu did offer one piece of testimony that came as a surprise to Richards—the recollection that Newman had told him that the "worst that could happen" in this kind of case was a "slap on the hand." Richards was alarmed, worried that the statement was evidence that Newman didn't realize he was committing a crime. But he pressed forward, and felt that Antoniu handled himself well during cross-examination.

Richards held one witness in reserve. Marc Glassman had been present at one meeting with both Antoniu and Newman where the scheme was discussed, and as a result, was the one other person besides Antoniu who could provide direct evidence of the flow of information from Antoniu to Newman. If necessary, Richards planned to call Glassman in his rebuttal case, after the defense witness testified.

The defensive case was anticlimactic. It consisted of only one witness, an expert who talked about the wide diffusion of inside information in the marketplace. Richards felt it did nothing to hurt his case. Newman himself never took the stand in his own defense, and, in reality, most facts of the case were never in serious dispute. Aside from the legal issues, the real questions were over more subtle nuances of knowledge and intent. Richards decided it wasn't necessary to call Glassman to the stand.

Both lawyers focused on these points in their closing arguments to the jury, and, curiously, both seized upon Antoniu's testimony about the "slap on the hand" to support their contentions. Velie argued that it showed they had no awareness of potential criminal liability; Richards, in turn, argued that by comparing their actions to serious crimes, they acknowledged that their own behavior was criminal.

The jury deliberated for a day and a half, a nerve-racking period for Richards, Velie, and, of course, Newman. Over the years, Richards felt he'd learned to read the clues from a jury. This time, the jury asked to have its instruction on the "alleged mail fraud" charge reread. Richards knew of another trial in which the jury had also asked for an "alleged" charge to be reread, and then had acquitted the defendant. "This convinced me we'd lost," Richards recalls. But when the jurors filed in and announced the verdict, it was guilty on all counts.

There was dead silence in the courtroom. Richards wanted to turn around to see Newman, who was sitting behind him, but he didn't. "I didn't want to be jubilant—I think it's inappropriate," he says. "It's a solemn, trying moment." Nonetheless, he says, "I felt exquisite relief."

BY the summer of 1983, much of the personnel in the Southern District office had changed. But despite Newman's conviction, the Morgan Stanley case dragged on.

Martin was replaced by Giuliani. After the trial, Lee Richards resigned to start his own firm, Grais & Richards. He could have parlayed his success in the Newman case into a lucrative position in a large firm, but like many Assistant U.S. Attorneys, he'd found the experience of running his own cases and having so much responsibility at an early age made him impatient with the team efforts and slow advancement that are the norm in large firms.

In some ways, however, the Morgan Stanley case had come full circle, since Larry Pedowitz—the prosecutor who began the investigation—had taken a leave of absence from Wachtell, Lipton in order to return as head of the criminal division of the U.S. Attorney's office under Giuliani. He was still keenly interested in wrapping up the case, although day-to-day responsibility for it was assigned to Peter Romatowski, a young assistant. Romatowski plunged into the case, even though he felt a bit peculiar about it—it was the first case where he actually knew one of the principal defendants, albeit slightly. Courtois's Colombian wife had been a Harvard classmate of his.

The major loose threads in the case were Courtois and the other foreign defendants, but progress had slowly been made. Only Luxembourg had proved to be a dead end. It refused to extradite Carniol on the grounds the Luxembourg law doesn't recognize insider trading as a crime. Switzerland had finally agreed to turn over various bank records, and as pressure mounted on Spyropoulos, who had fled to Greece, he finally capitulated. He returned to the U.S. and quietly entered a guilty plea.

Courtois had still eluded the prosecutors, although they had come close. While Courtois's wife's uncle remained president of Colombia, the extradition request had made no headway. But then he was defeated. Soon after, the request was granted, and Courtois was actually arrested and spent thirty days in a Colombian jail. But for reasons that are still unclear, he was released by the Colombian authorities and disappeared.

He soon learned, however, how difficult the life of a fugitive can be. Courtois returned to Canada, apparently because his wife needed sophisticated medical treatment unavailable in Colombia. He was arrested by Canadian police when he tried to renew his Canadian passport at a passport office in Toronto.

When Romatowski learned of Courtois's arrest, he called Courtois's lawyer and laid out a picture of the evidence that had been amassed against Courtois. Not only was there the damaging testimony of Antoniu, but the investigators had pieced together the elaborate trading scheme Courtois had created using records obtained from the Swiss and information about the Panamanian branch of the Union Bank of Switzerland, through which Courtois had traded, using an accomplice, Marcello Leon. Much to Romatowski's amazement, Courtois had continued trading on inside information taken from Morgan Stanley a full year after the SEC first called Antoniu. He used inside information about nine deals in addition to those he leaked to Antoniu.

But it seemed Courtois was intent on entangling himself even further in the web of lies he'd already spun. He argued that Antoniu had falsely accused him in order to protect his true source at Morgan Stanley, knowing that since Courtois was in Colombia, "I might not ever have an opportunity to defend" the charges. He claimed he "didn't need" Antoniu, because his wealthy father would give him "$50,000, $100,000, or $150,000" if he asked. Besides, he said, Antoniu was "very pushy" and a "social climber." Courtois's lawyer also made the point that Newman's conviction might yet be overturned on appeal.

That possibility soon evaporated. Following Newman's conviction, his lawyer, Velie, had appealed again to the Second Circuit, making many of the same arguments that had been made in his earlier motion to dismiss. Predictably, the Second Circuit again ruled that the indictment was sound and that the conviction was valid. This time Newman took his case to the Supreme Court and sought certiorari, though without the assistance of Velie. Apparently disenchanted, he replaced Velie with the prominent Washington firm of Wilmer, Cutler & Pickering. The prosecutors realized there was a reasonable chance the Supreme Court would review the case, despite their disclaimers that it was never intended as a test case. As promised, the Solicitor General filed a brief supporting the government's position that the Supreme Court should deny certiorari.

In October, the government's view prevailed. When the Supreme Court issued its list of the cases it would review that term, Newman's wasn't on it. That meant that his conviction stood, and that the government's misappropriation theory of the case, while not explicitly sanctioned by the Supreme Court, could be used in future prosecutions of insider trading.

The Supreme Court's decision not to hear the case gave Courtois an impetus to settle, and negotiations began again between him, his counsel, and Romatowski. But they made little progress, principally because Romatowski wouldn't give Courtois any guarantees about his potential sentence if he pleaded guilty. Prosecutors in the Southern District, in fact, aren't allowed to bargain for sentences.

Then Judge Haight urged at a pretrial conference that Romatowski waive the no-bargaining rule in this particular case. The judge felt it would be a waste of everyone's time and resources to litigate a case that was really no longer in dispute. So, with Giuliani's consent, Romatowski offered Courtois four years in jail and a $150,000 fine. Courtis rejected the offer, and it looked as if the trial would go forward.

On the eve of the trial, however, Courtois did an about-face and agreed to plead guilty to conspiracy and four counts of criminal fraud. In return the government agreed not to prosecute him for any other offenses committed in the course of the scheme. No sentencing promises were made. In a sworn statement to the prosecutors, Courtis finally admitted his role in the conspiracy and the full scope of his involvement.

The following year, Pedowitz, Richards, and Romatowski attended the annual reunion of the Southern District Assistant U.S. Attorneys. For the last ten years, the prosecutors involved in Morgan Stanley had joked about the agonizingly slow progress of the case. This year, they had a successful conclusion to celebrate—and toasted their mutual efforts for the last time.

THE prosecutors' efforts had a devastating impact on the lives of the defendants. Newman served thirteen months in a federal penitentiary and is barred from the securities business. Courtois served a year in prison, and is similarly barred from pursuing his once-promising investment banking career. He also paid fines of more than $150,000, although the prosecutors believe he made off with about $300,000 in additional profits from his insider trading. Neither their lawyers nor the prosecutors know the current whereabouts of either man, although Courtois is believed to be in Canada.

Despite his cooperation, Antoniu too was sentenced to a year in prison. As his incarceration approached, however, the prospect seemed to terrify him, and his lawyer feared that his lithe good looks would make him an immediate target of sexual molestation. Antoniu sank into a deep depression and his lawyer presented psychiatric testimony that he was suicidal. As a result, and principally because of his cooperation with the government, Judge Haight lifted Antoniu's prison sentence and placed him on probation. Antoniu returned all of his illicit profits and was left practically penniless.

Antoniu enjoyed one further moment of notoriety. In 1984, his former wife, Francesca Stanfill, wrote a novel describing characters and a series of events strikingly similar to her relationship with Antoniu, a point made by many reviewers. The book made clear that Francesca's bitterness hadn't subsided, and an angry Antoniu responded with a libel suit. In his suit, Antoniu demonstrated a peculiarly revisionist view of the entire matter: he claimed his marriage to Francesca failed because he wouldn't convert to Roman Catholicism, a claim that prompted considerable scoffing at the U.S. Attorney's office.

The lawsuit was eventually dismissed by mutual consent of Antoniu and Stanfill. Prominent libel lawyer Floyd Abrams, who represented Stanfill in the case, says Antoniu's allegations were "utterly preposterous." Nonetheless, he says Stanfill agreed to a "nominal payment" in order to get Antoniu to drop the case. At the time, Antoniu was working as a "consultant" to a small Minneapolis investment banking concern.

But part of the impact of the case wasn't so much on those individuals convicted, but on the people who now may never be convicted because they decide not to commit a crime—those who are deterred. It is this broad, social impact, many prosecutors say, that leavens the work of sending people to prison and that gives them their greatest satisfaction.

As Romatowski wrote in the sentencing memorandum he prepared in the case, the nature of the crime called for prison terms and meaningful penalities for Newman, Antoniu, and Courtois.

At least five members of the Harvard Business School class of 1972, equipped by their education and background with every advantage for succeeding in the legitimate business world, nevertheless chose to play a role in a criminal scheme. Sheer greed is one of the reasons for their gamble. But in view of their actual and potential salaries, business op-

portunities, and as Courtois pointed out in his own case, family resources, the question lingers: what else draws people of such means to
become traffickers in stolen goods?

The explanation for such persons' involvement . . . must lie in part in
the lack of a public perception of a meaningful penalty for this type of
conduct. Many of the persons involved in this particular case have at
least one characteristic in common: by training and experience, they are
consummate risk evaluators, who weight carefully the benefits against
the potential adverse consequences before acting. For Courtois and his
friends, some of whom took their chances for relatively modest gains,
the risks must have seemed small indeed.

But not everyone is deterred. In March 1984, Romatowski, recently
promoted to head the securities fraud unit, learned from the SEC that
a trading ring based on leaks from inside *The Wall Street Journal* seemed
to be flourishing. The scheme apparently involved a *Journal* reporter,
a top broker at Kidder, Peabody & Company and a Manhattan lawyer. Several months later, Romatowski obtained indictments against
R. Foster Winans, a *Wall Street Journal* reporter who wrote the paper's
"Heard on the Street" column, and obtained a guilty plea from Peter
Brant, the Kidder, Peabody broker, triggering another major scandal
on Wall Street. Winans was later convicted, and the Supreme Court
agreed to review the case.

AND the Winans case proved to be just a prelude to the biggest
scandal in Wall Street's history. In May 1986, Dennis B. Levine, an
investment banker at Drexel Burnham Lambert Inc., was charged
with reaping more than $12 million in profits from unlawful insider
trading. He in turn implicated arbitrager Ivan F. Boesky, who agreed
to plead guilty and settle SEC charges by paying $100 million, the
largest fine in the agency's history. The scandal quickly spread to
some of Wall Street's largest and most powerful firms, including
Drexel; Goldman Sachs & Co.; and Kidder, Peabody & Co.

Increasingly, insider trading seemed like a cancer that had spread
throughout Wall Street. And when government prosecutors were
asked for the legal precedent to support their massive crackdown, they
invariably cited one case: *United States* v. *Newman*.

Giuliani's response to his office's success in wrapping up the

Newman case was predictable: he called a press conference. He later became even more visible in the insider trading area. The arrest of Levine, the charges against Boesky and their subsequent guilty pleas established Giuliani in the public mind as the most effective prosecutor of insider trading ever.

If some of his colleagues, such as Richards and Pedowitz, felt the credit for the Newman case should have been shared more equitably, they didn't say so publicly. Within the office, however, there was considerable grumbling about Giuliani emerging as a champion of white-collar fraud prosecution.

In fact, Giuliani, shortly after taking office, had cut back the manpower devoted to fraud prosecutions from about ten full-time assistants to five, saying he wanted to devote more resources to the Mafia and drugs. "Even back when Giuliani was an assistant in the office," recalls one former assistant, "he wasn't that interested in white collar."

But then Giuliani learned that *The New York Times* was preparing a profile of him, and the *Times* reporter was asking questions about the new U.S. Attorney's dedication to prosecuting white-collar fraud cases. Suddenly Giuliani restored the fraud unit to its previous strength. After *The New York Times* piece—a typically glowing profile—the unit was again cut back to five prosecutors. "He didn't even wait a decent interval," says a former assistant.

Giuliani acknowledges that he reduced the size of the fraud unit and later increased it, but says that had nothing to do with the profile in *The New York Times*. "When I arrived in the office, I had to assess where the emergencies were," he says. "Organized crime and corruption were the areas where we had the worst problems. I put the brightest people we had in those areas. We had to be aggressive. As soon as I was able to hire more assistants, we restored all the people to the fraud unit." He says the timing of the *Times* article was coincidental, and says the personnel shift had nothing to do with his own commitment to fight white-collar crime. "We've prosecuted more white-collar criminals in this office than ever before," he says.

During the early stages of Giuliani's tenure as U.S. Attorney, there was much more for the assistants in the office to worry about than publicity. Despite the enthusiasm within the Justice Department, not everyone had been pleased when it was announced that Giuliani would be moving to New York to become the U.S. Attorney. For JoAnn Harris, the former head of the Fraud Section in Washington who had clashed with Giuliani over the McDonnell Douglas case and over his treatment of Lubin and Mendelson, Giuliani's decision to come to New York was a nightmare.

Harris, after deciding she had to leave the Reagan administration, had been appointed by Martin as a prosecutor in the Southern District. Harris had returned to New York in large part to get away from Giuliani. Now, once again, he would be her boss.

Harris had no way of knowing how the flap over McDonnell Douglas would hurt her career.

At the time Harris decided to leave Washington, she had made no secret of the fact that a cherished dream of hers was to enter the judiciary. The Deputy Attorney General asked her to give him a list of names of people she felt would be outstanding candidates for judgeships, and she gave him a list that included her own name. Unfortunately for her, she also had made no secret of her feelings about Giuliani's handling of the McDonnell Douglas matter and what she deemed his childish behavior toward Lubin and Mendelson. Word of her attitude had inevitably reached Giuliani, for whom loyalty was always a paramount virtue.

Others in the Justice Department at the time of Harris's resignation felt that she was an ideal candidate for a federal judgeship. Most importantly, she was competent. She had trial experience, she had dealt with sophisticated business and financial cases, and she was dedicated to her work. From a political standpoint, she was even better. She was a woman, and the Reagan administration had launched a drive to shore up its political support among women—a glaring weak spot in the otherwise remarkable popularity of the President. It was a drive that would culminate in the appointment of Sandra Day O'Connor to the Supreme Court. And Harris had an even more unusual characteristic: her husband is black.

Says one member of the Justice Department's Office of Policy Planning who served on the committee that proposed names for federal judgeships: "JoAnn Harris was almost unbelievably desirable. She is experienced and competent. She is a woman. She's married to a black. In one appointment, you blunt criticism from the two groups most hostile to the Republican Party: women and minorities. We were enthusiastic about her appointment, and saw it as an unusual political opportunity."

Harris's nomination, however, was vetoed. When committee members asked why, they were told that Giuliani had forbidden her appointment. While Giuliani had no formal authority over judicial appointments, his position was such that no appointments would be made over his strenuous opposition.

One lawyer involved in the judicial selection process recalls that Harris was on a "short list" of finalists for a federal judgeship. Soon after that list was prepared, however, the department official circulating the list for comment said Harris had been rejected. Asked why, the official said, "Rudi Giuliani told me she was a lib," meaning she was too liberal.

Some time later, the Justice Department began preparing a talent bank of potential judges for future appointments. Again, Harris's name was included on the list and, again, it was deleted after the list circulated within the department. The lawyer asked why, and this time was told by the previous official's successor that "Rudi hates her."

Giuliani, however, says he doesn't recall being asked for an opinion about Harris and doesn't recall that she was even under consideration for a federal judgeship. "I disagreed with her judgment at times, but these things happen. I don't resent JoAnn."

Although no federal judgeship had materialized, Harris was so busy working for Martin in New York that she didn't have time to be disappointed. She headed up the complex and difficult tax evasion prosecution of the Reverend Sun Myung Moon, a case that raised unusual church and state issues. Her success in that case was particularly satisfying since Moon had some of the best defense lawyers in the country, including Harvard law professor Laurence Tribe. At the time Giuliani was selected as U.S. Attorney, she was busy on litigation involving Westway, a controversial proposed highway for the West Side of Manhattan. Harris's success was such that she was named Martin's executive assistant.

That, she knew, would be coming to an end with the arrival of Giuliani. The transition period—the time when Giuliani had been named but hadn't yet come to New York—indicated to Harris how impossible her position had become. One of her responsibilities was hiring new assistant U.S. Attorneys. A number of new people had been given job offers, and others were being interviewed. Giuliani insisted on reviewing the offers outstanding, then did nothing. "He just sat on them," says one assistant. "He wouldn't approve Harris's choices. Martin was furious."

Harris finally threw in the towel and resigned. Martin offered her a position with his firm, where he was returning after his own resignation. Eventually she left there to form her own firm and to teach. Mendelson, Lubin, and now Harris—those who had crossed Giuliani in McDonnell Douglas—had all left government service.

By the time Giuliani actually arrived on the scene in New York, morale in the office was low. Harris was a respected, popular figure and her departure was a blow to the office. But there was worse to come.

SHIRAH Neiman, a prosecutor in the office for twelve years and the head of one of two major crime units, first learned that her unit was being merged out of existence. Then she was unceremoniously transferred to litigation counsel at a staff meeting where, according to those present, Giuliani conspicuously failed to praise her for her previous work. Gene Kaplan, a veteran deputy chief, was demoted and left soon after. And there were others.

Everyone expected some personnel changes with a change at the top, but a transition had never been like this. The office had always been collegial and nonpartisan: Giuliani's actions violated an unspoken code. Moreover, "There are ways of doing what Giuliani did gracefully," says one assistant. "We'd hear the rumors that somebody was out for weeks. By the time there was a memo or announcement, it was established fact. The person being fired was usually the last to know. Rudi's hatchet was bloody."

During this period, Larry Pedowitz, who had returned to head the criminal division, did much to ease the tension and anxiety. Giuliani recognized his contributions and importance to the office, and included him among his inner circle of advisers. "Larry Pedowitz was a saint," says one assistant. In one instance, an assistant who had to stay in the office longer than expected because of the demands of his cases, and who had been hoping to enter private practice to earn more money, complained about the financial hardship on his family. Pedowitz offered him a loan from his own savings. "Pedowitz had made a lot of money at Wachtell, and he knew he'd be making even more when he went back," explains a colleague.

But the unusually good judgment Giuliani displayed with Pedowitz wasn't consistently applied, prosecutors say. "Loyalty to Rudi was the supreme test," says one. Caruso, Giuliani's top aide in Washington, hadn't stayed with him in the U.S. Attorney's office, opting instead to join Shearman & Sterling, a prestigious Wall Street law firm. But he was easily replaced by a team viewed by many in the office as so sycophantic that its members were dubbed the "Yesrudi's" (Yes, Rudi), pronounced with a southern slave accent.

Foremost among these—and the most irritating to some of the rank and file—was Jane Parver, a prosecutor who replaced JoAnn Harris as the executive assistant. While indisputably intelligent, Parver, say some of her colleagues, managed to be rude, brash, and aggressive at the same time she was imperious and high-handed. She was fond of ordering other lawyers in the office to "make a note of it," as though they were her secretaries. Her attitude enraged some defense counsel who had to deal with the office. Giuliani seemed to love it. She became one of his closest advisers. In the view of most lawyers in the office, she told him everything going on in the office that she knew about.

It was, therefore, a further blow to morale when Parver began having an affair with Pedowitz, who had separated from his wife. "We all thought that Larry had the greatest judgment in the world, and then he went off and did this. It was bad enough that the head of the criminal section would have an affair with a section chief. But he also took up with the least popular woman in the office, who was a pipeline to Giuliani," says one assistant.

Pedowitz denies that the relationship had anything to do with his work. "It had absolutely nothing to do with any case I worked on, or my professional life," he says. He also disagrees with those in the office who dislike Parver. "I admire her as a person. She's a wonderful lawyer," he says.

Giuliani says "Parver is a genius," but acknowledges there were others in the office who clashed with her. "There was a lot of anger and jealousy," he says. "That was unfortunate."

The work of the office went on. "Thank God, these people are so competent and so professional that nothing really interfered with their work in court," says Harris. But morale suffered badly.

Nor were personal clashes confined to the U.S. Attorney's office. Giuliani wasted no time before tangling with the most powerful and respected figure in New York prosecution: Robert Morgenthau, the Manhattan District Attorney, and a former U.S. Attorney himself. The setting for what would become a fierce and enduring rivalry was New York's most sensational murder case of the year.

THE CBS MURDERS

THE piers of Manhattan that once berthed great ocean liners are gradually disappearing, many of them crumbling into decay or being converted to other uses. Pier 92, where West 54th Street meets the Hudson River, is now a multi-tier parking lot. It is especially convenient for employees of CBS News, which has its studio complex just around the corner on West 57th Street.

Angelo Sticca, a soft-spoken man in his late fifties who worked as an engineer with CBS's construction department, parked his car there. On April 12, 1982, he got off work a little later than usual, about 5:45 P.M., and hurried to catch up with three of his colleagues, all CBS technicians who parked their cars in the same area. His friends got to the pier before he did, but as they neared the area on the top deck, reserved for monthly parking, where they kept their cars, Sticca was only about twenty-five feet behind. He could hear them talking and laughing.

Suddenly, Sticca heard something else, a sharp noise—like "metal snapping," he later said. He looked south, in the direction of the sound, and could see the Manhattan ship passenger terminal in the background, one pier to the south. Silhouetted in the glow of a Hudson River sunset was what looked like a white van. Sticca saw a man dragging what looked like the body of a woman around the front of the vehicle, then the figures disappeared from view.

One of Sticca's colleagues, Leo Kuranuki, went toward the van. "What's going on?" he asked as he rounded the front of the van. "You didn't see nothing, did you?" a man's voice answered.

Sticca suddenly felt uneasy. Something about the answer—the tone perhaps—was chilling, even terrifying. He decided to get to his car right away. Probably this was just some squabble between a guy and his girl friend, and the others would take care of it. If not, Sticca didn't want to be there.

As he reached his car on the north side of the pier, Sticca looked back. There was the man again, now on the other side of the van, struggling with one of his friends from CBS, Robert Schulze. As Sticca watched in horror, the man pulled out a long-barreled handgun and held it directly against Schulze's skull. Sticca heard a short whistling sound. Then Schulze crumpled to the pavement.

Sticca panicked. He jumped into his car, started it, and put it into reverse. He was terrified the gunman would spot him, make eye contact, realize there was another eyewitness, and shoot to kill. As he backed out of his parking space, he saw the gunman grappling with the third of his companions, Edward Benford.

Sticca raced his car down the ramp from the third level to the street level, but the van was soon in close pursuit. Sticca pulled into traffic, managing to maneuver in front of another car. To his immense relief, the van turned right onto 12th Avenue, heading south. Sticca rushed back to the pier.

There, lying in small pools of blood, were the bodies of his three colleagues. Each had been shot once in the head.

New York, a city accustomed to violent crime, was rocked by what were quickly dubbed the "CBS murders." The killings seemed senseless, random. No motive could be discerned. Millions of New Yorkers use the city's parking lots every day. It seemed as though it could have happened to any of them.

Sticca vanished from public view. His identity was withheld. Because he was the sole eyewitness, police worried that his life was now in serious danger.

WHEN Allen Sullivan's phone rang at eleven-thirty the morning after the CBS killings and he heard the voice of Roger Hayes on the line, Sullivan groaned to himself. Hayes was chief of the trial division in the D.A.'s office, with responsibility for assigning new cases, and as soon as Sullivan had heard about the murders, he realized he was a likely candidate. And he was already working at near capacity on some of the office's most visible cases.

Sullivan was, in fact, the office's star homicide prosecutor. When John Lennon was shot outside the Dakota apartment building on Manhattan's Upper West Side, it was Sullivan who was dispatched to the 20th Precinct to oversee the investigation. He later prosecuted Mark David Chapman, Lennon's killer. He had recently handled the extradition to Utah of Mark Schreuder, the young man hired by his mother to murder his grandfather, a case that formed the basis for two nonfiction books and two made-for-TV movies. He had been working eighteen-hour days, six- and seven-day weeks, for the last six months. And his premonition was correct: Hayes wanted him for the CBS murders.

Sullivan's appearance and demeanor belie the image of the hard-driving homicide prosecutor. He is tall, wears glasses, and his light-colored hair is streaked with gray. His manner could be described as deliberative if he displayed a bit more animation. He has been known to punctuate his own discourses with occasional yawns. Says one assistant who worked closely with him, "He's so slow-moving there were times I thought I'd die." The night of the Lennon killing, frantic policemen dashed in and out of the office Sullivan occupied in the precinct house. Sullivan himself sat quietly, sipping a cup of tea.

Sullivan's demeanor has worked to his advantage as a prosecutor. His slowness, colleagues say, masks a sharp and quick mind. He is methodical nearly to a fault. But most importantly, he exudes credibility. Juries—and everyone else, for that matter—find it nearly impossible to disbelieve him. Sullivan seems far more like the Appalachian social worker he thought he was going to become than the top homicide prosecutor in the toughest district in the country.

When Sullivan graduated from the University of Wisconsin Law School in 1967, "The thought of being a prosecutor hadn't entered my mind," he says. He'd already accepted a job with an Organization of Economic Opportunity–funded group called Appalachian volunteers, based in eastern Kentucky, where he planned to do both legal and social services work for the poor. But he took the New York bar examination and discovered that it would be nearly a year before the tests were graded and he could become a member of the bar. To support himself during that interim period, he took a job with the D.A.'s office after being told that much of his work would be insuring that individual rights were protected. He spent his summer vacation doing volunteer work in eastern Kentucky.

It took the CBS murders to get him back to Kentucky. He found himself more and more absorbed by his work in the D.A.'s office, and after passing the bar, he stayed on. In 1970 he was assigned to the homicide bureau, since absorbed into the general trial bureau, where he had responsibility for cases from their inception. By April 1982, when he got the call from Hayes, Sullivan had more homicide experience than any other prosecutor in the office.

Besides giving him the assignment, Hayes told Sullivan there had been another development that morning that might be linked to the CBS murders. A surrealist painter had returned from his job as a part-time bartender at around 4:30 A.M. and took his dog out for a walk. He unleashed the dog, which quickly sniffed out what the painter at first thought was garbage. It turned out to be a woman's body, dumped just a block from the D.A.'s office. A triple murder now looked like it might be a quadruple murder, since an eyewitness had seen a woman's body being dragged into a van on the pier where the CBS technicians were shot.

Sullivan left immediately for the midtown north precinct station, where the investigation was being directed. More than thirty police detectives were working on the case, which had been assigned top priority within the police department. He was briefed by detectives Richard Chartrand and Richard Gallagher, who revealed some key information that had already been discovered.

At the pier itself, Chartrand had discovered a single .22 caliber shell casing next to each of the victims. There was indeed an eyewitness to the murders who provided an account of events on the pier the previous night. Unfortunately, the witness had said he'd doubted he could identify the killer; he had avoided looking at the man's face for fear that he would be recognized as a witness and pursued. However, he was able to describe the van in detail: he said it was a light-colored van with maroon or purple upper paneling. Sullivan was pleased there was an eyewitness, but initially dismayed that he wouldn't be able to identify the man who had pulled the trigger. That meant any future prosecutions would be purely circumstantial cases. Although circumstantial evidence played a role in most of his murder cases, Sullivan had never before obtained a murder conviction in a case built entirely on circumstantial evidence. He recognized that he and the police would have their work cut out for them.

The woman discovered that morning, Chartrand continued, was named Margaret Barbera, and she was almost certainly the woman whose body the eyewitness had seen being dragged into the van. It seemed plausible, though far from certain, that the CBS technicians were killed simply because they stumbled on the killing of Barbera.

Sullivan and the detectives decided to focus their initial efforts on that hunch by trying to learn everything they could as quickly as possible about Barbera. They also ordered that the records of the parking lot be obtained and scrutinized for clues relating to Barbera, the van, the van's owner, and patterns of their arrivals and departures. Sullivan wrote countless subpoenas enabling the police to have access to documents and records. During the next few days, an enormous amount of information poured into the precinct house. The disclosures about Barbera were particularly revealing.

After her body was discovered, the FBI had been routinely notified and had checked its records. Barbera, they discovered, was a key figure in an ongoing investigation into a diamond-district concern called the Candor Diamond Company. The previous August, Candor had filed for bankruptcy, the victim of a spiraling scheme in which fictitious invoices were sold to a factoring concern; those invoices were paid for with still more fictitious invoices. The fraud had gone on for a year, and Barbera was Candor's bookkeeper.

The head of Candor was Irwin Margolies, a fat, balding man who led the flamboyant life-style of the successful diamond merchant. His puffy fingers dripped with diamond rings; he took lavish trips abroad; he gave each of his children a new Porsche—all, apparently, with the proceeds of his factoring scheme.

Under questioning by federal authorities after the bankruptcy, Margolies had blamed everything on Barbera. He had become so suspicious of her, he said, that he had her followed by a private detective. What Margolies learned, and what the FBI later corroborated, indicated that Barbera was an unusual woman, to put it mildly. Chartrand filled Sullivan in on the details.

Attractive, independent, and bright, Barbera nonetheless fostered the illusion that she was dying of cancer. She worked at Candor at night, she had said, because her days were occupied with radiation therapy. She went so far as to have friends drop her off and pick her up at the Sloan-Kettering cancer institute in Manhattan; other times she drove herself there in her late-model BMW. But Barbera's name didn't appear in any of Sloan-Kettering's patient records.

Some, such as Margolies, were skeptical about Barbera's condition. But not the woman who rapidly became her best friend, Jenny Soo Chin. Chin, convinced that Barbera was dying, became her nearly inseparable companion. Barbera hired Chin as her personal assistant at Candor.

Despite Barbera's willingness to lie about her medical condition, the FBI had come to believe the important aspects of Barbera's version of the Candor fraud, which portrayed Margolies as the mastermind. Eventually, Barbera had agreed to cooperate and appear as a witness against Margolies. In return, she had pleaded guilty to a lesser charge. But the investigation into the tangled affairs of Candor languished in the Manhattan U.S. Attorney's office. Margolies was neither arrested nor indicted.

As soon as Sullivan learned that one of the murder victims was scheduled to be a witness in a federal case, he notified U.S. Attorney John Martin, who assigned an assistant to the case and several FBI agents. Sullivan recognized that there would soon be a tug-of-war with the federal authorities over who would take charge of the case, but for the time being, the D.A. and the U.S. Attorney agreed that it would be a joint investigation.

Sullivan was also intrigued by the relationship between Barbera and Jenny Soo Chin. For Chin, it was quickly learned from computerized police records, had disappeared in suspicious circumstances the previous January. Chin's car was found abandoned near the Lincoln Tunnel. Despite the blood-soaked upholstery, it was being used by prostitutes in the neighborhood whose clients were apparently New Jersey commuters. The case had been assigned to the 104th Precinct in Queens, but little effort was made and Chin's fate was still a mystery. However, Sullivan immediately recognized one piece of possibly significant evidence: in searching Chin's car, police had found a .22 caliber shell casing, just like the ones on the pier.

Barbera, too, had feared that Chin's disappearance was murder and was linked to the federal investigation of Margolies. Soon after Chin vanished, Barbera told the assistant U.S. Attorney in charge of the case, Stephen Schlessinger, that she was terrified and, as a cooperating witness, asked for police protection. Her request had been denied.

Meanwhile, detectives pored over documents obtained from the parking facility, and there too Sullivan found some intriguing leads.

Police officers had interviewed employees of the parking facility immediately after the killings and learned that the area of the murders was reserved for monthly parking leases. So they obtained copies of all the monthly leases. Margaret Barbera's was among them. Applications for leases included vehicle descriptions, so the police scrutinized those to determine whether there were any vans owned by monthly parkers. There had turned out to be three, two of which could be quickly eliminated. The third looked suspicious: a gray van owned by Donald Nash.

The lease application signed by Nash indicated that he had submitted the application on April 6, just a week before the murders and five days after Barbera submitted her parking application. He had written a false license-plate number on the application after crossing out what turned out to be the license number actually issued to the van. His business and address—Rubin Construction at 436 West 45th Street—seemed to be false. Police found no sign of the business at that address and neighbors knew nothing about anyone named Donald Nash.

Police also sifted through heaps of daily parking tickets collected from the monthly parkers, painstakingly piecing together a record of Barbera's and Nash's comings and goings at the lot. On several days, Nash arrived at the lot shortly after Barbera or left the lot soon after she departed. Even more significantly, despite paying for a month of parking, Nash hadn't returned to the lot after the evening of the murders.

Sullivan was deeply suspicious of Nash within three days of taking on the case, but the mystery was far from solved. Who was Nash? What possible motive might he have? Had he any connection to Candor or Jenny Soo Chin? The questions raced through his mind as the focus of the investigation shifted to Nash.

There was considerable information about Nash, it turned out, already in the police records. He'd served two jail sentences; he'd recently been arrested for forging a Manhattan taxi medallion and running an illegal taxi service. In fact, he had pleaded guilty to a misdemeanor charge for the offense and had been scheduled to appear for sentencing on April 13, the day after the murders. He didn't show up.

The next day, a routine examination of FBI license-plate records turned up another clue. The Queens neighborhood where Barbera lived had been under surveillance by the FBI during March for reasons that had nothing to do with Candor or the CBS killings. An FBI agent had noted the license numbers of vehicles that were parked for any significant amount of time in the area. One of those license numbers was that of Nash's van, parked only a block from Barbera's apartment building. With the evidence from the parking lot, it looked as if Nash was following Barbera. On April 17, five days after the murders, the FBI began twenty-four-hour surveillance of Nash.

Sullivan spent the weekend in the midtown precinct office, continuing to examine documents and ticket stubs, and he received regular reports from the three teams of FBI agents who, in rotation, were shadowing Nash.

The agents started at Nash's house in Keansburg, New Jersey. During the day, Nash and a young man later identified as his nephew Thomas Dane shopped for camping equipment. Then Dane drove Nash to a long-term parking lot at Newark International Airport. Shortly after, the FBI agents excitedly reported, Nash drove out of the lot in a van that closely resembled the description of the van used by the killer except for one respect—it was solid black.

Nash drove south on the New Jersey Turnpike, stopping for the night in Lancaster, Pennsylvania. He continued west the next day, passing through West Virginia, and crossed the Kentucky border on the morning of April 19.

Sullivan and the police detectives shared the FBI surveillance teams' concern that the longer Nash's exodus continued, the greater the likelihood he would elude his pursuers. And the farther he moved from New York and New Jersey, the less likely it seemed that he would lead them to evidence linked directly to the CBS killings. Sullivan thought it was time to stop Nash.

Early on the nineteenth, FBI agents contacted the Kentucky state police and told them Nash was a suspect in the CBS murders. If possible, they wanted him stopped so they could check the vehicle identification number, or VIN, of the van to see if it matched that recorded on the pier parking records.

Nash eluded a roadblock that was hastily set up, but a state trooper later spotted the van parked just beyond an entrance ramp to an interstate highway—a technical violation of Kentucky law, which forbids stopping on interstate highways. The trooper asked Nash what the problem was, and asked to see his driver's license and registration. The trooper immediately radioed the VIN to headquarters, but he let Nash go on. He also reported that the black van looked as if it had recently received a "home paint job." The FBI quickly confirmed that the VIN matched that of the van parked on Pier 92 the evening of the murders.

The question Sullivan and the federal prosecutors now faced was how to arrest Nash. In most cases, it is the arrest that triggers a panoply of constitutional protections for the accused. The searches that often accompany arrests have probably given rise to more constitutional litigation than any other police activity, and the remedy for mistakes by the police is usually to allow the accused to go free. Evidence seized in the course of a search following an arrest that is itself improper, for example, is generally excluded in court. Otherwise, the courts have reasoned, police would be free to launch searches based on any frivolous pretext for an arrest.

In Nash's case, the Kentucky police had several options. Nash could be arrested for the CBS murders, but Sullivan and the federal prosecutors were apprehensive. Despite the circumstantial evidence they had obtained, they weren't sure they could satisfy a court that they had "probable cause" to believe Nash had committed the crimes. Probable cause is a complicated judicial doctrine that has evolved to justify arrests and searches.

Besides, there was a simpler option: when the Kentucky police fed the van's VIN into the National Crime Information Center computer, they discovered that the van was stolen. Shortly after 10 A.M., Nash stopped at a rest area along the freeway and was arrested by state troopers for possession of stolen property. They gave no hint that Nash was suspected of far more heinous crimes.

In what would later prove to be an event of crucial significance for Sullivan and other prosecutors, Nash, just after he was arrested and handcuffed, asked the trooper to retrieve his eyeglasses from the van. The trooper did so, noticing a spent .22 caliber shell casing on the floor behind the driver's seat. But the trooper didn't conduct a search. Although searches made at the time of an arrest without a search warrant have sometimes been upheld, police have learned through numerous painful examples that the warrantless search poses extreme risks to any subsequent prosecution. Instead, the trooper had the van sealed and towed to a police garage.

The trooper's restraint proved remarkably fortuitous. By twelve-thirty that afternoon the Kentucky police learned from New Jersey authorities that Nash's van wasn't actually stolen. It had been reported stolen, but the report had been corrected. The NCIC computer had failed to disclose the correction. Nash's arrest wasn't valid.

In New York City, there was a brief panic, since technically Nash should be allowed to go free. But the New York City police quickly called the Kentucky authorities and told them that Nash had failed to show up for sentencing in the taxi medallion forgery to which he had pleaded guilty. It was on that charge that Nash was rearrested later that afternoon, having never left police custody.

Meanwhile, Sullivan and the two federal prosecutors working on the case, Ira Block and Stephen Schlessinger, plunged into drafting a search warrant application so that Nash's van could be searched.

The task wasn't an easy one, since the search of the van wasn't related to the fugitive charge on which Nash was being held in custody. That meant that the prosecutors had to convince a judge that there was probable cause the van contained evidence related to the CBS murders. As the Fourth Amendment states bluntly, "no warrants shall issue, but upon probable cause."

The prosecutors decided to focus their application on the role of the van and the likelihood that it contained evidence rather than on Nash's role in the crime. After all, Sullivan recalls, they really didn't know what Nash's precise role was. They had found no connection linking Nash to Barbera. Was Nash actually the trigger man? Was he just the driver of the van? A lookout?

The evidence linking the van to the crimes had to be spelled out in detail. After all, the van in the garage was black, and the eyewitness had specified a "light-colored" van. In exhaustive detail, the prosecutors cited the parking records, the VIN identification, the eyewitness's recollections, the trooper's observation that the van looked as though it had received a home paint job. They worked on the document until 4 A.M., went home for a shower, and then met at the airport. Sullivan and Block flew in one of the FBI's planes to Kentucky.

Once they arrived, Block went before a federal judge to obtain the search warrant, while Sullivan went to the Kentucky police to check on the condition of the van and prepare for a search.

Block quickly discovered that the judge wanted a faultless search warrant. After all, the CBS murders had been highly publicized, and any evidence later suppressed might reflect directly on his actions in approving the warrant and on the Kentucky police who carried it out. Despite the prosecutors' intensive efforts the night before, the judge wasn't satisfied with the application, demanding more specific information identifying the van and its present location. Search warrants

have occasionally been rendered invalid by descriptions that give policemen too much latitude to roam through a suspect's personal property. Fortunately Block was able to gather the needed detail, such as
the address of the garage where the van was being held, and later that
afternoon, the judge signed the warrant.

Sullivan describes the search of the van itself as "one of the finest
pieces of forensic work I've ever seen." It began about 4 P.M. and
didn't end until 1 A.M. the next morning. Every item in the van was
inventoried, catalogued, and packaged for transport to New York.
There were two serologists (specialists in blood types), forensic technicians, photographers, and policemen participating. Sullivan, who
had been up all the previous night, had had nothing to eat. When the
search was finished, he discovered that Frankfort's one "all-night"
restaurant had chosen that night to close early.

Sullivan's only solace was that the search of the van had turned up
some promising clues. The .22 caliber shell that had been spotted
earlier by the state trooper when he retrieved Nash's eyeglasses looked
identical to those found near the bodies of the CBS technicians. Numerous small bloodstains had also been found and lab scrapings had
been taken.

The next day Sullivan attended Nash's arraignment in a Kentucky
court where he was formally charged with being a fugitive. Since he'd
already pleaded guilty to the misdemeanor charge, he had no right to
bail. There was no mention of the CBS murders, and Nash seemed
calm and unruffled. It was a process he had been through several
times before.

The presence of so many New York officials had aroused the cu-
riosity of the press, and after the arraignment, the Kentucky police
held a press conference. At Sullivan's request, they said little about
the real evidence against Nash. Instead, Sullivan tried to deflect questions by heaping praise on the work the Kentucky authorities had
done. But after repeated questioning, he acknowledged that Nash was
going to be prosecuted in New York, and for that reason, he couldn't
say more at the time. The next day, Sullivan and Block returned to
New York, and Nash followed soon after. He made no effort to resist
extradition from Kentucky.

Once he was back in New York, Sullivan knew he and the detectives had to work quickly. Nash was sentenced to a ninety-day prison
term for forging the taxi medallion, which meant that he'd be out in
sixty days for good behavior. Unless they were prepared to indict

Nash for the CBS murders by then, they would have no grounds for holding him in custody. There seemed every likelihood that he'd escape.

Sullivan spoke first with the eyewitness, Angelo Sticca. Sticca was nervous and apprehensive, still afraid that Nash had seen him and that Nash would arrange to have him eliminated. Sullivan showed Sticca pictures of Nash, but to no avail. Sticca couldn't identify him as the man on the pier. In fact, Nash didn't match the description Sticca provided the day of the murders, when he described the gunman as tall, heavyset, and possibly Hispanic.

Detectives continued to pursue every lead. There were rumors Barbera was linked to a Mafia family in Philadelphia; they couldn't be substantiated. Police talked to Nash's wife; Dane, the young man who had driven him to Newark airport; and officials linked to Candor. They subpoenaed Nash's telephone records and obtained a search warrant for his house in New Jersey.

But time was running out. A new homicide grand jury had just started its term, and over the next nineteen days, Sullivan brought fifty-one witnesses to testify about Nash and his involvement in the events of April 12. But the most crucial evidence was scientific: the police lab had determined that the .22 caliber shells found on the pier, in Jenny Soo Chin's car, and in Nash's van had all been fired from the same weapon. And blood tests showed that many of the bloodstains in the van had all the genetic characteristics of Barbera's blood—characteristics that would be expected to occur in only 1 percent of the population. Two of the stains were consistent with the characteristics of Chin's blood.

Certain key witnesses weren't called before the grand jury, since under New York law, anyone who testifies is granted full immunity from prosecution. The law was passed to correct what were perceived as prosecutorial abuses of the grand jury proceeding, in which prosecutors induced witnesses to testify with a variety of promises, many of which became the subject of later litigation when prosecutors decided to prosecute former witnesses. So neither Nash nor Margolies, for example, was asked to appear. Two others whom Sullivan suspected might be criminally involved—Mrs. Nash and Dane—were given immunity. Sullivan's reasoning was that even if culpable, they played small roles and their testimony might be indispensable. Despite the grant of immunity, Dane lied repeatedly, though neither Sullivan nor the grand jury knew it at the time.

Three days before he was scheduled to be released from prison, Nash was indicted for the murders of Barbera and the CBS technicians.

The following day, New York City District Attorney Robert Morgenthau called Sullivan into his office and asked him if he'd be interested in heading a new bureau that would handle extradition requests and insanity hearings—two subjects in which Sullivan has a special interest. Sullivan says he thought about the offer for a few days.

"I enjoyed the investigative and trial work," he says, "but there were other things I wanted to do. And I was tired. The previous winter was exhausting." Daniel LaBelle, a young Assistant D.A. who helped Sullivan on the Nash investigation, recalls that Sullivan rarely had a weekend off and complained that he feared he was losing his concentration. Like a star athlete, he wanted to leave trial work with his reputation at a peak.

SULLIVAN told Morgenthau he'd accept the position, but only if he was relieved of trial responsibilities, including the Nash case and the continuing investigation of the murders. Morgenthau mulled that over for a few days, and agreed. He recognized that it was time to groom a successor to Sullivan as the office's star homicide prosecutor, and the Nash case would provide as good a vehicle as any.

THE day after the murders on the pier, Assistant District Attorney Gregory Waples glanced at his watch: 5:45 P.M. Early, but not too early to leave his office for the day. As on most days, the then 31-year-old prosecutor shed his suit, donned running clothes, and laced up his running shoes for the six-mile distance between the District Attorney's office at One Hogan Place in lower Manhattan and his modest apartment uptown on West End Avenue. It was a cool, clear spring evening, near sundown, so Waples opted for the most scenic of his routes home. He headed due west toward the Hudson River, then north, passing the old shipping piers.

At West 52nd Street, a cruise ship was in port. Two blocks north, he glanced at the Kinney's parking lot pier for signs of police activity—he'd read the newspaper accounts of the CBS murders that morning. But he paid scant attention. If there were any breaks in the case, he'd know soon enough.

In any event, Waples was preoccupied with his own cases, which, though less sensational than the CBS murders, were relatively serious, high-profile matters. As a member of what is called the career criminal unit in the District Attorney's office, Waples gets cases involving repeat offenders and, in most instances, serious crimes. At the time, he was preparing for hearings in the seemingly random murder of a young attorney in a Manhattan park near the East River. And in a relatively short period of time, Waples had established a reputation as one of D.A. Robert Morgenthau's most promising young prosecutors.

That Waples was a prosecutor at all was surprising to friends and colleagues who knew him at Yale University and Columbia Law School, where he was a member of the *Law Review*. Few top Ivy League law graduates end up in the rough-and-tumble, comparatively low-paying field of prosecution. Indeed, Waples is something of an anomaly among New York City Assistant District Attorneys. A detailed sociological profile of New York prosecutors in 1978 concluded that they "are generally young, white males of Catholic or Jewish background. They are second- or third-generation Americans and New York City born and educated. They have attended local colleges and law schools, usually not the ones with Ivy League or national reputations. They came from lower socioeconomic origins more than is typical of the legal profession." The study noted, however, that the "tendency" is toward prosecutors with fewer ties to the community and with more prestigious academic credentials. Waples himself had spent a summer clerking at Cravath, Swaine & Moore, one of the country's most prestigious law firms, and he'd gone to work there full time after graduating and clerking for a federal judge. At Cravath, he was known as one of the brightest and most promising young associates, but after a scant four months there, "I knew I wanted out," Waples recalls.

Working as part of a large team of lawyers assigned to what seemed an interminable antitrust case alienated him from Cravath, but he had few alternatives in mind. Almost instinctively, he applied for a position as an Assistant U.S. Attorney in the Southern District of New York, more because it is a prestigious training ground and stepping-stone to the loftier reaches of the profession than because of any inherent interest in prosecution. He went through the elaborate series of interviews required by Robert Fiske, then the U.S. Attorney in Manhattan, but was turned down.

Waples was ostensibly rejected because of a hiring freeze in the office, but he feels he may well have alienated Fiske at his last interview when he bluntly told him that he hated his work at Cravath. Fiske, who had been and is now a partner at Davis, Polk & Wardwell, a firm that shares the same building with Cravath and is often compared to it, didn't respond favorably to the criticism of a sister firm. He suggested Waples look elsewhere for a job. The incident illustrates one of Waples's distinguishing characteristics: candor that can, at times, seem blunt. He is not inherently political.

Waples turned next to the U.S. Attorney's office in the Eastern District of New York based in Brooklyn. There too he was rejected for reasons he was never told. Finally, almost "out of desperation," he says, he wrote a letter to Morgenthau.

Among prosecutors in the U.S. today, Morgenthau's reputation is formidable. He presides over one of the largest staffs of local prosecutors in the country—recently there were 371—who handle about 100,000 cases a year. He was a prominent figure even before becoming Manhattan District Attorney in 1975: his father was Henry Morgenthau, Jr., Secretary of the Treasury under President Franklin Roosevelt, and he was U.S. Attorney in Manhattan from 1961, when he was appointed by President John F. Kennedy, until 1970, when he was replaced by Republican President Richard Nixon.

Like his well-known predecessor, Frank S. Hogan, who served as Manhattan D.A. for thirty-two years, from 1942 until 1974, Morgenthau has come to personify the office.

Unlike federal prosecutors, but like most state prosecutors, the District Attorneys in New York are elected. Like judgeships, they are posts that coexist uneasily with partisan politics, and political considerations have sometimes ill-served the pursuit of justice. Morgenthau, as he did while he was U.S. Attorney, has tried to de-emphasize the political aspects of his office. He had no opponent in both the 1977 and 1981 elections, and most New Yorkers are hard pressed to say what political party he belongs to. As one Assistant District Attorney recalls, "In 1981 I didn't even realize there was an election." The assurance that their performance won't be measured by political standards has been a key factor in Morgenthau's ability to attract high-quality career-minded prosecutors to the office.

Still, Waples had reservations about applying to work there. "Its image was seedy. I knew the quality of the office had nose-dived under Hogan," he says. But Waples wrote his letter on a Monday, and

Wednesday morning Morgenthau called him to invite him in for an interview that very evening.

Morgenthau isn't known for his personal skills. Tall and patrician-looking, he seems distant and aloof to many of the lawyers who work under him. Close colleagues say he is, in fact, almost painfully shy. But Waples felt an immediate rapport—Morgenthau does project integrity and determination, especially in one-on-one situations. And Morgenthau recognized an intensity in Waples that the U.S. Attorneys had ignored, or found discomfiting. That very night, Waples received a job offer. After checking with some people he knew who were familiar with the office, he accepted. "I had no place better to go," he recalls, "so I decided to gamble." His salary immediately dropped by 50 percent—to $18,500—and he was assigned a cramped office with no secretary, an abrupt change from the comparative luxury of Cravath.

Waples's first jury trial was a burglary case, and it seemed an easy case to win, since the defendant had been found inside a funeral parlor at 105th Street and Amsterdam Avenue at 2 A.M. His sole defense was that the door to the building had been standing open and he had wandered in. The jury found him not guilty.

"I was so upset I nearly quit," Waples recalls. "If that was the mentality of juries, then I wanted out. I took it personally." But Waples stayed on to obtain ten convictions in a row, and his attitudes matured. "I don't take the verdicts so seriously," he says. "Now, verdicts run off me like water off a duck's back. My feeling is, if the jury wants these people walking on the street with them, that's fine."

Waples was in the midst of preparing for hearings in the stabbing murder of a young lawyer in a park near the East River when he got the call from Roger Hayes telling him he was now wanted for the Nash case. The office had been impressed by Waples's work on the stabbing case, especially his ability to handle the press. When a murder victim is a white upper-middle-class professional, the New York press, especially the influential New York Times, gives the story major attention.

Waples plunged into the Nash investigation enthusiastically. He spent four full days with Sullivan, a prosecutor he knew mostly through reputation, reviewing in detail the evidence and the progress of the investigation so far. Nagging at Waples, as it had with Sullivan, was the question of motive. Why was Nash interested in Barbera? It isn't necessary to prove motive to obtain a murder conviction, but in a purely circumstantial case, a conviction is unlikely without a plausible explanation.

Waples and Sullivan agreed that Barbera's status as a witness in a federal case and her relationship to Candor made Margolies a suspect—someone who, they theorized, must have hired Nash to do the killing. But Sullivan was far from convinced. Margolies had been offered a plea bargain of a three-year term in a relatively comfortable federal prison in return for a guilty plea to the factoring fraud; federal prosecutors had offered his wife probation. The Margolieses had turned down the offer. Was this a motive for murder? And the execution of the killing by Nash was highly unprofessional. It all seemed too stupid to be true.

Waples too was mystified by aspects of the case. As he took charge in mid-July, he had two objectives: to continue the investigation of Nash and to find out who had really masterminded Barbera's murder.

In mid-August, Waples flew to Kentucky with a New York City detective and the chief laboratory technician on the case. Waples had drawn up a warrant application to search the van again and then bring it back to New York, and he wanted to meet and get to know the Kentucky authorities involved in the case, since many of them would later be witnesses at Nash's trial.

Waples was at the Kentucky Attorney General's office after completing a second search of the van when he received a phone call from one of the policemen who had helped conduct the search. As he had been resealing the van with tape, the policeman reported, the tape had struck a bulge. It looked, he thought, like a bullet fragment lodged near a front-door window.

Waples told him not to touch the lodged bullet—to extract something from the structure of the van hadn't been specifically authorized by the search warrant. Waples went back before the judge, got his approval, and returned to the garage. When the fragment was withdrawn and tested, it showed traces of gunpowder and might have been a .22 caliber bullet.

The discovery caused Waples to ruminate. Based on the evidence, it seemed clear that Barbera and the three CBS technicians had all been shot outside the van. Yet the bullet could have lodged in the panel only if it was fired from inside. Waples wondered if the bullet might be linked to the still unexplained disappearance of Jenny Soo Chin.

Since the discovery of Barbera's body had triggered renewed interest in Chin's disappearance, police detectives had reconstructed Chin's movements the day of her disappearance in considerable detail. In reviewing the reports, Waples learned that Chin spent the evening of January 5 at Barbera's house on Grandview Avenue in Queens. Chin sometimes spent the night with Barbera, but that day she had told her daughter she would be home that night.

About 7 P.M., two teen-agers sitting on a stoop in the neighborhood saw a woman open the door of a maroon station wagon parked on the street. Suddenly, a man walking behind her grabbed her and pushed her into the car. The woman screamed, then disappeared from view. The station wagon, with the man at the wheel, drove off.

The teen-agers reported the incident, but it was apparently dismissed as a lovers' quarrel; only later was it linked to Chin's disappearance and the discovery of her blood-spattered maroon station wagon. Many of the details of the abduction emerged, in fact, only after the teen-agers were hypnotized. Laboratory analysis of the bloodstains and hairs in the station wagon established that they were almost certainly Chin's.

Other evidence too began to suggest ties between Nash and Chin. Since the incident with the mistake over whether the van was stolen, intensive efforts had been made to discover why the van had been listed as stolen and how it had come into Nash's possession.

It turned out the van had been reported stolen on January 7 by Robert Dane, Nash's nephew and the brother of Thomas Dane, who had accompanied Nash to the Newark airport. Dane said that the van had been stolen between 4 P.M. on January 5 and 5 P.M. on January 6—precisely when Chin was abducted.

On January 11, the van was found abandoned in the Bronx. It was reclaimed by Dane, who collected several thousand dollars in insurance for damage to the van, then sold it to his uncle.

Waples wondered: Had Nash "stolen" his nephew's van January 5? Was the man seen by the teen-agers abducting Chin actually Nash? Might Chin have been shot first in the station wagon, then finished off in Nash's van?

Waples had other reasons for worrying about Nash's connection to Chin. Nash had been indicted by the grand jury for four murders, but not for any charges related to Chin. Under New York laws of evidence, information related to crimes not charged is excluded unless it can be linked directly to the charges in the indictment. Judges fearful of reversal of convictions on appeal, Waples knew, tend to be cautious and exclude such evidence. That meant that the mounting evidence related to Chin—which looked as if it might be essential for a full understanding of Nash's crimes—might not get before a jury.

In November, Waples took evidence related to Chin before the grand jury and obtained a new indictment charging Nash with the four murders and conspiracy to kill Chin and Barbera. He stopped short of charging Nash with Chin's abduction—the conspiracy charge would suffice to bring in all the evidence Waples wanted. By the time of the new indictment, trial of the case was rapidly approaching, scheduled for mid-January. Then, in what Waples deemed a stroke of good fortune, Nash's defense lawyers asked for a postponement.

Ordinarily, Waples would have opposed the request. Despite a constitutional right to a speedy trial, defendants often seek to delay, hoping that time will diminish the memories of witnesses and lead to contradictions in their trial testimony. Such is often the case. But as Waples notes, "This was an exception to the conventional rule. Most cases weaken with time; most evidence is available right away. Here, there were still enormous areas to explore."

Some of those took tremendous efforts for relatively small gains. For example, Waples wanted blood and hair samples taken from Mrs. Nash and Thomas Dane in order to distinguish them from the samples taken from the van. "I didn't want them saying they cut themselves in the van," Waples says. Both refused to cooperate. So Waples had to file a lawsuit in New Jersey to compel them to submit to tests. It was a case of first impression there, raising the issue of whether nonsuspects can be forced to submit to such tests. The case ultimately rose to the U.S. Supreme Court, which refused to hear it, leaving in place a New Jersey court's order granting Waples's request. But the effort consumed many hours of research, writing, and argument.

Other efforts, though, produced breakthroughs. Waples began to spend his free evening hours and weekends poring over the voluminous phone records of everyone involved in the case, especially Nash's. Sitting in his apartment hour after hour, Waples wrote down every one of Nash's calls, looking for patterns. One Saturday night in late December Waples noticed a call Nash made on March 2 to an unfamiliar number that Waples could tell was a Queens exchange.

He was curious, so he went down to the precinct where the files identifying phone numbers were kept. The number wasn't there. He mentioned to the detective on duty that he'd have to subpoena the phone company to learn whose number it was, and the detective asked what the number was. He went to another file, then triumphantly pushed a folder in front of Waples. The number was Barbera's! "Holy shit," Waples recalls. "This was the first direct evidence linking the two." "My God," the detective said, "he's going to be convicted."

On close examination, the phone record showed that the call lasted less than a minute. Frightened by the disappearance of Chin, Barbera had been spending a lot of time out of the city then. Waples guessed that Nash had gotten tired of hanging around her empty house, and had become incautious. He apparently called her number from New Jersey to see if she was home, and hung up when she answered.

Waples was also concerned that the call hadn't been discovered earlier, even though all the phone records had been examined. He personally reviewed them all, spending twenty-hour days checking every phone number. By doing so he discovered that Thomas Dane had made calls to various mail-order outlets selling parts to gun silencers (silencers themselves can't be sold legally to the public, but the parts necessary to assemble them are readily available). When he called and interviewed the outlets, he learned that Dane had placed orders for the parts; a COD receipt was later found signed by Dane.

Waples now worried that Dane—who had been immunized for what now seemed to be patently false grand jury testimony— was "up to his ears" in the scheme, Waples says. At the least, Dane was trying vigorously to protect his uncle. Waples could have prosecuted Dane for perjury, but decided instead to use the new information to surprise Dane at trial. Perhaps by doing so he'd get uesful admissions against Nash.

In early March, pretrial hearings began, hearings Waples knew would be of crucial importance. Nash's defense lawyer, Lawrence Hochheiser, had moved to suppress all the evidence obtained from the van, as well as all the evidence that had been discovered later as a result of clues in the van.

Defense lawyers made much of Nash's arrest based on erroneous information that his van was stolen. "The arrest was totally unfounded," they wrote in papers submitted to the court. "The Nash vehicle was not stolen and the officers used this explanation as a ruse to obtain custody of the defendant and his van. Sham arrests have been universally condemned by the courts."

Waples recognized that the entire case probably turned on the outcome of the suppression hearing. The evidence that defense wanted suppressed "was practically our whole case. The warrant for the search of Nash's house was based on the evidence of the van; it would have been like dominoes falling."

Such evidence is typically excluded under one of the most controversial doctrines of criminal law, one that has spawned countless appellate opinions and has been the bane of many prosecutors' existences—the exclusionary rule. There are other remedies for violations of constitutional rights, for example, civil tort suits for damages and criminal prosecutions of officials who violate civil rights, but exclusion of illegally obtained evidence is by far the most common remedy. The principle of the rule is simple: constitutional violations can best be deterred by denying police and prosecutors any benefits obtained from those violations.

The exclusionary rule has been extended, principally by the Supreme Court under Earl Warren, to exclude evidence that wouldn't have been uncovered but for some previous evidence uncovered in violation of the Constitution. This exclusion is often called the rule against admission of the "fruits of the poisonous tree," and the Supreme Court has ruled specifically that any evidence eventually found as a result of an illegal arrest must be suppressed.

The current Supreme Court has taken some steps to cut back on the exclusionary rule, and it has been the subject of heated attack by the Reagan Justice Department. The Nash case shows exactly what has caused the greatest hostility to the rule. If the point of the rule is to deter improper police conduct, then the police must be able to know they are doing something wrong. Yet, when the Kentucky police arrested Nash for possession of a stolen van, they had no way of knowing they were acting on erroneous information. They believed they had probable cause for making the arrest. Moreover, they could have arrested him legitimately as a fugitive.

Another issue was the .22 caliber shell spotted by the state trooper when he retrieved Nash's glasses at the time of the arrest. The trooper had no search warrant for entering the van. Indeed, the existence of the shell had been cited by the prosecutors in making their application for a search warrant, which meant that if the shell were suppressed, the warrant itself might be rendered invalid as the fruit of an unlawful act. Waples had cause for concern: evidence had been excluded, and defendants freed, for what seem to be far less serious invasions of constitutional rights. They are the kinds of cases that enrage a substantial portion of the population that believes constitutional rights have been allowed to undermine law and order.

Waples recognized that the legality of the trooper's discovery of the spent shell would turn on two doctrines: those of "consent" and "plain view." Courts have consistently ruled that if a suspect agrees, a search without a warrant doesn't violate any constitutional rights—the suspect is presumed to have waived those rights. Nash, after all, asked the trooper to go into the van to retrieve his glasses. Ordinarily that should satisfy the consent requirement, Waples thought, but Nash was in handcuffs at the time. Could he be deemed to have "consented" to the search when he didn't have the option of getting the glasses himself? As defense counsel noted in their motion, "With guns pointing to his head, the defendant was placed under arrest, handcuffed, and hauled off to the local police facility."

The trooper had also spotted the shell, he testified, as he stepped into the vehicle. Waples thought he could argue that the shell was "in plain view." Courts have ruled that evidence in the plain view of the policeman who has a right to be where he spotted it is admissible. Opinions have held specifically that evidence seen through a car window may be admitted in court.

Waples spent days researching relevant case law and preparing his argument. He wanted to leave as little as possible to chance. Given the complexity of the case law that has grown up around the Fourth Amendment, judges have wide latitude in deciding whether or not to suppress evidence, and it is always difficult to measure how the prospect of freeing an alleged quadruple murderer affects their decision. And in the argument itself, the judge hearing the motion made short shrift of the defense motions, rejecting them all. Waples could proceed to trial, with all his evidence intact.

HIS hand strengthened considerably by the failure of the motion to suppress, Waples had to consider the possibility of approaching Nash for a guilty plea. Nash still had some bargaining power: there was, of course, the risk that Waples would lose at trial. More importantly, Nash had information.

From the day of his arrest in Kentucky, Nash hadn't revealed anything to police or prosecutors. All the evidence suggested that he had no personal motive for killing Barbera or Chin, and must have been hired to carry out the murders. His testimony against the mastermind of the plot would almost certainly convict whoever had set the tragedy in motion.

While Waples would have loved a confession from Nash, he decided not to even enter into negotiations. This was not so much because Waples doesn't believe in confessions—a position he had held during law school. Prohibiting confessions has had wide support among civil libertarians and others, since historically, the extraction of confessions has probably given rise to more violations of civil rights, indeed, to torture, than any other activity engaged in by police or prosecutors. But Waples's years as a prosecutor have softened his own opposition. As a practical matter, confessions can be the sole means of achieving some convictions. And, he feels, abuses can be, and have been, curbed by regulating the conduct used to produce confessions rather than by prohibiting confessions entirely.

His decision not to seek a confession from Nash, however, was based on purely practical reasons. Waples couldn't in good conscience offer Nash any jail sentence short enough to produce his release during his natural lifetime. Life in prison was the most serious sentence Nash risked anyway, so there wasn't any incentive for him to bargain. And Waples was just too filled with revulsion for Nash and his crimes. "He was a four-time murderer. I never have and I never will bargain with someone like that," he says.

Waples also wondered if he might be able to get the testimony of one other person who, he suspected, could identify who hired Nash.

In examining Nash's telephone records, Waples had discovered that Nash had placed four long-distance telephone calls to a number belonging to Henry Oestericher. Oestericher, it was quickly established, was a Manhattan lawyer whose principal client was Irwin Margolies.

Investigation into Oestericher had revealed the lawyer to be a chronic loser. His legal practice had gone nowhere, so he went into real estate. That venture ended in bankruptcy. He went into the diamond trade and failed. Then he went back into private practice, joining a lawyer named Norman Schwartz. Schwartz, it turned out, was the uncle of the Assistant U.S. Attorney assigned to the Candor diamond fraud, Stephen Schlessinger.

Margolies had his offices in the same building at 19 West 44th Street as Schwartz and Oestericher, and retained them as his lawyers. Having Margolies as a client, in fact, seemed to bring Oestericher the greatest prosperity he had ever known.

Police detectives had first approached Oestericher in mid-September. Oestericher said he wasn't inclined to be interviewed, but he wasn't adamant. He'd seemed calm; he made references to concerns about attorney-client privilege, and he said he'd think about it. But then his behavior turned evasive. He canceled one interview because of Yom Kippur, another because he "changed his mind." Finally Waples had subpoenaed him to appear before the grand jury.

Waples, however, had no idea what, if anything, Oestericher's involvement in the case actually was. He was convinced he knew something, based on the calls from Nash. Yet there was no obvious motive for Oestericher to be involved—he wasn't a suspect in the diamond fraud, and Barbera and Chin posed no apparent threat to him.

Waples almost put him on the witness stand before the grand jury, which would have given him full immunity from prosecution. At the last minute, he decided to ask Oestericher to waive the immunity. Oestericher refused, which intensified Waples's suspicions. He didn't want to inadvertently immunize a conspirator to murder, so he decided not to call Oestericher as a witness. He thought he could convincingly establish Nash's guilt even if he couldn't provide the jury with a certain motive. With the pressure of Nash's trial approaching, further investigation of Margolies would have to wait.

The trial of Donald Nash began in Manhattan State Supreme Court on March 30. During the previous week, Waples and Hochheiser, the chief defense lawyer, considered six hundred prospective jurors before settling on twelve and two alternates. Waples says he relies largely on instinct in choosing a jury—he doesn't use the elaborate statistical analyses and sociological profiles favored by some trial experts.

For his opening statement, Waples delivered the most elaborate presentation of his career, working from nearly three hundred pages of notes. He began working on it in February, spent every night and weekend on it, and estimates it took at least two hundred hours of preparation. The circumstantial evidence amassed had to be painstakingly pieced together so the jury could understand the case. Over the course of the seven-week trial, Waples presented 140 witnesses.

In some ways, Waples felt that the circumstantial aspects of the case helped him. Referring to the chief defense lawyer, for example, he says that "Hochheiser is a master of cross-examination. He's especially good at destroying sleazy witnesses. But I had a high-quality group of witnesses, and you can't really argue with the facts."

And with one witness where he was vulnerable to Hochheiser's approach—Nash's nephew Thomas Dane—Waples took the offensive. As he had planned after discovering the mail-order purchases of the silencer parts, Waples used the information to force an admission from Dane that he'd lied before the grand jury. Dane appeared deeply shaken and wept at the conclusion of his testimony. Hochheiser, in turn, tried to suggest that Dane was himself the killer—but the suggestion was far less plausible after Waples demonstrated that Dane had tried to protect his uncle by lying under oath.

After his testimony, Dane's house was searched. Inside an attaché case, police found another .22 caliber shell casing that, after being tested by lab technicians, was shown to have been fired from the same gun as that used on the pier. Since the murder weapon was never found, Waples thought it was crucial additional evidence linking the weapon to Nash, and he recalled Dane to the stand to explain the shell's presence. In retrospect, Waples thinks that was a mistake. Dane claimed that the shell must have been planted by the police—a claim repeated by Hochheiser.

The contention was just plausible enough that Waples feared the defense had managed to create doubts in the jury's minds about the quality of the prosecution's evidence. "Beyond a reasonable doubt"— the state of mind required for conviction—is a difficult standard.

Late in the trial, there was an even more threatening development. Though neither a witness nor a defendant, Irwin Margolies managed to throw a wrench into Waples's carefully planned case.

The previous November, Margolies had agreed to plead guilty to the federal fraud charges in connection with the Candor bankruptcy and was sentenced to twenty-eight years in jail—twenty-five years longer than he would have gotten had he accepted the earlier plea bargain. His wife, Madeleine, pleaded guilty to tax evasion and was sentenced to three years in jail for her part in the scheme. The anger over the demise of Candor that Margolies had at first apparently directed toward Barbera and Chin was now focused on a New York lawyer who had investigated Candor, David Blejwas, and Ira Block, the federal prosecutor in charge of his case.

According to an inmate at the Metropolitan Correctional Center, the federal prison in New York City, shortly after Margolies arrived at the center, he offered the inmate $15,000 to arrange the murders of both Blejwas and Block. The inmate reported the matter to federal authorities, and to substantiate the claim, they wired him for sound and he secretly recorded conversations with Margolies. In one of those conversations, Margolies turned to the subject of the CBS murders, saying he knew that Nash "wasn't the trigger man."

Margolies's statement was annoying not just because it cast doubt on Nash's role in the crime. Waples was also worried that he would be required to disclose the statement to Nash's lawyer, who could be counted on to use it effectively at trial. As Waples reached the close of his case, he had still made no mention of the matter to Hochheiser.

In a line of cases nearly as controversial as those involving the exclusionary rule, the Supreme Court has ruled that prosecutors must disclose possibly exculpatory evidence to defendants, and that failure to do so is a violation of a defendant's right to due process of law. In what has become known as the "Brady doctrine," the Supreme Court wrote flatly that "the suppression by the prosecution of evidence favorable to an accused . . . violates due process."

The disclosure of the statement from Margolies, however, posed a difficult dilemma for Waples. On the one hand, disclosing the statement and how the government had obtained it jeopardized the ongoing use of the informant and his investigation of Margolies. In fact, the U.S. Attorney's office insisted that Waples not reveal the activities of the inmate and an undercover informant working in the Metropolitan Correctional Center with him. On the other hand, by not making the disclosure he risked a mistrial.

Waples thought he might risk nondisclosure on the ground that Margolies's comment wasn't really exculpatory. Under New York law, Nash would be guilty of the offense of murder if he aided and abetted it, whether he was or was not the "trigger man." Waples felt there was ample evidence implicating Nash without the claim that he actually pulled the trigger. Still, the cornerstone of the case in the jury's mind was undoubtedly the image of Nash holding the gun to the heads of the CBS technicians. Waples felt he couldn't risk withholding the evidence.

On the last day of his case, in an in camera, secret hearing before the judge, Waples revealed the existence of the informant and Margolies's statement. Hochheiser was furious, insisting that he should have been told immediately. Hochheiser tried to interview the inmate and the undercover operative, but they wouldn't talk to him. He didn't dare call Margolies to the stand, but he did demand a mistrial. To Waples's relief, the judge overruled the request. The undercover operation against Margolies, however, had to be dropped now that it had been disclosed.

The jury knew none of this. Hochheiser called only one witness in Nash's defense—an ophthalmologist who testitifed that Nash had poor vision. The defense lawyer noted that the eyewitness at the pier and those at Chin's abduction hadn't mentioned that the killer wore glasses. Hochheiser also attacked Waples's case as "totally circumstantial."

In his two-day closing statement, Waples argued that "in this case the circumstantial evidence is more convincing and more persuasive than direct evidence." He noted that there were no eyewitnesses to Barbera's killing because the "three men who stood face to face with Donald Nash" were brutally killed. Though Waples acknowledged that he had no direct evidence that Margolies had hired Nash, he suggested that as the motive. And he described as the single most important piece of evidence the phone call to Barbera's number from Nash's phone. Waples avoided histrionics. As Murray Kempton wrote in *Newsday* at the time, "Listening to Waples has all the excitement of watching your car rust . . . the power of Waples's exposition was in the very tedium of its progress toward the irrefutable."

After thirteen hours of deliberations after the close of argument, the jury convicted Nash on all counts. On the way out of the courtroom, Nash looked at Waples and smiled almost inperceptibly. Shortly after, the court clerk gave Waples a note handwritten to him by Nash. "Nice job. Too bad you got the wrong guy." Waples framed the note, along with a clipping of the blazing headlines that announced Nash's conviction, and hung it on his office wall.

Waples, his assistant LaBelle, and a group of the detectives went out for drinks to celebrate the verdict. It seemed fitting that fireworks were going off to commemorate the centennial of the Brooklyn Bridge. Congratulations poured in from others in the office. "Greg did an absolutely superb job," says Sullivan, who says it didn't bother him that Waples got all the credit for the verdict. "I thought we had enough to convict when I left the case," Sullivan says, "but there was a tremendous amount left to be done. Waples deserved all the credit he got." For Sullivan, the case was a reminder that his new position wouldn't bring him the limelight that trying murder cases had, but celebrity "was never the reason I chose this line of work," he says.

For Waples, however, the conviction of Nash meant that only half his work was done on the case. In his closing argument to the Nash jury, he had told them he believed Margolies was the mastermind of a scheme to murder two witnesses to the Candor Diamond Company fraud. Now he intended to prove it.

All he needed was evidence. For in fact, as he had implicitly acknowledged to the Nash jury, the theory of Margolies's guilt was little more than plausible conjecture. Of the innumerable people interviewed in connection with the case—practically everyone who had ever had any significant dealings with Barbera and Chin—only Margolies had a motive to murder both. Nevertheless, Waples had no direct evidence that Margolies and Nash had ever met, let alone that Margolies had hired Nash for a contract murder.

Evidence wasn't the only obstacle Waples faced to convicting Margolies. Even before the arrest of Nash, the U.S. Attorney's office had insisted that it would be the office to handle any prosecution of Margolies. After all, Margolies was already under federal indictment on federal fraud charges. Barbera was going to be a witness in a federal case. Nash himself could have been prosecuted on federal charges of obstructing justice. The far greater severity of the state crime of murder, however, persuaded the U.S. Attorney to cooperate in the Nash investigation but leave the prosecution of Nash to the District Attorney.

Since then, however, Margolies had entered his plea on the fraud charges, received a twenty-eight-year sentence, and promptly solicited the murders of Block, the Assistant U.S. Attorney, and the lawyer involved in the fraud case. This was an attempt to strike at the heart of law enforcement—tantamount to trying to murder an FBI agent, and few crimes enrage prosecutors and law enforcement personnel more. In the wake of these events, U.S. Attorney Martin insisted that his office be the one to handle Margolies. Waples was equally convinced that Margolies should be prosecuted on the graver state crimes of murder and solicitation to commit murder, especially since so much of the case rested on evidence that he had already developed in conjunction with the Nash proceeding.

The conflict triggered a high-level conference at the U.S. Attorney's office between Martin and Morgenthau, who had been Martin's boss when Morgenthau was the U.S. Attorney and Martin an assistant in his office.

Martin says that when he took office as U.S. Attorney, he vowed he wasn't going to get into jurisdictional battles with the District Attorney and other federal prosecutors. But they had proved impossible to avoid. "Margolies was typical," Martin says. "There were real federal interests here. Margolies was in federal prison for a federal crime when he put out a murder contract. We had to take stringent measures to punish this and to deter it."

These were interests that Martin felt would be ignored in the context of a state prosecution. "They were just interested in the murder case," he says. "This was just another bad act, a spillover from their main case. They weren't interested in the federal crime per se."

Despite Morgenthau's pleading and cajoling, Martin held firm, saying that he was prepared to file federal charges against Margolies and would do so with or without the cooperation of the District Attorney. Waples was alarmed by the prospect. If the federal case went to trial, the District Attorney might be barred from prosecuting Margolies under New York State's double jeopardy provisions—no one can be tried twice for the same acts, even if they give rise to multiple charges, some of which weren't lodged in the first trial. Waples thought he was making some headway at persuading Block, the Assistant U.S. Attorney, that Waples should try the case.

But Martin followed through on his pledge. On June 3, roughly a week after Nash's conviction, Martin held a press conference to announce the federal charges against Margolies of attempted murder of a federal witness. The government charged Margolies with offering $15,000 to a gunman to carry out the murder.

As it happened, June 3 was also Martin's last day in office. Waples was convinced that Martin had clung to the case for publicity. "Martin wanted to go out in a blaze of glory," Waples says. "This was the crown jewel of his tenure."

Martin denies that publicity was a factor. "The decision wasn't etched in stone," he says. "At the appropriate time jurisdiction might have been ceded. I wasn't going to leave the investigation in their hands until we knew what had happened."

Since Martin was leaving and the District Attorney seemed to have the support of Block, Morgenthau decided to continue investigating and prosecuting the case as though the federal charges hadn't been filed. Perhaps Giuliani, the new U.S. Attorney, could be persuaded to step aside, especially if Waples was able to build a more convincing case in the meantime.

Moreover, the federal investigation into Margolies's activities in the Metropolitan Correctional Center had produced an unexpected clue to Margolies's involvement in the CBS murders. During the time Margolies had been secretly tape-recorded, Waples kept hoping that he would inadvertently say something that would implicate him in Nash's activities. Nothing had developed, however, partly, Waples believes with some annoyance, because the federal informant was told to elicit evidence into the federal, and not the state, crimes. Nonetheless, among the witnesses federal prosecutors called before the grand jury was Margolies's brother-in-law. He testified that he had paid Hochheiser, Nash's defense lawyer, $15,000 for Nash's defense on instructions from Margolies. Waples was electrified by the news. It was the first direct evidence tying the diamond merchant to Nash.

WAPLES promptly subpoenaed Hochheiser—a rare opportunity to question his former adversary under oath. But Hochheiser, invoking the attorney-client privilege, refused to provide any information about the source of his legal fees for Nash's defense.

There was nothing illegal about Hochheiser's accepting money from Margolies. But his doing so was risky and may have been unethical, defense lawyers say, because of the potential harm to his own client. For example, had Waples known that Hochheiser received money from Margolies at the time of Nash's trial, he could have introduced that fact as evidence to support his theory that Margolies hired Nash and now felt obligated to pay for his defense—possibly crucial evidence in the weakest area of the case against Nash, that of motive. A defense counsel is ethically obligated to do nothing that will damage his client's case.

Hochheiser won't say whether Margolies paid for Nash's defense, but says "if you print that, I won't say you're wrong." He defends the practice, saying that since Nash and Margolies were charged as coconspirators, it was in Margolies's interest that Nash receive the best possible legal defense. If Nash were acquitted, Margolies probably would have been as well, he reasoned. Moreover, Hochheiser says he didn't intend for Waples to find out about the fee arrangement.

The only other evidence Waples had that indirectly linked Nash and Margolies were the four phone calls from Nash's New Jersey home to Henry Oestericher, the lawyer who shared office space near Margolies.

Though he had earlier rejected the possibility of granting Oestericher immunity in order to obtain his testimony, Waples was now rethinking the possibility. The leads he had pursued in other directions hadn't produced much concrete evidence. The legal fees, though tantalizing, would hardly convict Margolies standing alone.

If the case against Margolies looked weak so far, that against Oestericher looked even weaker. Waples saw no way that, even if Oestericher was a coconspirator, he'd be able to prove it without the cooperation of Margolies himself, and that was out of the question.

And Waples's intuition told him Oestericher wasn't seriously involved. The man was a lawyer, after all, and he had no personal motive for killing Barbera and Chin.

Waples conferred with Morgenthau, and they decided to go ahead and immunize Oestericher. The day before Nash was scheduled to be sentenced, Waples granted Oestericher immunity and brought him before the grand jury hearing testimony with respect to Margolies.

Oestericher's testimony proved a great disappointment. He said little that wasn't already known about the case. He denied knowing of any contact between Margolies and Nash. And the phone calls on which Waples rested many of his hopes he explained as calls regarding some handyman work that Oestericher hired Nash to do.

Waples didn't know whether or not to believe Oestericher. He tried accusing him of lying—Oestericher remained steadfast. Waples couldn't understand why Oestericher would go so far as to commit perjury, especially after a grant of immunity, just to protect Margolies.

The next day was Nash's sentencing, and Waples urged Judge Scott to make "absolutely certain the defendant never sees freedom again in his natural life." Hochheiser told the judge that his client had asked him to say little on his behalf except that he maintained his innocence. Waples says the approach was consistent with the attitude Nash had displayed throughout—that a hired killer, if he blunders, must accept his fate stoically.

Judge Scott deplored the "senseless waste of human life" and said, "I find nothing which in any way mitigates the enormity of this man's crime." He sentenced Nash to four maximum terms of twenty-five years to life, to be served consecutively rather than concurrently. That meant a combined minimum term of a hundred years—one of the longest terms ever imposed in Manhattan.

Nash's sentencing, however, increased the public pressure on Waples to do something about Margolies. Margolies's alleged role had again been mentioned at the sentencing hearing, and the press was beginning to publicly question why Margolies wasn't being prosecuted. Waples finally decided he had to go forward.

All he had were the phone calls, the attorney's fee payment, the prison informants, and, of course, a motive. It was enough to satisfy the twenty-three-member grand jury, which indicted Margolies on July 15 for murder and conspiracy to murder Barbera and the lawyer representing the defrauded factoring company. Consistent with the government's theory that the CBS technicians had merely stumbled on the crime, Margolies wasn't charged in connection with their deaths. The indictment indicated as well that Oestericher and Thomas Dane may have participated in the conspiracy.

The indictment was announced publicly in a joint news conference by Morgenthau and the new U.S. Attorney, Giuliani. Since taking office, Giuliani had been persuaded to allow the District Attorney's office to handle the case. The federal charges against Margolies that Martin had insisted be filed were quietly dropped. In return, Giuliani was allowed to share the limelight generated by the new indictment.

Despite the public fanfare, Waples was worried about proving the case. Thus, he was excited to learn that he personally figured prominently in the latest scheme to emerge from Margolies's feverish imagination.

Soon after the indictment, Block called Waples from the U.S. Attorney's office to say that Margolies had approached yet another federal informant inside the Metropolitan Correctional Center. This time, Margolies had asked the informant to approach Waples with a substantial bribe, seeking to get Waples to drop the case or to "go easy" on him.

Waples and Block wired the informant and sent him back to try to solidify this new evidence of yet another crime by Margolies. But when Waples later reviewed the tapes, he decided against pursuing the matter because of problems the Hitachi investigators had anticipated. "The tapes sounded too much like it was the informant suggesting the scheme," Waples says. Nor was Margolies's acquiescence all that convincing. In any event, Waples thought the case already depended too heavily on prison informants, who are often destroyed on cross-examination by savvy defense counsel. Informants are usually so unsavory that they are rarely good witnesses.

Except for that flurry of excitement, little happened in the case until the fall. Then some new evidence surfaced implicating Oestericher further in the scheme.

Earlier in the investigation, police learned that the building on West 45th Street cited by Nash as his business address when he filled out his parking application for the pier parking lot had once been owned by Oestericher. That suggested another tie between Nash and Oestericher, so Waples decided to focus his investigation on the building. He subpoenaed all the phone records for all of the building's tenants. Despite hours of poring over them, Waples found they produced no breakthrough. But Waples also noticed that the building's superintendent, Alberto Torres, had been employed at the building for twenty years, dating back to the time Oestericher owned the building.

Torres is elderly, about sixty-five, and is a dignified, soft-spoken Hispanic immigrant whose demeanor, Waples says, is inherently trustworthy. He had been questioned earlier by police detectives, but had said nothing to give rise to any suspicions. He had seemed happy to talk to the police.

Now that Waples's interest had been renewed in the building on West 45th, he asked a police detective who spoke Spanish to try talking to Torres again, asking if there were anything else he knew about links between Oestericher and Nash.

Waples was at home one evening when he learned the results of the detective's efforts. He called Waples with the information that Torres had admitted for the first time that he knew Oestericher and that there was a link between Oestericher and Nash. Torres told Sanchez that Oestericher had hired him as the building superintendent, and that he had put Oestericher in touch with Nash when Oestericher needed an electrician.

Waples was so excited by the development that he joined Sanchez and personally tried to extract further information from the superintendent. But Torres suddenly became reticent.

Oestericher had said nothing about any ties to Torres, and Waples's suspicions that the lawyer had lied in his grand jury testimony mounted. Waples called the U.S. Attorney's office, and urged the assistant working on the case, Steve Schlessinger, to try to increase the pressure on Oestericher, threatening him with prosecution in connection with the bankruptcy fraud. (Oestericher's immunity granted by Waples extended only to acts in connection with the conspiracy to kill Barbera and Chin.) But to Waples's annoyance, Schlessinger did nothing. Waples's ally Block was busy on another case.

Out of frustration and almost on impulse, Waples decided to approach Oestericher again directly. The day after Thanksgiving, he wrote Oestericher a stern letter. In his grand jury testimony, Oestericher had denied that Torres had introduced him to Nash. Now Waples wrote that based on recent interviews with Torres, he believed Oestericher's testimony to be "materially false." Materially false testimony before a grand jury, Oestericher knew, is perjury—a crime not covered by his grant of immunity.

Waples carefully refrained from making any direct threat of prosecution, and, in fact, it was highly doubtful that Waples ever would have sought such an indictment against Oestericher. Perjury is probably the most underprosecuted of all crimes. The offense itself is rampant, occurring during the course of most investigations and trials. But prosecutors rarely seek indictments.

It is, for one thing, a derivative crime, one that usually occurs as an outgrowth of another offense. If it is the suspect or defendant who lies, a perjury case distracts from the principal, usually more important case. Only when the chief case is weak, as has been the case with some prominent organized-crime figures and labor leaders, does a perjury indictment sometimes serve as a substitute. And even in those cases, convictions are far from certain—probably because juries suspect that the perjury case is a surrogate for other charges that the prosecution can't prove.

When witnesses lie, as Waples believed Oestericher did, there is even less incentive to prosecute. Witnesses aren't the target in the first place—Waples had already given Oestericher immunity for the substantive crime. And their prosecution only diverts attention and resources from the chief suspect. As a result, the perjury charge is most useful as a threat.

Waples heard nothing from Oestericher. But unknown to the prosecutor, his letter corresponded with a significant development in the peculiar relationship between Oestericher and Margolies. Waples later learned that throughout Nash's prosecution and the investigation of Margolies, Oestericher had remained on retainer to Margolies, performing nominal legal services in return for substantial and regular cash payments. Just before Thanksgiving, Margolies had given orders from his prison cell that the payments to Oestericher be stopped. Oestericher was left in a financially precarious condition and, even more significantly, was personally wounded and hurt by the abandonment of a man to whom he had shown extraordinary loyalty.

Two weeks later, Waples got a call from Oestericher's lawyer, Charles Clayman. "I've an attorney who wants to come in from the cold," Clayman told Waples.

An excited Waples quickly called the U.S. Attorney's office and arranged a meeting there with Clayman and Ira Block, who had replaced Schlessinger entirely on the case in the U.S. Attorney's office. Clayman confirmed Waples's greatest hopes—Oestericher did, in fact, have critical information about Margolies and two other, unnamed people. Before Oestericher would disclose the information, however, he had a demand—he wanted complete immunity from prosecution for any crime, including perjury and any federal crimes. And he wanted to be able to continue practicing law.

Waples was dying to know what information Oestericher had, and wanted to grant most of the request. (He says he and the others had a good laugh over the notion of Oestericher continuing to practice law. There was no way they could guarantee that or that the bar association would permit it, but Waples figured it wasn't a serious request.) Waples was also running out of time: Margolies's trial was scheduled for mid-February, and he felt he needed Oestericher's testimony.

But snags developed immediately. When Waples got back to the D.A.'s office, he learned that Morgenthau had just left for a two-week trip to Israel. He felt he'd be able to persuade Morgenthau to extend the grant of immunity as soon as he returned, but then further problems developed at the U.S. Attorney's office.

It had been one thing for Giuliani to step aside from a prosecution that had been launched by his predecessor in what was clearly a predominantly state case. He had done so quickly and graciously as long as he shared in the publicity. But Oestericher was another matter. The man had admittedly hindered a federal investigation—a crime that particularly angers Giuliani, since it strikes at the heart of the enforcement process. And Giuliani wasn't comfortable with an immunity grant. It cut completely against the grain of his notion of a tough prosecutor. Giuliani flatly told Block that he wanted a guilty plea to a felony out of Oestericher before they could discuss any kind of deal.

That decision was delivered to Clayman, Oestericher's lawyer, in what turned into a stormy session. Clayman rejected the prospect out of hand, furious that he'd been led to believe a deal was in the offing. Block and Waples both threatened that they'd haul Oestericher before a grand jury, seeking indictments. Clayman, the prosecutors recall, said his client would probably just lie again.

Clayman says he doesn't recall saying that Oestericher would lie, but "even if I said it, I wouldn't recall it." A lawyer may not knowingly place a client on the witness stand to commit perjury. But prosecutors say the practice is widespread.

Waples saw the prospect of his new star witness going up in smoke. Block hadn't succeeded in making any headway with Giuliani, so Waples turned to Larry Pedowitz, the Newman prosecutor and head of the criminal section. Pedowitz seemed sympathetic to Waples's arguments. Oestericher, Waples emphasized, wasn't the focus of the investigation and never had been. Even in an obstruction of justice case, Oestericher played a subsidiary role to that of Margolies. And murder was a far more serious charge. If Margolies were to be convicted, Waples argued, he needed Oestericher. Pedowitz went to Giuliani, and the U.S. Attorney finally deferred to Pedowitz's and Waples's arguments. A week later, Giuliani agreed to immunity for Oestericher.

Still, working out the terms of Oestericher's cooperation had taken three weeks, and Waples didn't want to lose a day. On Saturday, January 5, he finally sat down for a face-to-face session with Oestericher. And for the first time since the CBS murders in April 1982, he heard firsthand disclosures of how the whole scheme had come about.

Oestericher talked for six hours without interruption, "leaving us spellbound," Waples recalls. "He had more information than I'd ever dreamed. He told us how the murders had been planned and carried out, speaking clearly and dispassionately. It was like being inside the mind of a fiend."

Even Clayman was astounded. "I'd never heard Oestericher's story," he says of his client. "I didn't want to hear it. When I did, it was beyond my wildest dreams. I've never heard a more chilling story."

Some pieces of the puzzle that had persisted even after Nash's conviction fell into place. As Waples had long suspected, the scheme was born in conjunction with the collapse of the Candor Diamond Company and the fraud investigation of Margolies by federal authorities. In fact, Oestericher told Waples, Block, and others who gathered for the session, there was a chilling connection between the investigation mounted by the U.S. Attorney's office and the murders.

According to Oestericher, Margolies was worried about the evidence Margaret Barbera might provide federal authorites if she decided to cooperate. He knew, for example, that she had in her possession incriminating copies of the company's books and accounting records. His fears were heightened one day when the lawyer who was representing Margolies in the fraud investigation and who had shared office space on West 44th Street with Oestericher, Norman Schwartz, told Margolies that Barbera and another unidentified woman had signed cooperation agreements with the U.S. Attorney. Schwartz knew this information, he said, because the Assistant U.S.

Attorney in charge of the case, Steven Schlessinger, was his nephew, and had told him so.

The prosecutors were shocked by the disclosure. If what Oestericher was saying were true, Schlessinger probably should have disqualified himself from the case because his uncle represented the target of the investigation. Worse, it appeared that Schlessinger had broken a cardinal rule of prosecution—he had placed witnesses in jeopardy by disclosing their cooperation to a defendant's lawyer.

Indeed, Barbera's mother, Jacqueline, subsequently filed suit against Schlessinger, Martin, the U.S. Attorney who supervised Schlessinger, and Attorney General Smith. She alleged that Schlessinger's negligence in disclosing her daughter's identity as a cooperating witness had wrongfully caused her death, and that Martin and Smith had failed to adequately supervise Schlessinger.

In a February 1987 opinion denying the government's motion to dismiss the suit, presiding federal judge Shirley Wohl Kram wrote that "in effect, Schlessinger placed Barbera in danger by informing Margolies' attorney that Barbera was cooperating with the authorities and then denied her the ability to defend herself by refusing her request for police protection despite the unexplained disappearance of her co-worker." However, Judge Kram did dismiss the allegations against Smith. The government has appealed the decision, and the case was pending as of spring 1987.

Schwartz, who allegedly learned Barbera's identity from Schlessinger and told Oestericher, declined all comment. Schlessinger also declined comment, on the advice of his lawyer, assistant U.S. Attorney Peter Salerno. Salerno notes that neither the government nor Schlessinger has formally responded to the allegations made by Jacqueline Barbera. Asked specifically whether Schlessinger revealed Barbera's identity and whether Schlessinger was Schwartz's nephew and should have disqualified himself from the case, he declined comment. Schlessinger was working for the Justice Department in Miami at the time Judge Kram filed her opinion.

The disclosures about Schlessinger were a chilling reminder to Waples of the power prosecutors sometimes wield over the lives of witnesses and defendants. However Margolies found out, his knowledge that Barbera was cooperating had tragic consequences, which quickly became apparent as Oestericher continued his story.

According to Oestericher, upon hearing of Barbera's cooperation, Margolies immediately concluded that Barbera and Chin were plotting against him. He was partly wrong, as it turned out—the unidentified woman who was cooperating was actually another former employee and not Chin. Margolies told Oestericher that he wanted the two women silenced, and their bodies destroyed so that they'd never be found. He wanted Oestericher to find a hit man.

Much to Waples amazement, Oestericher admitted that it was he who had procured the services of Nash. Margolies had insisted that he make some effort to find a killer, so Oestericher said he phoned Alberto Torres, the building manager who had from time to time obtained handymen and craftsmen for him. Oestericher said he assumed Torres wouldn't be able to help, but that at least Margolies would have heard him make the effort. Soon after, however, Torres called back to say that Nash, who had done some electrical repair work for Oestericher and was now operating a construction business from a phone in Torres's building, was interested. Oestericher said he thought Nash was "the wrong man for the job," but Margolies was delighted that someone had been found.

The following day, Nash and Margolies met for the first time at Ike and Mike's Delicatessen in midtown. Oestericher said Margolies later told him that the two reached an agreement, using sign language to arrive at a figure of $8,000 per murder.

Waples was a bit taken aback by the disclosures. He had, as it turned out, immunized someone who was far more involved in the scheme than he had suspected, someone who would have been guilty himself of murder for his complicity. Torres too had been immunized early in the case, and now he seemed to be a knowing conspirator. But Waples consoled himself by acknowledging that he could never have proved these cases—indeed, he might never have known the full scope of each person's involvement—if this case hadn't taken the course it did. He had to keep his efforts focused on the prime culprit, Margolies.

Oestericher continued his narrative, mentioning that he knew Margolies had supplied Nash with information about Barbera and Chin: their addresses, telephone numbers, description of their cars. But after the delicatessen meeting, months went by and Oestericher had heard nothing further about the matter.

Then Oestericher revealed one of the most horrifying aspects of the crime. In January 1982, Oestericher said, an excited Nash had arrived at the 44th Street offices and conferred with Margolies. Afterward, Oestericher said, Margolies reported that Nash had "eliminated" Chin. To prove it, Nash had brought in a snapshot of Chin's bloody corpse.

"She died hard," Margolies quoted Nash as saying. Presumably, Nash also told Margolies what he did with the body, but neither has disclosed that information. Chin's corpse has never been found. (The most popular theory among police investigators on the case is that it is sealed inside one of the concrete piers supporting the convention center on Manhattan's West Side, which was under construction at the time of the disappearance. Chin's abandoned car was found near the site.)

Given the blunders he later made, Nash showed himself to be a surprisingly resourceful killer. According to Margolies's account to Oestericher, Nash had fixed Chin's car so that it wouldn't start. When Chin and Barbera arrived at the car and failed to start it, he had appeared and offered to help, quickly correcting the damage. His motive, he had told Margolies, was to make the two women comfortable around him. The element of recognition may have helped in his later abduction of Chin, witnessed by the two teen-agers.

Nonetheless, Margolies wasn't happy with the news of Chin's murder. He had wanted Barbera killed first—she was the most serious threat, and killing her, he felt, might have frightened Chin out of cooperating, making her murder unnecessary. Nash protested, saying he had to kill when the opportunity presented itself. Margolies seemed upset to Oestericher, but not so much that he rescinded the contract on Barbera.

Oestericher said he heard nothing further about Nash until the night of the CBS murders. Margolies called him at home. "Did you hear the news?" he asked, and Oestericher said yes. "*Oy vay*," Margolies replied. Nash was angry, saying that the murder went awry because Margolies had hurried him too much, and he was forced to kill the CBS employees because they'd gotten a good look at him. Margolies gave Nash an additional $5,000 to compensate for the complications.

That ended Oestericher's account of the crime, and it was enough, Waples felt sure, to convict Margolies. Given Margolies's demonstrated propensity for eliminating witnesses who turned against him—even operating out of his prison cell—Waples asked Oestericher if he wanted to enter the witness protection program. He refused then, but later accepted.

Waples returned the next day, Sunday, for another full day with Oestericher, and spent an additional three days with him, going over his recollection of events, learning more about the Candor bankruptcy and fraud, and the relationships among Margolies, Barbera, and other employees. Waples never fully understood the capacity of a man like Margolies to attract the loyalty and devotion of Oestericher, who was, after all, a member of the bar. Even after the Candor fraud was exposed, the two men were planning to use the proceeds of the fraud to embark on a new diamond business once Margolies emerged from prison. Only Margolies's decision to cut off Oestericher had turned the lawyer into a witness for the prosecution.

Torres's role was also baffling—someone with no criminal record had apparently procured a murderer and received nothing in return. A few days after the Oestericher interviews, Waples went back to Torres, and confronted him with Oestericher's disclosures. Torres finally broke, admitting his role and saying that he hadn't spoken sooner because he was afraid of retaliation by Margolies or Oestericher. He argued—unconvincingly, Waples says—that he didn't realize he was procuring a murderer until the day the killings actually took place. That afternoon, he said, Nash came rushing into his office, saying he needed money. "I just shot three people," Nash said to Torres.

AFTER several postponements, all at the request of Margolies and his defense counsel, Robert Hill Schwartz (no relation to Margolies's prior lawyer, Norman Schwartz), Margolies's trial began on May 5, accompanied by intense media coverage.

For Waples, it was the consummation of nearly a year of sustained, intense effort. Waples thought he had successfully bridged what is often the most difficult and frustrating gap a prosecutor faces: the knowledge of a criminal's identity and the ability to prove a case before a jury. That Nash and Margolies were the principal culprits in the CBS murders had been evident to Waples for some time. It was the painstaking and sometimes mundane accumulation of the evidence—the poring over phone records, the sifting through parking tickets, the detailed laboratory tests—that now made a conviction seem within reach. Although he was more confident than he had been before the trial of Nash, there was plenty that could still go wrong—as is the case in any trial. His task wasn't an easy one—it was still a complicated, high-pressure case, and Schwartz is a keen and experienced adversary, a former prosecutor in Queens. And anything can happen with a jury.

Oestericher was the star witness for the prosecution, and despite the high price Waples paid for him in terms of immunity and the importance of his testimony, he was hardly the ideal witness. Criminals rarely are. Oestericher had already lied repeatedly in the course of the investigation, including under oath before a grand jury.

Schwartz made much of Oestericher's unreliability, his complicity in the Candor fraud, his role in the murders, his unsavory past, including ownership of a Times Square hotel notorious for prostitution. He tried to paint Oestericher as the true mastermind of the killings.

In doing so, Schwartz was able to hammer at a theme that always makes coconspirators who have been immunized vulnerable on cross-examination: they have bargained for freedom by implicating the defendant. Schwartz got Oestericher to admit that if he was now lying in his testimony, to acknowledge it would subject him to prosecution for murder. At the same time, Schwartz says, he didn't want to go too hard on Oestericher, a "loser" who might arouse the jury's sympathy.

Schwartz also tried to take advantage of the fact that Waples had ordered that no notes be taken during the initial interviews of Oestericher. (Such notes might have been subject to disclosure to the defense before trial, and Waples wanted both to protect Oestericher and to preserve an element of surprise.) At trial, Schwartz argued that the absence of notes made it impossible to determine whether Oestericher had changed his story since the interviews, the clear implication being that he had.

Waples was anticipating a difficult cross-examination, and says that Oestericher, as a person, seemed "destroyed" by the time Schwartz was through with him. Schwartz was sufficiently effective that Murray Kempton, writing in *Newsday*, noted that Oestericher's "guilt in this affair does not seem markedly lighter than that of Margolies, and the unsophisticated may wonder how so towering a scoundrel can go free for no higher purpose than to add an infinity of years to the 28 to which Margolies has already been sentenced for fraud."

Torres made a more effective witness. Although he too lied before a grand jury, his immunity had already been granted before he changed his testimony—he hadn't used the truth as a bargaining chip with the prosecution. His motive for lying, fear, was more plausible and made him more sympathetic.

Still, Waples made sure the case didn't rest entirely on the jury's belief of Oestericher and Torres. He had all the phone records, the payment of Nash's legal fees, and other, independent evidence of ties between Nash and Margolies. He had solid evidence of motive, and perhaps most significantly, Schwartz wasn't able to muster any plausible alternative to the scenario Waples mapped out for the jury. Although it was possible that Oestericher took it upon himself to plan the entire scheme without Margolies's knowledge, that theory failed to explain the evidence of direct contact between Margolies and Nash. Margolies himself never took the stand.

However, Nash did make a very brief appearance at the trial. During the investigation, Waples had asked Nash's lawyer whether Nash would be willing to testify against Margolies. The lawyer sent a letter in reply, saying that if Nash were called to the witness stand, he would testify that Margolies wasn't involved in the murders. Waples thought it was a bluff, but as required by the Brady decision, Waples turned the letter over to Schwartz, since it was evidence that might tend to exonerate his client. Schwartz, in turn, called Nash as a witness for the defense.

Nash showed up, wearing dark glasses, prison garb, looking thinner and subdued. In the event, however, he didn't take the stand. Rather than exonerate Margolies, he told the judge that he would invoke the Fifth Amendment and refuse to answer questions. As a result, the jury never learned of the letter and Nash's lawyer's claim.

After closing arguments, the case went to the jury on May 30. The jury deliberated for twenty-five hours, spending much of its time debating the credibility of Oestericher and the charges that Margolies had tried to arrange the killing of an Assistant U.S. Attorney and another lawyer from his prison cell. According to Schwartz, who spoke later with a number of the jurors, they largely rejected Oestericher's testimony as unreliable.

But when the jurors returned to the courtroom, they announced their verdict. They found Margolies guilty of the murders of Chin and Barbera; they acquitted him of the attempt to kill Blejwas and Block. Margolies, standing for the verdict, flinched slightly as he heard the result, with his eyes closed and his hands clasped at his ample waist. He didn't look at Waples.

Waples sought the maximum sentence for Margolies, arguing at the sentencing hearing several weeks later that the crimes were "an affront to civilized society." Justice Eve Preminger, who presided at the trial, agreed that she found no mitigating circumstances. She sentenced

Margolies to two consecutive twenty-five-year-to-life sentences, to begin after Margolies finished his twenty-eight-year fraud term. Then forty-nine years old, Margolies seems destined to spend the rest of his life in prison.

THE successful prosecutions of first Nash and then Margolies, two of the most important and visible cases in the office, propelled Waples into the stardom that some in the office had anticipated. His colleagues and adversaries are unanimous in praising his work, his phenomenal energy, thoroughness, and dedication.

"Greg stands very high in my estimation in fairness and decency," says Schwartz, qualities he believes are important to an effective prosecutor. "The advocate in you says you should do everything you can to convict someone you believe is guilty. Yet you have a duty to do justice, to help the other side, even to tear down your own case. The potential is there for terrible conflict. Greg seems to cope with that well."

Waples's new stature has been amply acknowledged in Morgenthau's office. Waples is teaching trial tactics to less experienced Assistant District Attorneys, and was promoted to senior litigator (there was no accompanying pay raise, however). Perhaps the most telling symbol, however, is his most recent assignment—the prosecution of Bernhard Goetz.

After Goetz came to national attention for shooting four young black men on a New York subway train, allegedly in self-defense, Morgenthau's office took the case before a grand jury, which refused to indict Goetz. In an unusual step, Morgenthau asked Waples to search for additional evidence and take the case back to a grand jury. With his usual thoroughness and dedication, Waples produced the evidence—one of the victims who agreed to testify—and returned from the grand jury with an indictment for attempted murder. Although Goetz was ultimately acquitted on most charges, Waples says there was never any doubt in his mind that Goetz should be charged.

The Goetz case has already projected Waples into public view to an unprecedented degree, far greater than anything he coped with in the CBS cases. Waples says he has no real political ambitions and no desire to become a celebrity, but he is plainly pleased that others recognize his work as important. He is also aware of the negative aspects of publicity. Each week since the indictment of Goetz he has received stacks of mail, most of it negative and hostile, some of it threatening. He has received his first telephoned death threat.

Nor is Waples's life glamorous by any conventional standard. During the Margolies investigation, he and his wife were divorced. Waples plainly doesn't want to talk about it; his colleagues note that his work habits and the demands of his job left scant room for any family life. "I don't think it was ever much of a marriage in the conventional sense," says Dan LaBelle, who worked closely with Waples during this period, but says Waples told him virtually nothing about the divorce except that it happened.

Waples has none of the material amenities associated with the yuppies of his generation. He drives a battered car, usually grabs a cold piece of chicken and a beer for dinner after jogging home from work, and spends what little leisure time he has with a few friends and his cat.

None of this fazes Waples; what does affect him is his work. Even with the pressure of the Goetz case mounting, the CBS murder cases aren't over. Nash has appealed his conviction; Margolies hasn't yet appealed, but has filed a separate suit charging that Waples deprived him of his constitutional rights.

Of the two, the Nash appeal is the more serious. On appeal is the issue of whether Nash's arrest was illegal. And his principal claim is that Waples failed to turn over in a timely fashion possible exculpatory evidence, which he was required to do by the Supreme Court's Brady decision. Waples concedes that he withheld information at the request of the U.S. Attorney, though he doesn't think it was exculpatory and believes he will prevail, based on applicable case law. (Indeed, in 1986 the Court of Appeals upheld the conviction.) But Waples has agonized over the allegation that he behaved improperly.

"I believe I acted correctly," Waples says, "but I'm not proud of what I did. I find it a little embarrassing. I'd rather not have these conflicts. My reputation is for fairness. I value that and it's important to me that my word be trusted. So, even though what I did is legal, I don't feel comfortable with it as a human being." If he had to do it over again, Waples says, he would have turned over the evidence immediately despite the objections by the U.S. Attorney.

Perhaps such ruminations are healthy. "The prosecutors who agonize over their roles don't bother me," says Schwartz, the former prosecutor turned defense lawyer. "It's the ones who don't—those who put on the white hat and charge."

THE clash between Giuliani and Morgenthau over the handling of the Margolies prosecution, though no hint of it surfaced publicly, left some enduring bad feelings. Lawyers in the Manhattan D.A.'s office chalked up the case as a victory for Morgenthau, but Giuliani's assistants knew otherwise: it was just the opening skirmish in what promised to be a long-running contest.

Giuliani's opportunity to establish his superiority came a year and a half later. On a foggy January night in 1986, Donald R. Manes, the Queens Borough president in New York City and the powerful chairman of the Queens Democratic Party, was found in his car nearly unconscious, an ankle slashed and bleeding. The discovery of Manes, and the likelihood that he had tried to commit suicide, triggered the largest municipal corruption scandal of Mayor Edward Koch's administration.

Conducted in a blaze of publicity, the Manes and related investigations seemed tailor-made for a prosecutor like Giuliani. The only hitch, as had been the case with the CBS murders, is that bribery of a local political official—Manes' suspected crime—has often been prosecuted as a state, not a federal, crime.

Nonetheless, Giuliani sought and obtained permission from Washington to use the federal racketeering statute to indict municipal officials, especially Stanley Friedman, the Bronx Democratic leader and the most prominent official to be implicated after Manes himself. Giuliani had several arguments to support his jurisdiction. The case had originated with an informant in Chicago, and the FBI had been investigating the case for over two years. "This case was well under way before Morgenthau showed the slightest interest," Giuliani says. Moreover, Justice Department officials felt that a scandal within a Democratic administration in New York City called for a Republican prosecutor rather than Morgenthau, a Democrat. The political benefits were obvious.

The action was a shot across the bow of Morgenthau, who had already filed state charges against Friedman. Morgenthau, say colleagues, was furious at the intrusion, in part because duplicate prosecutions raised double jeopardy issues that might threaten the success of any convictions.

To head off a clash that might undermine both their efforts, Morgenthau agreed to have lunch with Giuliani. This time Giuliani refused to withdraw from the case and cede jurisdiction to Morgenthau, as he had in the CBS case. The two prosecutors announced, however, that they had reached a truce and would cooperate to determine whether federal or state jurisdiction in the case offered the best chance for a successful prosecution.

The truce lasted less than a month. In February, Giuliani publicly accused Morgenthau of "intruding" into his investigation and warned that the Manhattan D.A.'s efforts were frightening away potential witnesses. Then Giuliani's office succeeded in having a judge quash a subpoena from Morgenthau's office to a potential witness in both cases—an unusually strong move by one prosecutor to frustrate another. "Their subpoena threatened to harm very sensitive negotiations under way," Giuliani explains. "I saw nothing useful they could add to this case." Morgenthau had been restrained in his public responses, but he issued a list of offices and agencies with which he was cooperating. The list did not include the Manhattan U.S. Attorney's office.

Their rupture has since proceeded unabated, with squabbles over jurisdiction and scheduling of trials periodically surfacing in court. (Which political corruption case—Guiliani's or Morgenthau's—goes first will be a crucial battle in the ongoing war.) Who will ultimately triumph in a series of prosecutions that will probably take years is far from clear. Observers say that Giuliani's personality is better suited to this kind of conflict and that he has more experience at bureaucratic infighting. He is the odds-on favorite. But Morgenthau's prosecutors say his patience is wearing thin and that he can be fierce when aroused.

The feud with Morgenthau did invigorate some of the assistants working for Giuliani. By shifting his competitive focus on Morgenthau and the Manhattan D.A.'s office, and away from rivalries within his own office, Giuliani helped to boost morale. After two years of his administration, the tension and anxiety stemming from the early personnel problems had largely dissipated. Pedowitz left the office to return to a partnership at Wachtell, Lipton, easing tension over his affair with Parver (who, nonetheless, would frequently inject "Larry says . . ." into discussions of cases and policy). Eventually, their affair petered out, and Pedowitz again ascended into the pantheon of most-loved former prosecutors.

But as fears by assistants that they would lose their jobs or be banished within the office eased, a new morale problem took their place. It wasn't just that Giuliani was a media hound, or that he kept the public spotlight on their office. By and large, that was seen as a plus. It was that he took public credit at the expense of assistants at the office, and, in a few cases, undermined their authority.

A case that came to symbolize those problems was the massive prosecution of fugitive financier Marc Rich. The legendary commodities trader and his U.S. operations, Clarendon Ltd., had been charged with sixty-five counts of mail and wire fraud, racketeering, violating federal oil price controls, and tax evasion, and the case was among the most important and visible in the office.

The Assistant U.S. Attorney in charge of the Rich case was Morris "Sandy" Weinberg, Jr. He reported to Jane Parver, who in turn reported to Giuliani. Weinberg eventually worked out a potential plea agreement with Clarendon in which the company would plead guilty and the government would be able to levy massive fines.

Parver, however, opposed the plea and wanted to drive a harder bargain, say assistants in the office at the time. Over time, relations between her and Weinberg became increasingly strained, eventually erupting in frequent shouting matches. The assistants say that when Weinberg didn't do Parver's bidding, she complained to Giuliani, who usually backed her up. "Some lawyers in the office were appalled," says one assistant in the office at the time. "Parver only had oversight authority in the case, and Giuliani wasn't that familiar with the facts. Yet they were overruling the assistants who knew the most about it."

Nonetheless, eventually a plea agreement was reached: Clarendon pleaded guilty to making false statements and tax evasion and made payments of over $150 million. Though Parver had been adamantly opposed to settlement and stormed out of one settlement discussion, she says she supported the final plea agreement. And Giuliani was finally brought around by what one assistant characterizes as "strenuous argument. This was a great plea for the government."

Thus it was galling for Weinberg, the principal architect of the settlement, that it was Giuliani who announced the settlement at a press conference and got public credit for it. Although Weinberg and another assistant who had worked hard on the case, Martin Auerbach, were present with Giuliani at the time of the announcement, they were barely mentioned in the next day's press coverage. They were particularly upset that the article on the settlement in *The Wall Street Journal* the next day, the paper's lead story, made no mention of them. The article said Giuliani "held aloft a check made payable to the

United States of America" and quoted him saying the U.S. received "far more money" than it would have had the case gone to trial.

Giuliani recalls that the assistants on the case did complain to him about their lack of recognition, especially Weinberg. "Sandy was very concerned about this," Giuliani says, "but I think he was being immature. He had a hard time accepting that many other people besides himself were needed on a case this complex."

"It was a bitter experience for Sandy Weinberg," says one assistant. "He'd invested three years of his life in this case. He argued seventeen pre-trial motions. Giuliani did hardly any." As soon as possible after the end of the case, Weinberg resigned to go into private practice in Florida.

The situation was so demoralizing that some assistants went to Giuliani directly to talk about what they saw as an emerging pattern. Giuliani, they say, argued that it was in their own interest for him to take credit for every success in the office. "His argument," one recalls, "was that no one ever remembers a case, or who was responsible for it. What they remember is who you worked for. And if you worked for someone people view as a great prosecutor, then that rubs off on you. He always pointed to Levi [Edward Levi, former dean of the University of Chicago Law School and Attorney General in the Ford presidency] and how that's who appointed him and who he worked for and how he was remembered. What we didn't say was that most people don't even know who Levi is."

To others, Giuliani says that publicity is in the public interest. "You've got to get a big bang for the buck," he says. "Get attention. If no one hears about a tax prosecution, then it's not going to deter anyone. Get the information out. That translates into deterrence.

"I was on page one of The New York Times today," he continues. "It's true there's been some resentment from others in the Department of Justice and in Washington. There's cynicism about people who get publicity. Why are they doing it? I constantly get asked, 'What are you running for?' But I see this as a vital part of law enforcement."

Giuliani has achieved a public profile higher than any New York prosecutor since Thomas E. Dewey. Not all of the publicity has focused on the work of his office and its cases. Giuliani himself has been the subject of major profiles in most New York publications; nearly all of them have bordered on the adulatory. "Rudi has a remarkable rapport with the press," explains one of his aides.

But not all the publicity for the office was favorable. In May 1985,

Daniel Perlmutter, an Assistant U.S. Attorney in Giuliani's office, was arrested and charged with stealing cash, cocaine, and heroin being held as evidence in the U.S. Attorney's office. He was also involved in a prostitution ring, often using the names of other attorneys in the office to conceal his own identity.

It was an unheard of scandal in the Southern District U.S. Attorney's office. Colleagues, many of whom considered themselves close friends of Perlmutter, were deeply shocked. Opinions about the handling of the matter tended to divide into two camps: those who felt Perlmutter should have received more supervision and help from the office, and those who felt he should have been fired, or at least removed from sensitive drug cases, long before his arrest.

"It was obvious that something was terribly wrong with Perlmutter," recalls one of his friends in the office. "We all knew he was having some bad problems in his marriage, and he was often moody or depressed. Then he would disappear—there'd be a court appearance and he wouldn't show up, and we'd have to search frantically for him and try to cover for him. With the benefit of hindsight, something should have been done."

Giuliani wasted no time agonizing over what might have been done. He felt personally and professionaly betrayed, and denounced Perlmutter angrily and publicly. He wanted to prosecute Perlmutter personally, but was persuaded by his top aides to turn the case over to the Justice Department in Washington to avoid the appearance of any conflict of interest. Perlmutter eventually pleaded guilty.

Perlmutter wept openly at his sentencing in January 1986, saying that "the proudest day of my life was when I was sworn in as an Assistant United States Attorney. I disgraced that great office." In a letter to the judge, William Tendy, then Deputy Attorney General in Washington, wrote that he knew of no other incident that had so seriously challenged the integrity of the Southern District U.S. Attorney's office, which had "justifiably earned a reputation as the most respected prosecutor's office in the country. Dan Perlmutter's actions produced a shock wave through the office and throughout the office alumni that is impossible to describe."

Perlmutter was sentenced to a three-year prison term, which Giuliani denounced as too lenient. Twelve years would have been appropriate, he said.

Perlmutter was a dramatic example of a prosecutor turned criminal. It is a rare, but not unheard of, phenomenon. Prosecutors occupy positions of unusual trust and power; probably a Perlmutter wouldn't have been able to pursue his increasingly blatant crime spree for so long in any other position. Prosecutors spend their professional lives studying criminals, whose exciting if reprehensible careers can sometimes exert a fatal attraction.

Misconduct on the part of prosecutors, however, is rarely so clearcut. It is also far more widespread. In exercising the great discretionary power with which they are entrusted, prosecutors often find themselves in shadowy, shifting ethical territory, in which several false steps can transform them from the hunters into the hunted. Such was the case in what started as the largest tax fraud prosecution in history.

THE BANK OF NOVA SCOTIA
TAX SHELTER SCHEME

THE late-model station wagon gathered speed as Georgetown, the capital city, gave way to the parched, desertlike terrain of the Cayman Islands, a skin diver's paradise and one of the Caribbean's most popular tax havens. It was October 19, 1981. Jack Walker, the driver of the car, was a local restaurateur and businessman. He noticed that his heavyset passenger was still perspiring, despite the air conditioning. Walker wondered if it was from the physical exertion of getting the file drawers of documents into the back of the wagon or whether something else was worrying him.

Walker was sophisticated enough to be suspicious. Though he came across as an easygoing guy with a southern drawl who liked nothing more than a lively evening of drink and food at his restaurant, he was himself no stranger to the ways of financial fraud. Like some of his friends in the Cayman Islands, Walker wasn't an expatriate entirely by choice. He had fled his native Tennessee several years earlier when his construction business there collapsed. He was subsequently indicted for bankruptcy fraud.

His passenger was someone who had trusted him despite his legal problems—or maybe it was because of them. Walker had met William Kilpatrick at his restaurant when Kilpatrick hosted a gala celebration for investors involved in some Cayman Islands–based tax shelters. Kilpatrick was a Denver entrepreneur who had himself fallen into bankruptcy during the late sixties, only to rise again with spectacular success. Now he had made Walker an officer in one of his many Cayman Islands corporations and given Walker control of the hundreds of documents in the back of the car.

As he drove, Walker periodically eyed Kilpatrick with concern. Ordinarily loud, fast-talking, flamboyant, Kilpatrick seemed subdued. He still looked the part of the western success story, with the long, bushy silver sideburns curving back over his ears, flashy rings on his fingers, and expensive cowboy boots under his designer suit. But Walker sensed there was trouble, perhaps more than at any other time in Kilpatrick's career. Walker knew that his career had already had its share of ups and downs.

Kilpatrick had grown up near Lubbock, Texas, during the Depression, worked his way through college, and wound up in Colorado in 1962. He ran a helicopter service based in Denver, supplying local radio stations with airborne traffic reports and making a seasonal specialty out of dropping Santa Claus impersonators into shopping malls.

The venture was successful, but in 1966 he sold out, sank the proceeds into a transmission repair franchise operation, and promptly went bankrupt.

The setback had little visible impact on his life-style. He owned a large ranch house and swimming pool, and had a country-club membership and a chauffeured limousine. Nor did it seem to bother his friends, some of whom were in high places. Not long after the bankruptcy, Kilpatrick showed up with General Anastasio Somoza, the since-deposed and assassinated leader of Nicaragua. The two were in a land development deal together in Costa Rica, Kilpatrick said at the time.

By the mid-seventies, Kilpatrick was into tax shelter deals, a field that seemed a natural outlet for his outgoing, business-getting personality, the financial acumen he'd developed in his real estate and other ventures, and a westerner's natural distaste for Washington bureaucrats in the Internal Revenue Service. He flourished, and so did the number of prominent people he numbered among his friends: Representative Jack Kemp, astronauts Jack Swigert and Wally Schirra, Colorado Senator William Armstrong. One of his proudest possessions is a photograph of himself with a smiling President Ronald Reagan and Nancy at the President's first inaugural. Kilpatrick had been a major fund raiser for the Republican Party in Colorado.

But Kilpatrick's friends had done little to help him this time. The

Securities and Exchange Commission had been investigating his tax shelter promotions, specifically his sales tactics and disclosure statements. Now a criminal grand jury had subpoenaed documents from Cayman Islands corporations allegedly controlled by Kilpatrick; some of those documents, Walker strongly suspected, were at that very moment piled up on the back seat of his car.

Those suspicions were quickly confirmed. Suddenly Kilpatrick shifted sideways in the front passenger seat, reached back, and grabbed a piece of paper from one of the files. Walker glanced at it, but couldn't tell what it was. Kilpatrick gazed at the paper for a moment, then crumpled it tightly into a ball. "This goddamn piece of paper will send me to jail," Kilpatrick said angrily. He lowered the car window, then tossed the wad from the speeding car. It was one piece of evidence that federal prosecutors would never see.

JARED Scharf had just returned to Washington from San Diego when his boss called him into the office. He had what looked like two hot tax shelter scams, and he was offering Scharf his pick. Where did he want to spend the next year? Denver or Los Angeles?

Scharf groaned quietly to himself at the prospect of another out-of-town assignment. Scharf was one of about twenty trial prosecutors assigned to the criminal section of the Tax Division of the Justice Department, a group responsible for prosecuting all the government's major tax fraud cases. Although some cases are farmed out to individual U.S. Attorney's offices, and the tax prosecutors always work closely with U.S. Attorneys when their cases are in their jurisdictions, the subject matter is deemed so specialized that the Tax Division has its own crew of career prosecutors.

Scharf was one of the more experienced prosecutors in the group, having already tried twenty-five cases since he arrived in Washington in 1977. He was also quickly becoming something of an expert in tax shelters, an area that had been given scant attention, at least in terms of criminal prosecution.

Scharf had just conducted a six-week trial in San Diego against members of the Life Science Church, an organization whose members, by taking a phony "vow of poverty," had sought to evade paying any income taxes. That case had raised some delicate First Amendment issues, successfully overcome by Scharf. The case resulted in convictions.

Scharf carried files on both cases into his office for a quick examination before he made up his mind. Basically, he saw, the choice was between cattle or coal. The Los Angeles case was an alleged livestock fraud, involving huge, deductible "losses" on investments in cattle herds that allegedly never existed. The other involved alleged frauds in coal and methane tax shelters, with elaborate royalty and lease provisions that gave investors four dollars in tax write-offs for every dollar invested.

Prosecution of the Denver coal case looked as if it might have more widespread impact, but Scharf was used to being in Southern California. He was also concerned about the strength of the coal case. He'd never heard of the alleged mastermind, Denver entrepreneur William Kilpatrick. There was a good deal of material in the file, since the matter had come to the Justice Department from the Securities and Exchange Commission, which was conducting its own investigation. But some key aspects of the case, especially those involved in bringing criminal, rather than civil, charges, appeared to Scharf to be little more than informed speculation. Scharf opted for the cattle case and prepared to spend another year in California.

He wondered how he would break the news to his wife. The Life Science Church case had kept Scharf away from his home and family for most of a year. The San Diego case had ended on January 12. Scharf calculated that during the preceding 365 days he'd been away from home 150 nights.

He had managed to bring his family out to California for three weeks, but his employer, the federal government, did little to facilitate that experiment. The only economy of scale was his hotel room— the government picked up the tab for one room, as long as it cost less than the government's modest per diem, and whether or not Scharf was alone in it. But that was it. All meals consumed by his wife, for example, had to be paid out of Scharf's pocket. If the couple took a cab from the airport, Scharf had to pay the half of the fare attributable to his wife out of his own pocket. Bringing his family along hadn't turned out to be a financially viable option.

Still, there was an excitement about trying big cases out of town that Scharf had never tired of. There were few distractions, enabling Scharf to concentrate exclusively on the immediate case. Scharf had a romantic notion of himself as a modern cowboy, doing today's equivalent of frontier justice. "I rode into town, got the bad guy, and rode out of town. It was great," he says. It never occurred to him that he would ever be wearing anything but a white hat. Or that in the showdown with Kilpatrick, he himself would be the one who felt prosecuted.

Despite Scharf's choice of the cattle case, Kilpatrick's coal and methane shelter gradually came to dominate Scharf's life. It also brought his promising career as a prosecutor to an abrupt end.

AFTER Scharf initially turned down the Kilpatrick coal venture case, it was assigned to Stephen Snyder, a younger prosecutor in the office known to everyone as "Jake." Snyder plunged into the case with typical enthusiasm, loudly proclaiming it to be history's greatest tax shelter case.

Snyder fits the image of the tough prosecutor. He was born in Iowa—on a farm just up the road from the location for the movie *Country*. He was still in his teens when his father died of cancer, and he took over the operation of the farm. He later put himself through college and law school at Drake University, in Des Moines, working part time at a public defender's office.

He always wanted to do criminal law, practically the only kind of law he knew about in Iowa. He got little satisfaction from the defense work he did in the public defender's office, and turned with enthusiasm to prosecution, where he saw a real opportunity to do some good for society. The Tax Division was his first job out of law school.

Snyder still looks like a farmer. He's tall, stocky but not fat, round-faced, and easily excitable. He reddens easily when angry or, as is often the case, after he's been drinking. He was popular among other prosecutors in the office, and they usually knew what he was up to. His accounts of his prosecutorial exploits where generally delivered in booming tones that could be heard up and down the corridors of the office.

Says one of the agents who worked closely with Snyder, "He has a personal approach to the law—Jake was very aggressive in his approach. He could even be personally obnoxious. He saw this entirely as good guys versus bad guys. He was looking for liars, cheaters, and stealers. That's what he'd say: 'I'm here to get liars, cheaters, and stealers.' "

The coal shelter, however, was Snyder's first tax shelter case, and was both factually and legally complex. Snyder was aggressive but not foolish, and he knew when he needed outside advice. Snyder had not even taken a tax course in law school. After studying the files and gathering as much information about Kilpatrick and his operations as he could, he asked for a meeting with top-level people in the section to review the facts and help him decide if they added up to a crime.

Just a few weeks after relinquishing the case, Scharf was asked to sit in on a meeting with Snyder to go over the facts. Also attending were Glenn L. Archer, Jr., the Assistant Attorney General in charge of the Tax Division; Robert Davis, an Assistant Attorney General; and Stanley Krysa, the chief of the Tax Division's criminal section, responsible for approving all prosecutions.

It was an unusually high-ranking group, but the Tax Division was eager to determine whether the Kilpatrick case might be the vehicle for a major tax shelter crackdown. The Reagan administration had given illegal tax shelters high priority, both as a means of raising millions in uncollected tax revenues and as a way of deterring unwitting taxpayers who were being lured into schemes promising three-, four-, even eight-to-one write-offs. The Tax Division had become convinced that civil tax cases, in which participants were simply made to pay taxes owed and appropriate penalties, were simply a slap on the wrist, and that shelter schemes were mushrooming.

Statistics pretty much told the story. In 1973, the IRS had examined a mere 400 tax shelter operations. In 1980 the number jumped to 174,000; it was 300,000 in 1982. The increase could be attributed in part to recent tax laws that, by providing special benefits for real estate, oil and gas, and other energy sources, invited abuse. But for every civil case filed, new, dubious tax shelters sprang up. A more effective deterrent was needed.

Criminal prosecution seemed the obvious answer. But finding the right case hadn't been easy. The tax lawyers in the division acknowledged among themselves that given the complexity of the tax laws it is sometimes very hard for them to figure out whether a scheme was legal or not, let alone criminal. And successful criminal prosecution depends on proving that the defendants themselves knew of and willfully violated the law.

The facts in the Kilpatrick case were so complicated that Snyder brought a blackboard into the conference room and diagrammed the transactions involving the coal and methane, to the extent he'd been able to figure them out. And he included in his presentation what he knew about the background of Kilpatrick and his operations.

Kilpatrick's coal and gas operations had grown out of federal tax policy during the mid-seventies, which, in the wake of soaring oil prices due to the OPEC oil cartel, was intended to provide tax incentives for developing alternative fuel sources. One such incentive was the ability to deduct payments of advance minimum royalties, a common practice in coal operations.

Payments of advance minimum royalties, Snyder explained, tended to produce large deductions for the operator of the coal mine. The operator paid an advance minimum royalty to holders of royalty interests even if no coal was being produced and no income generated. The losses represented by the payments were fully deductible.

Kilpatrick moved to exploit the provision in the late seventies when he bought leases to coal-producing properties in West Virginia, Tennessee, and South Dakota. Then, through a new corporation he created called United Financial Operations, Inc., he sold the properties in parcels to limited partnerships of investors seeking tax deductions. In order to make the necessary payments of advance minimum royalties, each investor was required to pay $45,000 a year for eight years, a total of $360,000. All the advance minimum royalty payments were deductible against the investors' ordinary income. That plan, standing alone, probably wouldn't have attracted much investor interest. It required large payments, generated only a dollar deduction for each dollar invested, and made sense only if the coal mine proved economically viable, returning profits to the investors.

So Kilpatrick had enhanced the tax aspects of the partnerships by taking them a step further. Of the $45,000 in annual advance minimum royalty payments, only one-fourth, or $11,250, was paid in cash by the investor. The remainder was borrowed from Kilpatrick. The investor could still deduct $45,000. An investor otherwise in the 50 percent bracket emerged with a net gain of $11,250 even if no coal was produced: a $22,500 deduction minus the $11,250 cash outlay.

In 1977 Kilpatrick and his Denver lawyer/partner, Declan O'Donnell, began selling units in the partnerships to the public. Within nine months, the offer had come to the attention of the Securities and Exchange Commission in Washington, which issued a subpoena for Kilpatrick's documents and records related to the partnerships after Kilpatrick refused to provide them voluntarily. The ostensible basis for the SEC probe was that Kilpatrick and O'Donnell were selling unregistered securities in violation of the federal securities laws.

EVEN as the SEC's investigation continued, Kilpatrick launched another tax shelter scheme. This one took advantage of 1978 legislation that provided tax credits (even better than deductions) for investments in plant and equipment used to develop synthetic fuels.

Kilpatrick bought from a Denver inventor the rights to a process that was supposed to convert coal into methanol. Unlike the coal operation, the financial arrangments were far more complicated.

Allegedly for legitimate tax reasons rather than secrecy, Kilpatrick established a Cayman Islands corporation named International Fuels Development Corporation, which he and O'Donnell sold to a friend of Kilpatrick's named Wilson Quintella. Quintella was well known in his native Brazil, where he was a retired admiral of the Navy. IFDC then bought the rights to Kilpatrick's methane formula for $10 million. Kilpatrick, in turn, sold general and limited partnerships that entered into licensing agreements with IFDC, allegedly to develop the process. The bottom line for investors in this scheme was another four-dollar deduction for each dollar invested, again by borrowing much of the investment required from Kilpatrick.

In both the coal and methane gas schemes, a key role was played by another Cayman Islands entity called Marlborough Investments Ltd., run by another friend of Kilpatrick's, a Costa Rican named Adrian Paris Arana. Marlborough was a financing source for many of the loans provided by Kilpatrick; Kilpatrick arranged a large line of credit for Marlborough with a Dutch bank by pledging as collateral the assets of Clalite Concrete Block Company in Denver, another business he controlled.

Sales of the coal and gas partnerships cost the IRS $123 million in lost taxes in 1978 and 1979 alone.

Meanwhile, the SEC's investigation continued, and it wasn't hard to see why the agency's suspicions were aroused. Given the presence of so many entities owned or controlled by Kilpatrick, the potential for abuse was high. The SEC was also interested in the economic viability of the operations. Was there any chance that they would produce profits for the investors? Did disclosure materials accurately and fully convey the risks to potential investors?

Kilpatrick fought the SEC's efforts to learn the answers to those questions. He refused to turn over records in the U.S. Others were already in foreign countries. Then, two months after the SEC issued its subpoenas, Kilpatrick transferred the accounts of the tax shelter entities to the Cayman Islands branch of the Bank of Nova Scotia, a place he felt sure would be beyond the reach of the SEC.

Despite its suspicions and discovery efforts, the SEC produced no firm evidence that Kilpatrick had done anything wrong. The investigation was concluded when Kilpatrick finally entered into a consent decree agreeing not to sell unregistered securities.

The consent decree had little impact on the coal shelter partnerships. Demand and prices for the kind of coal to which Kilpatrick's ventures had leases collapsed in the late seventies. No coal was ever extracted, and Kilpatrick stopped selling coal partnerships, turning his attention to the methanol deals.

The SEC turned over the materials it had collected on Kilpatrick's operations to the IRS, which was already looking into the returns of individuals linked to the Kilpatrick partnerships.

At about the same time, in August 1980, IRS agents in Denver received a tip from an informant. The informant leveled all kinds of charges against Kilpatrick—that he had ties with organized crime, that he had drug contacts in Central America, and that he was marketing fraudulent tax shelters. IRS agents in Denver decided to follow up, but none of the claims seemed to pan out—except the one involving the tax shelters. Gradually, more confidential informants supplied information—including the claim that Kilpatrick was traveling to the Cayman Islands to destroy evidence. Even though they would have preferred to keep developing the case quietly, the IRS agents immediately notified the criminal section of the Tax Division in Washington, asking that a grand jury be convened and subpoenas issued to Kilpatrick. That way, if he destroyed subpoenaed documents, he'd be guilty of obstruction of justice. This was the case that landed on Snyder's desk.

The IRS investigators had suggested, and Snyder agreed, that there were two potential criminal aspects of the Kilpatrick shelters. The first was economic viability. If the coal and methane ventures were never intended to produce any economic benefit, and were created solely to avoid payment of taxes, then they were illegal. There was also the matter of the loans from Kilpatrick entities to investors, which provided the leverage necessary to yield such high write-offs.

As Snyder explained to the group the nature of the payments, he took to the blackboard, using information supplied by the IRS and the

SEC. A key question was, where was the money coming from to provide the loans for the advance minimum royalty payments?

Snyder diagrammed the first entity: P&J Coal Company. P&J, owned by someone named John Pettingill, purportedly made the loans to participants in Kilpatrick's coal shelters. The investigators, however, had determined that P&J was near bankruptcy. Pettingill had acquired the company and its assets for a mere $3,000. It couldn't possibly make the loans required by the shelter scheme. Nonetheless, P&J in 1978 issued checks to the coal companies totaling more than $18 million, representing the loans to investors. During their audits, many of the investors had produced copies of the checks to substantiate their deductions.

That money had apparently come from a mysterious entity named Big C Companies Ltd., another Cayman Islands corporation. Finally Snyder connected the chain to a Kilpatrick entity, Marlborough Investments. Big C had evidently gotten the $18 million from Marlborough.

Although there was yet no firm evidence, the diagram looked suspiciously like what is known as a "money circle." In such a scheme, checks are written and deposits made, but the money ends back where it began—presumably, in this case, in the Marlborough account. In the end, no money changes hands. What was needed was evidence that the coal companies returned the advance royalty payments to Marlborough. Snyder's question: Was such a financing system a violation of criminal law?

The group reached no firm conclusions, but the consensus seemed to be that it was. Deductions ordinarily depend on a payment being made that is for a deductible purpose. Even if Kilpatrick's ventures, though shaky, were for legitimate tax deductible goals, if no real payments were actually made, the deduction would presumably be illegal.

In any event, all agreed that a grand jury should be convened to continue the investigation of Kilpatrick and his colleagues. Beyond the specific evidence presented, the whole thing smelled bad. Snyder thought it might even be the big case the department had been waiting for. Perhaps a grand jury, possessing greater jurisdiction and subpoena power than either the SEC or the IRS, could uncover additional evidence and pierce the elaborate structure of offshore corporations erected by Kilpatrick. They knew, however, that it wouldn't be easy.

THE following month, a grand jury was convened in Denver to conduct the criminal investigation into Kilpatrick's affairs.

Technically, grand juries aren't permitted to investigate on their own. For example, recent indictments in New York against police officers accused in the beating death of a black youth were dismissed when it was revealed that the foreman of the grand jury had undertaken his own investigation out of a belief that prosecutors weren't investigating the case with sufficient zeal. Grand juries aren't supposed to be advocates, but impartial judges of whether charges should be lodged. Nonetheless, the line is an increasingly fine one, particularly in cases where the grand jury begins hearing evidence at the same time an investigation is commenced. Defense lawyers argue that in such cases, as a parade of witnesses is brought before the grand jury and is questioned by prosecutors, the jurors come to identify with the investigators and, for all practical purposes, might as well be doing the questioning themselves.

For the next few months, however, the grand jurors had few witnesses to occupy their attention. Snyder and another Tax Division prosecutor assigned to help him on the case, Thomas Blondin, faced the same problem that had stymied the earlier investigations by the SEC and the IRS: the presence of most key witnesses and documents outside the U.S.

The prosecutors notified Kilpatrick and O'Donnell that they were the targets of a grand jury criminal investigation, but that only seemed to harden the targets' resistance to providing any documents or making witnesses available. So the prosecutors had the grand jury issue subpoenas calling for the production of all the bank and other financial records pertaining to the coal and methanol shelters.

Kilpatrick flatly refused, arguing that he didn't own or control most of the corporate entities whose records the prosecutors wanted. IFDC, for example, was owned by Wilson Quintella, the Brazilian admiral; Big C Companies was owned by Oliver Hemphill; P&J Coal Company, by John Pettingill; and Marlborough Investments, by Adrian Paris Arana. Kilpatrick insisted he had only "arm's length" transactions with them, and had no power to make them produce records and documents.

Snyder denounced Kilpatrick's response to his colleagues as patent dissembling. He knew already that the four "owners" of the companies were all friends and business associates of Kilpatrick's who he suspected were nothing but nominal owners for the very purpose of frustrating inquiries into Kilpatrick's affairs. It was annoying, but it also whet his appetite for more information. Why would Kilpatrick go to such lengths unless he had something substantial to hide?

Snyder was also intrigued by another fact that seemed to link the corporate entities in the Cayman Islands. All four of them had accounts at the Cayman Islands branch of the same bank—the Bank of Nova Scotia, headquartered in Halifax, Canada. The bank was in many ways ideal for someone like Kilpatrick, since it was both a major foreign bank, largely beyond the jurisdiction of U.S. courts, and its Cayman Islands branch was bound by the strict bank secrecy laws that have made the Cayman Islands such a popular haven for foreign investors.

Since Kilpatrick was resisting, Snyder decided to try another route to his bank records. He subpoenaed the Bank of Nova Scotia itself, hoping that a major international bank would feel obligated to comply with a legitimate inquiry.

Those hopes were quickly dashed. The bank's lawyers refused, saying that the Cayman Islands' laws specifically prohibited such disclosure of customer records. And they argued that such a request shouldn't even be enforced by the U.S. courts, which are obligated under a principal called comity to honor the laws of foreign sovereigns.

Snyder threatened both the bank and Kilpatrick with contempt proceedings for defying the subpoenas; both remained adamant in their refusal to cooperate. He decided to move first against Kilpatrick, who couldn't invoke complicated doctrines of international law. The prosecutors filed a contempt motion against Kilpatrick, asking for a trial to demonstrate that Kilpatrick did, in fact, control the network of Cayman Islands corporations whose records they wanted. The case was assigned to a federal District Court judge in Denver, Jim Carrigan.

Even before making the contempt motion, Snyder had compiled a list of names of individuals involved in the Kilpatrick companies and operations. He or one of the IRS agents working with him made phone calls to all of them, seeking their cooperation in the investigation.

An interesting fact turned up about one of the people they called—Jack Walker. Agent Paul Raybin had reached Walker by phone in the Cayman Islands, and unlike most of the potential witnesses, Walker was friendly and cooperative. He agreed to accept service of a subpoena, thereby eliminating the problem of serving him outside the U.S., and agreed to testify in Denver.

The day Walker was supposed to appear, however, he didn't show up. His lawyer called and explained that Walker was wanted on a federal bankruptcy fraud warrant in Nashville and couldn't come into the country without risking arrest. The lawyer indicated that Walker was willing to talk if they met on neutral territory, and Raybin said they'd consider that. But at the time Walker seemed just another of many potential witnesses whose testimony would be difficult to obtain, so he and Snyder let the matter drop.

Several months later, they got around to following up on Walker's offer. Raybin called his number in the Cayman Islands, and learned from Walker's housekeeper that Walker was off the island on a business trip. Raybin immediately went into action. He knew from previous inquiries that the Cayman Islands are connected by direct air service to only three places: Miami, Houston, and Jamaica. Since he was a fugitive, Walker could be arrested in all three (Jamaica, unlike the Cayman Islands, has an extradition treaty with the U.S.).

Raybin called Cayman Air and got a phone number where Walker could supposedly be reached. It was a Denver number—and turned out to be that of the travel agency used by Kilpatrick. Raybin called the travel agency and learned that Walker was meeting with Kilpatrick that day in Amsterdam. He was scheduled to return to the Cayman Islands via London and Jamaica.

Raybin reported his findings to Snyder, and they immediately notified the FBI, which in turn contacted Scotland Yard. Walker was arrested by British police as he passed through London on April 1, a Thursday.

Snyder, who was in Washington at the time, was ecstatic at the news. He ran down the corridor shouting, "I'm going to London," then realized he didn't have a passport. He managed to get one on an emergency basis and left for London that night. Raybin joined him the next day. Much to the annoyance of his superiors, Snyder didn't bother to go through the formal approval process required by the department for all international travel.

Snyder and Raybin met with Walker and his lawyer for the first time on Saturday morning. The trip turned out to be a stroke of good fortune. Walker not only knew a good deal about Kilpatrick's operations, but he was carrying a briefcase of documents, some of which he showed Snyder and Raybin. They showed the movement of funds among the Kilpatrick entities and demonstrated the real ownership and control of the companies—critical evidence for Snyder's contempt motion and for the case as a whole.

Snyder was desperate to get Walker into the U.S. to testify. The extradition proceedings in Britain, however, could take months. So Snyder acted as an intermediary between Walker and the U.S. Attorney in Nashville to work out a plea agreement for Walker that would leave him free to return to the U.S. Walker, who was anxious not to be imprisoned in Britain while awaiting extradition, agreed to plead guilty to one count of bankruptcy fraud. In return, Snyder promised to make sure the sentencing judge knew that Walker was cooperating in another important federal case. The prosecutor couldn't make any sentencing promises, but he felt confident the judge would be lenient under those circumstances. Snyder reminded Walker that the more cooperative he was, the more impressed the sentencing judge in Tennessee was likely to be. And Snyder promised Walker that he wouldn't be prosecuted for his own role in the Kilpatrick tax shelters.

Walker agreed to cooperate fully. As a measure of his good faith, he had his wife transfer the Kilpatrick documents he had in his custody to his lawyer in Nashville, who turned them over to a federal agent. And Walker turned out to be Snyder's star witness in Kilpatrick's contempt hearing in May.

At the hearing in Denver, Walker told the story of Kilpatrick's trip to the Cayman Islands and how he wadded up the document that he feared would send him to jail—crucial evidence that indicated Kilpatrick knew he was engaging in criminal fraud. Walker confirmed that he was, in fact, just a front for Kilpatrick, acting on Kilpatrick's instructions. After hearing Walker's testimony, Judge Carrigan ordered Kilpatrick to comply with the subpoenas. When Kilpatrick still refused, the judge ordered a federal marshal to take Kilpatrick into custody and lock him up until he decided to cooperate.

After just one night in Denver federal prison, Kilpatrick capitulated. He agreed to turn over the documents, and asked the Bank of Nova Scotia to comply with the subpoenas for his records.

Snyder and Blondin were suddenly confronted with masses of documents both from Kilpatrick and the bank—documents they had never really expected to get. There were so many that the prosecutors couldn't organize them properly in the small space they'd been allocated inside the Denver U.S. Attorney's office.

E V E N without the space problems, Snyder and Blondin had been coexisting rather uneasily with their colleagues in the Denver U.S. Attorney's office. Robert Miller, the Denver U.S. Attorney, a Republican Reagan appointee and former Greeley, Colorado, prosecutor, had originally tried to wrest control of the case away from Washington. After being rebuffed by the Justice Department, relations between most of his staff and Snyder had cooled markedly. Miller had assigned an Assistant U.S. Attorney to act as a liaison with the prosecutors from Washington, but otherwise the office provided little support.

Nor did Snyder's style or diplomatic skills do much to improve relations. Snyder favored blue jeans, work shirts, and cowboy boots; he avoided the office altogether, preferring to interview witnesses at the Landmark Inn, a bar near the hotel where he stayed while in Denver.

When Miller told Snyder and Blondin he couldn't give them any more space for their operations, the two prosecutors thought they would have to move into the post office. But there was only slightly more space there, and it was less convenient. Soon after, however, they were rescued by one of the leading figures of the Denver bar, Fred M. Winner, the chief judge of the federal court for the District of Colorado.

Judge Winner is probably the best-known jurist in the mountain states, and he is highly controversial. A 1970 Nixon appointee, he was named the worst federal district judge in the Tenth Circuit, a large area of the western U.S. that includes Colorado, by the *American Lawyer* magazine in 1983.

No one denies Winner's intelligence, wit, knowledge of the law or ability to write well [the *American Lawyer* noted]. Rather, lawyers contend that Winner is dangerous because he is cunning enough to stay just within the bounds of judicial discretion. This, they argue, allows Winner to harass lawyers, break rules, and almost always get away with both. "He's Machiavellian," says a former Denver public defender who is now in private practice. "He can twist and distort and pretty much cover anything up."

But Winner couldn't have been nicer to Snyder and Blondin. One day he came up to them in the courthouse and put his arm around

Snyder. "The U.S. Attorney doesn't understand you guys," he told Snyder in fatherly tones, and invited them to move their operations right into the federal courthouse. In fact, on that and other occasions, Judge Winner was so friendly that Snyder worried. He didn't want defense counsel charging judicial favoritism toward the prosecution if any of the Kilpatrick cases ended up in Judge Winner's court.

Once settled in their new quarters, the prosecutors were able to pore over the records produced by the bank. Unfortunately, they seemed entirely innocuous. There was nothing to suggest the circular payment scheme that Snyder had suspected at the outset. Worse, there wasn't even much to suggest that Kilpatrick was the real owner of the corporate entities, such as corporate checks bearing his signature. Either Kilpatrick was much cleaner than the prosecutors had ever suspected, or he had been much more clever in directing these enterprises.

Then the prosecutors made a startling discovery. The documents that had been in Walker's custody—minus the paper tossed out the window by Kilpatrick—included a large number of canceled checks and other records from the Bank of Nova Scotia, presumably duplicates of the records that had just been turned over by the bank.

For example, in sifting through the Walker materials, Snyder came across a check that caught his attention because it was for such a large amount. It was for $18,855,600 drawn on the Bank of Nova Scotia from the account of Marlborough Investments, and signed by Adrian Paris Arana. It was payable to the Big C Companies, dated December 29, 1978. Curiously, there was also a stop payment order dated February 12, 1979, on a check for the same amount—even though the Marlborough check had been stamped by the bank as paid on December 29. But what was remarkable was not so much the mystery surrounding the check and the stop payment, but the fact that there was no trace of either document in the documents the Bank of Nova Scotia had provided in response to the subpoena. It looked as if the bank hadn't complied fully with the subpoena.

Moreover, as Snyder and Blondin went carefully through the checks provided by Walker—but not the bank—they felt they were finally able to piece together how the shelter schemes had been financed. And coupled with the bank's failure to disclose the evidence, disturbing questions about the role, even complicity, of the Bank of Nova Scotia were raised.

Much of the activity relating to the 1979 tax year coal deductions had taken place in a single day—December 29, 1978—in the bank's Cayman Islands branch. The canceled checks indicated that Marlborough Investments issued a check for the $18.85 million to Big C Companies. Big C Companies issued a check, also drawn on the Bank of Nova Scotia, to P&J Coal Company for the same amount. P&J Coal, in turn, made the advance royalty payments to twenty different coal companies, all of which had accounts at the same branch of the bank. Finally—and this was the crucial evidence—the coal companies, either directly or indirectly through another Kilpatrick entity, issued checks totaling $18.85 million back to Marlborough Investments, completing the circle. The payments were allegedly made to purchase corporate debentures of Marlborough.

The prosecutors were ecstatic at the discovery of the documentary evidence, which they recognized would form the core of their criminal case. At the same time, they pressed their efforts to bring witnesses before the grand jury to buttress the case.

A key part of that effort involved persuading associates of Kilpatrick and O'Donnell to appear and testify. Their first effort was a series of letters, which created quite a stir in Denver and elsewhere among clients and business associates of Kilpatrick and O'Donnell.

Written on stationery from the Denver U.S. Attorney's office the letters read:

> The United States Department of Justice is conducting a Grand Jury investigation of the business activities of William A. Kilpatrick, Declan J. O'Donnell, John Pettingill and Sheila C. Lerner [Kilpatrick's secretary] for the years 1977 through 1980. The Grand Jury is attempting to determine whether these individuals, through Financial Operations, Inc., P&J Coal Co., Inc., Marlborough Investments Ltd., International Fuels Development Corp. Ltd., and International Block Construction Co. Ltd., have committed violations of Title 18 and Title 26 of the United States Code.
>
> The Grand Jury has obtained information which indicates that you have had and/or currently do have a business relationship with one or more of the individuals and/or entities listed above. It has been determined that your testimony will be helpful in resolving questions which still face the Grand Jury. Subsequently [sic] the United States Department of Justice cordially invites you to appear and testify before the Federal Grand Jury in Denver, Colorado (U.S.A.) at your convenience.

Transportation, lodging and meals will be arranged for and paid by the United States Department of Justice.

We look forward to your response.

Sincerely yours,

> STEPHEN L. SNYDER, Trial Attorney
> Criminal Section, Tax Division,
> by PAUL E. RAYBIN, Special Agent.

Despite the cordial wording, the prosecutors assumed there would be no doubt in the reader's mind that serious business was afoot, given the multiple references to the Department of Justice and the grand jury. The message did get across—Kilpatrick later complained that his business associates and clients were so stunned that his business career was nearly ruined. But the letters produced little in the way of cooperation.

Many of the recipients of the letters hired the same lawyer, Bernard Bailor, who called Snyder to say that his clients weren't going to testify voluntarily. They were particularly wary of waiving any Fifth Amendment rights in a field like tax, where they weren't even sure what might be construed as a crime.

The prosecutors were in something of a bind. Unlike Walker, who they could entice into testifying by promising assistance with his other legal problems, they lacked leverage with these potential witnesses.

Grants of immunity seemed to provide the only practical way for the prosecutors to overcome the witnesses' reluctance to speak. The law governing grants of immunity is different in the federal court system than in New York and some other states. In New York, a witness who appears before the grand jury is automatically immunized from future prosecution unless he specifically waives his Fifth Amendment rights and waives immunity from prosecution. In federal court, a witness may be compelled to testify if he is given a grant of use immunity for his grand jury testimony; he may nonetheless be prosecuted based on other evidence. A federal statute outlines the procedures used for the granting of such immunity. Because of the frequent arguments that often later arose between defendants and prosecutors over exactly what was promised in return for a witness's testimony, the procedure requires Justice Department approval of all immunity agreements.

In practice, however, the approval process has proved cumbersome for federal prosecutors, who often want to offer immunity on the spur of the moment, often while engaged in delicate negotiations with a potential witness. Snyder, on the phone with Bailor, spontaneously suggested what are known as letters of assurance, even though he wasn't entirely sure he had the authority to do so. The letters assure the witness that he won't be prosecuted. Though not phrased in terms of immunity, the letters have the same practical effect—if a defendant can't be prosecuted the defendant is effectively immune.

Bailor seemed to grab at the suggestion for his clients, and Snyder tentatively agreed to such an arrangement. He checked with the Tax Division in Washington, which okayed the arrangement as long as it complied with the department's internal guidelines.

In retrospect, Snyder may have embraced the arrangement with a bit too much abandon—in all, twenty-three witnesses were given such letters of assurance, including one witness who, it later emerged, hadn't filed tax returns at all for several years and could otherwise have been prosecuted. But it seemed at the time the best way to get the witnesses' testimony—after all, they seemed to want the letters.

(Unlike the more cumbersome process of statutory immunity, which requires Justice Department review, witnesses aren't required to accept such letters if offered. Witnesses must accept immunity if statutory procedure is followed. That feature of the statute was included primarily as a means to obtain the testimony of organized-crime figures, who frequently used the Fifth Amendment as a means not to prevent self-incriminating testimony but to protect others.)

Getting the witnesses before the grand jury, however, didn't mean that they would be cooperative, volunteering valuable information that wasn't specifically asked for. For example, John Jewell, a general partner of Kilpatrick's in one of the ventures and who was given immunity, was talking outside the grand jury room with Raybin, the IRS agent who was acting as an investigator and grand jury agent in the case. Raybin mentioned that he'd been out to Jewell's house, and Jewell bluntly responded, "If I catch you on my property I'll shoot you." Snyder later tried to calm Jewell, commenting during his testimony, that "as the investigation continues, nerves are getting a little frayed, I think, on both sides, correct? I think we just both—all parties concerned have to be maybe a little more cautious in our words and deeds so as not to convey something we don't mean to somebody else." Jewell apologized for the remark to Raybin (which the agent took as an actual murder threat), but remained a hostile witness throughout.

Snyder also got into an argument with Roland Hjorth, a professor at the University of Washington called as an expert in tax law who wasn't involved in any of Kilpatrick's activities. Hjorth claimed that after his testimony, Snyder, within the hearing of several grand jurors, threatened to sue Hjorth for perjury. (Snyder concedes that in a discussion after Hjorth's testimony that he did say to him, "I'll see you in court," but that he only meant he'd see Hjorth when he testified—it wasn't meant as a threat to sue Hjorth himself. He adds that he wasn't aware any grand jurors were present at the time.) Hjorth later said that Snyder was so rude, abusive, and insulting that he'd never appear as an expert witness again.

His colleagues acknowledge that the coddling of witnesses isn't one of Snyder's strengths as a prosecutor. As Scharf explains, "Jake loves to debate. He'll argue anything—like how many aircraft are there in the U.S. Navy—whether he really knows what the facts are or not. Witnesses don't realize that he enjoys this sort of thing. He's not attacking them personally."

Meanwhile, the supposedly secret grand jury investigation seemed to be the talk of Denver. The resulting pressure appeared to be having an effect on O'Donnell, a key potential defendant, and some witnesses. Among the witnesses called before the grand jury was O'Donnell's former secretary, who had left his employ soon after O'Donnell remarried. Defense lawyers later claimed that she was questioned about her sexual relations with O'Donnell. Prosecutors denied that, but there was speculation that the two had been romantically involved, and she was the kind of witness whose testimony would undoubtedly have worried O'Donnell. Two witnesses died, one from a heart attack and another—the original informant—from poison. An investigation ruled it suicide.

Early that summer, O'Donnell's lawyer, Robert Grossman, asked for a meeting at the Justice Department in Washington in an effort to head off what seemed to be a growing probability that the grand jury would indict his client, O'Donnell. It was at this point that the Kilpatrick case again entered Jared Scharf's life.

Prior to the meeting, Grossman, himself a former IRS lawyer, had insisted that someone in the department with higher rank than Snyder or Blondin be present; he figured—rightly—that prosecutors with as much invested in the case as those two prosecutors had wouldn't be receptive to appeals to drop it. The Justice Department has a formal procedure for such conferences, and ordinarily will assign another attorney to hear the defense lawyer's pleas. The lawyer is called a reviewer, and in this instance, Scharf, as a more senior attorney, was assigned that function.

He wasn't impressed with Grossman's presentation, which focused on the law rather than the facts in the case. The department had already determined that the acts alleged, if true, constituted a crime. If anything, O'Donnell seemed so desperate to avoid prosecution that it made Scharf skeptical of his claim to innocence. Grossman actually encouraged the prosecutors to bring his client before the grand jury—an extremely rare occurrence, since defense lawyers generally want their clients to avoid such testimony at all costs unless there's been a grant of immunity.

Grossman said he wanted O'Donnell to testify because he could produce two of the country's top tax experts—Mortimer Caplin, a former IRS Commissioner now in private practice, and James Eustis, a tax professor at New York University School of Law—both of whom would testify that the facts didn't amount to a crime. Snyder was skeptical, but impressed nonetheless. He said that if Grossman followed through on that promise, he would drop the investigation. In return, Snyder understood that O'Donnell would testify before the grand jury.

His expectations in that regard were quickly dashed. Grossman did produce an "expert," but he was neither Caplin nor Eustis (the expert was Hjorth, who later got into the argument with Snyder). And he sent a letter to Snyder "confirming" that O'Donnell would testify before the grand jury in return for a grant of immunity. Snyder was annoyed and astounded by Grossman's audacity, since immunity hadn't even been discussed in the course of their meeting. (Grossman says that it was "implicit" in the conversation.)

DESPITE the breakdown of negotiations with Grossman, and much to Snyder's surprise, O'Donnell actually responded to his grand jury subpoena and showed up at the courthouse to testify, unescorted by Grossman. Snyder immediately sensed trouble, even though O'Donnell was himself a lawyer and surely knew that he shouldn't be testifying before the grand jury, especially without his lawyer present. Ethically, lawyers may not contact an opposing party in a lawsuit;

they are required to communicate through the party's lawyer. And in criminal cases, the prohibition is more than an ethical one. Targets of grand jury investigations, as well as defendants, have a constitutional right to counsel, and prosecutors may not question suspects outside the presence of their lawyers, unless those rights are waived. Those rights are what gave rise to the well-known Miranda warning, which is read to everyone arrested.

Snyder faced a situation where he wasn't sure O'Donnell could waive those rights, since his lawyer had already said that he couldn't testify in the grand jury. "Did you talk to your lawyer?" Snyder asked him. O'Donnell said no, but he wanted to testify. He wanted to make a clean breast, he insisted. But Snyder, knowing how furious Grossman had been when their negotiations broke down, didn't want to arouse further protests if he had O'Donnell testify without Grossman being there. So he gave O'Donnell a quarter and told him to call Grossman right away. O'Donnell returned, saying that Grossman was out of his office and couldn't be reached. And he still wanted to testify.

At this point, prudence suggested that Snyder wait. What was one more day or two? But he felt that a rare opportunity to get O'Donnell's testimony was at hand. Given the man's emotional state, he could change his mind at any moment. He was sure that Grossman wouldn't let his client testify. And after all, O'Donnell was a lawyer himself. Snyder brought O'Donnell before the grand jury and, on the record, warned him repeatedly about the hazards of testifying.

At that point Snyder figured he had done enough. When O'Donnell insisted that he knew what he was doing, Snyder plunged into a direct examination of O'Donnell that continued for several days, eliciting valuable information about Kilpatrick's operations. His premonition that Grossman would be furious was amply borne out. Grossman was not only furious; he encouraged O'Donnell to sue Snyder in a civil suit for violation of his civil rights. O'Donnell and Kilpatrick later did file suit against Snyder for $4.5 million in damages. (The case was pending in 1987.)

At about the same time, the prosecutors informed the Bank of Nova Scotia that it too had become a target of the investigation and was no longer being considered simply an important source of evidence. Snyder and Blondin had agonized over the decision to make the bank a target for some time. After all, there were four banks involved in Kilpatrick's operations, and it was initially hard to justify targeting one bank over the others. Nor was it customary in such cases to pursue financial institutions. Even if the facts suggested they were something more than innocent conduits for funds, to prove the requisite criminal intent on the part of the institutions is very difficult. Usually such institutions argue that any criminal aberration was due solely to the unauthorized activities of one or more individuals, and those arguments are often successful in front of juries.

The discovery of the records and check from the Bank of Nova Scotia that turned up in Walker's custody and hadn't been turned over the bank, however, had suggested to the prosecutors that the bank's culpability was strong. They reasoned that such a response required the knowing complicity of the institution, as well as the unlawful conduct of a few employees. And they had long wanted an institutional case to enhance the deterrent effect of the prosecution.

The bank was surprised and disturbed by the notice, and sent its outside counsel from the large New York City law firm of Shearman & Sterling to Washington for a conference with the prosecutors. This meeting too was attended by Scharf in his capacity of reviewer. The Shearman & Sterling lawyers argued that the bank's failure to produce the records was an oversight caused by a combination of warehouse storage problems and illegible microfilm. Somewhat to the prosecutors surprise, they didn't argue that responsibility should be confined to just a few individuals in the bank rather than the bank itself. The prosecutors weren't impressed—the coincidences explaining the nonproduction of damaging documents were too incredible.

Shortly after that conference, the bank hired a criminal lawyer, Robert Morvillo, a New York lawyer and former Assistant U.S. Attorney in Manhattan whose specialty now is the defense of white-collar crime cases. He made what the prosecutors conceded was an interesting argument—that the bank couldn't have intended to commit a crime because it didn't know specifically that the object of the activity going on in its Cayman Islands branch was tax fraud.

THE prosecutors had to acknowledge that the law in that area is unclear. Ordinarily, a defendant is guilty of conspiracy only if the defendant knows the object of the conspiracy. (There were no allegations that the bank itself filed false or fraudulent tax returns, so its liability would be only as a coconspirator.) But it wasn't clear whether the bank would have to know that the object was tax fraud specifically, or if it would be enough that it knew the object was fraud. The prosecutors and Scharf thought the latter interpretation was correct, and that the checking account pattern showed clearly that some kind of fraud was taking place. But they acknowledged that the department might disagree, and agreed that Morvillo could take his case to higher levels in the department. Morvillo met with Rudi Giuliani (then still the Associate Attorney General).

Naming the Bank of Nova Scotia as a target had increased the visibility of the investigation within the department in other ways too. The bank is 20 percent owned by the government of Canada, which was furious at the allegations of criminal wrongdoing. The Canadian embassy in Washington conveyed its concerns in strong terms to the State Department, which in turn notified the Justice Department that there was strong Canadian opposition to any indictment of the Bank of Nova Scotia. And Canada was in an unusually good position for extracting favors from Washington. There was still considerable goodwill and a sense of obligation remaining from Canada's role in first hiding and then aiding the escape of several Americans from Iran at the time of the Islamic Revolution.

Scharf, Snyder, and Blondin were aware that numerous meetings were being held between the two departments, but never received any direct pressure not to pursue the case. "We felt the vibes," Scharf says. But they reasoned that if the Canadian government knew as much about the case as they did, it wouldn't oppose the indictments.

The prosecutors' judgments were also influenced by the evidence that was being amassed from the grand jury investigation. The mystery of the $18.85 million stop payment order was finally solved, and it provided the most convincing evidence yet of the bank's criminal culpability.

According to grand jury testimony of Richard Bell, one of Kilpatrick's associates who had been immunized by Snyder, on about February 2, 1979, Kilpatrick had arranged for Adrian Paris Arana, the nominal owner of Marlborough Investments, to be given sole signature authority over Marlborough's account at the Bank of Nova Scotia in the Cayman Islands. Kilpatrick, Arana, and Bell had then met with two of the bank's officers, C. M. Smith and M. J. Raynes, at the bank's offices.

At the meeting, Kilpatrick had Arana make out a Marlborough check for $18.85 million on the account of Marlborough, payable to the Big C Companies. Handwritten by Arana on the check was the date—not February 2, but December 29, 1978. The check was stamped as paid by the bank officers, and the stamp too had been altered to reflect the false date. It was that check, in fact, that had appeared in Walker's files. The stop payment order was for the original check in the same amount that the backdated check replaced. That check, also drawn on the Marlborough account, had been signed by William Kilpatrick. It was an obvious attempt by Kilpatrick to disguise his own control of Marlborough and his role in the scheme.

The evidence also established that the various Kilpatrick entities engaged in the schemes wrote millions and millions of dollars' worth of checks on their Bank of Nova Scotia accounts, even though the balances in those accounts had only modest amounts in them. Marlborough, for example, issued $57.7 million in checks in 1979. Its account balance was zero.

Snyder and Blondin were now convinced that they had all the elements necessary to prove the commission of a crime: the phony payment, evidenced by the check "kite," or swap, and criminal intent, evidenced by the elaborate schemes to hide Kilpatrick's involvement and by the efforts to obstruct the government's investigation. By the end of the summer, Snyder and Blondin were ready to recommend prosecution to their superiors in Washington.

In the first instance, their recommendation went to Scharf, who remained with the case as a reviewer. He examined their memos carefully, doing some additional research of his own, and prepared a lengthy review memo for the head of the Criminal Division. He strongly agreed that indictments should be sought and that they had a strong case. He disagreed only with respect to some of the individual defendants—he thought, for example, that Wilson Quintella, the Brazilian admiral, would be hard to convict because, confined to a wheelchair, he'd attract sympathy from the jury. And he wasn't sure Sheila Lerner, Kilpatrick's secretary, should be indicted. It seemed she knew what was going on, but would it serve the interest of deterrence to indict a principal wrongdoer's secretary? Was she too small a fish in the scheme?

The question of whether to indict the Bank of Nova Scotia was deemed so sensitive that Stanley Krysa, head of the criminal section, wrote a separate confidential memo on the subject to Bob Davis, an Assistant Attorney General. In it, Krysa argued that the policy reasons for prosecuting the bank outweighed opposition by the Canadian government.

The IRS has had substantial compliance problems with Americans using the secrecy laws of the Cayman Islands in tax evasion schemes. These banks, in one form or fashion, have someimes corroborated [*sic*] with tax evaders but usually not to the extent of the fraud conducted here by the Bank of Nova Scotia. This case presents a unique opportunity for the government to inform the banking community and American tax evaders that secrecy laws can be broken and their conduct is not outside the reach of the United States.

Further, this prosecution should not alarm legitimate international banks. The creation of fictitious paper purportedly representing loans is serious, fraudulent conduct, in which legitimate banks would not engage . . . Further, the creation of a back dated check and the destruction of the original canceled check, goes far beyond what any legitimate institution would even consider. Indeed, the Bank's representatives candidly state that they had no explanation for this conduct. In short, this prosecution will only reinforce what is acceptable banking practices, as distinguished from fraud.

Snyder and Blondin got the go-ahead to proceed with indictments against Kilpatrick, O'Donnell, Pettingill, the bank, C. M. Smith, a bank officer, even Sheila Lerner, the secretary. But the grand plan for reining in international banks outlined by Krysa soon foundered on treacherous shoals.

THE indictment finally drafted by Snyder and Blondin had twenty-seven counts charging tax fraud, mail and wire fraud, and conspiracy, both to commit the substantive crimes and to obstruct the government's investigation. Soon after the grand jury returned the indictment, the prosecutors got an unexpected bonus: Pettingill's lawyer called to say his client wanted to discuss a guilty plea.

The prosecutors don't know exactly why Petttingill, the nominal owner of the P&J Coal Company, decided to throw in the towel. But from time to time, defendants who have vigorously resisted every step of an investigation pleaad when an indictment is handed down. The psychological stress of facing trial can be great, especially when a defendant has already expended considerable financial and emotional resources trying to stave off indictment.

Pettingill indicated that he was worried about the effect of a trial on his health—he weighed more than three hundred pounds. Nor did he want to hold out for Kilpatrick's sake. The two had been rivals of a sort ever since they both worked as salesmen for a Los Angeles tax shelter promoter. They used each other and competed, but had never had much affection for each other. And Snyder promised that if a court ruled that Kilpatrick's ventures were legal, Pettingill could re-open his plea.

The other defendants, however, posed far greater challenges. Two defendants, including Smith, the bank manager, lived outside the U.S. and opted to become fugtives. Kilpatrick and O'Donnell both responded with extensive motions to dismiss the indictments, both on substantive grounds and—of particular concern to Snyder and Blondin—because of alleged prosecutorial misconduct.

Dismissal of an indictment because of misconduct is most often associated with police misconduct, not misconduct by a prosecutor. Increasingly, however, courts have been turning to dismissals as a means to exercise control over the conduct of prosecutors, with ac-companying public outcries that criminals are being allowed to go free because of minor errors on the part of prosecutors.

As the Third Circuit Court of Appeals has explained, however,

> the right to indictment by an unbiased grand jury is guaranteed by the fifth amendment. When the framers of the Bill of Rights placed that requirement in the fifth amendment, they were not engaging in a mere verbal exercise. The fact that grand jury proceedings are secret . . . , and largely under the control of the federal prosecutor, magnifies this concern.
>
> We recognize that dismissal of an indictment may impose important costs upon the prosecution and the public. But the costs of continued unchecked prosecutorial misconduct are also substantial. This is partic-ularly so before the grand jury, where the prosecutor operates without the check of a judge or a trained legal adversary, and virtually immune from the public scrutiny . . .
>
> Certainly the constant flow of cases to this court involving prosecutorial misconduct before petit juries demonstrates that judicial tongue clicking and adjurations as to the better practice are likely to have little impact on the problem. On the other hand, we think that the prospect of cases lost because of attorney misconduct is likely to produce a sharp improve-ment in the procedures adopted by United States Attorneys to control attorney conduct before the grand jury.

A prosecutor's precise ethical obligations before a grand jury aren't legally clear and are often complicated. But essentially, they are commonsense requirements for insuring that targets of investigations get a fair hearing. Snyder and Blondin, once the motion was made, took comfort from their own belief that they had tried to be fair—allowing O'Donnell, for example, to provide his own self-serving and exculpatory testimony, and allowing his tax expert to appear in an effort to make sure the jury heard both sides of the case.

The kind of blatant prosecutorial misconduct most feared by the public—personal vendettas launched by prosecutors resulting in ransacked homes and offices and ruined careers—is rare, though not unheard of. Not many cases alleging such behavior have been filed. Still, sanctions for such conduct are severe; the result can be civil damage awards against the prosecutor in ruinous amounts. The courts are replete with charges of less blatant, but nonetheless serious instances of misconduct, most arising from zealous prosecutors' failure to bear in mind that prosecutors are constitutionally required to seek justice in their pursuit of convictions.

A survey of recent reported cases, for example, indicates that prosecutors can't mention inadmissible evidence in opening statements or closing arguments; can't misstate or mischaracterize facts; can't offer personal opinions about whether evidence is reliable or witnesses credible; can't comment on a defendant's refusal to testify; can't call a witness knowing he will invoke the Fifth Amendment (on grounds that the jury might infer the defendant's guilt from the witness's silence); and can't introduce evidence of prior crimes to suggest the defendant's willingness to engage in criminal conduct.

Taken in context, such misconduct can at times seem insignificant, even harmless, to the defendant, and it is up to the presiding judge in each instance to decide whether the appropriate remedy for disciplining the prosecutor is to dismiss an indictment against the defendant. Defense lawyers, predictably, claim that judges err on the side of lenience in dealing with prosecutors.

From a defendant's point of view, a more serious problem is finding out about a prosecutor's misconduct, especially since grand jury proceedings, and even the identities of the grand jurors, are secret. Grand jurors aren't allowed to discuss the case; witnesses are sometimes instructed not to disclose what transpired during their testimony. Snyder and Blondin, for example, swore some of their witnesses to secrecy.

Their admonitions apparently had little effect, however. The defendants later said that one of the witnesses, Richard Birchall, a lawyer who advised Kilpatrick on one of the tax shelter programs, was left alone by Snyder and Blondin in the office where secret exhibits and transcripts related to the investigation were stored. Birchall said he took the opportunity to read through much of the material.

As a result, defense lawyers were able to mount an unusually detailed assault on the prosecutors' handling of the grand jury investigation. The defense motions were a veritable catalogue of alleged abuses before the grand jury.

The defendants charged that using the letters of assurance violated statutory immunity procedures. They claimed that witnesses before the grand jury, such as Hjorth, were "systematically badgered, ridiculed and embarrassed." They charged that the grand jury was used improperly to gather information that was subsequently turned over to the IRS, information it couldn't have obtained through ordinary civil process. They claimed the prosecutors violated statutory secrecy provisions by, among other things, allowing Birchall to ransack their files. And, predictably, they charged that O'Donnell's testimony had been improperly solicited outside the presence of his lawyer. The defendants asked that the indictments be dismissed and that, in the alternative, they be allowed to scrutinize the grand jury transcripts for other evidence of misconduct and be permitted to interview members of the grand jury.

Nor were their notions confined to the issue of misconduct. The defendants also argued that as a matter of substantive law, the indictments failed to allege a crime. Their principal contention was that the indictment didn't allege that the underlying business—coal mining and methanol development—were without "economic merit," the traditional standard for fraudulent tax shelters. They argued that the method of financing couldn't form the basis for a criminal violation of the tax laws.

In Washington, the motions were viewed with concern, though not undue alarm. Defendants routinely file such motions, and they are usually denied. But this was developing into an important, high-visibility case in an area of great political concern to the administration. The legal principles were admittedly relatively untested. And the allegations of government misconduct, while sweeping and in some instances unsubstantiated, were unusually detailed. If true, there was the real chance that some of them would lead a judge to dismiss the indictment.

Snyder and Blondin were somewhat baffled by the attack on their behavior—they believed firmly they had done nothing wrong. But they weren't that experienced—it was only Snyder's second grand jury investigation. Because the two prosecutors were now personally under attack, the Tax Division decided they needed more assistance and supervision. The cattle case Scharf had opted for in Los Angeles had just ended in a plea, so he was available. He was the acknowledged master of tax shelter prosecutions in the office, and he was also familiar with the case, having served as the department's reviewer. And he was willing—Kilpatrick was rapidly developing into the most important case in the office. Shortly after the motions were filed, Scharf became lead counsel for the government.

Soon after joining the case in an active capacity, Scharf was confronted with the disappearance of a possibly key witness, Malcolm Haynes, an employee of the Bank of Nova Scotia who had been present at some of the meetings between Kilpatrick and Smith, the branch manager for the bank in the Cayman Islands. Haynes hadn't cooperated or appeared before the grand jury, but since the events involving Kilpatrick, he had been transferred to the bank's branch in San Juan, Puerto Rico. That meant he could be subpoenaed and compelled to testify, since Puerto Rico is a U.S. territory.

Scharf, however, learned from an FBI agent in Puerto Rico that there were signs Haynes was moving again—in fact, Scharf was told, Haynes may have already fled the island.

Scharf was alarmed for two reasons. First, Haynes might slip beyond his grasp. In addition, he didn't think that the Bank of Nova Scotia yet knew that Haynes was likely to be a key witness. It looked now as though the bank might have caught on. Scharf didn't want Haynes being coached by the bank's lawyers about what to say and how to say it.

Scharf's first impulse was to fly to Puerto Rico immediately and try to surprise Haynes before he left. But he adhered more closely to department guidelines than Snyder had when he flew to London; he first sought and obtained Justice Department approval for the trip and related expenses.

Approval in hand, Scharf embarked on what later became known as the "Puerto Rican affair" and a cause célèbre in the trial of Kilpatrick.

When Scharf arrived at the bank office in San Juan, he learned that he was too late—Haynes had already left for a new assignment in Canada. Haynes's family, however, was still in San Juan. Scharf figured that if he questioned Haynes's family members he might at least be able to pinpoint Haynes's whereabouts.

Scharf went to Haynes's home address, but the house had a "For Rent" sign outside and looked vacant. So in what he thought was a bit of resourceful detective work, he decided to check at the nearest school to see if the Haynes children were pupils there. It turned out they were, and Scharf says the principal of the school was eager to help. He offered to get the Haynes children out of class. Scharf said that wasn't necessary, but the principal had the teachers of the two Haynes girls come to his office, and one of them knew the Hayneses were currently living in the Holiday Inn before moving to Toronto.

Mrs. Haynes wasn't at the Holiday Inn, but Scharf and the agent with whom he was working spotted her driving out of the parking lot. They assumed she was going to pick up the girls at school so they went back expecting to find her there. Instead, they saw the Haynes girls walking toward the house where they had lived, and Scharf followed them there. Mrs. Haynes was outside in the front yard, and Scharf introduced himself and explained why he was there.

He made no headway with Mrs. Haynes. She was polite and a bit nervous, but said she'd been told not to discuss the case with anyone and refused to provide information about her husband or his where-abouts. She directed Scharf back to the bank, urging him to speak with a bank officer there.

Scharf finally gave up the effort and flew back to Washington. The next day he was feeling a little worried about Mrs. Haynes's reaction to his questions and the manner in which he had located her, and he also wanted to make one last effort to obtain her cooperation. So he wrote the following letter:

DEAR MRS. HAYNES:

I thank you for your friendliness yesterday, even if I cannot thank you for your cooperation. I hope that neither your daughters nor you were frightened by our unscheduled appearance. At your suggestion, we spoke with Mr. Rector about your husband's present address. He told us where he is working, but not where he is residing. We do not believe that any efforts we might make to contact Malcolm at work would be fruitful because, in the presence of his employer's representatives, we cannot be sure that what he tells us would represent a thorough response to our questions.

I presently have the power to serve a subpoena on you requiring you to come to court in Denver in late February, where a judge would probably order you to answer this and many other questions. I am reluctant to use that power because I do not want to take you away from your children for several days, especially when you are in the midst of moving to Canada. Also, I appreciate the difficult situation you described when you explained your refusal to reveal where we could get in touch with Malcolm. It is not important enough to me to force you, an innocent third party, to do something which you believe might jeopardize your husband's employment by violating his employer's instructions not to talk to us. Therefore, I have decided not to serve you with a subpoena now. This means that I will lose the power to do so beginning the day you leave Puerto Rico to return to Canada.

If my actions in this regard persuade you that I am trustworthy, then I would ask only that you talk to your husband, tell him about our conversation February 8, show him this letter, and ask him to decide whether it is best to remain silent so as not to offend the bank or whether it is best to tell us what happened in Georgetown.

I would be anxious to hear from you or Malcolm . . . I cannot offer Malcolm his career, as the bank can; I can only offer him immunity from prosecution if he speaks candidly, probable confidentiality of his communications if he does not testify in court, and the knowledge that he has done the right thing.

Thank you very much.

Sincerely,
JARED J. SCHARF
Trial Attorney, Department of Justice.

Scharf never heard directly from either Haynes or his wife. But Mrs. Haynes followed his suggestions in at least one regard: she showed the letter to her husband, who promptly turned it over to the bank, which immediately showed it to defense counsel. The letter would come back to haunt Scharf.

MEANWHILE, the defense motions to dismiss the indictments because of prosecutorial misconduct were assigned to Judge John Kane, Jr., an appointee of President Jimmy Carter, a former deputy director of the Peace Corps in Calcutta, India, and a judge known generally as a political liberal. Oral argument on the motions was held on Washington's Birthday 1983, and lasted for three hours. As an indication of the importance of the motions to the government, there were four prosecutors from Washington present, as well as Linda Surbaugh, an Assistant U.S. Atorney in Denver who had now been assigned to the case.

Judge Kane gave no clue to his thinking on the motions; he asked virtually no questions during the arguments. Scharf, Snyder, and Blondin were consequently stunned when, several days later, Judge Kane delivered an opinion dismissing twenty-six of the twenty-seven counts against Kilpatrick on the ground that the indictment had failed to make out a criminal offense. All that remained was one count of obstruction of justice, a count that was concededly collateral to the main thrust of the indictment and had nothing to do with tax law per se.

Scharf and Snyder went out to a local bar and got drunk. In the parking lot outside, Snyder let off steam by throwing down his suit jacket and loudly denouncing the outcome with colorful language.

The decision was a setback for the prosecutors, but they had understood from the outset that the case would be precedential and, as a result, would probably require appeals. There was no hesitation in Washington about granting the prosecutors' request that Judge Kane's ruling be appealed to the Tenth Circuit Court of Appeals. The judge's ruling also rendered moot the allegations of prosecutorial misconduct; he said that since he was dismissing most of the indictment on grounds of substantive law, he had no need to address those contentions. At least the appeal would focus on the law rather than on Snyder and Blondin.

A decision still remained, however, about what to do with the one remaining count. One option was to simply drop it; another was to wait for a ruling on appeal, and then try that count with the others if they were reinstated. A final alternative—one the judge probably never dreamed would be adopted—was to go ahead and try Kilpatrick on the one count.

The prosecutors were feeling petulant. They were angry and frustrated about the dismissal of the other twenty-six counts. They knew that Judge Kane was presiding over another long and complex case, and they strongly suspected that part of his motive in dismissing the charges was simply to rid his court calendar of another burdensome proceeding. The prosecutors now saw one way that, in small measure, they could retaliate against a judge who otherwise seemed entirely beyond their reach.

"I realize now that it would have been prudent to await the results of the appeal," says Scharf. "But we were upset. We said among ourselves, 'We're not cleaning your calendar at our expense.' " So the prosecutors demanded that Kilpatrick be tried immediately on the lone remaining count. "We took the macho approach," says one of the agents.

Judge Kane dismisses the allegations that he dismissed most of the counts to clear his calendar as "absurd," noting that he has numerous long, complex cases and one more or less would have little impact. He adds, "I'm sickened by the thought that prosecutors would seek to use the courts to punish a judge," noting that that is precisely the kind of attitude that leads to prosecutorial misconduct.

In any event, the prosecutors' tactic failed in its intended effect. Judge Kane agreed to let the trial of the remaining count proceed, but with a different judge presiding—Judge Winner.

Since helping Snyder and Blondin move their materials into the courthouse, Judge Winner had been in Wyoming, serving temporarily on the district court there (federal judges often fill in on other courts when needed). He was about to assume senior status, however, and was scheduled to return to Denver. When he asked Judge Kane for a case to work on when he returned, Judge Kane offered him his choice of three. Judge Winner chose Kilpatrick. Trial was scheduled for May, little more than a month away.

Despite Judge Winner's prior friendliness to Snyder and Blondin, the prosecutors weren't delighted by the assignment. The judge was known to be fickle in his affections toward lawyers. Assistant U.S. Attorneys in Denver had plenty of stories about lawyers in the office whom the judge praised openly in one case, then denounced in the next. A former District Attorney in Denver told the *American Lawyer* that "he [Judge Winner] polarizes every case. In one case I couldn't do anything wrong and the other guy couldn't do anything right. He's sent people out of there vomiting." And Scharf, Snyder, and Blondin knew that a hostile judge can do enormous damage to even the best-prepared case.

The first indication that Judge Winner's friendly attitude might have changed came during some of Kilpatrick's pretrial motions. In what the prosecutors viewed as a patently frivolous demand intended to harass, Kilpatrick's lawyer, Denver attorney William C. Waller, Jr., asked for photocopies of all documentary evidence the government might introduce at trial. What annoyed the prosecutors was that they had already provided copies of all the documents on microfilm.

They assumed Judge Winner would deny the request. Instead, he asked for argument on the motion. Scharf was in Orlando, Florida, at the time preparing for another case. He asked for time to fly out to Denver for the argument. Judge Winner denied it. Instead, the judge arranged a multiparty conference call. "There were ten people talking at once," Scharf says. "It was ridiculous—no one could understand anything. It was mass confusion." Then the judge granted the defense motion, consigning the prosecutors and their assistants to hours at photocopying machines.

Soon after, defense lawyers protested that the prosecutors had dropped as a witness Wilson Quintella, the Brazilian admiral, who they now said was essential to their case. Judge Winner called a hearing on the matter.

Scharf explained that Quintella had been subpoenaed, but that they had been notified by his lawyer that if questioned he would invoke the Fifth Amendment. The government wasn't prepared to offer Quintella immunity (Quintella had barely escaped indictment). Since Quintella was confined to a wheelchair, and the government would have had to fly him to Denver from Brazil, a prospect that was uncomfortable for Quintella and expensive for the government, Scharf decided to release him from his subpoena.

Judge Winner was furious. He blasted Scharf and the prosecutors, and demanded that they show him a court case that gave them the authority to release a witness from his subpoena. The prosecutors couldn't—because the proposition is so obvious that it was never litigated, they say.

The defense lawyers seized on this theme by saying that the two defendants who were fugitives were also necessary to their case. In an extraordinary move, the prosecutors agreed to give the fugitives safe passage in and out of the country for their testimony rather than risk further wrath from Judge Winner. "It's practically unheard of to let an indicted defendant remain free like that. But we bent over backwards," Scharf says.

The prosecutors were even more amazed at the reception accorded one of the fugitives, Michael Alberga, when he arrived in Denver to testify. Alberga was a lawyer in the Cayman Islands, which inherited a British legal system. During his testimony, he was extremely deferential to Judge Winner, always addressing his as "M'Lord." "Winner lapped this up," Scharf recalls. "It turned into mutual admiration. Pretty soon Winner was arranging tours of the courthouse for Alberga, showing off the computer system. It was incredible." Scharf says the prosecutors later discovered that "M'Lord" isn't even the proper form of address for a trial judge in the Cayman Islands. The title is reserved for appellate judges.

As the trial of Kilpatrick continued, relations between the prosecutors and the judge deteriorated steadily. The judge's remarks to the prosecutors became more biting, and the prosecutors felt more angry and frustrated. At one point, a witness later testified, Snyder became so angry that after the jury left the courtroom, Snyder threw his suit jacket on the floor, stomped on it, and mouthed what the witness thought were "cuss words" at the judge as he walked out. (Snyder denied the charge. Scharf, who says he never saw such an incident even though he was in the courtroom every day, wonders if the witness wasn't confusing the instance with Snyder's outburst in the parking lot the night most of the indictment was dismissed.)

The judge also evidenced a growing interest in some of the defense's allegations of prosecutorial misconduct. The day after testimony by Richard Bell—a crucial witness who testified about the backdating of the $18.85 million check—the defense lawyers informed Judge Winner that Snyder had threatened Bell that unless his testimony was harmful to Kilpatrick, Bell's letter of assurance would be revoked. Specifically, the defense charged that Snyder told Bell that "all bets were off" if his testimony was favorable to Kilpatrick. The allegation admittedly raised legitimate concerns about the credibility of Bell's testimony and the propriety of Snyder's conduct, and Kilpatrick charged that it amounted to an obstruction of justice by Snyder.

The judge took a keen interest in the allegation, interrupting the trial to hold an impromptu evidentiary hearing. Snyder said that he didn't recall making such a remark, but if he had, he meant only that if Bell lied he would be subject to prosecution for perjury. Malcolm Bell, Richard Bell's brother and lawyer, testified that Snyder made such a comment, but volunteered that "this has all been very negative about Jake Snyder, and I wish to say he has behaved admirably in this case and I would not criticize him at all." Judge Winner didn't seem happy about Snyder's explanation, but allowed the trial to proceed and didn't let defense lawyers present the alleged threat to the jury. But the incident also seemed to arouse the judge's interest in the subject of letters of assurance, which had figured in the earlier defense allegations of prosecutorial misconduct.

The judge asked Scharf why, given the 1970 statute outlining requirements for grants of immunity, the prosecutors had instead used letters of assurance. Scharf explained the practice, saying it was authorized by Department of Justice guidelines. The judge opined that he thought it was unlawful to circumvent the statute, so Scharf produced two court cases endorsing the practice, which, "to avoid embarrassing the judge," Scharf says, he passed to the judge's law clerks. The next day, Judge Winner announced that he realized the practice was lawful, but that "Griffin Bell [the former Attorney General] promised that it wouldn't be done." He also critized Scharf for talking to his clerks.

Animosity continued to mount. One day, Blondin mentioned in passing that the judge had said he couldn't refer to the earlier proceedings in which Kilpatrick was held in contempt for refusing to produce documents. The judge interrupted, "I surely have, and if you refer to the contempt proceedings, there are going to be some new contempt proceedings."

The growing tension finally exploded on May 5, when the fugitive witness Alberga concluded his testimony. During his testimony, a letter from Snyder to Alberga was introduced that mentioned Kilpatrick was being investigated by the grand jury and seeking cooperation from Alberga. Although the letter was written prior to indictments in the case, the judge apparently misread the date on the letter and assumed that Snyder had made direct contact with a defendant without going through his lawyer, a practice ruled by the Supreme Court in a well-known case, *U.S.* v. *Massiah*, to be an unconstitutional deprivation of counsel. Once the jury was out of the room, the judge, bristling with anger, launched into a lecture.

"I can't believe it's necessary to mention this, but in view of some of the things that have happened in this case, I'm going to mention it." Then he practically shouted: "No representative of the United States government, even including special agents of the United States Attorney's office, are to talk to any person under indictment out of the presence of their lawyer. That is a direct order of the court."

Judge Winner stood, turned on his heel, and began to leave the courtroom.

At that point, Scharf, who had been sitting in the spectator section near the rear of the court, concedes that he boiled over. Jumping to his feet and, according to others present, screaming, he said, "Can we inquire if there's any indication whether that has been done, Your Honor?"

"I'll find out," the judge angrily retorted, and again turned his back.

"There hasn't been any, Your Honor," Scharf shouted to a now vanished Judge Winner. The judge promptly got on the telephone to the U.S. Attorney's office, complaining about Scharf's conduct.

Scharf concedes that he was shouting during this exchange, but says he did so only because the judge was about to leave the room and he wanted to be heard. The next day, despite the fact that the judge was obviously in a bad mood, Scharf again asked if there was any evidence the prosecutors had violated the Massiah rule. "I'm not going to respond to your question," the judge snapped. "I'm not here to be cross-examined."

The judge proceeded to make mincemeat of Blondin's summation before the jury. Referring to one of the defense witness's statement, Blondin mentioned that "I believe that." Defense counsel didn't object—if anything such a statement helped their case—but the judge pounced. He interrupted the statement and had Blondin come to the bench.

"I have no idea how many times the Tenth Circuit has eaten government lawyers alive for saying what testimony they believe," he said. "They have reversed repeated cases for doing that. You are treading on extraordinarily thin ice by saying what evidence you as a lawyer believe. If you wish to continue putting error in this case, go ahead."

Then Blondin summarized a witness's testimony, and the judge again interrupted. "I have no recollection that he so testified, but the record will speak for itself." He added bluntly, "If he didn't so testify, I will grant a new trial."

And with increasing frequency, Judge Winner was referring to the prosecutors as "the lawyers from the banks of the Potomac," as though that were the capital of a totalitarian police state.

By the end of the case, Blondin felt shattered; neither Scharf nor Snyder expected a conviction, given the atmosphere in the courtroom. Much to their surprise, and the evident dismay of the judge, the jury found Kilpatrick guilty of obstructing justice. Judge Winner dismissed the jury, omitting the customary thank-you for their time and care in deliberating. He then invited defense lawyers to submit posttrial motions for a new trial. It was clear to the prosecutors that, despite the conviction, the case was far from over. Nonetheless, they clung to one reed of hope. Judge Winner was due to retire in August, less than three months away.

Scharf left Denver for a trial in Orlando, and says it took days to shake off the atmosphere of tension and hostility that prevailed in Denver. The prosecutors began referring to Judge Winner as "Ayatollah Winner."

Following up on Judge Winner's suggestion, the defense lawyers filed a barrage of posttrial motions, seeking not only a new trial but dismissal of the original indictment. They renewed many of the earlier claims of prosecutorial misconduct that had been filed before Judge Kane, adding new ones that had surfaced during the trial. And Judge Winner granted their requests for a full-scale evidentiary hearing into the conduct of the prosecutors in the case.

SCHARF and the other prosecutors dreaded the prospect, and felt they had little chance, given the judge's open hostility. It had reached the point where they felt they had to move to disqualify Judge Winner, and they even prepared a draft brief on the point. But they were overruled by their superiors in Washington, who didn't want to offend a judge who had presided over many tax cases, and were also concerned that, given the strict standards for such motions, the effort would fail. Blondin, Scharf, and Snyder filed a last, desperate memo with Archer, the Assistant Attorney General.

"We hereby beg reconsideration of the Tax Division's decision not to file the motion to recuse Judge Winner from further action . . . it is our opinion that it would be a grave error not to proceed with the motion for recusal." Scharf, in particular, remains bitter about the decision. Even if the chances were slim, a successful motion would have avoided the nightmare that soon followed.

BECAUSE the prosecutors were now likely to be witnesses in what was rapidly turning into a trial of them rather than the defendants, the defense lawyers also moved to disqualify Snyder, Blondin, and Scharf from prosecuting the case, triggering a high-level meeting in Washington.

Krysa, head of the criminal section, agreed that the disqualification motion was a defense ploy that could have far-reaching damaging effects on the government's prosecutions. Defendants would simply allege prosecutorial misconduct, demand a hearing, and then move to disqualify the prosecutor on the grounds that he'd be a witness. It also posed a practical problem: no one else in the department was familiar enough with the complicated facts and procedural history to step effectively into the case.

Nor was U.S. Attorney Miller any help. Although his office had once been eager to wrest control of the case away from Washington, it now wanted to wash its hands of what was rapidly developing into a messy situation. Miller, of course, had been kept apprised of Judge Winner's actions, and it was clear that more trouble lay ahead. Much to the annoyance of the prosecutors in Washington, he ordered Linda Surbaugh, the Assistant U.S. Atorney in Denver who had been acting as a liaison with the Washington prosecutors, not to assume responsibility for the case. Miller "stopped talking to us," Scharf says.

Krysa and the prosecutors decided that Blondin and Snyder would voluntarily withdraw from the case, because their conduct was the focus of the hearing and they would be major witnesses (the Code of Professional Responsibility does require lawyers to withdraw as counsel in cases where they are likely to be witnesses, the theory being that they can't be detached advocates when their own conduct is called into question). But Scharf was determined to stay. He argued that there was nothing alleged by the defendants for which he was the sole witness—others could provide whatever proof was necessary. And Scharf had been a prosecutor on the case only after the grand jury handed up the indictment. He couldn't have been guilty of grand jury abuse.

Then the Puerto Rican matter surfaced. Robert Morvillo, the lawyer for the Bank of Nova Scotia and, ironically, the former prosecutor who had once argued the Massiah case for the government, claimed that Scharf's interviews with bank employees and attempt to contact Haynes without going through the bank's lawyers violated the bank's Massiah right to counsel. Scharf objected that such claims weren't relevant to Kilpatrick's demand for a new trial, but Judge Winner was plainly unhappy when Scharf showed up in Denver to represent the government in the hearings. "He made me feel like a pervert for following the two girls," Scharf says of Winner.

The judge called U.S. Attorney Miller again to complain. He threatened to report Scharf to his local bar association for violating the Code of Professional Responsibility. Finally, midway through the hearings, Scharf bowed to the pressure and disqualified himself. He asked for a one-week pause so the government could bring in new counsel; Judge Winner refused. For a full morning, the hearings proceeded without any effective counsel for the government. A fresh lawyer from Washington, Charles Alexander, arrived that afternoon.

In the prosecutor's eyes, it hardly mattered whether or not they had counsel. The hearings had turned into a field day for the defense lawyers and for Judge Winner.

On the first day that Alexander, the new prosecutor, appeared to represent the government, he was greeted with this anecdote from Judge Winner:

"We used to have a lawyer in Colorado named Jim Kelly. Jim was colorful. He was on the civil service commission, and if one wanted to be appointed to the police department, one left a specified amount of currency in a milk bottle during the days that they had milk delivery. Jim could bring the most scurrilous pleadings I thought I had ever read."

Then, to make his point, the judge added: "Your office exceeds Jim."

Even something as seemingly innocuous as Judge Winner's former friendly invitation to move materials into the courthouse now became a point of hostile contention. As one of the IRS agents was testifying, Judge Winner interrupted, lambasting the government for not providing adequate security for the secret grand jury materials.

"Wait a minute. Was there any representation made to the judge who provided that space that it was for grand jury materials? . . . Well, the record should reflect that I am the judge that provided that space, and at no time was there any suggestion made to me that it was grand jury materials. We evicted some shorthand reporters to give you that space . . . There is no security whatsoever in that space. There were passkeys to that space on the third floor floating all over this building. And under no circumstances would we have approved storage of grand jury materials there." The prosecutors insist that the judge was told what was being stored—he had to have known they were conducting a grand jury investigation—and in any event, if the issue was important, they say the judge should have stepped down because he was now becoming a witness in the proceeding.

Other incidents too came back to haunt the prosecutors. During one discussion, the judge interrupted: "What about this lady who, according to your file—and I'm interested in this—this lady who makes certain accusations against Mr. Snyder about throwing his jacket on the floor and mouthing profanities at the court? I'd like to hear that," he said, adding later, "But there has been testimony that a lawyer from your office, Mr. Snyder, had a temper tantrum after I left the courtroom and threw his jacket on the floor in the presence of all of the spectators and mouthed obscenities . . . That really does increase the stature of a lawyer to do that in a United States district courtroom. I really think he ought to get the Legion of Merit."

At one point Alexander, the government lawyer trying to defend the prosecutors' conduct, said he wasn't aware that prosecutors swore in witnesses who appeared before the grand jury (the prosecutor isn't supposed to do the swearing). "He said, 'Raise your right hand,' " the judge said, referring to Snyder. "I'm sure he wasn't telling them to reach up to the Mexican thing that drops candies on their heads." (Snyder says he only swore an agent to maintain grand jury secrecy—he didn't "swear in" a witness.)

The judge asked Scharf at one point if it was true that he had stood up and screamed at him in court.

"I raised my voice because the court was halfway out the door," Scharf replied.

"I was right there and turned and looked at you, and in one of the greatest exhibits of control, I didn't say anything," the judge retorted. "Competent counsel don't stand up in the spectator section and scream."

Scharf, on the witness stand, was questioned at length about his trip to Puerto Rico, a narrative the judge listened to with mounting anger. "Is it standard practice for the Internal Revenue Service to surveil the houses of potential witnesses?" he finally asked. "No, Your Honor," Scharf replied. "I know I have my house surveiled," the judge continued, "and I get tired of the neighbors calling me up and saying, 'Hey, somebody is spooking your house again.' It's not a very pleasant thing . . . In fact, I think it's something that is dubious judgment when you're looking for a witness . . . I'll say this. You would have gotten fired . . . if you had done it that way."

If there was any doubt about the likely outcome of the hearings, the judge put those to rest.

"I have heard it said in this courtroom that this [the hearings and defense motions on prosecutorial misconduct] represents a ploy on the part of defense counsel. This is no ploy. They raise very, very, very serious matters which in my judgment go to the heart of the administration of justice in the United States of America and which in my judgment demand an extremely thorough investigation by the Department of Justice because it holds up to the public our Department of Justice as being a vehicle for depriving people of rights for which many people have given their lives and a few others have spent weeks and months and years away from home.

"Then," the judge continued, "the [government] brief which was filed makes the statement that, the snide statement, I might add, that there is little chance of success in this, in these posttrial motions. Don't count on that."

The prosecutors had one hope. As the hearings wore on through the summer, Judge Winner's retirement date loomed ever closer. It was becoming obvious that the hearings couldn't be completed before Judge Winner was scheduled to step down. Perhaps he wouldn't have the chance to deliver the blow to the case he was evidently preparing.

Their hopes in that regard were soon dashed. Even though the hearings weren't complete—the government hadn't even presented its witnesses—Judge Winner announced that he had heard enough to reach a decision.

Judge Winner's opinion is a sharply worded condemnation of prosecutorial misconduct, and it soon became the subject of yet another controversy in the already controversial case. The judge lost no time in going after Scharf, Snyder, and Blondin.

In summarizing the case, he noted that

> it was prosecuted by three attorneys employed by the Tax Division of the Department of Justice in Washington. The single remaining count of the indictment had absolutely nothing to do with tax law, and the trial could have been handled competently and with aplomb by any Assistant United States Attorney living in Denver, but the administrative decision of the Department of Justice was to send three lawyers from the Tax Division to try an obstruction of justice case, a prosecution unrelated to their professed area of expertise . . . the Colorado United States Attorney's office is absolutely blameless in this case so fraught with problems. . . .
>
> To fully cover all the headaches of this case would require a volume, and I don't plan to write that book for reasons which will appear presently. Instead, I shall highlight some of the things which occured during the investigation and during the trial of the case. But, there are so many things to cover that this opinion won't be short. Many of the accusations are disputed by the accused government counsel and agent, but they are forced to admit a few instances of "mistake," and their denials run contrary to testimony of a large number witnesses.

Judge Winner then went through a litany of nearly every allegation made against the prosecutors, mentioning the Richard Bell incident, the claims of Richard Birchall, the screaming fits, obscenities, the Puerto Rican escapade, the "swearing in" of agents of the grand jury, the informal grants of immunity, the use of O'Donnell as a witness in the absence of his lawyer, and Blondin's comment that he believed a witness.

He referred to a request by Scharf as "the most ridiculous demand I have ever heard in the almost fifty years since I graduated from law school" and said of Scharf's "discourtesy" in raising his voice: "I thought that my court reporter's comment as we left the courtroom was discerning. She said that if her five-year-old son did something like that he would be sent to bed without his supper."

Since the hearing couldn't be completed, the judge said he wouldn't rule on motions to dismiss the entire indictment—including the twenty-six counts on appeal for other reasons to the Court of Appeals—but would remand the case to Judge Kane so that he could make that determination. And Judge Winner granted Kilpatrick a new trial on the obstruction count, throwing out the verdict.

The Justice Department prosecutors were stunned. They had expected an adverse verdict, but not an opinion that would soon be published in official court reports that lambasted them personally for more than eighteen full pages of text. And the entire tax shelter case now looked as if it was in shambles.

The battered prosecutors convened in Washington to plot strategy.

The atmosphere was gloomy. For, no matter how much they attributed the disastrous results to the bias of Judge Winner, the fact remained that there were some fairly serious allegations of prosecutorial misconduct. Snyder, in particular, was beginning to worry that he had been too careless, too cavalier in his handling of the grand jury investigation. But, they insisted, whatever errors had been made were highly technical, didn't hurt the defendants, and probably happened in most grand jury investigations.

"In any major grand jury investigation there are errors," Scharf says. "Snyder and Blondin did a clean job. No grand jury investigation has ever been scrutinized like this one was. Every minute instance of misconduct was dredged up and thrown at us. None of the mistakes called for this kind of punishment."

But the prosecutors were further demoralized when their superiors in the department decided that the matter had to be brought to the attention of the department's Office of Professional Responsibility, which investigates and handles internal disciplinary matters. Nonetheless, Archer and Krysa, their superiors, said they would stand behind them. The department decided to file a motion with Judge Winner asking that he reconsider his opinion or at least withdraw those portions attacking the prosecutors, which he himself had admitted weren't proved and were only allegations. The judge refused.

The prosecutors and their superiors in the department now faced the dilemma of what to do about Judge Winner's order. They could appeal his granting of a new trial and/or his refusal to withdraw or modify the opinion attacking the prosecutors to the Tenth Circuit, but opinion was divided. The chief counsel of the IRS opposed any appeals. Scharf and Blondin wanted to appeal both aspects. Snyder wanted to appeal only the judge's refusal to modify his opinion.

Approval for any appeal had to come from the Solicitor General, Rex Lee. Archer, the Assistant Attorney General, prepared a confidential memo for the Solicitor General, outlining the case, and recommending appeal of the judge's refusal to withdraw his opinion, but not of the decision to grant a new trial.

> Judge Winner, without any need to do so, has effectively condemned professionals and potentially damaged their careers without a full hearing in which all of the evidence is presented and in a manner which deprives them of review of legal conclusions. Such action is clearly inconsistent with notions of basic fairness . . . In essence, the court by publicizing unsubstantiated allegations may become an instrumentality by which innocent persons are defamed and maligned.

Archer also pointed out that the opinion could do widespread harm to the government's prosecution efforts.

> Allegations of professional misbehavior by Government prosecutors, particularly allegations coming from the bench in the misleading form that the allegations here took on, inevitably injure the Government by calling its actions in other matters to be called into question. Thus, quite apart from the damage to the prosecutors' individual reputations, which we believe we also have an obligation to defend, the Government has suffered real harm, harm that is compounded with each day that the memorandum opinion is not withdrawn.

Surprisingly, there is nothing in the memo to indicate that Archer realized that an effort to have a judicial opinion withdrawn might give rise to a First Amendment question about the judge's right to free speech, particularly since the prosecutors were government officials and public figures. Nor is there any evidence that the issue was discussed with Solicitor General Lee before he gave his approval. In any event, the appeal was filed, arguing that Judge Winner violated a judicial duty to keep court records free from "scandalous matter."

Had the matter stopped there, the motion might have been ruled upon in the ordinary course and little attention paid to an ancillary matter in an already complicated case. But the Justice Department didn't stop with its motion. It went ahead and shot itself in the foot.

Soon after the motion was made, the prosecutors were startled to see that Judge Winner had already submitted a copy of the offending opinion to West Publishing Company, which publishes all judicial reports in the United States. West is a private (and highly profitable) company, but it enjoys a monopoly on such reporting and acts in a quasi-official capacity. Its reports are heavily relied upon by the legal profession, judges, and courts. Prior to issuing large bound volumes of collected opinions, West keeps lawyers up to date by issuing paperback, loose leaf "advance sheets" of recent opinions. Late in the year, Judge Winner's opinion showed up in the advance sheets, complete with his denunciation of the prosecutors.

The prosecutors were indignant, since a motion was pending to block issuance of the opinion. Once disseminated in the advance sheets, the very damage they were trying to prevent was done. They brought the matter to the attention of the department's appellate division, which was handling the appeal in the Tenth Circuit.

The assistant chief of the Tax Divison's criminal section called West, asking if it would omit the opinion from the bound volume (the advance sheets are customarily thrown out when the bound volume arrives, and the prosecutors assumed that most lawyers would simply discard Judge Winner's opinion without having discovered it was there).

West said that it exercised no discretion in what it printed, and would drop the opinion only if it was asked to do so by the District Court of Appeals. Two days before the volume was scheduled to be published, the Justice Department drafted a motion asking the Tenth Circuit to halt publication of the opinion, mentioning that West had no objections. On January 3, 1984, the Court of Appeals granted the request.

Scharf says he was barely aware matters had reached this stage until a morning in early January when *The New York Times* emblazoned the story on page one, accusing the Justice Department of exercising a prior restraint on publication—a blatant violation of the First Amendment. "My God," Scharf says, "they treated this like it was the Pentagon Papers."

That morning was apparently the first time that it had occurred to anyone in the Justice Department, or the Tenth Circuit Court of Appeals, for that matter, that there might be a First Amendment dimension to the remedy they sought. All concerned beat a hasty retreat.

The Justice Department, after launching an internal investigation, responded to congressional inquiries into the matter by saying that it had now determined that the motion requesting that the opinion not be published was "contrary to the Department's policy against seeking the imposition of prior restraints on the press." And the Tenth Circuit promptly issued a new order, overruling its previous order to West halting publication.

The effort to suppress Judge Winner's opinion had by now precisely the opposite effect—as is so often the case—ensuring that the alleged prosecutorial misconduct was now known to a general public of millions rather than to the handful of lawyers who would probably have read the opinion before the Tenth Circuit decided the govenment's appeal. But the damage to the department's own cause was hardly confined to *The New York Times*, the Washington *Post*, and other newspapers. *The New York Times* article was read by producers at CBS, and it wasn't long before Scharf was contacted by the most potent force in investigative jouralism—*60 Minutes*.

ALL the while media controversy was swirling about the case, Scharf, Snyder, and Blondin were preparing to be witnesses into new hearings into prosecutorial misconduct ordered by Judge Kane—the full-scale hearings that Judge Winner hadn't been able to complete. Even more was at stake now, since Judge Kane was facing motions from all the defendants to dismiss all counts of the indictment (including the twenty-six that had already been dismissed on substantive law grounds, but could be reinstated by the Court of Appeals). The hearings were being handled by Alexander, who had stepped in after Scharf's ouster in Judge Winner's proceedings.

This time, the defendants were armed with even more allegations, since Judge Winner had ordered that they be allowed to pore over all the secret transcripts of the grand jury proceedings, looking for even more instances of error and misconduct.

Now that they were back before Judge Kane, the prosecutors didn't have to face the overt hostility of Judge Winner. Still, they doubted that Judge Kane, despite his overall courtesy and good humor, had forgotten their insistence that the trial of Kilpatrick go forward on the obstruction of justice count. Nor did they enjoy being in the position of defendants.

"As a lawyer, I'm used to my word being accepted in court. I resented that everything I said was challenged, the implication being that I was lying," Scharf says. "I resented having to testify at all. I had had twenty-five jury trials. I was never treated like this."

Scharf, Snyder, and Blondin all testified, and tried to put their actions in the best light possible. All three were convinced that they had only acted zealously in order to do justice, and had somehow fallen victim to a nightmarishly successful effort by the defense lawyers to shift the focus of the case onto them and away from the real defendants. Nonetheless, by the end of the hearings, they weren't optimistic. Their anxiety mounted as months passed and still there was no opinion from Judge Kane.

Scharf finally wrote a despairing memo to his superiors in the Justice Department.

> There are many convincing indications to support a belief that the Motion to Dismiss on grounds of grand jury abuse will be granted (even though there is no legal justification), that the case will be lost irretrievably, and that an embarrassing widely publicized opinion will be issued. Some of these indications include Judge Kane's comments from the bench, rumors of his comments to the national media, his comments to the local (Denver) media . . . and his delay in issuing his decision in this matter. There are rumors that he said he will not decide the motion until September. Such delay could be to assure wide publicity when *Sixty Minutes* resumes in the fall.

The situation looked so bleak that the prosecutors were considering some desperate strategic maneuvers, the ostensible basis for which would be the Speedy Trial Act.

The act implements a criminal defendant's right to a speedy trial, requiring trial within seventy days of a federal defendant's first appearance in court. The time can be extended at the defendant's request or with the defendant's consent, and it usually is. But in the case against Kilpatrick, the Bank of Nova Scotia, and the others, the clock was ticking away.

To the prosecutors, this dilemma offered two admittedly risky possibilities. They could make an emergency motion, calling for Judge Kane to decide the defense's motions to dismiss immediately, on grounds that the Speedy Trial Act was about to be violated and would require dismissal of the indictments. If their emergency motion were granted, the prosecutors hoped the judge might be forced to issue a decision without an opinion because of lack of time.

An alternative—and even more drastic approach—was for the government to ask Judge Kane to dismiss the indictments because it couldn't provide a speedy trial, in effect, sabotaging its own case. The thinking here was that the case would simply disappear without further embarrassment, and the prosecutors could try to refile the charges in some state other than Colorado, where the atmosphere toward them wouldn't seem so poisoned.

Scharf also wanted to move to disqualify Judge Kane, on the grounds that he had been commenting on the case to *60 Minutes* and because there were media reports that Judge Kane was a likely Supreme Court nominee if Senator Gary Hart, then running in the Democratic primary for President, were elected.

He recognized that all three steps were radical steps for the Justice Department to be taking. Nonetheless, so sure was he that the case was about to be lost and his own reputation irreparably damaged, that he felt desperate steps were in order, and he formally recommended that any or all three be taken. "Despite the obvious outcry this would cause, I would go along with this move, and do it myself if so designated," he wrote to Archer and Krysa in June.

Cooler heads in the department prevailed. And, in fact, Scharf was rapidly losing the ability to affect any decision about the case. His superiors were becoming concerned about what they feared was his and the other prosecutors' loss of judgment with respect to a case that still had the potential to generate embarrassing publicity for the government. They rejected all his emergency measures, and they specifically forbade Scharf, Snyder, and Blondin from going on *60 Minutes*.

Judge Kane finally issued his opinion on September 24. It was, if anything, more damning than Judge Winner's had been, because it was less rhetorical and emphasized the facts uncovered about the grand jury investigation. It granted the defendants the relief they sought—dismissal of all counts of the indictment—effectively leaving the prosecutors without a case.

Judge Kane ruled that the indictment had to be dismissed for two of the alleged examples of misconduct alone: the violation of grand jury secrecy proceedings and swearing some of the grand jury witnesses to secrecy. The judge wrote:

> Several instances demonstrate blatant disregard for the time-honored tradition of grand jury secrecy. As discussed below, such violations were utilized by the government, not only to gain what was certainly perceived as an advantage in connection with the intended prosecution, but were also apparently part of an improper attempt to embarrass the targets and hinder the ongoing operation of their business during the course of the grand jury investigation.

Judge Kane cited the letters sent to potential witnesses that identified the targets, interviews by agents with investors in the shelters that mentioned the grand jury investigation and the targets, and lax security over grand jury materials, including the incident where Birchall allegedly rummaged through the file drawers.

The judge was also sharply critical of swearing some of the grand jury witnesses to secrecy, especially lawyers for two of the defendants in what the judge concluded was an effort to prevent anyone from finding out that the prosecutors had tried to pierce the attorney-client privilege in their questioning.

> Indeed, during these hearings, the Department of Justice attorney involved acknowledged that at the time he imposed the improper obligations he was aware of the *United States Attorneys Manual* provisions prohibiting the imposition of an obligation of secrecy upon a witness. Yet, although provided with ample opportunity, he was unable to offer any legitimate reason for his transgressions.

In addition, Judge Kane acknowledged that use of the letters of assurance, calling witnesses who the prosecutors knew would plead the Fifth Amendment, improper comments by the prosecutors, and attempts to interview witnesses outside the presence of their lawyers, while not in and of themselves requiring dismissal, contributed to his decision.

> The grand jury is more than a symbol of the limitations the Constitution places on the government's power [the judge concluded]. When the government usurps the grand jury and destroys its independence so

that it looks and acts like an arm of the prosecution, the very essence of a government of limited powers is destroyed.

In addition to the abuses detailed in this memorandum opinion, numerous other instances of misconduct are recounted by Judge Winner in his August 25, 1983, Opinion. In sum, the substantial departures of prosecutors in this case from established notions of fairness, from clearly articulated rules of law, from specific rules of procedure and, indeed from the Department of Justice's own manual and operating directives constitute systematic and pervasive overreaching. There is no doubt that the indicting grand jury was usurped and that time-honored constitutional principles were sullied.

Some of the violations, standing alone, require dismissal. Others, while not singularly requiring dismissal, when combined with one another amount to travesty. What is perhaps most alarming is that even in the very last of so many hearings, one of the prosecuting attorneys continued to refer to the challenge to his and colleagues' conduct as "silly" and "frivolous." The supervisory authority of the court must be used in circumstances such as those presented in this case to declare with unmistakable intention that such conduct is neither "silly" nor "frivolous" and that it will not be tolerated.

THAT blow was no sooner absorbed than the prosecutors were again faced with a barrage of calls from *60 Minutes* seeking comment on the case and the allegations of prosecutorial misconduct. In fact, Scharf hadn't even seen Judge Kane's opinion when he got the first call from *60 Minutes* producer Ira Rosen, leading him to suspect that *60 Minutes* was being kept apprised of developments sooner than the government lawyers were.

Scharf, Snyder, and Blondin wanted to go on the show. Even after the department had concluded the previous March, in response to requests from the show, not to provide a departmental spokesman for comment, the three prosecutors had written a memo to Archer asking that they personally be allowed to go on the program. Their request was denied. And the ban was renewed in the face of fresh questions from the show following the issuance of Judge Kane's opinion.

This time, however, Scharf was inclined to ignore the department's injunction. He was tired of being the human sacrifice in the case, and even if the show was unfair—which he believed it would be—he wanted the chance to have his say. And, in any event, he didn't much care any longer about the response of the department. It had ignored his strategy suggestions. It had launched an inquiry into his conduct, which made him feel even more like a defendant. Despite words of support, the department's actions had been unconvincing. The Justice Department was beginning to act, he thought, like the Denver U.S. Attorney's office, which was plainly backing away from the case as fast as it could. He felt his career in the department was in a shambles. And perhaps more than anything, he was tired. Tired of the case, tired of traveling, tired of the Denver judges, and maybe most of all, tired of having to shoulder the extraordinary burdens required of prosecutors. Within a week of Judge Kane's opinion, he announced his resignation.

He didn't even have another job lined up. But he felt better, and he told *60 Minutes* that he would appear on the show as soon as his resignation was effective on October 26. He even agreed to be interviewed by Mike Wallace the week before his resignation as long as the program wasn't aired until the week after he resigned. The interview was scheduled for October 25.

The day before, however, Archer notified Scharf in no uncertain terms that he could not grant an interview while still employed by the government. When Scharf called Ira Rosen, the producer, to tell him he'd have to reschedule the interview, he says Rosen exploded. Scharf claims Rosen accused him of being part of a government effort to delay the broadcast until after the presidential election date. He also claims Rosen warned him that "people in high places" within CBS would be very upset, adding that Mike Wallace was a friend of Attorney General William French Smith's and the two often had dinner together.

According to a memo Scharf made of the conversation, "Mr. Rosen said that Mr. Wallace will be very angry. He asked me if I would have anything 'good' to say that could be harmful to the government if the interview were delayed until the following week. I told him that I would respond truthfully to any questions asked of me, and if truthful answers were harmful to myself, to my colleagues, to the government, to the defendants, or to the judges, then so be it." (Rosen declined comment on the memo, but says Scharf "has no credibility.") The interview was rescheduled for a week later, but Scharf had the sinking feeling that he was going on trial once again.

That interview, however, never took place. Scharf had lost any trust he had in Rosen, and made a series of demands that any reputable news organization would reject, including the right to review any editing of the video tape made of his interview. He also demanded what he called a "bond" of $25,000, to be returned to CBS if it lived up to its agreements with him. Rosen angrily rejected Scharf's demands out of hand; once again, Scharf, acting with what he thought were good intentions, had made the situation worse than it would have been had he done nothing from the outset.

The *60 Minutes* broadcast was finally aired in early 1985, and it was a classic *60 Minutes*–style exposé—of the three prosecutors, not of Kilpatrick's tax shelter activities. Although Kilpatrick said at the outset, "Make no mistake about it, I was guilty of everything they charged me with," the show was entirely sympathetic to Kilpatrick, portraying him as a law-abiding citizen who simply got caught up in the intricacies of the tax code, much like the average American might in setting up an Individual Retirement Account. CBS portrayed him as a man driven into bankruptcy by prosecutors pursuing a vendetta.

Scharf fared particularly badly on the program. CBS lumped him with Snyder and Blondin as one of the prosecutors on the case, never mentioning that he joined the case only after the grand jury investigation was over, and had nothing to do with any of the incidents of misconduct that figured in Judge Kane's dismissal. Furthermore, CBS described his list of conditions for being interviewed and his demand for $25,000 as collateral. In context, it made his refusal to appear on camera appear venal.

Neither Snyder nor Blondin appeared, nor did their superiors at the Tax Division. Brief footage of Denver U.S. Attorney Miller made Miller seem as if he didn't understand why Kilpatrick's activities violated the law. And footage of William French Smith saying the department was investigating the charges against its prosecutors was out of date.

In fact, that investigation was over, and the prosecutors had been largely exonerated by the Justice Department. On October 22, before *60 Minutes* had aired its program, Department of Justice spokesman Tom DeCair issued this statement to *60 Minutes*:

> This is a very important prosecution aimed at allegations of extraordinarily serious, large-scale tax fraud. Involving some $122,000,000, it is one of the largest tax fraud prosecutions in United States history. We have carefully reviewed the decision and opinion of the trial court, and we feel strongly that we must proceed with this case either through appeal or by seeking reindictment from a new grand jury. We have a

responsibility to all honest taxpayers to protect the integrity of the tax system.

The rulings and statements of Judges Winner and Kane are extreme and unjustified. We are convinced that, on the whole, they do not fairly reflect either the facts or the law in this case. That does not mean that we have failed to take the charges of prosecutorial misconduct seriously. The matter was referred to the Office of Professional Responsibility, a watchdog unit charged with investigating allegations of misconduct by Department of Justice professionals. After an extensive and independent investigation, that Office concluded that, although there may have been instances in which the prosecutors did not fully comply with certain rules of criminal procedure, those instances did not prejudice the rights of the defendants, undermine the independence of the grand jury, or even warrant disciplinary action.

CBS, however, made no mention of the statement or the conclusions of the Office of Professional Responsibility in its broadcast.

Rosen says he was aware of the Justice Department's conclusions, but didn't mention them because he was assured by Justice Department sources that the internal investigation was merely a "cosmetic job" intended to protect the government in case any of the defendants filed lawsuits.

Judge Kane, too, characterizes the Justice Department's investigation as a "total whitewash. I was never asked a single question," he says, "and neither was Judge Winner."

As the statement to *60 Minuters* indicated it would, the Department of Justice appealed Judge Kane's dismissal of the indictments, bringing to three the appeals from the case pending before the Tenth Circuit. Also awaiting decision were the motions to withdraw Judge Winner's decision attacking the prosecutors and Judge Kane's initial dismissal of twenty-six of the twenty-seven counts on grounds of substantive tax law. The Court of Appeals heard arguments in the appeals in August 1985; eighteen months later there was still no decision.

Despite the harsh language of the opinions from Judges Kane and Winner, the prosecutors may be vindicated in the appellate court's decision. Robert Morvillo, the former prosecutor who represents the Bank of Nova Scotia, concedes that most of the alleged instances of prosecutorial misconduct are "highly technical. I don't believe they did anything out of an evil motive. It was overzealousness and lack of judgment."

The Court of Appeals ruling will, in practical terms, have little effect on the government careers of the prosecutors. Snyder left Washington during the summer of 1985 to join the U.S. Attorney's office in San Antonio. Blondin remained in Washington, but was looking for another job. Scharf moved with his family to White Plains, New York. He is trying to develop his own private practice—a concededly slow process while he remains in the shadow of the Kilpatrick case. At least he now spends most evenings at home—even while admitting he misses the pace and drama of his job as a prosecutor. All three believe strongly that they have been victims and deserve vindication.

The truth, of course, probably lies somewhere between their own sense of righteousness and the vendetta portrayed on *60 Minutes*. Scharf, Snyder, and Blondin aren't Big Brother incarnate. They are, on the contrary, bright, personable if headstrong lawyers who thought they were acting out of the purest of motives—the desire to stop crime and apprehend criminals, in Snyder's terms, to catch the "liars, cheaters, and stealers." In a world sharply divided into the good and the bad, they always saw themselves in the white hats.

That, of course, was part of the problem. Henry Singer was Brooklyn District Attorney during the Depression, and he himself was later prosecuted on criminal charges. Having been on both ends of prosecution, Singer often warned that the most dangerous quality in a prosecutor was zeal. "Anyone who seeks to become a prosecutor," he once said, "should be disqualified on that ground alone."

BEING on *60 Minutes* to explain prosecutorial misconduct was agonizing for Attorney General William French Smith. Tax fraud prosecution was supposed to be a symbol of the Reagan administration's attack on budget waste, and instead, the premiere case had turned into a forum on misconduct. It was galling for Smith's aides to watch Giuliani reap the publicity he was getting in New York, and then have to suffer through this with the Attorney General.

Moreover, the unfavorable publicity was in an area—criminal law— in which the Attorney General had little experience and interest. But Smith's cautious reserve—so different from Giuliani's natural ebullience—had attracted little other publicity of any kind. Even within the administration, he was viewed at times as colorless and bland. In a magazine article, one unidentified White House source was quoted

as saying that Smith was "a major disappointment" to the administration and a "somnambulist" because he had "no known view on any
issue."

In fact, the characterization wasn't entirely fair. Smith had duti-
fully put into practice much of President Reagan's ideology. Under
his guidance, the Justice Department reversed its position on major
civil rights questions, antitrust law, and abortion, and cracked down
on government leaks to the press.

Even more significant, however, was what Smith hadn't done.
Within his department was a cadre of hard-core, ideological conservatives who sought radical change in the nation's law enforcement.
Their standard bearer was William Bradford Reynolds, the head of
the Justice Department's Civil Rights Division, where he had launched
an all-out assault to block affirmative action in all its forms. He and his
allies had far more ambitious goals, particularly in the criminal area,
where they felt those accused of crime had long been favored at the
expense of victims and law enforcement officers. The Bill of Rights,
they argued, was never meant to handicap police officers, and should
never have been imposed on the states by the Supreme Court through
its so-called incorporation doctrine. It was, to say the least, a radical
reinterpretation of constitutional law.

Smith never became a convert. At the morning meetings, Reynolds
and allies such as Charles Cooper would constantly push for radical
change, particularly in determining positions to be taken before the
Supreme Court. But Smith's inherent cautiousness and legal training
led him to reject such suggestions. He and Rex Lee, the Solicitor
General, argued repeatedly that such efforts were doomed to failure in
the Supreme Court even if, as Reynolds and his allies argued, their
positions were good policy.

Reynolds was also a pipeline to the White House, particularly to
Edwin Meese, counselor to the President. If Smith was relatively
indifferent to issues of criminal law enforcement, Meese seemed practically obsessed with it. Reynolds hammered away with Meese, criticizing Smith and especially Lee for their opposition. Gradually,
Justice Department lawyers got the sense that Lee had been targeted
by administration conservatives for elimination; he eventually announced his resignation.

They didn't have that sense about Smith. The Attorney General, as
Reagan's personal lawyer, had a relationship with the President that

existed independently of his official position. While they couldn't be sure what damage Meese might be trying to do to that relationship, they assumed any such effort would fail. Reagan simply didn't respond to criticism of such long-standing friends and supporters, particularly when the attack was intensely ideological and hinged on abstract arguments about constitutional law. Under William French Smith, the Bill of Rights stayed intact.

Then, in January 1984, Smith announced his resignation. Schmults, his deputy, followed suit, leaving a yawning hole at the top of the department.

At a news conference to explain his action, Smith said that he told the President he was resigning so he could return to his law firm, Gibson, Dunn & Crutcher, in Los Angeles. In his letter of resignation, he wrote that he had been involved in every one of Reagan's election campaigns, and "I do not want 1984 to be an exception. This would not be possible in my present position." He added that "it is now time for me to return to private life."

Even Smith's announcement attracted unfavorable comment. "His tenure has been lackluster," Senator Joseph R. Biden, Jr., the ranking Democrat on the Senate Judiciary Committee, told *The New York Times*.

In any event, Smith's announcement was overshadowed by the far more electrifying announcement of his successor. On the same day he made Smith's resignation public, President Reagan announced that Smith's successor would be Edwin Meese.

The announcement was a surprise, it seemed, to almost everyone but Meese himself, for whom the position of U.S. Attorney General seemed the pinnacle of a lifetime in public service and law enforcement. Meese was born and raised in Oakland, California. His father was a public servant, the Alameda County treasurer and tax collector. His grandfather had been Oakland's treasurer, as well as an Oakland city councilman.

Meese showed an early interest in the criminal justice system, deciding to pursue a career in law and taking criminal courses at the University of California at Berkeley, where he graduated in 1958. His wife, Ursula, was a probation officer in Oakland. Curiously, they spent their honeymoon on a tour of the California state prison system. Law enforcement became both a hobby and a career for the young Meese. He listened to police radio broadcasts for entertainment, cultivated friends on the police force, and eventually landed a job as an Assistant District Attorney in the Alameda County prosecutor's office. There he worked closely with another prosecutor, Lowell Jensen.

After Reagan was elected to his first term as California's governor, Meese applied for the then relatively obscure job of extradition and clemency secretary, and got it. He promptly turned the position into a clearinghouse for criminal justice policy in the governor's administration, and he gradually became a close confidant and ally of Reagan's. In 1969 Reagan made Meese his executive secretary and chief of staff, a position relinquished by William Clark when Reagan named the future national security adviser and Secretary of the Interior to a Superior Court judgeship. Meese had arrived at California's inner sanctum of power. In the years to come, he would rarely be far from Reagan's side. Now he was in the White House, the Attorney General–designate.

The conservative coalition within the Justice Department was ecstatic. The revolution they thought the President had been elected to bring about could finally proceed. Liberals, recalling such remarks as Meese's denunciation of the American Civil Liberties Union as "an ongoing lobby opposed to law enforcement," were predictably dismayed. Judiciary Committee members vowed that Meese would receive intense scrutiny before being confirmed for such an important position. Even a top Republican aide predicted there would be "rough sledding" in the confirmation hearings.

At the time, few realized how rough, or time-consuming, the scrutiny of Meese would be. More than a year later, in February 1985, months after Reagan had been re-elected and the campaign finished, Smith was still the Attorney General.

"It is purely rumor that the movie *The Long Goodbye* is a Department of Justice documentary," Smith quipped to Department of Justice employees assembled for what seemed like the fifth or sixth farewell party for Smith.

About a year earlier, at a glittering farewell party for the Smiths— one of the first—given by the Italian ambassador to the U.S., the comments had been different in tone. "There's a time to come and a time to go," Smith said. "This just seems the time to go."

A featured guest was the Attorney General–designate, who seemed much less at home in the black-tie crowd than Smith, but who obligingly posed for photos with the Attorney General and socialite guests. Meese said he wasn't nervous about the confirmation hearings. "It's one of those things you have to go through," he breezily told a reporter. He said he was confident he would be easily confirmed.

But Jacob Stein, an iconoclastic Washington lawyer who had never set foot in the Italian embassy, would see about that.

THE INVESTIGATION OF
EDWIN MEESE

JOHN R. McKean, a San Francisco certified public accountant, made something of a specialty of
helping clients out of what were euphemistically
known as cash-flow problems. In blunter terms, they couldn't pay
their bills. But even he had to admit to a certain amount of surprise
when his newest client turned out to be one of the most highly placed
men in America: Edwin Meese, counselor to the President. As he
examined the documents spread out on his desk, McKean marveled
that Meese's financial affairs could be in such a mess.

McKean had never met Meese and his wife, Ursula, before that
morning, June 13, 1981. President Reagan had been in the White
House less than five months. But that spring, Michael Deaver, another of the President's closest advisers, had called McKean with the
information that several people in the Reagan administration were
having some "serious problems" with their move to Washington.
Deaver had been impressed with the assistance McKean had given
him when the Deavers moved to Washington, and he had hired him
to prepare his tax returns and to help him with the elaborate financial
disclosure forms now required for most people elected or appointed to
high national office. Deaver explained that one of the people he wanted
to refer to him was Ed Meese.

Several months passed. Then McKean received a phone call from
Meese's secretary: Meese and his wife would be in California that

week. That morning Meese and his wife had arrived at McKean's offices at One California Street in San Francisco, armed with financial records, some handwritten calculations, and the growing sense that they desperately needed some expert financial planning: "We have to hang tough" for four years, Meese told McKean.

"Hanging tough"—a typical Meese response to any kind of adversity—was not going to solve the problems that McKean immediately perceived. Cash needs over and above monthly expenses were estimated by Meese for the rest of the year to total $41,200. His after-tax take-home pay at the White House would barely cover that. Though it was June, the Meeses hadn't even yet paid their 1980 taxes (they'd gotten an extension).

Though the Meeses didn't seem to be living lavishly by the standards of wealthy members of the Reagan entourage, they were plainly living beyond their means. They still had a large house near San Diego. They'd purchased another home in the Virginia suburbs of Washington, D.C.

Meese never asked directly for a loan, but that seemed an obvious corollary to the request for financial planning. McKean could offer Meese several advantages over a commercial bank, most notably, confidentiality. With McKean acting as an intermediary for a loan, the name of the real lender—and Meese's embarrassing financial plight—would never actually have to be disclosed. McKean mentioned the disclosure statute, and what Meese would have to say about their transactions, but to McKean, Meese seemed unconcerned; he "simply wanted to resolve his financial affairs promptly."

Nothing was decided that day; Meese, without his wife, returned four days later to continue their discussions. Eventually McKean arranged $60,000 in loans for the Meeses, and did nothing when Meese missed his interest payments.

A few months later, one of McKean's teen-age children thought someone was playing a prank when the phone rang and someone on the other end of the line said the White House was callling. It was Deaver on the phone, this time offering McKean a high-level appointment to the United States Postal Service Board of Governors. Later, McKean spoke directly to Meese on the phone about the prestigious appointment.

"As you know," he told Meese, "Mike [Deaver] called me on the Postal Service thing and I've now heard from White House counsel that it's going through. I appreciate any role you've played in this."

"We need good people back here," Meese replied, according to McKean.

In his euphoria over his new job, it never occurred to McKean that somewhere along the line his relationship with Meese might have turned criminal, or that some day he himself would be investigated to determine if his loan to Meese was in fact a bribe to get the appointment.

But months later, when deputy special prosecutor Richard L. Beizer pored over the accounts of the McKean dealings, he saw the same pattern that appeared in so many other Meese transactions: an amazing sloppiness about his personal financial affairs, a casual disregard for what most regarded as serious and important disclosure laws to maintain the integrity of government, and a curious blindness to the way such dealings would look to those who weren't his friends and cronies. Here was a dangerous confluence of qualities, one that all too often led people, wittingly or not, into criminal activity.

Now Meese had been tapped to be, of all things, Attorney General, the nation's highest law enforcement official and its top prosecutor. How ironic that Meese was himself, in a sense, about to be prosecuted by Beizer and his colleagues in the special prosecutor's office.

O F all the nation's top prosecutors, the special prosecutor is the most unusual and possibly the most powerful.

All prosecutors, as essentially law enforcement officials, are members of the executive branch. In the federal government, they are appointed, directly or indirectly, by the President, and they carry out their functions subject to his supervision and subject to his dismissal. If they commit improprieties, break the law, or otherwise misbehave and aren't suitably disciplined by the President or his appointees, it is a problem for the political process to correct. The President can always be voted out of office, or so the theory goes.

It is debatable whether the theory ever truly functioned in practice. But the public became acutely aware of its inherent problems during the Watergate scandal, as the realization spread that the suspects were President Nixon himself and many of his top aides, including the Attorney General, and that they could hardly be expected to carry out the investigation needed and file any appropriate criminal charges. The investigation that was launched was derided for its lapses and had no credibility with the public.

Arguments have since been made that in the case of Watergate, the system actually worked quite well. The threat of impeachment, a quasi-criminal proceeding against the President, forced Nixon's resignation. At the same time, however, it was apparent that crimes less severe than those giving rise to Watergate would probably be swept under the rug under the guise of executive privilege.

The result was legislation called the Ethics in Government Act of 1978, the omnibus legislation that remains as the most enduring landmark to the Watergate scandal. The act authorized the appointment of a special prosecutor to investigate and, if necessary, to prosecute high-ranking executive branch officials.

The concept of a special prosecutor wasn't new. After all, a special prosecutor had been appointed by Nixon in an attempt to lend credibility to the White House investigation. But that special prosecutor, Harvard professor Archibald Cox, also earned a place in history when Nixon fired him because he was investigating too thoroughly.

That problem was solved in the new legislation by insulating the special prosecutor from the dismissal power of the President. Special prosecutors were always "special" in the sense that they were supposed to operate independently of the executive branch; this act simply institutionalized that aspect by transferring the power to appoint and remove the special prosecutor from the executive to the judiciary, the least political of the three branches of government.

Since the passage of the act until 1982, there had been only four special prosecutors appointed and three investigations conducted. Special prosecutors were named to investigate allegations of cocaine use by Hamilton Jordan and Tim Kraft, both former White House aides to President Jimmy Carter; to investigate corruption allegations against former Carter Budget Director Bert Lance; and to investigate corruption charges against President Reagan's former Secretary of Labor, Raymond Donovan. No charges were brought against any of the three by the special prosecutor. However, Lance and Donovan were subsequently indicted by other state and federal prosecutors. (Lance was acquitted; and in mid-1987 Donovan too was acquitted.) In addition, a number of requests were made for appointments of special prosecutors that were denied. Those requests, as required by the statute, remained confidential.

Inevitably, those investigations led to charges that the special prosecutor statute was vulnerable to political abuse; that simply by leveling charges, no matter how unfounded, opponents of the President

could subject him to prolonged and embarrassing public investigations. Much of the criticism was prompted by a realization long known
as a truism to professional prosecutors: the lodging of charges over
which prosecutors have nearly unfettered discretion is the essential
source of their power.

And yet the process seemed to work. With Watergate fresh in the
memories of the public, the special prosecutor's investigations, by and
large carried out in a dignified and professional manner, provided
needed reassurance that the executive branch of government was not
above the law; that America was governed by laws, not men.

WASHINGTON lawyer Jacob Stein wondered why the U.S. Court
of Appeals for the District of Columbia circuit was calling him. One
of the country's most influential and distinguished appellate courts,
the Court of Appeals spent much of its time on the kind of important
cases unique to Washington: crucial tests of federal power, many
arising from the myriad federal agencies based in the nation's capital.

Stein is an oddity among lawyers in Washington, which boasts the
densest population of lawyers of any city in the U.S., and probably in
the world. The overwhelming majority of those lawyers are tethered
to the federal government, either serving it or, in the case of the
private bar, persuading and attacking it. With a few prominent exceptions, Stein's practice could have been duplicated in any large-to-
medium-sized city in the country. Stein is a criminal defense lawyer,
most of whose clients are more familiar with the dark and seedy
sections of Southeast Washington than the Northeast quadrant that is
the preserve of official and affluent Washington. Maybe it was that
experience that helped Stein win the only acquittal for a Watergate
defendant, his client Kenneth Parkinson.

Even within the ranks of Washington criminal lawyers, Stein is
viewed as peculiar. Members of the Washington bar describe him
affectionately as a "character." He is the best-known lawyer in a small
firm, Stein, Mitchell, & Mezines, where his office is legendary for its
disarray. Crowded with a hodgepodge of antiques, artifacts, and fur-
niture, it looks a bit like a nice-quality secondhand or antique shop.
Books are everywhere; on shelves, on surfaces, even on the floor.
Stein himself is the centerpiece, usually wearing a three-piece tweed
suit, a bow tie, and relishing opportunities to display a sly wit and a
vast storehouse of literary and historical trivia. Stein has what he says

is the largest collection of epigrams and aphorisms about the law. He loves to fling an old gypsy curse: "May you have a lawsuit—when you're in the right." He describes himself as one of the "odd birds of passage" that in an earlier time were drawn to the practice of law. In short, he has made himself into someone who could be a character in one of his beloved nineteenth-century novels.

When Stein took the call, the secretary to Court of Appeals Judge Roger Robb was at the other end. Without providing an explanation, she asked Stein to send over a statement of his background and experience. Though she evaded his efforts to divine the reason for her request, he'd been reading press accounts of problems with the Meese nomination to be Attorney General and demands for the appointment of a special prosecutor. Since it was the Court of Appeals that would choose the special prosecutor, he assumed its request for a résumé might be related.

Stein was slightly amused by the prospect of his being named to the position. In a few respects, he was an obvious candidate: few Washington lawyers had spent more time in the federal courts of the capital; Stein had even helped draft the rules of procedure for them. He knew the Court of Appeals judges well from his frequent appearances there. (A peculiarity of the District of Columbia court system is that there are, obviously, no state courts. As a result, even small, local matters end up in federal court and are appealed to the Court of Appeals. As a result, Stein's practice had brought him before the D.C. federal courts with a frequency that wouldn't be possible anywhere else in the country.)

But apart from his trial experience, Stein seemed a highly unlikely choice to be named a special prosecutor, or any kind of prosecutor, for that matter. "I don't like prosecutors," he says matter-of-factly. Unlike most criminal defense lawyers, Stein didn't cut his teeth in court as a prosecutor. "I've never been a prosecutor," he says with pride. "I've never held any kind of government position.

"From time to time," he says, "I've thought prosecution might be interesting work. I've wondered about the nature of the job. But I've never moved in that direction. I've seen too much prosecutorial oppression.

"If I ever was a prosecutor, I'd hope I wouldn't act like most of the prosecutors I've seen. They display all the affectations of temporary power. They have tremendous power. Many prosecutors are very young, with narrow experience in life and the world. Most have come from academic backgrounds, and that's not a good qualification for a prosecutor.

"I've dealt with many prosecutors over the years," he continues. "Most of them are inconsiderate—of other people's schedules, of the trepidation that others feel in approaching them. They're overbearing, lazy. Every human defect is exaggerated by power."

Stein didn't give the matter much more thought. Then, a little more than a week later, Judge Robb's secretary called again asking him to come in for an interview with the three judges who had been appointed to the selection panel. There were a few questions about his experience, but clearly he would pass muster on that score. And Stein cut short questions about what was clearly a more sensitive area, his political affiliation and leanings. It was crucial, the judges felt, that someone be appointed who would be perceived as nonpartisan, given the intensely political nature of the allegations against Meese.

Stein leaped on the questions with inner delight, for the judges couldn't have found a more nonpartisan candidate anywhere. Stein told them that he is not, nor has he ever been, a member of any political party. He has never made a campaign contribution of any sort. In fact, to preserve his ideological purity, he has never even voted. For years, he was spared that citizens' duty by his residence in the District of Columbia, whose citizens didn't have a vote in federal elections. But since the electorate has been expanded to include D.C., he has chosen not to vote. "I'm not at all political," he says, a state of mind he attributes, in part, to a lifetime in Washington where he has seen politics amply displayed in both its highest and lowest forms.

And finally, Stein had the stature the Court of Appeals knew that this special prosecutor would need to withstand the intense pressures that could be expected to emanate from the White House and the press. At fifty-eight, with experience as a Watergate defense lawyer and a term as president of the District of Columbia bar behind him, he fit the bill.

At the end of the hour-long session, the judges announced that they were going to appoint Stein to the position, making him the nation's fifth special prosecutor. They gave him only one piece of advice: be discreet with the press.

Stein could have pulled out then and there, he supposed, but he felt his long-dormant interest in prosecution quickening. "I've so often criticized prosecutors," he says. "Would others now find those failings in me?"

JACOB Stein took the oath of office on April 2. Immediately deluged with requests from the press for interviews, he turned them all down. "I thought that I couldn't even start down that road," Stein says. "I knew there'd be no end to it. I wanted to conduct this with as few dealings with the press as possible. It's unseemly for witnesses to read in the paper that they've appeared before a grand jury. I wanted to keep this dignified."

On April 4 he met with two of his predecessors, Arthur Christy and Leon Silverman. Christy had run the Jordan investigation; Silverman, the recently ended Donovan investigation. Both pressed upon him the need for a top-quality support staff, especially FBI agents and lawyers to serve as deputy special prosecutors.

Stein's next official appointment was with William Webster, the FBI director, whom he found extremely cooperative. If there was going to be any official foot dragging in the investigation, it was obvious that it wouldn't be coming from the FBI. Apart from his professional integrity, Webster was a potential ally in another sense: there was no love lost between the FBI director and Ed Meese. Webster gave Stein his choice of agents, including several who were already working on FBI investigations of some of the Meese allegations.

Stein insisted on only one possibly contentious point: once the agents were selected, he wanted them to report directly to him, the special prosecutor, and not to Webster. As the investigative arm of the special prosecutor's office, Stein believes it to be essential that agents be detached from the FBI, an agency of the executive branch even though it enjoyed quasi-independent status.

Finally Stein turned to the task of choosing a staff of lawyers. There was no shortage of candidates. As soon as it was made public that Stein had been named the special prosecutor, he'd received more than two hundred résumés from lawyers around the country hoping to be named to the special prosecutor's staff. But he wanted people he knew and knew he could trust. And he wanted some real prosecutors.

EVEN though Richard Beizer was in private practice with a large Washington law firm, he started thinking like a prosecutor again as soon as he heard a special prosecutor was going to be appointed to investigate Meese. He got on the phone immediately with some of his friends from the District of Columbia's U.S. Attorney's office, speculating on the identity of the still-unnamed lawyer. Was there any chance, he wondered, that he might be involved himself? He knew he should be concentrating on defense work, but still, serving as a special prosecutor would be a nice way to round out a career in prosecution. A nice postscript, he thought.

Until the previous summer, Beizer had spent nearly all of his professional life as a prosecutor, a career that during law school had never even occurred to him. Beizer attended the University of Virginia Law School from 1964 to 1967. While the high points of the student "revolution" were still to come, and never reached Virginia in the way they did in some schools in the north, almost no one in those days wanted to be a prosecutor, or at least admitted it. Prosecutors were agents of the government, the state, the Establishment. They were one step removed from the police, and in the eyes of many students, they were agents of oppression. "I think there were only two guys in my class who were even remotely interested in criminal law," Beizer recalls. "And that was so they could do a little pro bono work for criminal defendants. Personally, I didn't want to touch it."

After graduating, Beizer wasn't even sure he wanted to practice any kind of law. Like many his age, he joined the Peace Corps and was stationed in Calcutta. After several years in India, he decided it was time to re-enter American society, and landed a clerkship with the prestigious Fourth Circuit Court of Appeals in Richmond.

While clerking, his attention focused more and more on the trial courts. One day one of the Appeals Court judges mentioned that if trial work was what he really wanted he should seek a position with a prosecutor's office, especially one of the U.S. Attorney's offices.

Almost by default, Beizer applied to the District of Columbia's U.S. Attorney's office when his clerkship expired. He was turned down. The setback gave him new determination. He took an academic writing job for a year, and reapplied. This time he was accepted.

Beizer was plunged into a world as different from Calcutta as from the staid confines of the Court of Appeals. Rotating through the general crimes unit, he was assigned to everything from rape and murder to minor probation violations. In the District of Columbia, the U.S. Attorney's office handles everything.

Beizer was so fascinated by his work that what he thought might be a short stay to gain some trial experience turned into years. Beizer eventually gravitated to the sophisticated fraud cases, the white-collar cases that many prosecutors find to be the most intellectually challenging. And he outlasted five U.S. Attorneys, staying longer than he probably should have if he ever intended to establish a high-paying career in private practice.

Now his life as a prosecutor seemed behind him. But, on April 2, he read that the new special prosecutor was none other than Jacob Stein. Having come up against a defense lawyer as shrewd and colorful as Stein would have left an impression in any event. But Stein had been a defense counsel in the biggest case of Beizer's career as an Assistant U.S. Attorney.

It was a fraud case, a bribery case involving a Washington real estate magnate and local government official. Besides Stein, one of the defense lawyers was Edward Bennett Williams, one of Washington's best-known power brokers. Working closely with two other prosecutors, Beizer conducted a complex sixteen-month investigation, and after a lengthy, exhausting trial, the defendants were convicted in 1978.

Beizer had little time to savor his victory. The verdict was overturned on appeal because of a voir dire problem with one of the jurors, a complex and shifting area of the law at the time. Beizer and his colleagues moved to Philadelphia for the retrial, and this time the jury reached a verdict of not guilty.

Beizer was philosophical about the disappointing outcome, "I wasn't overjoyed," he says. "I thought we'd done our best." Like many career prosecutors, he'd learned not to dwell on the vicissitudes of juries. "That's a short-timer's game."

A by-product of the long case was a close relationship with and respect for Stein. So when he read of Stein's appointment as special prosecutor, he called immediately to congratulate him and chide him a bit on his shift to the other side of the criminal system, one for which he had had such disdain. Beizer realized too that Stein would be needing assistance; the topic wasn't broached, but Beizer figured it couldn't hurt for Stein to have a reminder that he was around.

Sure enough, a couple of days later, one of Stein's partners called Beizer and asked him if he'd be interested in helping out. "I'd love to," Beizer said, then set about trying to explain to his new law firm, Crowell & Moring, that after being there less than a year, it was already necessary for him to take a leave of absence.

GEORGE Frampton was in Colorado when he heard another special prosecutor had been appointed. The news brought back memories of his own work. One of the high points of his career—certainly one of the most intense, exciting stretches—was his time as an assistant special prosecutor from 1973 to 1975 investigating the Watergate scandal.

In fact, it had been hard to duplicate that excitement in private practice. Frampton had been blessed with a keen mind, all-American good looks, and a glittering résumé that included Harvard *Law Review*, an advanced degree from the London School of Economics, and a Supreme Court clerkship under Justice Harry Blackmun. He'd gone almost directly from the Supreme Court to the special prosecutor's office. A few years later, he was named to a task force investigating the Three Mile Island nuclear accident. With such a high-powered beginning to a career, what, really, was left that would be a challenge?

Frampton wondered. He'd just finished most of his work on a lengthy tax case for the state of Alaska, one that had raised important constitutional issues, but had taken him far from the centers of political power. He'd been in private practice with one of Washington's young, "hot" firms, Rogovin Huge & Lenzner, for seven years. He was feeling restless. Seven years was the traditional period preceding academic sabbaticals, and Frampton had decided that the concept was what he needed, to relax, do some reading, and think about his own future. That's why he was in Colorado.

But when he received a phone call from a partner of Stein's one day, he could feel his pulse quickening. The lawyer had a few questions for Frampton about the mechanics of setting up such an investigation, and Stein had urged him to call Frampton. Frampton and Stein knew each other from the Watergate trials; Frampton had prosecuted Stein's client, in fact. The two developed a rapport, and they had continued to trade favorite books long after Watergate was over. Stein's partner didn't mention the possibility of Frampton's actually joining the investigation, but Frampton mentioned that he was coming back to Washington for a while anyway, and why didn't he stop by for a chat with Stein. Not long after, Stein himself called Frampton asking him to join the team. Frampton hesitated. This wasn't exactly what he had in mind for his sabbatical. Still, he felt himself being drawn to some of the issues he knew would surface in the case. Maybe he could work on some of the legal issues, perhaps an "of counsel" role to the investigation. Ultimately he couldn't resist the possibility. He said yes, and arranged a flight back to Washington. At least for now, the sabbatical was over.

TOWARD the end of April, Stein gathered his staff in his office for their first meeting together. Besides Beizer and Frampton, he'd tapped David Austern, a partner in a small Washington firm, Goldfarb, Singer & Austern, who'd been an Assistant District Attorney in New York City as well as an Assistant U.S. Attorney in Washington. An honors graduate of Yale Law School, he was now teaching criminal law part time at Georgetown. Also on board was Terry Duggan, who would act as an administrator for the investigation. She has the distinction of having worked on every investigation by a special prosecutor, and has developed a reputation for being indispensable in what is concededly a highly specialized line of work.

Stein told the group that he would be relying heavily on them, and that he hoped to work through consensus. He had every qualification for the investigation but one, his lack of experience as a prosecutor, and that's where the staff would be most important.

That said, it was time to figure out what had to be investigated and how.

THE official executive order providing for Stein's appointment had spelled out six allegations against Meese that had prompted the need for an investigation. They had emerged already in press accounts and in the course of congressional hearings examining Meese's fitness to be Attorney General. The six areas to be investigated were:

1. Meese's failure to include in financial disclosure statements a $15,000 loan made by one Edwin Thomas to Mrs. Meese;

2. The connection between that and other loans to the Meese family and certain appointments to federal jobs;

3. Stock trading by Meese and members of his family;

4. Whether Meese obtained special treatment from government agencies for businesses in which he had a financial interest;

5. Meese's military reserve status and promotions; and

6. Meese's statements under oath about the alleged theft of Carter campaign materials.

The special prosecutors were, to varying degrees, familiar with the allegations, but knew nothing beyond what they had read in press accounts. Moreover, the mandate didn't indicate what, if any, criminal laws had allegedly been violated by the conduct in question. Matters that might lead one to question Meese's qualifications to be Attorney General might nonetheless have little relevance to a criminal investigation. Indeed, Senator Joseph R. Biden, Jr., wrote Stein a letter asking explicitly that he render an opinion concerning the "propriety or ethics" of Meese's conduct, and not limit the investigation to allegations of criminal conduct. Meese's own lawyer even asked for a declaration that "the evidence does not substantiate the loose charges of moral turpitude against Mr. Meese," a conclusion that went far beyond the question of whether criminal laws had been violated.

Thus, at the outset, the prosecutors were faced with defining the scope of their inquiry, a task that they knew would have profound implications for Meese's fate and for their stature. While their investigatory power seemed unlimited, they recognized that exceeding the scope of their authorized mandate would make them vulnerable to political attack, and could even bring down the tradition of the nonpartisan special prosecutor.

"The most important decisions in any investigation are at the outset," Frampton says, "when you define the scope of your authority and jurisdiction. Then you have to decide what to investigate and how, acting on very little information."

Since the order appointing Stein failed to identify the criminal laws allegedly violated, it was tempting to broaden the inquiry. But the statute itself posed an obstacle. The statute had been amended in 1982, providing, among other things, that the special prosecutor should be called "independent counsel," a less threatening term, but one that has failed to enter popular usage. It also explicitly limits investigations to alleged violations of "federal criminal law."

Moreover, for the intensely nonpartisan Stein, any evaluation of fitness, in the abstract, was political, subjective, and made him uncomfortable. He felt confident that evaluation of Meese's conduct could be carried out by others, such as the Senate Judiciary Committee, which had already displayed such interest in the Meese nomination. Stein made the mission clear: the prosecutors' "sole question" was to be whether the evidence warranted prosecution under federal criminal statues.

Even with that limitation, the investigation would be complicated. With a few exceptions, the core charges against Meese involved the payment of some kind of favor, financial or otherwise, in return for appointments to public office. In essence, it was one of the oldest political crimes known to man, but one that nonetheless arises persistently: bribery.

The federal bribery statute, the prosecutors discovered, makes it a crime for any public official "corruptly" to solicit or receive anything of value in return for being influenced in his performance of any official act. The penalty: up to fifteen years in prison and a $20,000 fine.

The presence of the word "corruptly" has always been an oddity, invoking as it does the state of mind of the alleged wrongdoer. It has always been a thorn in the side of prosecutors, and generally, judges have always treated it simply to mean that the recipient of a bribe must intend to be influenced in taking some official action. In that regard, the criminal state of mind required for bribery is the same as the criminal intent required for other crimes.

Besides the bribery statute, there is also another federal "gratuity" statute arguably covering much of the same conduct. It forbids public officials from soliciting or receiving anything of value in return for some official act. The maximum penalty for conviction: two years in prison and a $10,000 fine. In keeping with the lighter penalty, various courts have ruled that the standard of proof necessary to convict under the gratuity statute is lower than under the bribery statute, pointing to the absence of the word "corruptly." But the precise relationship of the two statutes has never been clear; indeed, there have been few prosecutions under either.

Bribery and its related crimes have always given rise to complicated case law, relying as they do so heavily on state-of-mind aspects, which are always highly subjective and difficult to prove. A peculiarity of the law is that it isn't necessary even to show that any action was taken in return for a bribe—only that the parties to the bribe understood and intended that such an action be taken. The crime requires, at a minimum, only that something of value was taken, and that the person conferring it did so with the expectation that influence would be exerted on his behalf.

As a result, the crime is very much one involving two parties. Prosecutors rarely attempt to make a bribery case against only one defendant. Invariably, juries wonder where the other participant is, why he or she hasn't been charged, and conclude that it is unfair for only one person to be on trial. The prosecutors realized that any investigation of Meese for bribery would necessarily become an investigation of everyone who had allegedly participated with him in the alleged influence peddling.

In their survey of the applicable law, the prosecutors also stumbled on a law making it a criminal misdemeanor for a public official to solicit or receive anything of value in return for an appointment to a federal job—a situation very close to the allegations against Meese. The language of that statute was even less precise than the bribery and gratuity statutes, and there had been virtually no prosecutions under the statute. Still, it was another law to keep in mind as the investigation progressed.

As Frampton had suspected, the case against Meese would pose some thorny legal problems. But before plunging into active investigatory work, he and other members of the team began collecting the masses of information regarding Meese that had already been collected in other agencies, storing it and filing it in new offices Stein had rented for their work on I Street in Washington. They'd decided that they couldn't use any space in the Justice Department in order to preserve their independence, and they needed the confidentiality of their own office space. Their presence would have disrupted Stein's modest law offices.

Frampton assumed the Justice Department had already gathered extensive files on Meese; he knew from his experience as a Watergate prosecutor that at a minimum the department maintained an elaborate file of newspaper clippings that would simplify their research. But when he called, Justice Department officials turned down every request for assistance. The Justice Department, it was clear, would provide no assistance whatsoever, taking literally the provisions requiring that the special prosecutor be independent. The special prosecutors wondered whether this was an expression of the department's high regard for the niceties of conflict of interest, or whether it was deliberately trying to make their work more difficult. Time would tell, they supposed. Meanwhile, the research went forward on other fronts.

FOR Frampton, the situation reminded him very much of the Watergate scandal. Now as then, the key witnesses were all in the White House itself. They would be Meese's colleagues and members of the White House personnel office, which had overseen the appointments process. Moreover, Meese himself was only one rung below the President in the chain of executive authority, a level above the potential witnesses.

"The nature of an investigation isn't that different, except that the subject is very powerful," Frampton says. "It's hard to launch an investigation from three rungs down the ladder of authority."

The special prosecutors quickly concluded that the White House personnel office would have to be a key focus of the investigation. In order to see if there was any connection between financial benefits alleged to have been bestowed on Meese by some people, and their subsequent appointment to official positions, the prosecutors felt they had to determine how each of them came to be considered and appointed to office. They wanted to know whether these people had been considered for any position before the dealings with Meese, who in the administration first proposed them for a position, who supported or opposed the appointment or nomination, who their competitors were for the job, why these people were chosen over others, and who ultimately decided whether a person was named or not.

The lawyers weren't familiar with the appointments process in the White House. Frampton agreed to take the lead in that portion of the investigation, since he wasn't extricating himself from another full-time job, and he plunged into research and some interviews with people who had been involved in the process.

Frampton learned that to an unusual degree the Reagan administration had centralized the appointments process inside the White House, in an office called the White House Office of Presidential Personnel. From January 1981 to July 1982, the head of the office was E. Pendleton James; he was succeeded by Helene von Damm, who was subsequently named ambassador to Austria.

The OPP, as it was called, was in charge of identifying vacancies, then preparing what were called "long lists" of candidates to fill them. Names on each long list might come from a wide variety of sources:

OPP staff members, previous lists, members of Congress, Cabinet officers, Republican fund raisers and contributors, even direct applications from people interested in a job. OPP winnowed each long list to a short list of two to four names in discussions with White House staff and other members of the administration.

Once one or more candidates was chosen by OPP, the name was submitted to the Senior Staff Personnel Committee. Throughout the time period being investigated, the same people made up the committee: James Baker, Michael Deaver, the director of OPP, and, Frampton was keenly interested to discover, Edwin Meese. During the first few months of 1981, the committee met nearly every afternoon to review appointments. Once it made a decision, it submitted a memorandum to President Reagan recommending an appointment. It was extremely rare for such a memorandum to recommend more than one name for a single job; in most respects, the committee made the decision for the President's approval.

It was clear that Meese occupied a central position that at least made the allegations of influence peddling a possibility. Frampton concluded that a visit to the White House would have to be his next step. How he was received would provide important clues not only to the merits of the allegations against Meese but to the administration's attitude toward the investigation.

From his Watergate experience, Frampton knew that his targets had no incentive to give him the evidence he wanted. On the contrary, they're usually trying to destroy it, hide it, or obfuscate it. But access to the records of OPP and the personnel committee was obviously crucial, and one way or another, Frampton intended to get it.

For his first visit, Frampton didn't want to start at too high a level; he didn't want to confront immediately the awkward situation of investigating a superior. So he met with a lawyer in the office of the President's counsel, Fred Fielding, but not with Fielding himself.

Frampton asked a few general questions about the workings of the appointments process, then zeroed in on the question of access to records in the White House. The lawyer reacted coolly. Internal memoranda evaluating the qualifications of those appointed to high office in the administration could obviously prove embarrassing. They undoubtedly contained sensitive political material, as well as evidence that some appointments had hardly been doled out for pure reasons of merit. The lawyer said that the White House had "some problems" with what Frampton and the other special prosecutors wanted.

Frampton didn't doubt that. He recognized that had he been in the Justice Department, talking with a White House official in a position to fire him, the inquiry might well have been stifled at that very point. But he wasn't. He noted that he had the subpoena power to obtain the records from the White House, and he was confident he would succeed even if there was a prolonged court fight over the scope and validity of a subpoena of White House records. Did the lawyer's superiors want the Meese nomination further delayed while this wrangling took place in court? Even more to the point, did the Reagan administration want the publicity suggesting it was resisting efforts of the special prosecutor to obtain evidence relating to the allegations against one of Reagan's trusted advisers? Frampton suggested that the White House solve its "problems" with his request, and left.

MEANWHILE, back in the offices on I Street, more Meese allegations had poured in in the wake of Stein's appointment, and the prosecutors were trying to sort them out and divide up the work. They'd already added another lawyer to their ranks, James Bensfield, a former public defender in Washington and an adjunct law professor at Georgetown, who, like Stein, was largely an expert in criminal defense work. Stein asked another Washington lawyer, John Aldock, to lend some assistance.

The new allegations seemed, at least on the surface, less serious than those mentioned in the mandate from the federal court. For example, CBS News reported that Meese had accepted a pair of jade-and-gold cuff links from the South Korean government on a Far Eastern trip in 1983. Unlike others on the trip, Meese hadn't turned over the cuff links to the White House gift unit until the day CBS called him with inquiries about the matter. In a similar vein, there were allegations that Meese's financial disclosure statement didn't report reimbursements for various travel expenses.

Taken individually, the new charges weren't earthshaking. Would Meese knowingly have violated a criminal law for a pair of cuff links? Still, the prosecutors were intrigued by the pattern of the allegations: the same curious negligence, if that was the word, with which Meese seemed to engage in official business. It hardly matched the portrait of the efficient administrator and executive secretary to Reagan that they had been given by others who knew him. They decided that the allegations, even if trivial, warranted investigation for the light they might shed on the broader questions about Meese.

While Frampton concentrated on the operations of the White House appointments committee, Beizer started gathering the information that had already been collected on Meese by other branches of government. He had particularly good luck with Senator Howard Metzenbaum's office. Senator Metzenbaum had been one of the most vigorous critics of Meese on the Senate Judiciary Committee, and one of his aides had taken the lead in gathering material related to the various allegations that had surfaced.

He agreed to give Beizer access to whatever the Judiciary Committee had collected. And that was just the prelude to an avalanche of additional information. On Frampton's next visit to the White House, he was told the order had come down to cooperate fully with the special prosecutors, though some limits might have to be imposed on access to a few documents—they couldn't be copied or leave the premises. Jubilant from that success, Frampton returned to the I Street offices to discover a messenger with a shopping cart full of documents.

The messenger was from the office of Meese's defense lawyer, Leonard Garment, well-known Washington attorney and former counsel to President Richard Nixon. The cart contained piles of documents from Meese's own files that might bear on the investigation, including Meese's own annotated newspaper clippings.

The prosecutors were amazed—they hadn't even had a chance to ask Meese or his lawyers for production of the documents. Obviously, Garment and Meese had made a fundamental decision early on: they weren't going to be accused of a cover-up, as Nixon had been.

"This was amazing," Frampton says. "It suggested—as I'm sure it was intended to—a great willingness to cooperate. It was a strategic legal and political decision made early on by Garment. He was going to sell us. It was a sales job."

In some respects, the great display of cooperation was worrisome to the prosecutors. It did further their work quickly. On the other hand, could the appearance of cooperation be deceptive? Might they be lulled into complacency? Stein, in particular, knew that one of the many ploys adopted by defense lawyers is to drown the prosecution in documents, sometimes omitting some. "We had to be skeptical," Frampton says.

The reaction of the prosecutors to all the cooperation, in fact, led to a clash with Stein. Despite the pledges of cooperation, Frampton and

Beizer wanted to draft a discovery letter to the White House, formally asking for access to everything they thought they needed. Under the circumstances, Stein thought they were being excessively adversarial.

"This was one place where we felt it was important to have experience as a prosecutor," one of the staff says. "Jake had a defense orientation ingrained in him. He didn't realize the need to ask for everything that we needed to cover our bases. This was in many respects the most important letter in the investigation. The White House might assert executive privilege; there might be highly political documents in there. We had to ask for them, and we had to insist on looking at them before they claimed they weren't relevant." Ultimately, Frampton and Beizer won out, and the letter was sent.

Surprisingly, it caused no hard feelings at the White House counsel's office. In fact, in conversations with the special prosecutors, lawyers in the office made some comments that put the Meese investigation, and the White House's cooperation, in an entirely different light: they indicated they wanted Meese out of the White House. Either he would go as the new Attorney General, or he would go under the cloud of a possible criminal indictment. The important thing was to get him out.

Three weeks into the investigation, the prosecutors felt they had enough information in hand to divide up the work among themselves. Frampton, because he still hoped to limit his involvement, took jobs that would largely keep him in Washington: acting as liaison with the White House, investigating the Army Reserve issues and the cuff links. Beizer and Bensfield took the lead on what still seemed to be the most complicated and serious charges, those involving possible bribery and influence peddling in the appointments process. That work, they realized, would take them to California and to the heart of the West Coast culture that had spawned so many top officials in the Reagan administration.

Beizer and Bensfield divided the bribery issues into three broad categories: those involving Edwin Thomas, one of Meese's top aides in the White House, and members of his family; those involving Meese's accountant, John McKean; and those involving Meese's house near San Diego and bank officers involved with the mortgage and sale of the house.

The allegations were straightforward, but the facts the prosecutors had already assembled looked complicated. In January 1981, Thomas lent $15,000 to Ursula Meese, who used the money to buy stock in a new biotechnology company called Biotech Capital Corporation. In return, it was alleged, members of the Thomas family were rewarded with federal appointments. Thomas himself served as an aide to Meese in the White House, and was then appointed administrator of the San Francisco office of the General Services Administration. Thomas's wife was named to a post with the Merit Systems Protection Board in San Francisco. Thomas's son, Tad, got a job with the Labor Department in Washington. Moreover—and this was what the prosecutors found most intriguing—there was no mention of the loan in Meese's 1981, 1982, and 1983 financial disclosure forms, nor was the stock mentioned in the 1981 and 1982 forms, although it did appear in the 1983 and 1984 forms. As is so often the case in such investigations, evidence that something is being concealed is often the red flag that a crime has been committed.

McKean had made two loans totaling $60,000 to Meese. In return, he had allegedly been named to the Postal Service Board of Governors. Although the loan was initially not included on Meese's 1981 disclosure form, the form was amended to include it in 1982. It did appear in 1982 and 1983, in fact, its presence there was what had caused the Washington *Post* to break the story about the loan and McKean's appointment. The allegations involving the Meeses' house in La Mesa, California, were more complicated, but seemed to lie at the heart of the Meeses' financial troubles. In 1981 and 1982, the San Diego Federal Savings and Loan, subsequently called the Great American First Savings Bank, made three loans on the Meeses' sprawling house outside San Diego, and one of which was secured by their home in McLean, Virginia. The bank had also allowed Meese to get away with late payments.

In return, it was alleged, the Great American bank had proved to be a veritable gold mine of talent for the Reagan administration. Gordon Luce, the bank's chairman and chief executive, was first named to the President's Commission on Housing, then was made an alternate delegate to the United Nations. Edwin Gray, the bank's director of public affairs, became deputy assistant to the President; he was then named the powerful chairman of the Federal Home Loan Bank Board. Marc Sandstrom, the bank's general counsel, became a director of the beleaguered Legal Services Corporation; he resigned in 1982. And Clarence Pendleton, a member of the bank's board of directors, was appointed chairman of the Commission on Civil Rights. With so many officers in sensitive, high-level positions, some of the prosecutors wondered how the bank itself had managed to function.

Beizer and Bensfield concluded that the place to begin their formal interviews was at the bank. Their goal: to assess the extent of the Meeses' financial problems, to determine what role the officers receiving appointments had played in the Meese loans, and to see if the treatment accorded the Meeses differed significantly from that extended by the bank to its other loan customers. Beizer began by issuing subpoenas for the Meeses' bank records—bank privacy laws would have prohibited the bank from voluntarily turning over the records.

When the prosecutors examined those and other documents, it was clear that the Meeses had fallen on difficult times, the beneficiaries and then the victims, like many other upper-middle-class Californians, of the boom and bust in Southern California real estate that took place during the late seventies and early eighties.

The Meeses had moved to the San Diego area in 1975 when Reagan's term as governor ended. Meese had taken a job as a vice president at Rohr Industries, a manufacturer of aircraft and jet engine components, but the work had proven unsatisfying. He left to pursue his true interest: criminal justice. He founded the Center for Criminal Justice Policy and Management at the University of San Diego Law School, and did some private work as a lawyer. It was not particularly lucrative work.

The Meeses bought their house the year they moved to the San Diego area for $132,000, using a $104,000 loan at 8.5 percent interest. The monthly payments totaled $799.76. Meese had no trouble getting the loan from what became Great American. Many of its top officers, including its chairman, had worked with him during the Reagan administration in Sacramento. Meese obtained another loan, of $16,000, in 1979.

After Meese was asked to join Reagan in Washington, he put the La Mesa house on the market for $319,000. Great American provided a "bridge loan" and another mortgage loan so the Meeses could buy a $265,000 house in Virginia. The bridge loan would presumably be paid off promptly when the La Mesa house was sold—it was payable in full by February 1982. Monthly payments on the new $150,000 mortgage alone were $1,659.30, added to the existing mortgage on the California house.

But the California real estate market was sinking. From January to June, real estate agents reported some interest in the Meese property, but there were no bids. The Meeses lowered their asking price to $298,000. The house remained unsold. By early November, realtors had given up with no prospects in sight. The loan payments fell into arrears. Given the gloomy outlook, the prosecutors wondered, would the bank have foreclosed on the property if anyone but someone working in the White House had owned it?

When Beizer and Bensfield arrived at the Great American bank, they weren't exactly greeted with open arms. Though San Diego bankers pride themselves on their friendly relations with customers and their relaxed, low-keyed approach to business, a federal investigation is another matter, and one conducted by a special prosecutor was unprecedented. "They were nervous," Beizer recalls.

A key witness was James Schmidt, the bank's president, who had been a senior vice president at the time of the Meese loans and Meese's principal contact at the bank. Schmidt had known Meese during the Reagan governorship, since he had been Luce's deputy and had followed Luce to Great American.

At the interviews, Schmidt was extremely nervous and seemed very high strung. He seemed a fastidious type, one for whom order and routine were important, and being interrogated by a Washington prosecutor was plainly a prospect that upset him.

Schmidt told a story that suggested that far from trying to curry favor with Meese, the bank had come to view him as a liability, and simply wanted the loans paid off. He described the long campaign to get Meese even to acknowlege his financial obligations.

In late 1982, he said, he had the bank send a letter to Meese, a copy of which was turned over to the prosecutors:

> I call your attention to the two loans on your La Mesa home which are now substantially in arrears. We fully understand the difficulty you have had in selling your home in this market, and I assure you it is our policy to assist our good borrowers while their homes are on the market. However, due to the length of time since your property has been listed and since the last escrow was cancelled, I must ask that the two loans be brought up-to-date as soon as possible.

Meese didn't answer the letter. In internal discussions, the bank decided to extend some of the Meese loans, and mailed modification agreements for Meese to sign. Again, there was no response. In June, the bank sent a letter mentioning, for the first time, the possibility that the bank would have to foreclose on the property if it didn't hear from the Meeses. There was no reply. In July, the bank sent Meese a certified letter demanding payment and asking whether Meese was receiving his mail.

A few days later, on July 22, the Meeses' son Scott was killed in a car accident. Under the circumstances, the bank decided to drop its collection efforts.

BEIZER had no reason to doubt Schmidt. He had copies of many of the letters, and their tone was forceful—if anything they would have seemed threatening to Meese, who was ignoring them. There was never any implication that the bank would work something out in return for any favors from Meese. And Schmidt himself was inherently credible—he hadn't received any appointment from Meese.

The bank's chairman, Luce, was another matter altogether. He had received prestigious appointments. But in his interviews, Luce, a patrician and polished witness who seemed far more confident and at ease than Schmidt had, seemed indignant at the mere implication that he would have curried favor with Meese in order to obtain a federal appointment. In Governor Reagan's administration, he pointed out, Meese was a glorified administrative aide, while he was a Cabinet officer. He remained a close friend of both President Reagan and Nancy. He was an executive committee member of Reagan for President and was a member of the finance committee for the 1981 Reagan inauguration. It was clear to Beizer that Luce considered himself Meese's superior. He would never, he suggested, grovel before Meese for any reason, least of all for a federal appointment that was his simply by placing a phone call to the President.

Indeed, Luce claimed that he had been turning down repeated requests to accept a high-level position in the administration ever since Reagan's election. He had told the transition team, for example, that he didn't want to be considered for a Cabinet post, and had later withdrawn his name for consideration as an ambassador. He had finally accepted the U.N. appointment, he said, only because it was a part-time job. Even then, another of Luce's friends, national security adviser William Clark, had done a little arm twisting to persuade Luce to accept the position.

Beizer didn't accept or reject Luce's account at face value—it would require extensive corroboration. But in interviewing potential witnesses, he always tried to size up their future performance at a trial. And he had to concede that Luce would be a formidable witness before a jury.

He would be an even more formidable defendant, another possibility that Beizer considered in all his interviews with the bank officers. If Meese had accepted a bribe, then someone at the bank had offered it. "A bribery case only sings," Beizer explains, "if you can bring both people to trial. It was always a question in my mind whether we could prosecute the donor."

By the time they left San Diego several days later, Beizer and Bensfield were worrying about the bank case against Meese. Whether or not it eventually proved to be true, the bank's explanation was one that would make common sense to a jury. There wasn't any doubt that there was a real estate crisis in Southern California in the early eighties. The bank had shown them file after file of lenders in straits similar to those of the Meese family. Many of them too had had their payments extended. While not all of them had received treatment as favorable as Meese—especially after behaving as irresponsibly as Meese—none of them had had a son killed in the midst of the bank's efforts to collect. The prosecutors knew how those facts would play before a jury.

But the interviews with the bankers had turned the prosecutors on to another person who seemed intriguing: Thomas Barrack, the man who eventually bailed the Meeses out of their house troubles, and had then received an important appointment.

Barrack was now living in Southern California, and it was he, it turned out, who saved the Meeses from the predicament caused by their failure to sell the San Diego area house.

The prosecutors learned from Barrack that he and E. Pendleton James, head of the White House personnel office, had been friends for many years. James, in turn, was a close friend of the Meese family; he'd been a college classmate of Ursula Meese's. James had been at a cookout with the Meeses soon after their son was killed, and James was distressed that in addition to that tragedy the family was plagued by the inability to sell their house. James asked Barrack to help.

Eventually, through a complex series of transactions in which some investors would buy the Meese house, fix it up, and try to resell it at a profit, Barrack managed to sell the house. He contributed $83,000 of his own funds toward the transaction.

Barrack said that James had subsequently made any number of efforts to interest him in a position with the Reagan administration. Finally, in 1982 Barrck said he had resigned from his enormously successful real estate development company. He was subsequently offered a job by Interior Secretary James Watt. He added, much to the prosecutors' interest, that while talking with James about the appointments process, they had decided that Barrack wouldn't mention anything about his role in selling the Meese house. "They didn't want it to seem they were using this as a lever," Barrack said. Either that, the prosecutors thought, or they were trying to conceal it. It remained to be seen whether Meese himself had had any role in Barrack's getting a job.

The prosecutors headed for San Francisco.

THERE was so much to investigate in the San Francisco area that Frampton and Austern flew out from Washington to link up with Beizer and Bensfield. The most intriguing areas of investigation were the allegations involving the Thomas family, and Edwin Thomas's $15,000 loan to Ursula Meese.

From the beginning, it had been that loan that most fascinated Beizer. It was the only one that was not reported on Meese's financial disclosure forms and Beizer wanted to know why. Experience had taught him that the most important evidence of wrongdoing was often concealed.

On the other hand, he knew that a straightforward case of failing to disclose required financial data was not as simple to prove as it might appear. The statute requires a knowing failure to disclose, which means that the defendant can simply claim that he forgot, or didn't know something was required. A subjective state of mind is an essential part of the crime. Many jurors, who have had their own problems wrestling with the tax forms from the federal government, are sympathetic to defendants' disclosure problems. Beizer didn't particularly want to move against Meese for disclosure problems alone.

But if the failure could be linked to some other wrongdoing—fraud, for example—then the disclosure case fell into place too. There was a motive. And while motive is not an essential element of most crimes, it is the evidence that often allows a juror to conclude that a required state of mind actually existed.

From the records supplied by the banks and by Meese's lawyers, the prosecutors knew what Mrs. Meese had done with the $15,000. In January 1981, shortly after receiving the loan from Thomas, she bought 2,000 shares of stock in a company just going public called Biotech, and placed the shares in custodial accounts for her children. Like so many of the Meese investments, the stock purchase turned sour. Immediately after the public offering at $7.50 a share, Biotech plunged, hitting a low of $2.25 a share. Mrs. Meese eventually sold the stock in 1983 for $6 a share, incurring a loss of $3,000. That, however, was offset in profits from stock she purchased on Thomas's recommendation in another company, American Cytogenetics, when Biotech acquired it. What, Beizer wondered, was Thomas's link to Biotech and American Cytogenetics, and what did he know about the companies? Were Thomas and the Meeses part of an insider stock-trading ring? And was that why the original $15,000 loan was concealed on the reporting form?

At the center of this tangled situation was Dr. Earl Brian, who was a key figure in the rapidly developing biotechnology field in and around San Francisco. Dr. Brian had made immense amounts of money forming venture capital groups to invest in emerging technology like gene splicing, and he had taken on the aura of a business and medical genius. A group of stockbrokers and investors had developed whose principal preoccupation was Dr. Brian and his endeavors; they called themselves the "Earl watchers." Thomas was a member. Dr. Brian was high on the prosecutors' list for interviews.

Also in San Francisco was John McKean, now ensconced at the General Services Administration regional office there. His situation was also intriguing, given the proximity of his loan to Meese to his appointment to the Postal Service Board of Governors. He'd gotten his job just two months after making the payments to Meese. Beizer had trouble deciding which case was more promising, McKean or the Thomases.

Beizer, Frampton, Austern, and Bensfield set up operations in an inconspicuous motel on the outskirts of San Francisco. Beizer took the lead in interviewing Thomas; Frampton concentrated on McKean, although each dropped in on the other's interviews when he had a chance. Each night, they'd compare notes, trying to fit the evidence they'd collected into the puzzle, looking for holes that could be filled in the next day's questioning.

Beizer spent three days with Thomas, and began by quizzing Thomas about how he came to receive his federal appointments, first the position as counselor to Meese, and then the position with the General Services Administration.

Thomas's demeanor was surprising. He seemed much less nervous than many of the others; in fact, he was indignant at the suggestion that he had loaned Mrs. Meese the money in order to get a federal post. Thomas told the prosecutors that he had worked with Meese during the transition period, and he hadn't liked the "atmosphere" in Washington—either the climate or all the political backbiting. He didn't even want to stay on, but was persuaded by members of his family and Meese to take the post in the White House.

Moreover, he insisted, his dislike of Washington only intensified as time passed. Determined to return with his family to California, he kept an eye out for possible jobs there, but without even telling Meese, because he knew Meese would try to persuade him to stay in the White House, and might even block his efforts to leave. He didn't even tell Meese that he'd been offered the General Services job until after the offer was made, and then he recalled that Meese was rather contemptuous that he hadn't managed to get something higher ranking. "It's not even a presidential appointment," he recalled Meese saying, implying that Thomas could have done much better.

It was an interesting defense theory, Beizer thought, the notion that Thomas hadn't wanted the very job he had supposedly bribed Meese to receive. His reluctance to go to Washington could also be conveniently corroborated—by members of his family and Meese himself. Thomas seemed less self-assured when the questioning turned to the loans themselves and the stock trading. Thomas explained that his family and the Meeses had been close for many years, and frequently got together for social occasions. He said that he and Ursula Meese shared an interest in the stock market and would chat about investment opportunities, particularly those involving Dr. Brian, whose activities Thomas followed closely. In one such conversation, they talked about Biotech, and Mrs. Meese said she'd invest for her children's college education if only she or her husband had the money. Thomas assumed that it was then that he'd offered her the loan.

After that Thomas didn't recall mentioning the loan to Meese until

February 1982, when he needed money to buy a house in the San Francisco area in connection with his move there from Washington. He took Meese aside at a going-away party for the Thomases at the Army-Navy Club and suggested Meese just sell the stock at a loss, return the proceeds, and Thomas would forget about the loss. Meese said no, that he'd accepted the loan in good faith, and he intended to repay it in full. Again in October, at a breakfast in the Stanford Court Hotel in San Francisco, Thomas asked for some of the money. Meese agreed to give him a check for $5,000. Thomas recalled no further discussion until he sold his Biotech stock in 1983 and urged the Meeses to do the same.

There were also, of course, the allegations that the Thomas and Meese trading in Biotech and other stock involved insider trading. There was little to suggest any inside information was involved in the Biotech purchases and sales, particularly since the shares were sold at a loss. But another company in which Thomas and Mrs. Meese invested, American Cytogenetics, was acquired by Biotech. Mrs. Meese bought 200 shares; Thomas bought a total of 4,600. The stock price more than tripled after the announcement of the acquisition. This looked, on its face, like a classic instance of insider trading, especially since Thomas acknowledged being a close friend of Dr. Brian's, the head of Biotech who negotiated the American Cytogenetics acquisition.

During his questioning, Thomas explained that he and Dr. Brian had become close friends during the Reagan governorship. Brian was Governor Reagan's Secretary of Health and Welfare (at age thirty), while Thomas was the Cabinet secretary.

But Thomas insisted that Brian had never told him about his plan to acquire American Cytogenetics. On the contrary, he insisted, Brian had said he thought the company's president was a "genius," but that he looked at the company and decided against buying it. Moreover, Thomas said he didn't mention anything about American Cytogenetics to Mrs. Meese and was, in fact, surprised to learn later that she had bought stock in the company.

Perhaps the most intriguing aspect of the Thomas interviews was the closeness of the relationship between Thomas and Dr. Brian. When Beizer asked Thomas whether he had any direct financial ties to Brian, Thomas seemed ill at ease. Thomas admitted that in 1981, as he was moving to Washington, Brian had loaned him $100,000, which he needed at the time for a down payment on a new house. Although he didn't buy the house, he kept the money, and agreed to repay it and pay 14 percent interest. He said he used the money for improvements on the Thomases' Squaw Valley vacation home and to buy more stock.

Then, in the spring of 1981, Brian was nominated for a nonpaying but highly prestigious post on the National Science Board. His candidacy had been championed by both Thomas and Meese. But for reasons that have never been publicy disclosed, Brian withdrew his name from consideration after the FBI conducted an investigation and its finding caused the White House counsel's office to question the appointment.

This was potentially the most damaging testimony that Beizer had heard. The timing of the Brian loan, the appointment, and the sharing of information about companies in which Brian was involved looked egregious on its face. That Thomas was talking at all to Brian about the possibility of acquiring American Cytogenetics, and then investing in the company, was getting perilously close to insider trading. Then came the attempt to name Brian to the National Science Board.

Thomas's insistence that he hadn't spoken to Mrs. Meese about American Cytogenetics would certainly bear further checking. If Thomas hadn't told her about the obscure stock, then who had? Beizer doubted that she had chosen it out of the blue.

On the other hand, the investigation was beginning to roam far afield from the original charges against Meese. Thomas was not the target of the investigation. Even if he or Mrs. Meese had done something wrong, it remained to be seen whether Meese himself knew anything about it. Nor were the amounts of money involved all that substantial, though that was no defense if indeed the conduct was a crime. Still, like much of the evidence being accumulated, there was something deeply troubling about these tangled relationships within the family of the man who was being named as the country's top law enforcement officer.

During evenings at the motel, Beizer shared the results of his interviews with Thomas and his thoughts on them, and Frampton, in turn, told of his own interviews with McKean, the accountant who had earlier tried to help the Meeses out of their mounting financial problems.

Frampton explained that according to McKean the Meese loan hadn't come from McKean himself, but from other investors—raising the possibility that there were others who had received some kind of

preferential treatment from Meese because of their financial relationship. But McKean insisted that he hadn't told Meese the names of the
investors, nor had he told the investors that the funds they invested
with him would be loaned to Meese. He said he didn't want the
investors to be tempted by the possibility of seeking influence with the
federal government, and he certainly didn't want them engaging in
any casual boasting that they were bailing out the counselor to the
President. In fact, McKean emphasized that he had seemed far more
concerned with this possibility than Meese himself. He said he mentioned that the lender's name would have to appear on Meese's financial disclosure form, and Meese had seemed unconcerned. "He just
wanted to resolve his financial affairs promptly," McKean had said.

Like the loans from the bank, Meese did not pay the interest or
repay the principal on time. McKean discussed the matter with Meese
periodically, arranging new payment terms, which in turn weren't
met. Meese had seemed particularly embarrassed, McKean recalled,
that he couldn't repay the loan even after he finally sold the house
outside San Diego. But McKean insisted that the extensions were
never granted in return for his appointments to the Postal Service
Board of Governors; he simply believed that Meese remained a reasonably good borrower who would eventually repay. McKean reiterated that in fact he was surprised when Michael Deaver called him
offering an appointment to the Postal Service Board of Governors and
didn't even know what the organization did. Why hadn't Meese made
a full disclosure of the circumstances of the loan on his disclosure
forms? McKean had no idea.

McKean made a credible witness. Still, there was the same troubling pattern: McKean had offered the Meeses something of value by
arranging for them, quickly and on an informal basis, an unsecured
$40,000 loan, later increased to $60,000, with no interest payable for
at least a year. Eventually interest payments were waived for fourteen
months.

Toward the end of the stay in San Francisco, Beizer scheduled an
interview with the vaunted Dr. Brian. Brian proved to be the most
difficult of the California witnesses, surrounded as he was with lawyers. He obviously had no intention of allowing special prosecutors to
probe his lucrative and convoluted business dealings, nor would he
discuss the reasons he withdrew his name from consideration for the
National Science Board. Though his limited answers did little to shed

light on the case, most of them corroborated the information Thomas had provided about his investments and stock trading. But in one respect there was a contradiction: Brian denied that he had ever discussed American Cytogenetics with Thomas, just as Thomas had denied discussing the company with Mrs. Meese.

But that and other questions and puzzling inconsistencies would have to be pursued in Washington, where most of the documents and the remaining witnesses were located. After a week of intense questioning and discussions in San Francisco, the exhausted prosecutors returned to Washington, where they reported their findings to Stein.

Over the next week, during a particularly hot period in the summer, they turned their attention once again to the documents provided by the White House and to interviews with the White House personnel involved in the appointments. Focusing on Thomas, McKean, Dr. Brian, and the bank officers, they wanted to know exactly how they had come to be nominated, who had suggested them, and whether Meese was involved.

The answer to the last part of their inquiry was readily available. Meese was, to varying degrees, involved in all the appointments.

In the case of Brian, the prosecutors had a copy of a memo initialed by Meese. "I would like to recommend Dr. Earl Brian for consideration as a Presidential appointee to the National Science Foundation," it began. It concluded: "Please see that Dr. Brian is given the fullest consideration."

But for some reason, Brian had run afoul of George Keyworth, then the President's science adviser, who played a major role in appointments to the National Science Board. On one list of candidates, someone had written "not a good fit for NSB" next to Brian's name. A staff member recalled discussing the Brian nomination and Keyworth's opposition with Ms. von Damm, a member of the appointments committee. She had insisted that because Brian had the support of Meese and Deaver he would "have" to be on the list submitted to the committee. According to another member of the committee, Brian's nomination was a "do." Any former Cabinet member in the California Reagan administration, he explained, whose name Meese and Deaver wanted to "see at the table," was going to "get to the table." "Getting to the table" meant being considered by the committee, which included Meese and Deaver, so once their candidates got to the table, their appointments were almost assured. Obviously, however, a Meese recommendation didn't overcome serious problems uncovered by the FBI, and there was no evidence that when the Brian nomination foundered, Meese did anything to press his candidacy.

Still, the prosecutors felt Meese's power in the appointments process was enormous. In interviews with staff members, it became clear that even their perception that Meese was promoting a candidate made them wary of anything that might frustrate the appointment. All the lip service paid to "merit" selection in the Reagan administration seemed absurd, but then, it was probably not much different in previous administrations. Appointments are inherently political.

The Thomas appointment was even more directly tied to Meese; Meese had personally hired him as his assistant at the outset of the administration. But nothing in the documents indicated any Meese involvement with Thomas's subsequent appointment to the GSA position in San Francisco, which tended to corroborate Thomas's claim that he didn't want Meese to know that he was applying for the position because he'd try to talk him into staying in Washington.

Documents also indicated that Meese was present at the meeting where McKean's name was first proposed for the Postal Service Board of Governors; McKean's name hadn't been on the original typed list of candidates. But witnesses at the meeting recalled that it was Deaver who first suggested McKean (McKean was Deaver's accountant). Deaver himself confirmed that, and recalled that he had turned to Meese in the meeting, saying, "Ed, you know him." Meese had acknowledged that, adding that McKean would be good for the job. No one suggested that Meese should disqualify himself from voting on the McKean nomination.

There was no indication that Meese had had any involvement in the initial appointment of Great American bank chairman Luce to the part-time housing commission position other than voting as a member of the committee; Luce's name had first been proposed by Edwin Gray, the head of the Federal Home Loan Bank Board who had worked under Luce. Ms. von Damm had played an active role in Luce's nomination to the United Nations. But so had Meese, it seemed. A senior staff memo listed Meese and William Clark as "recommenders" of Luce for the post. Meese's involvement in other appointments of bank officers seemed relatively minor.

Finally, there was Barrack. Although Meese and Barrack had frequently been in contact with each other, there was no indication that Meese had anything to do with Barrack's appointment to an Interior post by Secretary of the Interior James Watt, who appeared to have acted almost impuslively in offering Barrack a job. Meese had passed on a later nomination to a Commerce post, but Barrack had decided to return to California rather than accept it.

The prosecutors found no "smoking guns" in their interviews or documents searches regarding how the appointments had come about. But there were some consistent patterns. The Thomas, Brian, and McKean matters, which had aroused the most suspicion at the outset, also suggested the greatest involvement by Meese in the appointments process. The bank appointment and the Barrack appointment looked much less promising. Nonetheless, there was one striking aspect: never, in any of the conversations, documents, or witnesses' statements they examined, did anyone ever suggest that Meese might have been engaging in a conflict of interest by passing on the appointments of people who had granted him loans or favors. There was certainly no indication that Meese himself had ever raised the question, or even that Meese was aware such conduct might be wrong or even criminal. It was, some of the prosecutors thought, rather appalling in a moral sense. But from the point of view of criminal prosecution, it worked in Meese's favor. They had yet to find any evidence of any criminal state of mind on the part of Meese.

It was time for Stein and his deputies to assess the evidence with an eye to two major upcoming events: the possible convening of a grand jury and what they expected would be the climax of the investigation, the interview with Meese himself.

Stein had indicated at the outset that he had no intention of convening a grand jury simply to go through the motions if the evidence clearly didn't warrant it. On the other hand, he was equally determined to have a full grand jury presentation if there were matters that turned on the credibility of witness testimony. Grand jury testimony is taken under oath; all the interviews they'd completed to date were not.

By the summer, the prosecutors were able to rule out some of the charges against Meese that had been contained in their original mandate from the Court of Appeals. In these matters, the evidence was so filmsy or so insignificant that there seemed no point in burdening a grand jury with additional charges that would only confuse it. Moreover, it is strategically often a mistake to present a patently weak case; it arouses the sympathy of the jury for the target of the investigation.

The first charge to be discarded was the cuff-links claim. That

Meese had accepted some cuff links from South Korea and failed to relinquish them on his return to the U.S. had already been hashed over in the Judiciary Committee, and the prosecutors had examined the evidence closely. A major problem with any prosecutions: the Foreign Gifts and Decorations Act, which Meese allegedly violated, isn't even a criminal statute. It provides only for civil penalties. Moreover, it was too difficult to tell whether the value of the links was sufficient to bring them into the range of the statute. Meese could simply assert that he believed them to be of minimal value, and that assertion would be virtually impossible to disprove. It was, in any event, a trivial matter, the prosecutors thought.

Next to be discarded were allegations that Meese received a promotion from lieutenant colonel to colonel in the Army Reserve in return for the nomination of General William Berkman to be chief of the Army Reserves.

These allegations, like the cuff links, were rather hard to take seriously. Could Meese really have cared that much about his Army Reserve status? Nonetheless, an intensive investigation of the matter had already been conducted by the Army's inspector general after press reports linking the promotion to General Berkman's nomination appeared. The special prosecutors studied those findings, and conducted thirty interviews of their own.

The army investigation had concluded, and the prosecutors agreed, that Meese's promotion had been riddled with irregularities. He'd obtained special consideration, it seemed, because of his national prominence and not because he met the military qualifications for the appointment. Applicable laws were misapplied, ignored, or violated in transferring Meese to active status in the Reserve. But was a crime involved? Only, the prosecutors thought, if Meese's favorable treatment could be linked to the nomination of General Berkman, and even then, it would make a relatively weak bribery case.

The prosecutors could find no evidence that Meese knew any improper action was being taken on his behalf. Nor was there any evidence that anything Meese did had any material effect on Berkman's appointment. Finally, the prosecutors discovered in their interviews that the press report in the *Army Times* linking the two developments contained serious error and had been leaked from the White House by someone trying to block General Berkman's nomination. If anything, the whole matter seemed likely to generate sympathy for Meese, and they couldn't find any basis for criminal charges.

Investigation into Meese's role in the alleged theft of Carter campaign materials for use in Reagan briefings—the so-called "Debategate" scandal—had also proved disappointing. How those materials ended up in the Reagan camp seems destined to remain an enduring mystery of the 1980 presidential campaign. In Meese's case, the question was whether Meese had lied about seeing the briefing materials when he told House and Senate committees that he didn't recall seeing them. FBI, House, and Senate investigations had already failed to find any convincing evidence that Meese was involved. Nonetheless, the prosecutors had re-examined the whole matter.

While they didn't discover anything new, they did learn a good deal about Meese's work habits. Ever since he had become a close associate of then-governor Reagan in California, Meese had developed and encouraged a reputation for being a ruthlessly efficient administrator, one who could tame and streamline even the most unruly bureaucracy. But the evidence given the prosecutors by those who worked with Meese in the White House indicated the contrary. In fact, evidence that Meese was an almost hopelessly inept administrator was the most convincing indication that he was indeed telling the truth when he said he couldn't remember the campaign briefing materials. According to these witnesses, there was much else that Meese couldn't remember.

Carol Patrick, one of Meese's secretaries, seemed to be the person who kept her finger in the administrative dike. She told the prosecutors that an enormous amount of paper flowed into Meese's office— more than a thousand separate documents a day during the campaign. Although she tried to segregate material into organizational folders, the system didn't always work. Meese was frequently out of the office, and then Meese's desk, as well as the credenza just behind it, would become "completely covered" with masses of paper. She said that she had no recollection of Meese ever sitting at his desk reading anything; she estimated that, in total, he read less than one-quarter of the material that was sent to him. She had to file much of the accumulated material, even though she realized that Meese hadn't seen much of it. Others corroborated her story, sometimes in even more derogatory terms. There had been many complaints that material sent to the White House got bottled up in Meese's office. It seemed to be one of the main reasons that some White House personnel wanted Meese out, and had encouraged his being named Attorney General. "The stories of his incompetence were legion," says one of the prosecutors. "He was a major roadblock for domestic policy."

The prosecutors concluded that given Meese's work habits, it was entirely plausible that he had never seen the briefing materials, and, if he had, wouldn't have remembered them.

With those three areas disposed of, Stein was essentially left with the bribery and influence allegations involving Thomas, McKean, and the others, and the insider trading allegations. There had been some intriguing developments with respect to those claims, especially those involving Thomas.

After returning from California, Beizer had interviewed Mitchell Stanley, a special assistant to Meese at the time Meese was preparing his 1981 financial disclosure form—the one that had omitted the Thomas loan. Stanley said that he clearly remembered Thomas working with Meese on the disclosure form, something that Thomas had denied.

Beizer concluded that there were too many inconsistencies in Thomas's statements, and he decided to reinterview him. The effort produced a striking deviation from Thomas's earlier statement. Then, he had denied mentioning the loan to Meese in connection with preparation of the 1981 disclosure form. Now, Thomas said that he had reminded Meese of the loan. He said that he often briefed Meese hurriedly at the end of a day, and he recalled standing in the doorway to Meese's office one evening when he mentioned the loan.

Moreover, Thomas said the loan had again come up in a conversation he had with Meese in 1984 after a Washington *Post* reporter called him asking him about the loan. Thomas called Meese in Florida, where the Meeses were vacationing, to tell him about the call from the reporter, and Meese asked him why the loan hadn't been on the 1981 disclosure form. Thomas said he reminded Meese that he'd mentioned the loan to him at the time. Beizer found this disclosure striking because Thomas had been questioned extensively about the phone call to Florida in their earlier interview, and he'd made no mention of this information. Increasingly, it looked as if Thomas was trying to hide something.

As a result, Beizer and Frampton argued vigorously that a grand jury had to be convened. There were too many inconsistencies in the statements they'd received and too many issues that turned on matters of credibility. Stein agreed. Since Beizer had had the most grand jury experience by far, he assumed major responsibility for that part of the case. Frampton, meanwhile, began preparing for the key interviews with Meese and his wife.

Meese and his wife were scheduled for a full week of interviews beginning late that summer. Stein and his deputies had deliberately scheduled Meese's interview for late in the investigation, both to use as much information as possible in their questioning and because they knew the ongoing investigation would cause the pressure on Meese to mount.

By the time the interview date arrived, the prosecutors felt they knew Meese very well. In the hundreds of interviews they'd conducted, however, three distinct Meese personalities had emerged. There was the financial and administrative bungler. There was the right-wing ideologue, especially on matters related to crime and the police. And finally there was the man they referred to privately as the "country club" Meese—a charming, affable man who seemed to personify reasonableness and earned the loyalty and friendship of many associates.

Frampton interviewed Ursula Meese first. He adopted a gentle approach; she seemed more subdued than anxious; her friends had said she never really rebounded from the death of her son. Much of what she said corroborated what the prosecutors had learned in California. Frampton was especially interested in the insider trading allegations, and in one key respect, Mrs. Meese contradicted Thomas's statement: she said that Thomas was the one who recommended that she buy American Cytogenetics. She said she'd never spoken about the stocks to Dr. Brian; as far as she knew, neither had her husband.

For the Meese interview, the room was packed. Meese himself was surrounded by Leonard Garment and his other defense lawyers. Although Frampton did most of the questioning, Stein and all the deputy prosecutors crowded in to observe.

It was the "country club" Meese on display. He was remarkably affable, cool, and collected, the prosecutors thought, given that he was clearly fighting for his personal and professional reputation. In each case, he denied that he had appointed or approved anyone in return for any loans or other favors; in each case, he said he was simply trying to see that the best people were named to positions.

Such assertions were to be expected. The prosecutors were more interested in how he would deal with the failure to disclose the Thomas loan and ownership of the Biotech stock. This was one area where a possible motive was apparent: the loan had been concealed to hide the fact that there had been insider stock trading.

Meese's excuse was that he forgot both the Thomas loan and ownership of the Biotech stock. He added that in trying to figure out why he didn't recall the Thomas loan at the time, he didn't think it probably had to be disclosed because it was an informal family transaction, without any written documents. He repeated that he'd simply forgotten the loan and that it had never "registered" that it was the kind of thing that had to be disclosed. But he also said that he would have disclosed both the loan and the stock if he'd remembered them—he had no reason not to.

With Meese staking his defense on the plausibility of his failure of memory, Frampton unveiled what might be the most devastating information they'd uncovered—Thomas's statement that he'd reminded Meese of the existence of the loan at the very time the forms were being prepared, and reminded him of that incident as recently as 1984. It was a classic prosecutorial maneuver.

But Meese didn't flinch. He seemed unconcerned, even puzzled, but said he had no memory of Thomas ever having reminded him of the loan. Nor did he recall Thomas mentioning the matter during their March 1984 phone conversation. The testimony was the clearest contradiction the case had yet produced.

Another contradiction emerged in Meese's testimony about the McKean loan. During his interviews, McKean had insisted that he was not personally the source of the money being loaned; he had arranged the loan through other clients of his who were the actual sources of the funds. He had explained this to Meese, he said, because he didn't want Meese to know the sources of the funds nor the sources to know that they had loaned money to Meese. Yet in his financial disclosure forms, Meese had listed the source of the loan as "J. R. McKean." Moreover, in the documents provided by the White House, the prosecutors had found a memo from Meese to Fred Fielding, counsel to the President, in which Meese said that the loan was "from McKean personally and not from any company, group, or organization."

In his interview, Meese said once again that he couldn't recall what conversation with Fielding might have led to the memo, but said he had always regarded McKean as his "contact" with respect to the loan. Nonetheless, he said he always understood that the money for the loan came from McKean's "firm sources" and not from McKean personally. Still, he felt it likely he would have identified McKean as the source if asked whether McKean or "anyone else" had provided the funds; he wouldn't have known any other names to suggest. The explanation, the prosecutors thought, seemed unconvincing on its face. Unfortunately, it was also consistent with McKean's comments that Meese had seemed singularly uninterested in the steps he had taken to insulate Meese from any improper influence or conflict of interest that might otherwise arise from the loan or its sources.

In an area that the prosecutors thought was bristling with possible wrongdoing—the stock trading in American Cytogenetics and Meese's relationships with Dr. Brian—the interview proved frustrating. Meese acknowledged that he knew Brian from the Reagan governorship, and had seen him maybe a dozen times since 1974. But he said he knew nothing about Biotech's acquisition of American Cytogenetics until long after the transaction had occurred. Nor was he aware that Brian had loaned money to Thomas. He added that although he had been willing to support Brian for the position on the National Science Board, he had never attempted to recruit him or interest him in that or any position. He assumed that it had been Thomas who took the lead in recruiting Brian.

In discussing the problems with his loans from Great American, Meese was at his most persuasive. He played the role of the typical American homeowner and underpaid public servant, overextended through events over which he had no control. Meese acknowledged that he had been to varying degrees involved in the appointments of bank officers to federal posts, but he tried to minimize his role. It had never entered his mind, he said, that his participation in the appointments might be linked to the treatment of his loans; he had certainly made no connection.

Over and over again he reiterated a theme of his testimony: as counselor to the President, he had thousands of important matters on his mind. Personal finances was last on his list of priorities. He conceded he was not a good money manager and that the subject was of little interest to him. The prosecutors had to acknowledge that this aspect of his testimony had been corroborated thousands of times.

On the whole, the prosecutors felt that Meese had given a good performance as a witness. He had an ability to stick to his story and to move through questions in a deliberate, even plodding manner. While it didn't create an impression of any great mental acuity, it was effective. Many of the allegations against Meese required a reasonably sophisticated sensitivity for allegedly improper causal relationships. Meese gave a convincing portrayal of someone incapable, or unwilling, to recognize such complexity.

With the Meese questioning behind them, the prosecutors stepped up the pace of witnesses before the grand jury. Nearly all the major witnesses testified, including McKean, Thomas, and the Meeses themselves. There were no major deviations from the witness interviews, but part of the reason for the exercise was also for the prosecutors to assess the demeanor and credibility of the witnesses while they were on the stand, testifying under oath. In that respect too the performances were largely consistent with the interviews. Meese performed credibly. Thomas, on the other hand, forced to recognize that crucial aspects of his statements had changed from one interview to the next, seemed nervous and ill at ease. And there was one witness who aroused some tittering among members of the grand jury. He was apparently so nervous about the experience that his fly was unzipped during the entirety of his testimony.

During August, after some of the lawyers had a chance to take a week's vacation, Stein began a series of meetings at the I Street headquarters that had become the special prosecutors' summer home. The meetings were intended to assess the totality of the evidence gathered and to reach the most key decision in the investigation: whether they would seek an indictment of Meese at the end of the grand jury presentations.

As they took up consideration of the various allegations against Meese, memos prepared by the prosecutors became the basis for most of their discussions, and even before they had reached any final conclusions, the memos and discussions began to form the basis for a comprehensive written report summarizing their findings. Stein had decided early in the investigation that whether or not he and his colleagues decided to seek an indictment of Meese, he wanted a detailed, written account of the evidence to justify their decision. More than other prosecutors, special prosecutors operate in the court of public opinion.

In focusing their discussions, the prosecutors embraced what Beizer calls "Beizer's rules" of prosecution. The first of those rules was that there had to be enough evidence to get to a jury, what lawyers call a prima facie case. At the end of a prosecutor's case, a defense lawyer will often ask a judge to dismiss criminal charges on the grounds that so little evidence has been introduced that no reasonable person could conclude the defendant is guilty. If such a motion is granted, the jury doesn't even consider the question of guilt or innocence. Precisely how much evidence is required to survive such a challenge is vaguely defined; it certainly doesn't have to satisfy the proof-beyond-a-reasonable-doubt standard required for conviction, and doubts about evidence are resolved in the prosecution's favor. Bare allegations, obviously, aren't enough. If they don't believe a case can get to a jury, most prosecutors feel morally obligated not to seek an indictment, or to ask a grand jury that it not indict.

Beizer's second rule is that a prosecutor must have enough evidence to win a case. "I only prosecute cases I believe I can win. That's my responsibility. Prosecution is not just an exercise to take people to trial." In the case of Meese, the prosecutors wanted to feel a "moral certainty" about the charges before seeking an indictment. Without that degree of conviction on their part, they doubted they could win at trial.

Finally, the prosecutors asked whether the target of their investigation should be charged with a crime, even if the evidence was sufficient to meet the requirements of the first two rules. Prosecutors can't, and most don't feel they should, embark on a full-scale prosecution of every crime brought to them. They look at the broader policy implications: what is the law enforcement purpose of this prosecution? What is the perceived effect? In the case of Meese, this wasn't a terribly difficult aspect of their discussions, however, since deterrence of any crime at the highest level of the federal government was deemed a worthwhile public mission. It was the very reason for the existence of special prosecutors.

"What many people don't understand," says one of the special prosecutors, "is that our purpose wasn't to decide if Meese was innocent or guilty. That decision is for a judge or jury. Prosecutors have to divorce themselves from whatever personal feelings they have in that regard. We had to decide whether we had a winning case. It's easy to feel very strongly that all the evidence points to a crime, and yet to realize that the proof isn't there."

Some of the charges had already been disposed of, like the cuff links and the Army Reserve charges. Nothing new or startling had been uncovered since their last conversations about those charges. They saw no basis for charges.

Next they turned to the Great American bank loans and the appointments of various bank officials to federal posts. The prosecutors concluded that although it was a fairly close case, they did believe that the evidence would support the claim that Meese had "solicited and received something of value" from the bank within the meaning of the applicable criminal statutes. Their main problem for a jury, they felt, would be the bank's insistence—which they had corroborated—that many other customers received similar favorable treatment. This made Meese's treatment look like less of a "favor." They also concluded that Meese had been sufficiently involved in the appointments of the bank officers to satisfy the requirement that there be official action. In these respects, they thought they had a prima facie case.

There remained one other requirement under the statute: that what Meese received from the bank had to be "in consideration" for action on the appointments—what the prosecutors described as the "nexus" of the bribery offense. In other words, there couldn't be other explanations for the appointments other than the alleged bribe.

As they discussed the probable defense arguments on the nexus issue, the special prosecutors sensed their case was crumbling. Probably most damaging was the evidence that the bank officers didn't need Meese to secure their federal appointments. They had their own relationships with President Reagan stemming from his term as governor of California. In the case of some, such as the bank's chairman, Luce, they had resisted prior efforts to appoint them to high-level positions. Moreover, they had repeatedly dunned Meese to recover their loan principal and interest payments. This was not what would have been expected in a bribery scheme. Finally, the prosecutors felt that the bank officers had, for the most part, made effective witnesses.

No final decision about the charges was made yet, but a consensus was quickly forming. No one liked the way Meese had handled the loan situation, and they thought he should have withdrawn from considering bank officers for federal posts. But their sole purpose was to determine if they could charge Meese with a crime. He would not be on trial for bad judgment, or an insensitivity to potential conflicts of interest, neither of which is a crime. The prosecutors themselves didn't believe that the Meese loans had been part of a bribery scheme, so how could they ever convince a jury?

Next among what they had concluded were the serious charges was the McKean loan affair.

IN discussing the McKean allegations it didn't take long for a consensus to emerge. For one thing, the evidence seemed conclusive that it wasn't McKean's money that had been the source of funds for the loan. This didn't, in and of itself, eliminate the possibility of a bribery charge—the argument could still be made that arranging the loan for Meese was the "something of value" that McKean had provided in return for a job appointment. But it complicated and weakened the charges before a jury. Furthermore, the loan seemed to have been arranged on an arm's length basis. The interest rate Meese had to pay was higher than prevailing bank rates at the time. This just didn't fit the pattern of a bribe.

As in the case of the Great American bank officers, it also was plausible that McKean would have received his appointment to the Postal Service Board of Governors without any support from Meese. McKean had been Deaver's accountant, after all, and testimony had been uncontroverted that it was Deaver, and not Meese, who first suggested that McKean be appointed. There was no evidence that McKean had angled for the position. He had insisted that he was surprised by the phone call about the job and didn't even know what the job entailed. His later promotion too was largely attributable to Deaver, although he had also written two letters to Meese.

While the consensus developed quickly, there were some lingering doubts. Even if no explicit agreement existed, was Meese really in a position to block McKean's appointment or request for a promotion since he was in his financial debt? How could Meese exercise impartial judgment? The prosecutors strongly doubted that he could. But again, they had the problem of the nexus. The situation had to be explicit, or at least explicitly implied, at the time Meese was offered something of value and accepted it. The facts simply didn't seem to support the high standard required by a bribery charge. Again, the prosecutors were forced to remind themselves that bad judgment isn't a crime.

Much the same analysis produced the same result with respect to Barrack's appointment. Barrack had ultimately impressed and been appointed by James Watt. He had later been nominated for a position he didn't even accept. True, he had gone to extraordinary lengths to bail the Meeses out of the financial problems caused by their failure to sell their San Diego area house. The situation was messy. But not criminal.

By far the largest amount of time was spent on the Thomas loans and appointments and the related insider trading allegations. As they had long suspected, the case against Meese would stand or fall largely on the strength of that evidence.

They began with the insider trading charges, which might form a second or third count in any criminal indictment. While insider trading wouldn't be the main thrust of the indictment, it was important because it suggested a motive for Meese to have concealed the Thomas loan that was used to purchase Biotech stock.

Biotech was a problem in this scenario. The Meeses had lost money on their trading in Biotech stock. Although the insider trading statute doesn't require that the wrongdoers profit from their activity, the fact remains that there have been very few, if any, criminal prosecutions brought in circumstances where money was lost rather than made. Losing money is in itself usually a strong deterrent to that kind of behavior. Furthermore, the prosecutors had uncovered no direct evidence that Mrs. Meese received inside information from Thomas or Brian, or that she in turn had made her husband aware of it.

American Cytogenetics provided more promising material, but the link to the Thomas loan was more tenuous. Still, there was an interesting conflict in the evidence they'd obtained: Brian said he never discussed the company with Thomas, and Thomas said he did, although he claimed he hadn't received any inside information. Thomas had also denied discussing the stock with Mrs. Meese, whereas Mrs. Meese had identified Thomas as the source of the recommendation to purchase it. Thomas had also failed to disclose his $100,000 loan from Brian, a suspicious omission.

But as the prosecutors went over and over the inconsistencies, they weren't satisfied with the pattern they created. Though inconsistent in some telling respects, they nonetheless agreed with respect to the central factual element of the charge: no inside information had passed to Mrs. Meese or Meese himself. Even if an inference could be drawn that it had, the prosecutors knew how hard it is to convict defendants who trade on inside information who are far down the chain on which the information is passed. It is simply too difficult to prove that such "tippees" knew that what they were using was inside information and that their behavior was wrong.

The prosecutors reached no firm conclusions, but turned to the next discrete aspect of the Thomas charges, Meese's failure to report the loan on his disclosure form.

Here the prosecutors' instincts told them that they had at least a prima facie case: Meese had received the loan and he hadn't reported it. It was as simple as that. But to a greater degree than with the criminal bribery statutes and others involved in the investigation, they had conducted an extensive analysis of the law requiring the disclosure to determine what the applicable standards were for a criminal charge. The disclosure act itself provided only for civil penalties, and until 1984, when former Idaho Congressman George Hansen was convicted for filing false financial disclosure forms, there had never been such a criminal prosecution.

Stein and his colleagues concluded that there were five requirements for a criminal nondisclosure charge: (1) a statement (2) made to the federal government (3) of a "material" nature (4) that was false, fictitious, or fraudulent and (5) that was made knowingly and willfully.

Those standards complicated the matter considerably. In going through the analysis, the prosecutors were confident they could establish the first four elements of the charge. The evidence was incontrovertible that Meese had signed the forms and they were prepared by him or under his supervision. They were plainly intended for an officer of the federal government, the ethics officer in the White House. "Materiality" was a vague standard, but failing to report the existence of a loan, and, hence, the identity of someone to whom an officeholder might be beholden, was squarely within the main purpose of the statute. And there was no doubt that the statement was false.

That brought them to the final requirement, that the false statement be made "knowingly and willfully," a maddeningly subjective standard that enabled defendants to escape guilt by convincing a jury that they had simply forgotten. (It was the reason why, much later, the prosecutors doubted there would be a prosecution of Geraldine Ferraro for her failure to meet the disclosure requirements.)

Meese himself had attributed the omission to simple oversight, and there would be his testimony to contend with in any trial. Furthermore, the prosecutors had been briefed by the Justice Department that the department had informally adopted a policy that disfavored prosecutions under the disclosure statute except in the most egregious cases. The standard had been applied in two other cases referred to the Justice Department and the decision was made not to prosecute. Considering the policies of the Reagan Justice Department seemed in some ways a violation of the independence of the special prosecutor's office, especially since the department had decided to adopt rather lax standards with respect to a statute that the administration had viewed with thinly veiled contempt and that Meese himself had allegedly violated. Still, Stein had been asked to abide by Justice Department standards when he accepted his appointment. Just as Meese shouldn't receive lenient treatment because of his position in the executive branch, he shouldn't receive harsher treatment than anyone else would have under prevailing policy. That was the theory.

But the Justice Department guidelines aside, the nondisclosure charge came down to the key question of motive. If Meese's explanation that he had "forgotten" was to be rendered implausible, there had to be some other reason why he wanted to knowingly conceal the loan.

The prosecutors drew up a list of four possible motives, then turned to the evidence that might support each.

First was the possibility that Meese wanted to conceal the connection between the loan and his hiring of Thomas. But Meese hadn't bothered to conceal the McKean or Great American matters, suggesting that he wasn't sensitive enough to the possible conflict of interest to even recognize that disclosure might be a problem. And there were other plausible reasons for the appointment of Thomas: he and Meese had known each other and worked together for years. Presumably Thomas could have had the job whether he'd extended loans to Meese or not.

Another possibility was that Meese wanted to conceal the fact that he'd accepted a "gift" from a subordinate, a practice that is specifically forbidden in a section of the U.S. Code. Unfortunately for that theory, the portion of the code containing the law is obscure. Meese said he didn't even know the law existed. Furthermore, it wasn't clear that a loan would be treated as a gift under the language of the statute, so that theory was discarded.

Concealment of insider trading was the third possibility, but the prosecutors had already concluded that the existence of insider trading would be hard to prove. In addition, the initial failure to disclose the loan occurred before there was any trading in American Cytogenetics, making it implausible that Meese was trying to conceal something that hadn't even yet occurred.

Finally there was the possibility that Meese had failed to disclose the loan simply to avoid personal embarrassment. While it was the most benign of the possible motives other than forgetfulness, it probably would satisfy the "willful" aspect of the crime. While a plausible theory, there was no evidence to support it. Meese's financial problems were evident from other material in his disclosure forms. He'd disclosed the larger McKean loan.

Despite the lack of a convincing alternative motive, the prosecutors had one important piece of evidence that contradicted Meese's assertion that he'd simply forgotten the loan. It was Thomas's own admission that he'd stood in Meese's office doorway and reminded him of it at the time the disclosure forms were being prepared. How, then, could Meese have forgotten?

Beizer and Frampton, in particular, considered this significant evidence on which a grand jury might be willing to question Meese's assertions. But to pursue that aspect of the case would make Thomas— of all people—the star witness for the government's case. That raised two problems: Thomas himself was under suspicion, both with respect to the allegations that he had bribed Meese and for insider trading. That alone might bring his credibility into question. But worse was the fact that in their interviews and before the grand jury, Thomas had made the worst witness, hands down. A skilled defense lawyer, Stein in particular knew, would make mincemeat of Thomas on the witness stand.

For example, Thomas hadn't originally disclosed key information, including the claim that he reminded Meese of the loan. Why not? He had given other inconsistent testimony, or testimony that conflicted with statements of other witnesses. An example was his claim that he discusssed reminding Meese of the loan during a phone conversation while Meese was in Florida. Meese hadn't remembered such a conversation. The prosecutors had obtained copies of Meese's notes from that phone call, and there was no reference to the matter. And the prosecutors questioned Meese's secretary, who had participated in the conversation. She too had no memory of Thomas's alleged reminder. Who was a jury likely to believe, especially since Thomas may have been fabricating the reminder so he himself didn't appear negligent in omitting the information from Meese's disclosure form, which he helped prepare.

Thomas's performance was so bad, the prosecutors thought, that they briefly considered whether he should be charged with any crime. But the mandate for the investigation was clear: their task was to investigate Meese, and Meese alone. Leads relating solely to Thomas and Brian they had put aside, at times reluctantly.

Occasionally, one of the prosecutors says, he wondered whether they were being too circumspect. It almost seemed as though Meese could not have wound up with a more defense-oriented group of prosecutors if he had chosen them himself. Stein had been a defense lawyer all his life, and he was concerned—possibly too concerned— about the overzealousness he'd seen in other prosecutors. He had made clear that it was a charge he never wanted to face. Trained to see weaknesses in a case, had he overlooked the obvious strengths in a potential case against Meese?

Beizer had the most experience as a prosecutor, and the others usually looked to him for a prosecutorial view of the world. But he too was now a defense lawyer. And the major prosecution of his career had ended in a loss. Deep down, was one of his primary concerns not to undergo another loss, especially in an even more public arena with a big-name political defendant?

Frampton seemed the most determined to find a case. But his interest, at times, seemed to be waning. Compared to Watergate, the Meese investigation wasn't very glamorous. Frampton hadn't wanted to work on the investigation full time at the outset. Did he want to commit the time and resources necessary for a full-blown trial?

This lawyer says he never fully articulated those anxieties, because the evidence never quite coalesced into a case so strong that it was clear that the grand jury had to be asked for an indictment.

In fact, no final, formal determination was made with respect to the Thomas allegations or the others. The memos and discussions simply evolved, with little dissension, and pretty soon it became obvious what the outcome would be. The prosecutors could find no evidence of motive for why Meese had failed to disclose the Thomas loan, and without such a motive, Meese's claim that he forgot it seemed the only possible explanation. Deep down, some of the prosecutors never fully believed it. Most people remember $15,000 loans. There was evidence that Meese had discussed it with his wife, Thomas, and McKean on a number of occasions. And it was possible that Thomas had reminded him of it at the very time the forms were being filled out. But without any imaginable motive, the Meese memory lapse crumbled into insignificance.

For many prosecutors, the hardest decisions of their careers are those in which they don't prosecute. It is an abdication of their inherent power—the one decision over which they have virtually unfettered discretion. This was particularly true in the Meese case, since mere indictment would have doomed his nomination to be Attorney General and his political career. And several of the prosecutors were so appalled by what they had learned about Meese's administrative deficiencies and insensitivity to some of the very kind of conduct he would be expected to uncover and prosecute as Attorney

General that they thought it would be a public service to bring Messe down, even if he were eventually acquitted.

Stein didn't agree, and even the most zealous among them forced themselves to exercise restraint. In the draft of the final report that was taking shape, they wrote:

> Any evaluation of fitness for office must begin with a study of the published criteria for the post of Attorney General and must necessarily include a comparison of Mr. Meese's qualifications with those of others who have been nominated. There is always the danger that a finding based on such an inquiry would be the product of preconception rather than an objective statement. Furthermore, such a finding might create a precedent that should serve to distort the role of the independent counsel.

As a result, no findings were made on Meese's qualifications for the post of Attorney General. If the matter had been put to a vote, however, Meese wouldn't have passed muster.

As the drafts neared their final version, it was clear that there wouldn't be an indictment. Stein and his colleagues won't say whether the final decision of whether to indict or not was submitted to the grand jury, citing the secrecy laws that protect proceedings before the grand jury. Prosecutors have the option of simply dismissing the grand jury without seeking an indictment, asking the grand jury to vote on a possible indictment with a recommendation, or leaving the evidence to the grand jury to decide whether an indictment is warranted. It seems likely that in the Meese case the grand jury never voted. The draft report concluding that the evidence was insufficient was already well under way before the grand jury had finished sitting, nor is there any indication that any proposed indictment was drafted. Presumably, an indictment would have been drafted that the grand jury would have formally rejected or accepted. Some prosecutors say they feel they have a moral obligation not to submit indictments to a grand jury for a vote if they believe the evidence is insufficient; others take the opposite tack, believing that the representatives of the people should make that determination. Everything about Stein's philosophy suggests he would be in the former camp. The consummate nondemocrat, he wouldn't have wanted to leave so crucial a determination to the follies of a jury.

And thus the investigation came to an end. "We weren't happy about the outcome, at least I wasn't," Frampton says. "But we thought it was correct. We all believed we reached the correct decision."

Just before that decision was made public on September 20, 1984, the only major leak of the entire investigation appeared. The report was in its fifth draft with all the essential conclusions in it. Robert L. Jackson, a Washington-based reporter for the Los Angeles *Times*, reported that the special prosecutors had reached the decision not to prosecute Meese. The prosecutors insist that they were not the source of the leak, and speculate that one of the lawyers for Meese managed to glean their conclusions from their regular conversations about the progress of the investigation.

Jackson declines to identify his sources, but confirms the leak didn't come from any of the prosecutors. "It didn't come directly from Stein or anyone in his office," he says.

I T was certainly in Meese's political interest for the conclusions to be leaked as soon as possible. For despite the prosecutors' disclaimers that their investigation looked solely at the question of criminal conduct, and the fact that they invited the House and Senate Judiciary Committees to take up where they had left off in considering Meese's nomination, it was obvious that nothing would now block Meese's nomination. All investigations by a special prosecutor are inherently political, and the Meese investigation was no exception. Senate Majority Leader Robert Dole wasted no time in calling for Meese's "swift confirmation" after already having endured congressional scrutiny and a six-month special investigation. In a real if indirect sense, Stein and his deputies made Meese Attorney General. They waited with great anticipation to see what kind of Attorney General they had unleashed upon the nation.

That the special prosecutors reached the "correct" decision after their investigation was never called into question, either by Republicans or Democrats, and they take pride in that fact. On the other hand, there isn't much indication that their work was subjected to much scrutiny. The press, in particular, showed surprisingly little interest in their report or in the investigation beyond the result. "I really wonder if anyone bothered to read it," Stein says.

The New York Times in an editorial praised the work of Stein and his colleagues.

Mr. Stein, a Washington attorney who usually represents defendants, ably accomplished his narrow mission. His 385-page report does not answer every question that the Meese case raises, but it satisfactorily explains why no indictment is warranted.

. . . Mr. Meese has reason to be grateful [the editorial concluded] not only for Mr. Stein's work, but for the law that made it possible. The Reagan Administration scorns the statute as unconstitutional because in cases that pose a clear conflict of interest, it takes away the Attorney General's power to appoint a prosecutor and gives it to a special federal court. But if the independent counsel had been chosen by Attorney General William French Smith, an administration colleague and fellow Reagan campaigner, the quality of the investigation might forever be doubted, to Mr. Meese's continuing discomfort.

The law enabled Mr. Stein to perform a limited but important task, believably and well. For this the public can share Mr. Meese's gratitude.

There was no indication, however, that Meese ever felt any "gratitude" for the investigation. Stein, for one, never heard from him. He received not a word of thanks. Meese was swiftly confirmed as Attorney General, and the Judiciary Committees didn't even bother to call Stein to question him about his findings, nor was he called to testify.

As the Iran Arms/Contra scandal began to unfold in late 1986, the office of special prosecutor once again became a focus of public attention. The Court of Appeals named Lawrence Walsh, a New York lawyer, to lead a broad criminal investigation of the affair, including allegations against former National Security Council operative Oliver North.

North, in turn, seized upon the Constitutional questions inherent in the status of the special prosecutor. He filed a lawsuit to block the investigation, arguing that the office of independent counsel violated the Constitution's separation of powers. Though it was the first judicial test of the statute providing for an independent counsel, most experts felt the law would survive the challenge. Given that President Reagan had already hailed North as a "national hero" at the time he left the security council, it strained the public's credulity that President Reagan or Meese would conduct a thorough and impartial investigation followed by vigorous prosecution if warranted. Indeed, it would be hard to imagine a more compelling case for the appointment of a special prosecutor.

In mid-1987, Meese himself became embroiled in a scandal involving a government contractor, Wedtech. The allegations were strikingly similar to those investigated by Stein. This time the Reagan Justice Department said flatly that the special prosecutor law should be abolished.

But the sudden surge of interest in the office had little impact on Stein. After having been on center stage himself, Stein now felt nearly forgotten. He was once again the relatively obscure, if colorful, Washington defense lawyer.

The sudden transition gave rise to a few thoughts. "I've never had more power in my entire life," Stein says of his stint as a prosecutor. "I had an unlimited budget—that in itself is power. I had the subpoena power. I had the right to grant immunity. I could order phone taps. I had the right to add and investigate charges. Who could have more power?

"The way people react when you have power is easy to see. When you make a phone call, it's returned, and it's returned immediately." Those days, Stein says, are gone. "Now my calls aren't returned at all."

CONCLUSION

MEESE'S long-delayed confirmation hearings by the Senate Judiciary Committee were, predictably, an anticlimax. Despite Stein's carefully worded plea for a thorough investigation of some of the ethical questions raised by his own investigation, it was obvious that Meese's nomination to be Attorney General could not be defeated in the political arena. Only a knockout blow, such as a criminal indictment, would have enabled the Senate to deny President Reagan his choice for the job on ostensibly nonpolitical grounds.

Instead, the committee's hearings proved to be a forum for Meese to air his strongly held views on the subject of law enforcement and civil rights. Frequently pointing to his own background in prosecution and law enforcement, Meese pledged an unprecedented crackdown on crime. While continuing to emphasize the Justice Department's war on drug trafficking and violent crime—initiatives for which he had been largely responsible while he was at the White House—he pledged a new emphasis on white-collar crime. Ever since the McDonnell Douglas case, the Reagan administration had been dogged by allegations that its heart wasn't in white-collar prosecution; that the Republican Justice Department actually had a highly political view of what criminal laws merited enforcement and what didn't. Meese, as an unabashed champion of law and order, pledged to change that.

Meese also made no secret of the fact that the broad legal initiatives in areas of constitutional law that the administration at Justice had resisted would be a key part of his own tenure. He shocked some committee members, for example, by openly calling for the Supreme Court to overrule its own Miranda ruling and related cases that require police to read suspects their rights. He boldly endorsed efforts to overturn the court cases that applied the Bill of Rights to the states—a position that would constitute a revolution in the relationship of the federal government to the states and would undermine decades of jurisprudence in the criminal area. Such a step would overrule many of the important search-and-seizure and right-against-self-incrimination cases. For Meese, however, such so-called constitutional safeguards were little more than annoyances for the police and had achieved little beyond the unjustified release of countless criminals. For the most part, only the guilty get arrested, he told the Judiciary Committee, a hypothesis that, if pursued to its logical conclusion, would lead to the undoing of Anglo-American safeguards dating to the Magna Carta.

In early 1985, Meese's portrait was hung in the Justice Department corridor leading to the top departmental offices, joining such disparate figures as Robert Kennedy, Ramsey Clark, Nicholas Katzenbach, and John Mitchell. Jensen, whom Meese knew and respected from their days in California, was named Deputy Attorney General, the number-two position in the department, and responsibility for overseeing criminal law enforcement was shifted with him from the Associate Attorney General, the position that Giuliani had held. As Associate Attorney General, Meese chose Brad Reynolds, the controversial, intensely ideological chief of the department's Civil Rights Division, and the Justice Department official who had long championed a radically conservative agenda before the Supreme Court.

Given Meese's own views on the Constitution and the close relationship he had had with Reynolds while he was at the White House, Meese's choice of Reynolds wasn't suprising, but it was too much for the Senate Judiciary Committee, which balked at Reynolds's nomination and managed to defeat his confirmation. Meese simply named Reynolds to a position that didn't require Senate approval, then gave him expanded responsibilities that gave Reynolds as much authority as he would have had if he had been confirmed in the number-three post. As head of the Office of Legal Policy, Meese chose Charles Cooper, another conservative ideologue who is a close friend and habitual jogging partner of Reynolds.

Meese also surrounded himself with a group of newly appointed special assistants, one group of whom were so conservative and so rigid in their political views that other staffers jokingly called them the Nazi youth.

To underscore the importance he placed on law enforcement, Meese began a series of visits to U.S. Attorneys' offices around the country, sometimes dropping in on short notice and selecting a few assistants for one-on-one chats. Shortly after announcing the program of visits, Meese said he had already chosen the site of the first such visit, which he felt would be symbolically important. Most in the department assumed the visit would be the occasion for a ceremonial reunion and photo opportunity with Rudi Giuliani in New York. After all, Giuliani was the most visible U.S. Attorney in the country and he had come straight from the Reagan Justice Department.

But Meese's choice for his first visit was not Giuliani's fiefdom, the Southern District of New York. It was, instead, the Eastern District of New York—headquartered in Brooklyn—and the district viewed by the Southern District as its archrival. "It was a deliberate slap at Giuliani," says one Justice Department lawyer. Nor did Meese name Giuliani to the advisory group of U.S. Attorneys, deemed by Justice Department lawyers as a measure of just how far from favor Giuliani had fallen with the ideologically conservative group in the administration.

When Meese finally did arrive for his visit with Giuliani at St. Andrew's Plaza in Manhattan, relations between the two men were markedly cool. "Not hostile," says one assistant in New York, "but slightly strained. They are, temperamentally, not alike at all." Meese used the occasion of his visit to reaffirm his commitment to fighting white-collar crime, traditionally a focus of the Manhattan office. "We will vigorously prosecute economic crime," Meese told the assembled assistants.

But those inside and outside the administration who expected a crackdown on high-level white-collar crime from Meese were soon disappointed. Despite the rhetoric, Meese has declined to prosecute individuals in some of the highest-visibility and most important cases under investigation at the time he took office.

In May 1985, the Justice Department announced that E. F. Hutton & Company, one of the country's largest investment firms, had been engaging in a deliberate check overdrafting scheme that had defrauded more than 499 banks and financial institutions out of more than $4 billion. According to Albert Murray, an Assistant U.S. Attorney on the case, hundreds of Hutton employees had been involved in the scheme, and prosecutors had concluded that twenty-five individuals were knowing participants. Although a large number of those involved had been granted immunity in the course of the investigation, the top figures hadn't. Prosecutors working on the case strongly recommended that not only Hutton but the top individuals involved be indicted. It was a recommendation reminiscent of the prosecutors' recommendation to seek individual indictments in the McDonnell Douglas case, although the Hutton prosecutors thought they had a far stronger argument, since they were dealing with the long-standing crime of fraud, and not the more recent and less well-defined issues of corporate bribery that had been the focus in McDonnell Douglas. And at the heart of their recommendation was the argument that corporate charges simply do not deter crime. Individuals commit crimes, not corporations.

Meese overruled the recommendation of his own prosecutors. At a press conference to announce the disposition of the case, Meese said that "this was clearly a corporate scheme," noting that the individuals didn't "personally gain from the scheme themselves." Meese announced that Hutton would plead guilty to two thousand felony counts and would pay fines and costs totaling $2.75 million. Part of the agreement: no individual officers or employees of Hutton would be charged. "This makes it clear to the business world that white-collar crime will not be tolerated," Meese concluded.

Some Justice Department lawyers were appalled. For one thing, the individuals had benefited, if not directly, then by earning the approval of their corporate superiors. That motive is often at the heart of corporate crime. Moreover, Meese's statement about deterrence, in particular, was an example of his ability to simply declare that white is black with what appeared to be genuine conviction. The Justice Department lawyers were certain that Meese had just sent the opposite message: that white-collar crime would be tolerated. As *The New York Times* editorialized, "The pretense that no human beings operate E. F. Hutton makes it clear to the business world that if your company is shot through with managers involved in a huge swindle, not to worry—the Meese Justice Department will limit the liability to the corporation. None of the guilty officers will have to pay."

The plea prompted a storm of criticism of the Justice Department, and Democratic politicians found themselves in the unexpected position of criticizing the Reagan administration for going soft on crime. Fifteen Democratic senators sent a letter to Meese demanding an explanation of his "blatant failure to find individual liability in the affair." New York City Mayor Ed Koch weighed in on the issue, denouncing Meese for the decision not to prosecute individuals.

According to Justice Department officials, Meese was genuinely stung by the criticism. Jensen declines to discuss his own role in the decision not to prosecute individuals, including reports that he supported the prosecutors' recommendation that charges be filed. But he says, "The criticism of Meese has been unfair. Reasonable people can differ in deciding whether there is sufficient evidence to bring charges. You want the staff prosecutors to be aggressive, to act as advocates for prosecution. But the final decision must turn on whether the threshold of evidence has been met."

MORE worrisome to some lawyers in the department, however, was that Meese—for all his advocacy of law and order—seemed genuinely baffled by the criticism. "What concerned me," says one aide to Meese who later resigned, "was that I don't think Meese really felt these people had committed a crime. He didn't seem outraged about what they'd done the way he would if, for example, they'd been caught dealing in child pornography." (Indeed, Meese later announced a massive campaign against pornography. He did so in the Great Hall of Justice, where photographs showed him standing before the bare-breasted statue of "the spirit of justice.") Meese's attitude was a discouraging reminder of his earlier inability to grasp the ethical problems that had led to his investigation by a special prosecutor.

And it wasn't the last. Soon after the E. F. Hutton matter, Justice Department prosecutors recommended the prosecution of two of the country's largest drug manufacturers, Eli Lilly & Company and SmithKline Beckman Corporation. As in the Hutton case, their recommendations were overruled. No charges were filed, and neither company was prosecuted. Meese's judgments in the early days of the Iran Arms/Contra investigation have also been criticized. It remains to be seen whether the flaws in Meese detected by the special prosecutors led to any serious errors at a time of national crisis.

In the spring of 1986, Jensen announced his resignation from the department. It had been rumored that William Webster, whose wife had recently died, would retire as head of the FBI and Jensen would be named his successor. Webster—still on less than friendly terms with the administration—foiled that plan by indicating he had no intention of stepping down. Instead, Jensen was nominated to a federal judgeship in California. Jensen's colleagues say the resignation was timed so that his confirmation hearings could begin before the congressional elections in the fall of 1986, when control of the Senate might pass to the Democratic Party. (It did.) And they say his long-standing interest in becoming a judge motivated his decision to resign from a lifetime of criminal prosecution.

They concede, however, that Jensen was disappointed by the direction of the department under Meese. Among white-collar prosecutors in Washington, morale was debilitated by the decisions not to prosecute in the department's top investigations. Jensen had never been an ideological prosecutor. He had no taste for the growing politicization of the department. "He was a complete nonideologue," says one lawyer who worked with Jensen in the department. "He wasn't at all interested in Meese's top priorities—abortion, bussing, the whole conservative social agenda."

With the announcement of Jensen's resignation, the changing of the guard at the department was complete. Smith, Schmults, Giuliani, and now Jensen—the top four men in the department—were gone. In their place—in reality if not in actual title—were some of the administration's most fervently ideological bureaucrats: Meese, Reynolds, and Cooper.

It was ironic, some lawyers in Washington felt, that the prosecutorial torch seemed to have passed, at least in the public eye, from the Justice Department in Washington to Giuliani in New York. While Meese was dropping investigations and talking about pornography commissions, Giuliani was scoring major successes against the Mafia, against drug traffickers, against Wall Street traders on inside information, and against corrupt New York City politicians. If his record of successes continues he is likely to go down as the most effective prosecutor since Thomas Dewey. And it is a reputation that, like Dewey's, will be readily transferable into high political office, if Giuliani chooses to seek it.

Giuliani has been deluged with questions about his ambitions for higher office. He has repeatedly denied that he has any specific office in mind, and his denials ring true. He seems entirely absorbed in his current position, seems to revel in nearly every aspect of it, and shows every sign of retaining the position as long as the political climate permits.

Inevitably, however, he will have to give up the post. There will be another Democratic administration in Washington, and there are many—such as Iowa's Reynolds—who won't forget Giuliani's campaign to replace U.S. Attorneys with politically compatible lawyers. Giuliani would surely be replaced. When that happens, it appears likely that Giuliani would be pressed into running for higher office—mayor of New York, perhaps, or governor or senator.

As yet, Giuliani has had no firsthand taste of how politically treacherous his post can be. An egregious failure to convict could backfire with devastating consequencs for his political future. Nonetheless, Giuliani can't be faulted for avoiding risks. With the arrest of Robert Freeman, the head of arbitrage and a powerful partner at Goldman Sachs & Company, on charges of insider trading, Giuliani took on one of the world's wealthiest and most powerful financial institutions. "We're going to bring Giuliani down," a Goldman Sachs employee told *The Wall Street Journal* the day after the arrest. The gauntlet had clearly been thrown down.

So far, risk-taking has brought Giuliani an unprecedented series of courtroom triumphs. He has captured headlines with his victories in Mafia prosecutions—historically notoriously difficult cases to prove because of the willingness of witnesses to lie and their short life expectancy once they agree to cooperate. And while critics said Giuliani decided to personally try the case of Bronx Democratic leader Stanley Friedman because it was highly visible and a sure winner, knowledgeable observers disagree. They note that cases against elected political figures are often the most difficult for prosecutors to win because of the willingness of juries to believe the defendant is being tried for his political beliefs, not because he committed a crime. Friedman's lawyer did his best to exploit that theme in what was ultimately an unsuccesful defense.

"People misunderstand me," Giuliani says. "I'm not in this job to do the safe thing. If you never try to accomplish something, you never fail. I'd rather fail."

For all their differences, Giuliani and Meese share at least one important quality: zeal. They burn with an almost religious dedication to eradicating crime. As some prosecutors, like Jared Scharf, had to learn the hard way, zeal is dangerous to a prosecutor. For some observers, zeal has already been the undoing of Meese. By devoting much of his attention to a radically conservative agenda before the Supreme Court, he has diverted energies from other aspects of law enforcement. So far, his efforts to achieve sweeping constitutional reform must be labeled a failure. The Supreme Court explicitly rebuffed his attack on the Miranda decision, which Meese had called "infamous." Even a conservative justice, Reagan-appointee Sandra Day O'Connor, wrote that Miranda "strikes a proper balance." The Supreme Court declined to strike down its abortion opinion. Meese's efforts to ban affirmative action failed. Despite the acknowledged conservative drift of the Supreme Court, it pursued a largely moderate course and showed little sympathy, either in its opinions or in questioning during oral argument, for Meese's positions.

Indeed, in virtually unprecedented public pronouncements, both Justices William Brennan and John Paul Stevens criticized Meese's positions. Justice Stevens, in particular, said that Meese's reasoning ignored the Civil War and subsequent history, as well as "the last sixty years of Supreme Court precedents." Prominent Harvard Law School professor Laurence Tribe has denounced Meese, saying, "The Attorney General's public misunderstanding of fundamental constitutional principles is so widely known that even those who agree with him can hardly be proud of his flat-footed articulations of his position."

Meese hasn't responded directly to the criticism, but he is described as pleased that he has reopened a debate on some constitutional principles, such as Miranda, that were in danger of becoming taken for granted. The criticism has had no evident effect on the positions being taken during his tenure: if anything, he has become more radical, staffers say.

The Reagan administration, for the most part, is delighted. Meese is a rallying point for the right wing of the party, and so far he has achieved so little that there is slight danger of seriously alienating middle-of-the-road voters. Meanwhile, he is out of the White House, busy with his own agenda, and has played little policy-making role.

The qualities that handicapped Meese at the White House have also plagued him at the Justice Department, further undermining his effectiveness. Although he has a chief of staff whose primary function is simply to keep the paper moving across Meese's desk, the bureaucracy is close to paralysis.

"Look at the numbers under Meese," says one staff aide who says he is close to resigning in frustration. "If you divide the number of criminal cases by the number of people in the Criminal Division, you get less than one case a year. Before Meese, there was an effort to transfer many of these people to the field, where some Assistant U.S. Attorneys are handling more than a hundred cases a year. That effort has stalled. Meese won't do anything that looks like he's dismantling the division. It might undermine a budget request for more money. Meanwhile, nothing is being accomplished."

Meese's special assistants are as intensely interested in constitutional law reform as is Meese himself, aides say. The result is "virtually none of them knows anything about law enforcement." Results like the Hutton case, some aides say, are the inevitable result.

PROSECUTION has always been more political than most prosecutors would like to admit. During the Reagan administration it has become blatantly political, from the dropping of the individual cases in McDonnell Douglas to the corporate guilty plea in E. F. Hutton. Only time, including the length of Meese's tenure and the success of his assaults on Supreme Court precedent, will demonstrate the full impact of his politicization.

Giuliani's zeal has, so far, stood him in good stead. But some of his aides worry. His desire for publicity seems to grow by the day. During the summer of 1986, he went so far as to participate in an undercover mission, in which he dressed up in outrageous garb and went to Harlem, where he successfully purchased cocaine. He posed for photographs on his return.

No arrest resulted from the expedition. If there had been arrests, the charges probably would have been challenged on the grounds that the prosecutor had engaged in antics intended to gain publicity and deprive the defendant of a fair trial.

"So far, Giuliani has had the sense to listen to very good advice from his top people," says one assistant in his office. "They've been able to restrain him. But we're haunted by the prospect that somebody's rights are going to get trampled, and charges thrown out."

Giuliani himself, as well as his assistants, emphasize that, unlike Meese, Giuliani feels no deep-seated hostility toward the constitutional restraints within which he is expected to operate. By and large, he supports them. Rather, the danger is that in his enthusiasm during the thick of the chase, he is oblivious to some of them. "If Giuliani can continue to channel his zeal properly, and remain mindful of the need to contain it at times, he will be a great prosecutor. I hope and pray that he does," says one of his top assistants.

OF the prosecutors who have figured in this book, the one who comes across initially as the least zealous—at the furthest pole from a Meese or a Giuliani—is Greg Waples, the CBS murders prosecutor. In sharp contrast to the tenets of Meese and his allies, he finds no serious obstacles to law enforcement within the Bill of Rights, and says he has no trouble adapting his own work to the standards laid down by the Supreme Court. As his unpopular prosecution of Bernhard Goetz probably best illustrates, his prosecutorial agenda isn't shaped by politics.

There are those who question whether people with sensibilities as finely wrought as Waples's can be effective prosecutors over the long term. Waples himself says he isn't sure whether he wants to be a prosecutor for the rest of his life. But it most often seems to be the zealots who burn out on the job. Ironically, it may be the Wapleses among prosecutors—and in my experience there are many of them—who are the most effective. They are the prosecutors who aren't ideologues, who can see the often finely shaded lines between ethical and unethical behavior, between constitutional and unconstitutional conduct. Above all, they are as concerned with fairness as much as they are with putting criminals behind bars—recognizing that the two goals are complementary, not inconsistent.

One Assistant U.S. Attorney in New York says that every once in a while he tries to draw Giuliani's attention to a credo for prosecutors that was voiced by Whitney North Seymour, one of Giuliani's eminent predecessors in the office of U.S. Attorney. Copies of the credo hang, framed, on the walls of many of the assistants as well as on the office walls of many prosecutors who have moved on into private practice. It is a statement that makes perfectly clear that, with the possible exception of judges, prosecutors are the lawyers expected to be public servants more than they are advocates. Although it was written to apply to prosecutors in the Southern District of New York, it applies with equal force to any prosecutor, from the highest ranks of the Justice Department in Washington to the smallest rural courthouse.

It states that to be a prosecutor "requires commitment to absolute integrity and fair play; to candor and fairness in dealing with adversaries and the courts; to careful preparation, not making any assumption or leaving anything to chance; and to never proceeding in any case until convinced of the guilt of the accused or the correctness of one's position."

To be a prosecutor "demands unusual personal qualities—promptness; dependability; precision; thoughtfulness; decency; personal courage and conviction. One's basic credo should agree with Thomas Paine's: 'The world is my country, all mankind are my brethren, and to do good is my religion.' "

INDEX

INDEX

CETA funds, 71–72
Chapman, Mark David, 185
Chartrand, Richard, 186–87
Chiarella, Vincent, 136, 151–53, 155–56, 159, 166
Chin, Jenny Soo, 189, 194, 207, 224
  Barbera's relationship with, 188, 200
  disappearance of, 188, 199–202, 208–9, 213, 221
  Margolies's suspicions about, 219–20
  Nash's murder of, 220–21
  Nash tied to, 200–201
Christie & Viener, 163
Christy, Arthur, 299
Civiletti, Benjamin, 22, 53
civil rights, Meese's views on, 345
Clalite Concrete Block Company, 240
Clarendon Ltd., 229
Clark, Ramsey, 346
Clark, William, 315, 324
Clayman, Charles, 216–18
Clifford, Clark:
  on extensions of statute of limitations, 51
  plea bargains discussed with, 43–48, 59
Clifton, Lance, 170
  description of, 136
  insider trading investigated by, 136–37
  Newman case investigations of, 138, 141, 143, 148–49, 150, 163
Code of Professional Responsibility, 272
Columbia *Law Review*, 196
Commerce Department, U.S., 325
Commission on Civil Rights, 312
confessions, prohibition of, 205
Congress, U.S., 39–40
  crimes defined by, 15
  entrapment and, 95–96
  on foreign payments by corporations, 22, 80
  funds appropriated for sting operations by, 91
  on RICO statute, 49
  see also House of Representatives, U.S.; Senate, U.S.
Constitution, U.S., 95, 203
  First Amendment to, 235, 277–79
  Fourth Amendment to, 192, 204

Fifth Amendment to, 57–58, 138–39, 163, 224, 250, 259, 260, 267, 282
  Meese's views on, 345–46, 352–53
  status of special prosecutor and, 343
Cooper, Charles, 288, 346, 350
Country, 237
Courtois, Jacques:
  Antoniu's relationship with, 134–35, 150, 157, 159, 160–62, 173
  arrest of, 172–73
  guilty plea of, 174
  impact of prosecution on, 174–75
  indictment against, 166–67
  as insider trading source, 160–62, 164–65, 173–74, 175–76
  plea bargaining by, 174
  prosecutors eluded by, 172
  Richards's investigation of, 150–51, 153
Cox, Archibald, 295
Cravath, Swaine & Moore, 196–97, 198
Crime and Delinquency, 91–92
Crime Commission, Pennsylvania, 92
crimes, criminals:
  as congressionally defined, 15
  detection vs. instigation of, 95–96
  hiding misconduct as, 38
  high-tech, 90–91, 94, 103, 114–15
  legal technicalities and, 11
  white-collar, 10–11, 38, 345, 347–50, 353
  white-collar vs. street, 102–3, 177
Criminal Code, U.S., 338
  Hitachi's violations of, 112–13
criminal investigations, 10, 11
  grand juries used for, *see* grand juries
  presidential politics and, 15
criminal nondisclosure charges, requirements for, 337–38
Crowell & Moring, 301
Crowley, Christopher:
  Pedowitz's investigations and, 142
  Richards's investigations and, 151
currency reporting violations:
  as criminal fraud, 22
  Lubin's investigation of, 21–23
Curtis, Mallet-Prevost, Colt & Mosle, 113
Customs Service, U.S., 23

D'Amato, Alfonse, 130–31
Dane, Mrs., 201

INDEX

Dane, Robert, 200
Dane, Thomas, 190, 194, 200, 201
  gun silencer parts purchased by, 202, 206–7
  indictment against, 214
  testimony of, 194, 206–7
Danforth, John:
  Giuliani's conversation with, 68, 78–80
  McDonnell Douglas ties of, 64–65
Davis, Polk & Wardwell, 141–42, 151, 197
Davis, Robert, 238
Deaver, Michael, 292, 293, 308, 322–24, 335
Debategate scandal, 327
DeCair, Tom, 285–86
DeConcini, Dennis, 129
defense lawyers:
  as limits to power of prosecutors, 9–10
  Meese investigation and, 339–40
  prosecutors compared with, 9
  of white-collar criminals, 10–11
de la Renta, Oscar, 154
DeLorean, John, 96–97
Depression, Great, 234, 287
Dershowitz, Alan, 92
Deseret Pharmaceutical Company, 139–40
Dewey, Thomas E., 136, 230, 350
DiAngelis, Anthony, 116
Dirks, Raymond, 168–69
discovery process, 11
doctors and dentists case, *see* Newman case
Dole, Robert, 342
Donovan, Raymond, 295, 299
Douglas Aircraft Company, 18, 31, 42, 54, 70
Drexel Burnham Lambert Inc., 176
Drug Enforcement Administration, 132
due process clause, 57–58, 121–22
Duggan, Terry, 303

E. F. Hutton & Company, 347–49, 53
Eli Lilly & Company, 349
entrapment:
  predisposition to commit crimes and, 96
  settlement of, by juries, 96–97
  Supreme Court on, 95–96

Equity Funding scandal, 168
Ethics in Government Act, 295
Eustis, James, 253
exclusionary rule, 203, 208
Export-Import Bank (Eximbank), U.S., 36, 66–67
ex post facto laws, 58

Federal Bureau of Investigation (FBI), 23, 25, 132, 210, 227, 245, 327, 349–50
  anti–Vietnam War groups infiltrated by, 93
  Brian's nomination investigated by, 321, 324
  CBS murders investigated by, 187–91
  Hitachi sting operation run by, 89–90
  IBM's cooperation with, 94–95, 97, 106, 108–9, 119–25
  McDonnell Douglas defendants arrested by, 53–54
  Meese investigated by, 299
  as semiautonomous, 92, 299
Federal Home Loan Bank Board, 312, 324
Fielding, Fred, 308, 330
Financial Operations, Inc., 249
Fiske, Robert, 135, 151, 196–97
Fleming, Peter:
  Hitachi case settlement and, 124–26
  plea bargaining by, 117–18, 122–23
Ford, Gerald, 16
Foreign Corrupt Practices Act, 22, 50–51, 58–59
  Reagan administration reassessment of, 62, 64–65, 80
Foreign Gifts and Decorations Act, 326
foreign payments, 58
  grand jury investigations of, 23–27, 29, 34–35, 38–44, 46, 66–67
  see also currency reporting violations
Forsyth, Charles M., 18, 31
  background of, 20
  bribes paid by, 20–21, 32–33
  criminal fraud charges against, 21
  grand jury investigation of, 39
  indictment against, 50, 55
  in meeting with Bhutto and Raza, 19–21
  plea bargains discussed with, 43, 55

363